*Jordan L. Harding*

GEARY'S GUIDE TO THE WORLD'S GREAT APHORISTS

GEARY'S GUIDE TO THE WORLD'S GREAT

# APHORISTS

JAMES GEARY

BLOOMSBURY

Published by Bloomsbury USA, New York
Distributed to the trade by Holtzbrinck Publishers

All papers used by Bloomsbury USA are natural, recyclable products made from wood grown in well-managed
forests. The manufacturing processes conform to the environmental regulations of the country of origin.

LIBRARY OF CONGRESS CATALOGING-IN-PUBLICATION DATA

Geary, James, 1962–
    Geary's guide to the world's great aphorists / James Geary.—1st U.S. ed.
        p.   cm.
    Includes bibliographical references and indexes.
    ISBN-13: 978-1-59691-252-6
    ISBN-10: 1-59691-252-9
    1. Aphorisms and apothegms—History and criticism. 2. Aphorisms and apothegms. I. Title.
II. Title: Guide to the world's great aphorists.

    PN6269.G43    2007
    808.88'2—dc22
    2007006650

First U.S. Edition 2007

10 9 8 7 6 5 4 3 2 1

Designed by Sara Stemen
Typeset by Westchester Book Group
Printed in the United States of America by Quebecor World Fairfield

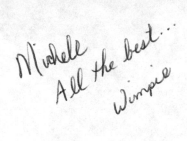

Every man is a quotation from all his ancestors.

—RALPH WALDO EMERSON

# CONTENTS

# BE SINCERE, BE BRIEF, BE SEATED

**W**HEN I lost my job, an aphorism by Vilhelm Ekelund was the first thing that popped into my mind.

I had been employed as a print journalist for almost seventeen years, the last ten of which were for the same publication. Over the decade I spent with that title, I had worked my way up from humble stringer—a kind of glorified gopher, the lowest form of life on the editorial food chain—to regional editor, the highest position I could attain without moving to another continent. Like a lot of my colleagues, I had watched the ructions and restructurings sweeping through the media industry with some trepidation. After a false start in the late 1990s, the Internet finally seemed to be changing the basic economics of publishing. By 2006, profits were plummeting, journalists were being made redundant left and right, and magazines and newspapers were folding at an alarming rate.

But thanks to that wonderful mechanism of psychological self-preservation we all share, I always figured job loss could never happen to me. I classed unemployment—along with other catastrophes like bankruptcy, disability, and terminal illness—in that category of ghastly events that were only visited upon the less fortunate. Middle age had yet to completely strip me of the foolish certainties of youth.

So when I was made redundant, the news came as a shock. Shock was swiftly followed by a torrent of other emotions: anger, foreboding, financial anxiety, grief, plus a weird sense of relief that a long period of tension and uncertainty was finally over. This whirlwind of emotion careened through my skull like a little localized tornado. I occasionally glimpsed pieces of my professional life as they flew past—the camaraderie of those late Friday nights in the office, a breaking story's adrenaline rush—and I waved good-bye.

I sat at my desk, stunned and disbelieving. My mind was blank, numbed by the strange banality that's wrapped around disaster. An unexpected crisis, a long-feared tragedy—both seem bizarrely ordinary when they finally happen. After a few minutes, when I was able to think again, it was of Vilhelm Ekelund, a reclusive Swedish aphorist who died in 1949, and his saying:

> To be placed on treacherous ground is good; generally, you learn to stand on your own feet only when the ground is rocking under them.

Ekelund's aphorism summed up the way I hoped to deal with the situation: recognition that the foundations of my professional life had been profoundly shaken, but determination to land softly and hit the ground running. Sometimes, you need a door slammed in your face before you can hear opportunity knock.

After talking with my wife that afternoon, I decided to tell our sons, who were aged eleven and eight at the time. Our daughter was just three, too young to understand. Of course, the last thing I wanted to convey to my boys was that the ground was rocking under their dad's feet. So I was careful to phrase the news in the most neutral possible terms. The boys were in their pajamas, lying in bed reading before turning out the lights for the night. I told them that there had been some changes at work, that I wouldn't be going back to the office anymore, and that soon I would start looking for another job.

But halfway through my little speech, my younger son interrupted and said: "You mean you're fired?"

For a moment, I was dumbstruck. My son was obviously way ahead of me, so I laughed and said: "Yes, I'm fired."

"Woohoo!" he shouted. "That means Dad is going to be home more often!"

I realized two things then: first, that my son sure has his head on straight; and second, that I still had plenty of solid ground beneath my feet.

## THE POINT OF THIS BOOK

Aphorisms have been a fixture of my thinking ever since I was eight, when I first discovered the form in the "Quotable Quotes" section of *Reader's Digest*. I imagine that Henry Scadding had predicaments like mine in mind when he published *A Pioneer Gathering of Books of a Sententious Character Comprising Proverbs, Parables, Sage Summaries and Saws, Being the Contents of the Log Shanty Bookshelf for the Year 1893 in the Pioneer's Lodge, Exhibition Park, Toronto.*

Scadding was a Canadian author and clergyman who emigrated from Devon, England, to Toronto in 1821, when he was eight years old. He wrote voluminously on a wide range of topics, but his greatest passion was for history, particularly that of his adopted hometown. Scadding also loved aphorisms, or "proverbs" as he called them. And given his historian's obsession with detail, he made a note of every book he owned that contained aphoristic sayings. When he was eighty, Scadding published this list as the *Pioneer Gathering*, which amounts to just a couple unbound printed sheets featuring works by authors ranging from Seneca to Shakespeare. In his preface, though, Scadding wrote the best ever description of an aphorism anthology.

> With homely primitive folk a small stock of proverbs is found to be very useful in emergencies of the head, heart and hands. In short, the compact set of sayings thus stored up might be compared to the old-fashioned pocket-knife which young lads aforetimes were so proud to possess, containing in its handle besides several blades a great variety of little implements—a corkscrew, button-hook, gimlet, turnscrew, tweezers, pincers, fleam or lancet, &c.

That's the point of this book: to be a Swiss army knife for the mind. For more than thirty-five years now, I've carried a small stock of aphorisms around in my head. When I was laid off, a blade with one of Vilhelm Ekelund's sharpest sayings flashed out. That aphorism didn't solve any of my problems, of course. But it did help me cut through the chaos of the moment to see a place where I could make a stand. Consult this set of sayings in emergencies of the head, heart, or hands.

This book is more than just a conventional anthology, though. It is also an encyclopedia, containing brief biographies and selected aphorisms of more than 350 authors—ancient and modern, famous and unknown—from all around the globe. It stretches back to the beginnings of the aphorism in the wisdom traditions of ancient Egypt and China, and it reaches right into the present day by featuring the contemporary writers currently engaged in a revival of the form. Some of the aphorists appear here in English for the first time.

I like to think of the book as a field guide, too, presenting aphorisms in their natural habitats: alongside their author, surrounded by his or her other aphorisms. The aphorism is our most intimate, idiosyncratic literary genre, so I've tried to give a glimpse of the lives and personalities behind the sayings through quick character sketches.

Previous anthologies have organized aphorisms under generic keywords or subjects. This is a fine way to find a saying when you need one. (Indeed, it is essential; that's why this book has two indexes, one organized by author and one by theme.) But to impose interpretations on sayings by placing them in subject chapters prevents readers from making their own meanings. I believe aphorisms are best when first read in the wild, free from the confines of any categories.

So I have organized this book by author, classifying the world's aphorists into eight different species based on my observations of their common concerns and shared characteristics.

*Comics, Critics, and Satirists*
*Icons and Iconoclasts*
*Moralists, Major and Minor*
*Novelists and Playwrights*
*Old Souls and Oracles*
*Painters and Poets*
*Philosophers and Theorists*
*Strange Beasts*

## HOW THIS BOOK WORKS

In compiling this book, I have tried to follow President Franklin Delano Roosevelt's advice to public speakers:

Be sincere, be brief, be seated.

This admonition applies equally to aphorists as well as anthologists. So my intention is to provide some context and connections, and then let the aphorisms do the talking. Each chapter begins with a short introduction to the species under consideration. Then each aphorist is described in an encyclopedic entry consisting of the following elements:

BIOGRAPHY    The Viennese author and critic Karl Kraus described the aphorism as what happens when "one thought becomes an abbreviated essay." My abbreviated biographies are anecdotal rather than academic. Where the writer is comparatively obscure, I have tried to provide some basic background information. For authors who are better known, I've tried to alight on some revealing detail or telling idiosyncrasy. Wherever relevant, I have included a consideration of the author's influences, too. Like all artists, aphorists often respond to or rebel against their predecessors, and these lines of literary influence can span centuries and cultures. As Henry David Thoreau wrote, "What the first philosopher taught the last will have to repeat."

ESSENTIAL APHORISMS    This section presents an essential selection of each aphorist's sayings. Mindful of Erasmus's admonition that "We should treat [aphorisms] not as food but as condiments, not to sufficiency but for delight," the selection is concise. If Erasmus had known about sushi, he might have preferred it rather than condiments as a metaphor. Like sushi, aphorisms come in small portions, are exquisitely formed, and always leave you wanting more. Readers hungry for another helping from specific authors should consult the bibliography.

PARALLEL LINES   Finally, where applicable, a group of related sayings is included. These are instances in which an aphorism from one author has been consciously or unconsciously reiterated, reinterpreted, or subverted by other authors. This list of parallelograms is far from exhaustive, however. Readers will no doubt discover their own relationships and similarities. French novelist Anatole France once quipped, "When a thing has been said, and said well, have no scruple. Take it and copy it." Parallel lines suggest just how often aphorists have taken this advice.

In *The World in a Phrase*, my history of the aphoristic form, I laid down the FIVE LAWS OF THE APHORISM: It Must Be Brief, It Must Be Personal, It Must Be Definitive, It Must Be Philosophical, and It Must Have A Twist. To this I now add the EIGHT TYPES OF APHORISM, the primary stylistic devices readers will encounter in this book:

THE CHIASMUS   The word *chiasmus* derives from *chi*, the Greek letter X, and means—appropriately enough—a crossroads or crossing. In literary terms, a chiasmus is a figure of speech in which the order of words in two parallel clauses is reversed. It is a popular aphoristic technique that often results in startling juxtapositions, such as Mae West's classic line:

It's not the men in your life that matters, it's the life in your men.

THE DEFINITION   The etymological root of the word *aphorism* also comes from the Greek: *apo* means "from" and *horos* means "boundary" or "horizon." So the original meaning of the term was "something that marks off or sets apart"— in other words, a definition. The definition is among the most durable forms of the aphorism, and English novelist Samuel Butler supplied a wonderful example of it:

A definition is the enclosing of a wilderness of idea within a wall of words.

THE JOKE   Many aphorisms are jokes shorn of everything except the punch line. Their humor, however, is often very dark. The best aphorisms—like the best jokes—are short, subversive, and sharp, as in the surreal one-liners of American stand-up comic Steven Wright:

When everything is coming your way, you're in the wrong lane.

THE METAPHOR   Many aphorisms are poems shorn of everything except the metaphor. Poetry and aphorisms vivify the language, and intensify our perceptions,

by finding similarities in unlike things. That's why so many poets have been practitioners of the form, and why so many aphorisms move us with their poetic
beauty, as in this citation from the *Upanishads*, an Indian sacred text composed
between 1500 and 500 BCE:

> One beam meets another in the dash of the great ocean and becomes immediately
> separated in the same manner; similar indeed is the meeting of beings with beings.

THE MORAL    The moral, or instructive lesson in life, is another of the oldest
forms of the aphorism. It began with the ancient Egyptians around the fourth or
third millennium BCE. Sage counsels, often written as a father's advice to his son,
were attributed to Egyptian rulers, such as this gentle admonition from Ptah-
Hotep, a regional governor:

> One that reckons accounts all the day passes not a happy moment. One that
> gladdens his heart all the day provides not for his house. The bowman hits the
> mark, as the steersman reaches land, by diversity of aim. He that obeys his heart
> shall command.

THE OBSERVATION    Normally formulated as simple declarative sentences,
these seemingly superficial statements contain hidden depths. At first sight, they
are often mistaken for truisms. But in the hands of a master, like popular romantic novelist and two-time British prime minister Benjamin Disraeli, this type of
aphorism is always acutely and astutely observed:

> The most dangerous strategy is to jump a chasm in two leaps.

THE PARADOX    The paradox is a specific form of observation, one that initially appears self-contradictory, illogical, or absurd. Like its ostensibly more prosaic relation, this form of aphorism trades in uncommon commonplaces and was
mastered by another popular author and two-time British prime minister, Winston Churchill:

> The further back I look, the further forward I can see.

THE PENSÉE    Pioneered by the French, the *pensée* is the most languid and
leisurely aphoristic form. In contrast to other types of aphorisms, which are usually no more than a sentence or two in length, *pensées* can be up to several sentences long, often reaching the outskirts of the paragraph. Typically, these long
aphorisms are made up of several shorter aphorisms, as evidenced by this example
from seventeenth-century Spanish Jesuit Baltasar Gracián:

Keep the extent of your abilities unknown. The wise person does not allow his knowledge and abilities to be sounded to the bottom, if he desires to be honored by all. He allows you to know him but not to comprehend him. No one must know the extent of a wise person's abilities, lest he be disappointed. No one should ever have an opportunity to fathom him entirely. For guesses and doubts about the extent of his talents arouse more veneration than accurate knowledge of them, be they ever so great.

## WHY THIS BOOK WORKS

When I was about eight, my father and I used to play a game every Sunday morning. It was a weekly ritual, performed after we got home from church and before everyone settled in to watch the afternoon football games on television. In our house, you could circle the ground floor by walking from the living room into the dining room, from the dining room into the kitchen, from the kitchen into the hallway, and from the hallway back into the living room again. My dad and I timed how long it took me to run this circuit: eight seconds.

Starting from the living room sofa, where my dad was comfortably ensconced, I sprinted into the dining room, proceeding through the kitchen and into the hallway. As I ran, my dad counted to seven, his right arm cocked in quarterback position, ready to release my miniature plastic Philadelphia Eagles football. When he reached the magic number, he threw the ball into the archway that led from the living room into the hall. I was nowhere to be seen at this point, still motoring down the hallway at full speed, headed straight for the front door. If we timed it right, the ball appeared in the living room entrance, hanging there in the air for a second, just as I ran past. More often than not, I caught it.

When my father died, this game of ours was my strongest memory of him. At home, he was a man of few words. "Little said, easily mended," was one of his favorite sayings. But he was a smooth talker, too, and as a salesman—of life insurance and aluminum siding—he made his living by being witty and persuasive. It seemed we had less and less in common, though, as I grew older, stopped playing football, and started getting into poetry and literature.

After his funeral, I sorted through his things. Since the early 1970s, when we moved into that house, he had kept a desk and a rusty metal filing cabinet in a little corner of the basement. I threw out loads of old insurance policies, claims forms, and brochures describing the wonders of aluminum siding. In one drawer, I found nothing but spent Sylvania flashbulb cubes. I dug up some treasures, too, including my dad's dog tags and a postcard from World War II. In another drawer, under a small stack of papers, I found a pile of aphorisms torn from one of those "Thought for the Day" desktop calendars.

I was astonished to discover that my dad was an aphorism collector, just like me. We had never discussed the subject, yet we both had been compiling our own anthologies all those years. My dad must have been working on his for a while, since the drawer contained dozens of little square sheets from what appeared to be calendars for several different years. One aphorism in particular leapt out at me because it was from one of my favorite authors, Ralph Waldo Emerson:

Life consists of what a man is thinking of all day.

Sifting through those sayings, I realized that my love for aphorisms was something else my father passed to me. Aphorisms are always in the air. When I need them most, they drop into my hands, seemingly out of nowhere. All I have to do is make the catch.

Over the past thirty-five years or so I've accumulated several desk drawers full of scattered sayings. This book is an attempt to put those words in order, just as English physician and vicar Thomas Fuller did in 1732 when he compiled *Gnomologia: Adagies and Proverbs, Wise Sentences and Witty Sayings, Ancient and Modern, Foreign and British*:

All that I take upon me here to do is only to throw together a vast confused heap of unsorted things, old and new, which you may pick over and make use of, according to your judgment and pleasure.

Read such of these as give you wisdom or pleasure, then pass them on.

# COMICS, CRITICS, AND SATIRISTS

**A**PHORISTS are not generally regarded as a jocular, lighthearted bunch. But aphorisms are very similar to jokes: both achieve their greatest effect by turning things on their heads. Prejudices and preconceptions, beliefs and expectations, conventions and consensus: these are just some of the things upended by aphorisms and jokes. It is no surprise then that COMICS, CRITICS, AND SATIRISTS specialize in wicked one-liners. "Abstracts, abridgements, summaries and c. have the same use with burning glasses, to collect the diffused rays of wit and learning in authors, and make them point with warmth and quickness upon the reader's imagination," is how Jonathan Swift described collections of such satirical sayings. But as any stand-up comic will tell you, being funny is a serious business. A smile looks a lot like a wince. For these aphorists, laughter is not just the best medicine; it is the last resort.

**ALLEN, WOODY** (United States, 1935– ) Allen was only sixteen when he began writing gags for popular 1950s television programs like Sid Caesar's *Caesar's Hour*, *Candid Camera*, *The Ed Sullivan Show*, and *The Tonight Show*. His films, like his aphorisms, mix slapstick with the sublime, like Ingmar Bergman wearing a Groucho Marx mask.

*Essential Aphorisms*

Sex alleviates tension. Love causes it.

Confidence is what you have before you understand the problem.

Eighty percent of success is showing up.

You can live to be a hundred if you give up all the things that make you want to live to be a hundred.

God is either cruel or incompetent.

My one regret in life is that I am not someone else.

**BALJAK, ALEKSANDAR** (Serbia, 1954– ) Baljak first came to prominence in the 1980s, writing about the last days of communism in the then nation of Yugoslavia. Taking his inspiration from great Polish dissident-aphorists like Stanislaw Jerzy Lec, as well as fellow Serbs like Rastko Zakic, Baljak tackles the bloody breakup of Yugoslavia and Serbia's bumpy transition to democracy in his darkly comic musings. He is a prominent member of the Belgrade Aphoristic Circle, an informal group founded in the early 1980s, and author of *Monumental Miniatures: An Anthology of Serbian Aphorisms.*

*Essential Aphorisms*

A dictator wants the same thing as the people: to decide everything himself.

A person whose appearance has considerably changed after the interrogation must file for a new ID card.

What's the use of democracy being on our doorstep when we are not at home?!

We introduced democracy painlessly. We didn't even feel it.

If everybody else agrees, I will also vote for change!

An aphorism is a dribbling of the spirit within a limited space.

An aphorism is proof that even great plays can be played on a small stage.

At any given moment, we know what we want. We just don't know when that moment is.

**BALZAC, HONORÉ DE** (France, 1799–1850) Balzac's appetites—for work, for food, for love—were prodigious. He wrote up to sixteen hours a day, often working through the night, keeping himself awake by drinking enormous quantities of a specially blended coffee. He ate a lot, too, once reportedly consuming 100 oysters in a single sitting. Yet he still found time for the incessant rounds of love affairs and socializing that provided him with so much material for his books.

Balzac conceived of his novels (there are more than ninety of them) as individual instalments in a unified work called *The Human Comedy*, a satirical sequel to Dante's *Divine Comedy*. He depicted the struggle for survival in bourgeois French society with both sympathy and cynicism. His cast of characters numbered in the thousands, covering every walk of life from humble *paysans* to Parisian politicians. "There is nothing left for literature but mockery in a world that has collapsed," he wrote in the preface to one of the books.

### Essential Aphorisms

Behind every great fortune there is a crime.

A lover teaches a wife all her husband has kept hidden from her.

A rent in your clothes is a mishap, a stain on them is a vice.

A married woman is a slave you must know how to seat upon a throne.

Life is simply what our feelings do to us.

With monuments as with men, position means everything.

The more you judge, the less you love.

A man's own vanity is a swindler that never lacks for a dupe.

Passion is born deaf and dumb.

The husband who leaves nothing to be desired is a doomed man.

Men may allow us to rise above them but they never forgive us for not sinking to their own level.

An entire city can slander a man but if he has no friends he will remain blissfully ignorant of it.

### Parallel Lines: Women and Love

In the first woman we love, we love everything. Growing older, we love the woman only.
                                                    —BALZAC

In their first affairs women are in love with their lover, later they are in love with love.    —FRANÇOIS, DUC DE LA ROCHEFOUCAULD

The desire of the man is for the woman, but the desire of the woman is for the desire of the man.

—ANNE-LOUISE-GERMAINE NECKER, BARONESS DE STAËL-HOLSTEIN

Woman is a fortress that lowers its drawbridge not to surrender to the enemy but to capture him.    —ROBERTO GERVASO

**BANKSY** (United Kingdom, 1974–  ) Banksy is the nom de plume of a British graffiti artist who tries to keep his identity secret in order to avoid police prosecution. His work combines street art and stenciling with trompe l'oeil: realistic images of rats, chimpanzees, and people are often accompanied by witty, aphoristic sayings. He's also fond of cultural pranks. He surreptitiously hung his own mock artworks in museums, including the Natural History Museum in London and the Metropolitan Museum of Art in New York. In 2005, he painted politically charged scenes on the thirty-eight-foot-high security barrier separating the occupied territories of the West Bank from Israel. One painting was of a hole in the wall through which a child could be seen playing in the sand with a pail and bucket.

*Essential Aphorisms*

Laugh now, but one day we'll be in charge. [Over the stencil of a chimpanzee.]

It's not a rat race. [Next to a stencil of a rat holding a paint-roller.]

I'm out of bed and dressed—what more do you want? [Next to a stencil of a rat holding a paintbrush.]

So little to say, and so much time . . . [Over a rat stencil.]

The joy of not being sold anything. [Spray-painted onto a blank street billboard.]

I need someone to protect me from all the measures they take in order to protect me.

**BEERBOHM, MAX** (United Kingdom, 1872–1956) Beerbohm was not averse to turning his sharp satirical wit on himself. His first book, published in 1896, was ironically entitled *The Works of Max Beerbohm*. He was a keen caricaturist as well, combining visual with verbal parody to devastating effect. In 1898, he succeeded fellow aphorist George Bernard Shaw as the drama critic for the *Saturday Review*.

## Essential Aphorisms

Anything that is worth doing has been done frequently. Things hitherto undone should be given, I suspect, a wide berth.

Good sense about trivialities is better than nonsense about things that matter.

To give and then not feel that one has given is the very best of all ways of giving.

There is much to be said for failure. It is much more interesting than success.

Only mediocrity can be trusted to be always at its best.

Nobody ever died of laughter.

**BILLINGS, JOSH** (United States, 1818–1885) Billings, whose real name was Henry Wheeler Shaw, called his sayings "affurisms." As part of the plain, straight-talking persona he adopted, he took to publishing some of his folksy observations using his own mangled phonetic spellings. But Billings was anything but a country bumpkin: his father was elected to Congress at the age of twenty-four, up until that time the youngest Congressman ever, and also served in the Massachusetts state senate for some twenty-five years. When the young Billings was expelled from college for climbing a lightning rod to steal the clapper from the chapel bell, he headed west to make his fortune. His father arranged for letters of recommendation—from presidents John Quincy Adams and Martin van Buren and Senator Henry Clay—to help him on his way. Still, Billings ran into trouble. Stranded in Napoleon, Indiana, without any money, he hit on the idea of giving lectures as a way to generate cash. He called himself Mordecai David, supposedly a direct descendant of the biblical David, and delivered an impromptu talk on mesmerism. Starting in 1870, after Billings had gained national fame for what he called his "short sentences, sharp at both ends," he earned a fortune from his books and lecture tours. Josh Billings, not Henry Wheeler Shaw, is the name inscribed on his tombstone.

Billings's homespun philosophy, and the witty one-liners in which he conveyed it, can be traced straight back to Benjamin Franklin, who invented the genre in America with Poor Richard and his almanacs. Like Franklin, Billings published almanacs, too, throughout the 1870s. Billings's career—and his caustic sensibilities—also resemble those of Mark Twain and Ambrose Bierce. All three men held a series of odd jobs (Billings was variously an auctioneer, coal miner, explorer, farmer, real estate agent, and steamboat captain) before landing in journalism, which provided the first outlet for their aphoristic musings. Billings was also a pioneer of cacography, or deliberately incorrect spellings, a stylistic device that was extremely popular in the late nineteenth century.

*Essential Aphorisms*

Brevity is power.

Adversity has the same effect on a man that severe training has on the pugilist: it reduces him to his fighting weight.

Genius after all ain't ennything more than elegant kommon sense.

Advice is like castor oil, easy enough to give but dreadful uneasy to take.

The best reformers the world haz ever seen are thoze who commense on themselfs.

As scarce as truth is, the supply has always been in excess of the demand.

Lazy men are alwuss the most posative. They are too lazy to inform themselfs, and too lazy to change their minds.

Flattery is like cologne water, to be smelt, not swallowed.

It's not only the most difficult thing to know one's self, but the most inconvenient.

Man waz kreated a little lower than the angels, and he haz been a gitting a little lower ever since.

Love looks through a telescope; envy through a microscope.

Most people when they come to you for advice, come to have their own opinions strengthened, not corrected.

There is no greater evidence of superior intelligence than to be surprised at nothing.

There is no revenge so complete as forgiveness.

The best way to convince a fool that he is wrong is to let him have his own way.

Mankind loves misterys—a hole in the ground excites more wonder than a star in the heavens.

The man who never makes enny blunders seldum makes enny good hits.

It ain't often that a man's reputation outlasts his money.

There are lots of people who mistake their imagination for their memory.

To bring up a child in the way he should go, travel that way yourself once in a while.

The top rounds ov a ladder are always the most dangerous.

Be like a postage stamp. Stick to one thing until you get there.

The rarest thing a man ever duz iz the best he can.

To finish is to win.

*Parallel Lines: Josh Billings and Mark Twain*

Put not oph till to-morrow what can be enjoyed to-day.          —BILLINGS

Do not put off till tomorrow what can be put off till day-after-tomorrow just as well.          —TWAIN

It is better to know nothing than to know what ain't so.          —BILLINGS

It ain't what you don't know that gets you into trouble. It's what you know for sure that just ain't so.                                                    —TWAIN

Remember the poor, it costs nothing.                                      —BILLINGS

To be good is noble, but to show others how to be good is nobler, and no trouble.                                                                              —TWAIN

**BÖRNE, LUDWIG** (Germany, 1786–1837) Among Ludwig Börne's many claims to fame, these two are perhaps the most unexpected: he was an important influence on Sigmund Freud, and the town of Boerne, Texas (population 6,019), is named after him. The former accomplishment has to do with Börne's literary self-help essay *The Art of Becoming an Original Writer in Three Days*, in which he advised: "Take a few sheets of paper and for three days on end write down, without fabrication or hypocrisy, everything that comes into your head. Write down what you think of yourself, of your wife, of the Turkish War, of Goethe . . . and when three days have passed you will be quite out of your senses with astonishment at the new and unheard-of thoughts you have had. This is the art of becoming an original writer in three days." The essay helped Freud develop his ideas about free association. German immigrants to Texas who admired Börne's liberal political views bestowed the latter honor. Born in Frankfurt as Lob Baruch, the son of a successful Jewish banker, Börne changed his name in 1818 when he became a Lutheran. He briefly had a job as a civil servant, but after the fall of Napoleon, Jews were no longer permitted to hold public appointments. So Börne became a journalist, editing a series of newspapers, including *Die Wage*, which was known for its lively, satirical political columns. The paper was perhaps a little too lively for the local authorities; the police shut it down in 1821. Börne went to live in Paris, where he wrote *Briefe aus Paris* ("Letters from Paris"), which criticized German despotism and espoused the rights of the individual.

*Essential Aphorisms*

When we are incapable of recognizing the laws of necessity, we believe ourselves to be free.

The Germans pride themselves very much on their modesty; to me that seems as if the hare wanted to pride itself on its timidity.

You can be honest after all, but it's stupid to let others notice.

You have no one to fear as much as yourself.

Ministers fall like buttered slices of bread: usually on their good side.

Reason is to intellect as a cookbook is to the pie.

They do not want freedom of the press because they believe that the wind will turn with the weathervane.

History teaches us virtue, but nature never ceases to teach us vice.

The light cast by so-called official announcements is often nothing more than a will-o'-the-wisp that leads us into swamps.

The secret of any power is this: to know that others are even more cowardly than we are.

**BOYD, ANDREW** (United States, 1963– ) Boyd describes himself as a "cultural activist, political organizer, performance artist, street theater producer" and "conceptual prankster." As a student activist in the 1980s, he became bored with handing out pamphlets and organizing rallies. So he began staging happenings that mixed performance art, media stunts, and theater of the absurd. His targets: economic inequality, large corporations, and President George W. Bush. Some of his high-concept high jinks include the Precision Cell Phone Drill Team, a squad of executives on military-style maneuvers, and Billionaires for Bush, an ironic grassroots political group. He also pens what he calls "postmodern maxims" that give a funny, fractured take on self-help books and inspirational literature, providing ample food for thought as we "navigate the jungle of existential terror and paradox that begins anew each day." Like Banksy, Boyd burlesques consumer culture in the spirit of Barbara Kruger and Jenny Holzer.

*Essential Aphorisms*

Need what recently didn't exist.

I choose how to live a life I didn't choose.

Irony is the only way I can take myself seriously.

Shop as though money were a consensual hallucination.

Accessorize your rebellion.

Take the kids to see a replica of what never was.

Be profoundly superficial.

Love the right wrong person.

It's not whether I arrive; it's how I lose my way.

The deeper my crisis, the clearer my choices.

**BRIE, ANDRÉ** (Germany, 1950–   ) Brie is a member of Germany's left-wing Linkspartei and has been a member of the European Parliament since 1999. He and his party are highly critical of contemporary capitalism, arguing that lack of state controls on the economy is destroying the European welfare state.

*Essential Aphorisms*

The atmosphere of Venus consists of ammonia, sulfur, and nitric oxide. Man must have lived there once.

Crime is rampant. We even steal away from responsibility.

I no longer come to blows with others. I've discovered that those I'd like to clout around the ears have nothing between them in the first place.

Why computers? Politicians are far more calculating.

We have nothing to say to each other. But we don't talk about it.

The spine is man's Achilles heel.

Jesus chased the moneychangers from the temple. Now they are everywhere.

God created the world. He was a satirist.

*Parallel Lines: Gray Cells*

The gray cells of dogmatists are completely escape-proof.            —BRIE

Thinking is criminal. After all, thoughts are born in gray cells.

—GABRIEL LAUB

**BRILLIANT, ASHLEIGH** (United States, 1933–  ) Brilliant started out as a painter rather than an aphorist. His paintings, however, never went over as well as the sharp, slightly loony titles he appended to them. So instead of working on canvas, he made quick pen-and-ink drawings to illustrate his aphoristic captions. "Soon, I was making lists of titles for pictures I had not yet painted," Brilliant has said. His drawings and aphorisms, known as "Pot-Shots," have been widely published since 1975, appearing on everything from coffee mugs to postcards. Brilliant's rules for "Pot-Shots" composition are strict: no saying can have more than seventeen words (seventeen is also the number of syllables in a haiku) and none can rhyme.

*Essential Aphorisms*

Life is the only game in which the object of the game is to learn the rules.

No man is an island but some of us are long peninsulas.

I feel much better, now that I've given up hope.

If we all work together, we can totally disrupt the system.

If you're careful enough, nothing bad or good will ever happen to you.

I could do great things, if I weren't so busy doing little things.

In order to discover who you are, first learn who everybody else is, and you're what's left.

If you can't learn to do it well, learn to enjoy doing it badly.

**BRUDZINSKI, WIESLAW** (Poland, 1920–  ) Brudzinski's first satirical broadsides appeared in 1936, in the Polish weekly *Kultura*. Since then, he has continued to publish his jocular jabs at politics, society, and human nature in the satirical magazine *Szpilki* ("Needles"), where he is also an editor.

*Essential Aphorisms*

The lesser evil usually lasts longer.

In life one has to go to the funerals of the people we like and the birthdays of those we don't.

Difficult questions should be answered before they are asked.

Sometimes difficulties come because you expect them.

Some take revenge before any harm is done to them.

Correcting old mistakes is often more costly than making new ones.

Some must live with the consequences of what they didn't dare do.

Exceptions spread word of the rule.

One day the truth will emerge, like a corpse in the water.

Better to be the servant of many masters than of another servant.

A view through bars can spoil the prettiest landscape.

A step back can be incautious, too.

The height of luxury: own car, own house, own opinion.

Friend: someone who does you harm completely selflessly.

Under certain circumstances a wanted poster is a letter of recommendation.

The most difficult thing to find is the way to the signposts.

**BUTLER, SAMUEL** (United Kingdom, 1612–1680) Most of Samuel Butler's writings were not published until almost eighty years after his death, in 1759. It's a strange fate for works by the author of *Hudibras*, a long satirical poem about the Puritans composed in a brilliantly compressed and aphoristic style. Published between 1663 and 1678, the book was widely admired, and imitated, during Butler's lifetime. Despite this success, Butler never won much favor at court, perhaps because his tongue was just a little too sharp. He coined some phrases that have gone on to become proverbial in English: "the Devil take the hin'most" and "spare the rod and spoil the child." His reputation was enhanced in death, however; Butler, the son of a farmer from Strensham, Worcestershire, England, has a monument in Westminster Abbey.

*Essential Aphorisms*

All a rhetorician's rules
Teach nothing but to name his tools.

What makes all doctrines plain and clear?
About two hundred pounds a year.
And that which was proved true before
Prove false again? Two hundred more.

Neither have they hearts to stay,
Nor wit enough to run away.

There are more fools than knaves in the world, else the knaves would not
have enough to live upon.

He is a fool that hath nothing of philosophy in him, but not so much as he
that has nothing else but philosophy in him.

Birds are taken with pipes that imitate their own voices, and men with
those sayings that are most agreeable to their own opinions.

**BUTLER, SAMUEL** (United Kingdom, 1835–1902) No relation to the author of
*Hudibras*, this Samuel Butler was born in Nottinghamshire, descended from a long
line of clerics. His grandfather was Bishop of Lichfield and Coventry, his father
was a vicar, and young Samuel was meant to be a vicar, too. But Butler came to
have increasingly serious doubts about his faith. Plus, what he really wanted to be
was a painter, a career his overbearing father wouldn't hear of. So Butler did what
any headstrong twentysomething in his situation would have done: he moved to
New Zealand to become a sheep farmer. Butler had a knack for sheep farming; his
business turned a healthy profit. Since there was not much else to do in New
Zealand, he had plenty of time for reading, most importantly Charles Darwin's
*On the Origin of Species*. He also began work on his satirical novel *Erewhon*. When
he returned to England in 1864, he was a gentleman of independent means—at
least until his money started running out. Butler took up painting again as well as
musical composition (his favorite composer was Handel), and he published
*Erewhon* to huge acclaim in 1872. It was his only real literary success, with most of
the rest of his books—several on evolution, one critiquing the Christian gospels,
some books about his travels in Italy, and a sequel to *Erewhon*—published at his
own expense. After his father died in 1886, Butler was financially independent

again, using the money to finance his idiosyncratic literary output. In the last few years of his life, he published translations of the *Iliad* and the *Odyssey*; a book arguing that the *Odyssey* was actually written by a woman; and a reconsideration of Shakespeare's sonnets. He spent an hour every morning revising and indexing the notebooks he had kept since he was a young man. His novel *The Way of All Flesh*, which had lain untouched in a drawer for almost thirty years, was published the year after his death. But it is the notebooks, edited by his lifelong friend Henry Festing Jones, that contain Butler's greatest aphorisms. "One's thoughts fly so fast that one must shoot them," he wrote, "it is no use trying to put salt on their tails." With *Erewhon*, Butler continued the tradition of picaresque satire that Jonathan Swift executed so brilliantly in *Gulliver's Travels*. He also shared Swift's gift for farce and acerbic wit. Like Ralph Waldo Emerson, Butler held radical, iconoclastic views for his time, yet managed to maintain a very respectable middle-class lifestyle. And like Arthur Schopenhauer, he was ornery and misanthropic, and pursued his philosophical investigations with a scientific meticulousness.

## Essential Aphorisms

We are like billiard balls in a game played by unskillful players, continually being nearly sent into a pocket, but hardly ever getting right into one, except by a fluke.

We are like thistledown blown about by the wind—up and down, here and there—but not one in a thousand ever getting beyond seed-hood.

All progress is based upon a universal innate desire on the part of every organism to live beyond its income.

The body is but a pair of pincers set over a bellows and a stewpan and the whole fixed upon stilts.

Morality is the custom of one's country and the current feeling of one's peers. Cannibalism is moral in a cannibal country.

Man is the only animal that can remain on friendly terms with the victims he intends to eat until he eats them.

Words are like money; there is nothing so useless, unless when in actual use.

Ideas are like shadows—substantial enough until we try to grasp them.

If we attend continually and promptly to the little that we can do, we shall ere long be surprised to find how little remains that we cannot do.

He alone can take well who can also make well.

The history of art is the history of revivals.

Hard-and-fast lines ever cut the fingers of those who draw them.

There is a miracle somewhere. At the point where two very large nothings have united to form a very little something.

It must be remembered that we have only heard one side of the case. God has written all the books.

Everyone should keep a mental waste-paper basket and the older he grows the more things he will consign to it—torn up to irrecoverable tatters.

Small things may be rehearsed, but the greatest are always do-or-die, neck-or-nothing matters.

To put one's trust in God is only a longer way of saying that one will chance it.

Paying debts is a luxury which we cannot all of us afford.

There is no such source of error as the pursuit of absolute truth.

Any fool can tell the truth, but it requires a man of some sense to know how to lie well.

Our understanding can burrow but a very small way into the foundations of our beliefs, and can only weaken rather than strengthen them by burrowing at all.

To know God better is only to realize more fully how impossible it is that we should ever know him at all.

You can do very little with faith, but you can do nothing without it.

To be dead is to be unable to understand that one is alive.

*Parallel Lines: Samuel Butler and Arthur Schopenhauer*

> People are lucky and unlucky not according to what they get absolutely, but according to the ratio between what they get and what they have been led to expect.    —BUTLER

> Virtue is a stranger in this world; and boundless egoism, cunning and malice are always the order of the day. It is wrong to deceive the young on this point, for it will only make them feel later on that their teachers were the first to deceive them.    —SCHOPENHAUER

> Pain consists not in that which is now endured but in the strong memory of something better that is still recent. And so, happiness lies in the memory of a recent worse and the expectation of a better that is to come soon.    —BUTLER

> All enjoyment is really only negative, only has the effect of removing a pain, while pain or evil, on the other hand, is the actual positive element and is felt directly.    —SCHOPENHAUER

> A man's style in any art should be like his dress—it should attract as little attention as possible.    —BUTLER

> *Style* is the physiognomy of the mind.    —SCHOPENHAUER

**BYRNE, DAVID** (United States, 1952–   ) Byrne, lead singer and songwriter with Talking Heads from 1977 to 1991, studied conceptual art at the Rhode Island School of Design, where he was in the habit of staging unusual "happenings." During one event, he had his hair and beard shaved off to musical accompaniment while a woman held up placards with Russian texts written on them. In addition to making music, Byrne also produces visual art and books that parody corporate management jargon and self-help nostrums. Like Barbara Kruger, Byrne often juxtaposes his aphorisms with iconic images—of Americana, consumer culture, medical implements, anonymous public spaces (he seems particularly fond of empty hotel meeting rooms)—that create a sense of giddy incongruity.

*Essential Aphorisms*

> Obstacles are those frightful things that appear when you take your mind off your goals.

You will never find the other ocean if you never leave the shore.

The difference between medicine and poison is the dose.

Hope allows human beings to suffer, daily and eternally.

To believe one knows is to err.

Winners are losers with a new attitude.

## Parallel Lines: In the Know

The more you know, the more you know you don't know and the more you know that you don't know.                     —BYRNE

In order to know, there is no need to know that we know, much less to know that we know that we know.            —BARUCH DE SPINOZA

**CHAMFORT, SÉBASTIEN-ROCH-NICOLAS** (France, 1740–1794) Chamfort was a changeling. Born to a mother descended from minor French nobility and a father who was not her husband, he was swapped by his mother for the stillborn child of a local grocer near Clermont-Ferrand in central France. Chamfort was informed of the identity of his biological mother when he was eight years old. The strange tale of his birth branded Chamfort for life. As an adult, he was both proud of his noble heritage and bitter at being deprived of the wealth and privilege he felt was rightly his. Despite his disadvantaged youth, he had established himself in Paris as a promising playwright and celebrated lover by the time he was twenty. In his mid-twenties, though, his luck changed. His plays bombed and he contracted a debilitating illness, possibly venereal, that ruined his looks. By the age of twenty-five, Chamfort was a has-been. During the French Revolution, he was a leading republican yet actively sought favor and patrons at court. Ironically, Chamfort's noble lineage came back to haunt him. He was accused of being an aristocrat and jailed for sedition. He was released after just two days but vowed never to allow himself to be arrested again. A few weeks later, Chamfort was in the middle of dinner with friends when the gendarmes arrived to take him in for questioning. He calmly finished his soup and coffee before withdrawing to his dressing room, where he took out a pistol, intending to kill himself. But he missed, merely smashing the upper part of his nose and bursting his right eye. He then seized a razor and tried to cut his throat and wrists, with similarly inconclusive results. Chamfort inflicted a total of twenty-two separate wounds on himself, none of which was immediately fatal. He lingered on for a few months, an invalid.

"What can you expect?" he said. "That's what it is to be clumsy with one's hands. One never manages to do anything successfully, even killing oneself."

*Essential Aphorisms*

Courtiers are poor men who have become rich by begging.

In a country where everyone is trying to be noticed, it is better to be bankrupt than to be nothing.

Celebrity: the advantage of being known by those who do not know you.

A man must swallow a toad every morning if he wishes to be sure of finding nothing still more disgusting before the day is over.

Society, which is called the world, is nothing but the contention of a thousand clashing petty interests, an eternal conflict of all the vanities that cross each other, strike against each other, are wounded and humiliated by each other in turn, and expiate on the morrow, in the bitterness of defeat, the triumph of the day before. To live alone, to avoid the bruises of wretched scrapes in which one attracts all eyes one minute only to be trampled on the next, is to be what they call nothing, to have no existence. Poor humanity!

Society is made up of two great classes: those who have more dinners than appetite, and those who have more appetite than dinners.

Love as it exists in society is merely the mingling of two fantasies and the contact of two skins.

Living is an ailment that is relieved every sixteen hours by sleep. A palliative. Death is the cure.

The nobility, say its members, are the intermediary between the king and the people . . . just as the hounds are the intermediary between the hunter and the hare.

For centuries public opinion has been the worst opinion of all.

The opinion of the public is a judgment which the honest man should never entirely accept and which he should never reject.

Not to be worked by anyone's hand, to be no one's man, to draw one's principles, one's feelings, from no one else, this is the rarest thing I have seen.

We must know how to perform the foolishness that our characters require.

There are few vices that will so readily prevent a man from having many friends as will the possession of inordinate talents or virtues.

Some things can be more easily rendered legal than legitimate.

To scorn money is to dethrone a king.

One is happy or unhappy as the result of a multitude of unseen things which one does not refer to and could not describe.

The contemplative life is often miserable. One must act more, think less, and not watch oneself live.

Persons of fashion have only to be herded together to fancy that they are in society.

Calumny is like some annoying wasp, against which one must make no move unless one is sure of killing it, or else it will return to the charge more furiously than ever.

Esteem is worth more than celebrity, respect is worth more than renown, and honor is worth more than fame.

He who leaves the game wins it.

## Parallel Lines: Happiness

"Happiness," said M—, "is not easily come by. It is very hard to find within ourselves, and impossible to find anywhere else."    —CHAMFORT

We owe happiness to ourselves; let us bestow ourselves upon it.

—BENJAMIN WHICHCOTE

We are no longer happy as soon as we wish to be happier.

—WALTER SAVAGE LANDOR

Most folks are as happy as they make up their minds to be.

—ABRAHAM LINCOLN

If you ever find happiness by hunting for it, you will find it, as the old woman did who found her lost spectacles, safe on her own nose all the time.                                    —JOSH BILLINGS

The secret of happiness is to admire without desiring. And that is not happiness.                                    —F. H. BRADLEY

Happiness cannot be pursued; it can only ensue.          —VIKTOR FRANKL

**COLEMAN, LES** (United Kingdom, 1945–  ) Coleman became enraptured by aphorisms in 1968, when he read Georg Christoph Lichtenberg for the first time. The acuteness of Lichtenberg's observations and the density of their expression made it seem to Coleman as if "literary osmosis" had taken place; for an instant, he became Lichtenberg. It was not until twenty years later, however, during a rainy holiday in Scotland, that he started writing aphorisms himself. "The essence or condensation of thought, and how language and image inform each other, has always attracted me," Coleman says.

*Essential Aphorisms*

True deception goes unnoticed.

Wind supports all flags no matter what the flag supports.

Headstone: death's bookmark.

A bridge has no allegiance to either side.

The distance a goldfish swims is not controlled by the bowl.

Audience: play watched from the stage.

The more a ball bounces the less it bounces.

Puppets go to sleep the moment they break free from their strings.

Each page in a book knows its opposite page by heart.

Glass is silent until broken.

**CONNOLLY, CYRIL** (United Kingdom, 1903–1974) Connolly was the archetypal man of letters: astute, astonishingly well read, and brilliantly argumentative. He wrote eloquently on the art of writing and the compulsion, even the duty, to produce masterpieces. As book critic for a variety of British newspapers, he wielded enormous literary influence. With Stephen Spender and Peter Watson, he founded and edited the journal *Horizon* from 1939 to 1950. *The Unquiet Grave*, which he published just after World War II under the pseudonym Palinurus, is a lively, stimulating mix of his own ruminations on writing and extracts by and about his favorite French aphorists. He was a bit of a depressive, though. At one point in his autobiography, *Enemies of Promise*, he writes: "I have always disliked myself at any given moment; the total of such moments is my life." Connolly gravitated to books that confirmed his gloomy view of the world, most notably Ecclesiastes and La Rochefoucauld's *Maxims*. In *Enemies of Promise*, he recalled on first reading La Rochefoucauld that he found "his opinions most reasonable for I was one to whom the existence of good seemed already more mysterious than the problem of evil."

*Essential Aphorisms*

Those who are consumed with curiosity about other people but who do not love them should write maxims.

Life is a maze in which we take the wrong turning before we have learned to walk.

Literature is the art of writing something that will be read twice; journalism what will be grasped at once.

An outside job is harmful to a writer in proportion as it approximates to his vocation.

There is no more somber enemy of good art than the pram in the hall.

Boys do not grow up gradually. They move forward in spurts like the hands of clocks in railway stations.

Promise is guilt—promise is the capacity for letting people down.

The fate of the entertainer is simply to go on till he wakes up one morning to find himself obscure.

Whom the gods wish to destroy they first call promising.

From now on specialize; never again make any concession to the ninety-nine percent of you which is like everybody else at the expense of the one percent which is unique.

**ČOTRIĆ, ALEKSANDAR** (Serbia, 1966–  ) Čotrić began reading and writing aphorisms as a boy, often scribbling sayings on the walls of his classroom. His teachers were so impressed with his initial efforts that they made him stay after school for extra instruction in Marxist education. They couldn't drill the aphorisms out of him, however. He was active in dissident politics during the 1990s, often involved in street protests against Serbian strongman Slobodan Milosevic. And despite being deputy minister in the Serbian Ministry for the Diaspora, he's still writing dissident aphorisms.

*Essential Aphorisms*

You are either with us or against yourselves.

How can we not be proud of our past when each new day is worse than the one before?

We should fight to the last man? Only the last man can say that.

We made many mistakes. Please arrest those who supported us.

**DARD, FRÉDÉRIC** (France, 1921–2000) Almost half of Dard's 300 or so books feature the hard-boiled, womanizing Paris police superintendent San Antonio. These ribald, racy detective stories have sold some 200 million copies, and Dard's San Antonio character has become as famous for his cynical sayings as for his crime-fighting abilities.

*Essential Aphorisms*

Women are exchanged; children accumulate.

In life, one is always alone. The important thing is to know with whom!

Real independence consists in choosing on whom we depend.

The future is nothing but some present rushing to meet us.

The feeling of superiority starts as soon as, exiting a cinema, your eyes meet the eyes of those waiting in line to get in.

Sincere people are executioners.

A boss: the less he speaks, the more he is heard.

One dies of everything, mostly of living.

**DOVLATOV, SERGEI** (Russia, 1941–1990) Dovlatov once said that as a short-story writer, he never needed to make anything up; he just needed enough time to write down everything that actually happened to him. He was never short of material, having been at various times a guard at a Soviet work camp, a journalist in Estonia, and from 1978 an immigrant in Vienna and New York. But his country-men in pre-glasnost Russia could only read his aphorisms and short stories in samizdat editions that were illicitly distributed in the country.

*Essential Aphorisms*

The opposite of love is not disgust, nor even indifference. It is lies. Accordingly, the opposite of hatred is truth.

Everyone is curious about what happens after death? After death, history begins.

Genius is an immortal version of an ordinary human being.

Humor is the inversion of life, the inversion of common sense, the smile of reason.

Tourism is the vital function of the idle.

Talent is like lust: hard to conceal and even harder to stimulate.

**FIORI, FULVIO** (Italy, 1955–   ) Fiori has written books of humor, plays (for both adults and children), and advertising copy. He's also a theater director and actor, performing regularly in his own one-man shows.

*Essential Aphorisms*

Numbers are the only thing mathematicians can count on.

The salmon swims against the current simply because he wants to be like the others.

The wrong I commit is that I'm right.

Lowering my head, I raise my salary.

All my slavery is the fruit of a free choice.

The ideal moments for thinking are the intervals between one thought and another.

Hope dies last but sickens first.

Admitting one's fear is already a good step toward panicking.

**FREDRO, ALEKSANDER** (Poland, 1793–1876) At the age of sixteen, Fredro left the comfort of his wealthy, privileged background to join Napoleon's army. He eventually served as a messenger for the general staff, often riding just a few horses behind Napoleon himself. He was decorated for bravery several times. When his fighting days were finished, Fredro returned to Poland to manage his family's estates. Though he had practically no formal education, he began writing comedies in verse, initially for his own amusement. Today, his aphorisms have become part of proverbial speech in Poland.

*Essential Aphorisms*

Not every improvement is for the better.

An apology—like a cleaned stain; some of it still remains.

The more you know, the more ignorant you should appear.

It is hard to get to the summit, harder to stay on it, but hardest to come down.

No man has yet died of love.

Where is the man who is not another man in his dressing gown than in a tailcoat.

There is no story stupid enough that someone somewhere won't believe it.

A rich man who doesn't squander his wealth robs the whole world.

It is better to wipe away a hundred tears than to make even one flow.

Many a great man, standing before the mirror, beholds a cheat.

A bankruptcy is the shortest way to a fortune.

A donation is an advance on ingratitude.

The debt of an obligation is difficult to calculate, that is why it is not easily paid.

Be thrifty to be thriftless.

There is no armor the bullet of injustice will not pierce.

Every owl is stupid by day.

**GERVASO, ROBERTO** (Italy, 1937–   ) Gervaso is one of Italy's best-known journalists and political commentators, a frequent guest on radio and television programs. He's authored more than forty-four books, including biographies of famous Italians like Casanova, the Borgia clan, and Claretta Petacci, Benito Mussolini's lover. "I'm a propagator and a polemicist," Gervaso has said about his aphorisms. "I need to have facts and to attack. I'm a bit like a public prosecutor in that I'm incapable of defending anybody but myself and therefore I defend myself by attacking."

*Essential Aphorisms*

Wealth doesn't make you happy but it helps you to endure unhappiness.

A woman in love is capable of anything. Exactly like a woman not in love.

In politics, you do not always have to keep your promises but you have to know how to make them.

Man is a death-row prisoner who has the good fortune to be ignorant of the date of his execution.

The most beautiful moment of love is when you have the illusion that it will last forever; the worst is when you realize that it has already lasted too long.

Paradise is full of saints who have never had occasion enough to sin.

He who loves his neighbor as himself either doesn't know his neighbor very well or doesn't love himself enough.

Common sense: the virtue of those who have no others.

Every time I gave my word to somebody, I never saw it again.

With a little luck, many martyrs would have become executioners.

**GRIBOYEDOV, ALEXANDER SERGEEVICH** (Russia, 1794–1829) Griboyedov was a soldier and diplomat, fighting against Napoleon and serving as ambassador at the Russian embassy in Tehran. He once fought a duel over an actress and was wounded in the left hand. Griboyedov's enduring fame in Russia rests not on his military or diplomatic exploits, however, but on the authorship of one play, *Woe from Wit*. The play doesn't have much of a plot, but it is a hilarious satire in verse on the stifling social conventions and intellectual conformity of the Russian empire under Tsar Nicholas I. The play itself was not published until 1861, but it was widely read in manuscript form. At one point, an estimated 40,000 handwritten copies were in circulation, mostly among supporters of democratic and constitutional reform. Many of Griboyedov's witticisms have become proverbial expressions in Russia. After war with Persia broke out, Griboyedov was involved in negotiating an end to the fighting. But anti-Russian feeling was running high, and Griboyedov and his staff apparently went out of their way to offend the local population. A riot ensued, and a mob attacked the Russian embassy. Griboyedov was among those killed. His body was so badly mutilated that the dueling wound on his left hand was the only way to identify it.

*Essential Aphorisms*

The houses are new, the prejudices old.

My eyes are dim.
My heart is blue.

The sin does not much worry me,
The rumors do.

Blessed are the credulous for they are carefree.

I'd love to serve. Servility is what I hate.

Drinking isn't bad as such.
A man may drink, though not too much.
It's education that's to blame
That many people go insane.

That which covers thee discovers thee.

**GUBERMAN, IGOR** (Russia and Israel, 1936–   ) In the 1960s and '70s, Guberman worked as an electrical engineer and wrote popular science articles on the side. But his verse always attracted attention in Russia (where he lived until 1987), often of the most unwelcome kind. The KGB became interested in his satirical quatrains around 1979. He spent five years in a labor camp in Siberia, an experience recorded in the book *Progulki Vokrug Baraka* ("Walks Around the Barracks"). Though writing was forbidden, he continued composing his poems, secreting scraps of paper in boots and under shirts—his own and those of his fellow prisoners. Throughout his ordeal, Guberman's aphoristic poems were available in handmade samizdat periodicals distributed among members of the dissident movement. His quatrains have even been given their own literary term: *gariki*, derived from Garik, a nickname for Igor. Although Guberman immigrated to Israel in 1987, he still has a wide and devoted following in Russia. "I belong to the people of the book, but still love the people of the bottle," he once quipped about his dual Israeli-Russian identity. During his days as a dissident poet, Guberman often wrote under pseudonyms, one of which was Abram Khayyám, an homage to the Persian poet Omar Khayyám. Guberman's verse, like that of Khayyam, is written in rhymed quatrains. It is bawdy, dark yet celebratory, and wonderfully irreverent.

*Essential Aphorisms*

Folk wisdom makes it very clear,
This truth for every soul:
However hard you wash your rear
You'll never make an eye from the hole.

The leaders of the working classes
Couldn't ever comprehend
That ideas thrown into the masses
Are like girls in the hands of lusty men.

In self-deceit and idle lament,
My dear boy, no longer dwell,
For life makes sense when it's compared
To death, disease and prison cell.

A man of bronze and mighty powers,
A monument to state obscurity:
A little fig leaf gently covers
An enormous organ of security.

**HOLZER, JENNY** (United States, 1950– ) Holzer, who was a student of abstract painting at the Rhode Island School of Design in the 1970s, gets her aphorisms off the page and into the environment. Her sayings have appeared on baseball caps, condom wrappers, retail receipts, T-shirts, the large LED displays in shopping malls and sports stadiums, the big electronic billboard on Times Square, and—using massive xenon projections—on U.S. national monuments and even mountains.

*Essential Aphorisms*

Being alone with yourself is increasingly unpopular.

Leisure time is a gigantic smoke screen.

Morals are for little people.

Protect me from what I want.

You are a victim of the rules you live by.

Playing it safe can cause a lot of damage in the long run.

The mundane is to be cherished.

Enjoy yourself because you can't change anything anyway.

**HUBBARD, ELBERT** (United States, 1856–1915) Hubbard was a born salesman and an instinctive philosopher, the epitome of America's self-made man. He got his start peddling soap. Then he joined a successful mail-order house and made it even more successful by introducing a line of high-quality merchandise. In 1893, he sold his interest in the firm and, at the ripe old age of thirty-six, retired to pursue an education and a literary career. He started with a grand tour of Europe, where he met and was greatly influenced by the English designer and ardent socialist William Morris. Inspired by Morris's arts and crafts movement, Hubbard founded Roycroft, his own thriving alternative community in East Aurora, New York. In the first fifteen years of the twentieth century, Hubbard was one of America's most renowned speakers and writers. He was sailing for Europe aboard the *Lusitania* when a German submarine sank the ship. L. Ron Hubbard, founder of Scientology, was Elbert's nephew. Like Benjamin Franklin, Mark Twain, Josh Billings, and Ambrose Bierce before him, Hubbard continued the uniquely American tradition of aphorist as folksy sage and homespun philosopher.

*Essential Aphorisms*

A conservative is a man who is too cowardly to fight and too fat to run.

A failure is a man who has blundered, but is not able to cash in on the experience.

A friend is one who knows you and loves you just the same.

Be pleasant until ten o'clock in the morning and the rest of the day will take care of itself.

Do your work with your whole heart, and you will succeed—there's so little competition.

Every man is a damn fool for at least five minutes every day; wisdom consists in not exceeding the limit.

He has achieved success who has worked well, laughed often, and loved much.

I would rather be able to appreciate things I cannot have than to have things I am not able to appreciate.

If pleasures are greatest in anticipation, just remember that this is also true of trouble.

Little minds are interested in the extraordinary; great minds in the commonplace.

Pray that success will not come any faster than you are able to endure it.

The greatest mistake you can make in life is continually fearing that you'll make one.

The world is moving so fast these days that the man who says it can't be done is generally interrupted by someone doing it.

Life is just one damned thing after another.

**HUBBARD, FRANK MCKINNEY** (United States, 1868–1930) Every day for more than a quarter of a century, Hubbard (no relation to Elbert) filled a regular slot on the back page of the Indianapolis *News* with the musings of Abe Martin and friends, residents of Brown County, Indiana. Hubbard's column—a humorous cartoon plus some witty wisecracks from the denizens of Brown County, a wild and remote area of Indiana—was syndicated in some 200 newspapers across the country. Abe Martin was a folksy philosopher, whose observations of his fellow men were wry and gently satirical. In a note on Hubbard published in the *New York Times* the day after the cartoonist's death, Will Rogers wrote: "Just think—only two lines a day, yet he expressed more original philosophy in 'em than all the rest of the paper combined. What a kick Twain and all that gang will get out of Kin." In 1932, the state of Indiana created a real monument to Hubbard's fictional characters: a state park was created in Brown County, with Abe Martin's Lodge situated in the middle of it. Hubbard's rustic, crusty Abe Martin is another direct descendant of Benjamin Franklin's Poor Richard. Like Franklin, Hubbard was a humorist who placed his words of wisdom in the mouth of someone who appeared to be a country bumpkin. Hubbard also compiled his sayings into almanacs, as had Franklin. And like Josh Billings, Hubbard often used countrified phonetic spellings for his aphorisms.

*Essential Aphorisms*

A good listener is usually thinking about something else.

An optimist is a fellow who believes what's going to be will be postponed.

Boys will be boys, and so will a lot of middle-aged men.

It ain't a bad plan to keep still occasionally even when you know what you're talking about.

It is pretty hard to tell what does bring happiness; poverty and wealth have both failed.

It's going to be fun to watch and see how long the meek can keep the earth after they inherit it.

It's the good loser who finally loses out.

Kindness goes a long ways lots of times when it ought to stay at home.

Laugh and the world laughs with you. Weep an' it keeps on laughin'.

Men are not punished for their for sins, but by them.

Nobody ever forgets where he buried the hatchet.

The hardest thing is to take less when you can get more.

The safest way to double your money is to fold it over once and put it in your pocket.

The world gets better every day—then worse again in the evening.

**JACKSON, HOLBROOK** (United Kingdom, 1874–1948) Jackson was perhaps the most devoted and accomplished British bibliophile of his day. He wrote relentlessly and engagingly on printing and typography, in addition to being a publisher and editing a series of literary newspapers and journals. He was great friends with two other accomplished aphorists: G. K. Chesterton and George Bernard Shaw.

*Essential Aphorisms*

Genius is initiative on fire.

Altruism is another name for egoism.

Originality is only variation.

Familiarity breeds not contempt, but indifference.

Forgive everybody but yourself.

Don't try to convert the elderly person; circumvent him.

Expedients are the only real substitute for morals.

He who reasons is lost.

**KRAUS, KARL** (Austria, 1874–1936) Kraus was an abrasive social critic, heaping scorn on everything from religion and patriotism to marriage, family life, and popular culture. For Kraus, civilization was in terminal decline, mostly because he believed crass consumerism was destroying art and culture. Kraus grew up in Vienna, a city that at the turn of the twentieth century was on the cutting edge of the most radical thinking in art, music, philosophy, and psychology. His father was a wealthy manufacturer who invented the paper bag, but Kraus loved literature, especially the theater. He founded, edited, and wrote most of the articles for *Die Fackel* ("The Torch"), a journal of literature and ideas that became hugely influential among Viennese artists and intellectuals, and *Die Fackel* was also the main outlet for his aphorisms. Kraus was fiercely independent of any dogma or intellectual clique. He ruthlessly attacked his perceived opponents and often declined to acknowledge greetings on the street. Kraus once wrote that his business was "to pin down the Age between quotation marks," but instead he drove an aphoristic dagger through its heart. Kraus was a devotee of Georg Christoph Lichtenberg, with whom he shared a bitter, piercing wit and a disdain for conventional social mores. He may have named *Die Fackel* with a Lichtenberg saying in mind: "It is impossible to carry the torch of truth through a crowd without singeing someone's beard."

*Essential Aphorisms*

An aphorism does not need to be true, but it should outwing the truth. It must get beyond it with a spin.

Society: everyone was there who was supposed to be there and who could not imagine Being having any purpose other than Being There.

A real man is someone who will never do the dirty deeds he is thought capable of. A half-man, someone never thought capable of the dirty deeds he does.

Social policy is the desperate surgical decision to remove corns from a cancer patient.

It is an enigma to me how a theologian can be praised because he has struggled his way to unbelief. The achievement that always struck me as most heroic and praiseworthy was struggling through to belief.

Grasping the world with a glance is art. Amazing how much fits into an eye!

Scarcely anyone would have become a great actor if the public had been born without hands.

What enters the ear easily leaves easily too. What goes in hard comes out hard. This goes for writing even more than music making.

Views reproduce by division, thoughts by budding.

With what the heart lacketh the mouth overfloweth.

Art serves to rinse out our eyes.

The mission of the press is to spread culture while destroying the attention span.

When someone has behaved like an animal, he says: "I'm only human!" But when he is treated like an animal, he says: "I'm human, too!"

Hate must make one productive; otherwise one might as well love.

Love and art do not embrace what is beautiful but what is made beautiful by this embrace.

Experiences are savings that a miser puts aside. Wisdom is an inheritance that a wastrel cannot exhaust.

Let language be the divining rod that finds sources of thought.

You don't even live once.

*Parallel Lines: Life*

Life is an effort that deserves a better cause.            —KRAUS

Life is a tragedy for those who feel and a comedy for those who think.
                                        —JEAN DE LA BRUYÈRE

Life is a progress from want to want, not from enjoyment to enjoyment.
                                        —SAMUEL JOHNSON

Life is not a problem to be solved, but a reality to be experienced.
                                        —SØREN KIERKEGAARD

Life is but an endless series of experiments.     —MOHANDAS K. GANDHI

Life is a series of collisions with the future; it is not the sum of what we
have been, but what we yearn to be.         —JOSÉ ORTEGA Y GASSET

Life is a dinner party without a host.
And, frequently, without a dinner party either.       —FRANK KUPPNER

**KRUGER, BARBARA** (United States, 1945–  ) Kruger started out in New York during the 1960s as a graphic designer working on women's magazines. She playfully parodies the arch-nemesis of the aphorism, the advertisement, by juxtaposing traditional advertising images with her own tart sayings. Kruger's work has become fodder for the commercial culture she satirizes. Her characteristic red border; her retro images of stereotypical family scenes from the 1950s; her big, bold typography—they're all used regularly in actual advertisements.

*Essential Aphorisms*

We don't need another hero.

When I hear the word culture I take out my checkbook.

I shop therefore I am.

God said it. I believe it. And that settles it.

**KUPPNER, FRANK** (United Kingdom, 1951–   ) Born in Glasgow, Scotland, Kuppner describes himself as "semi-employed"; that is, he's a full-time writer. Many of his volumes of poetry emerged from chance encounters in second-hand bookshops. *A Bad Day for the Sung Dynasty*, for example, is a series of more than 500 quatrains written as imaginary captions for the images in a Swedish book on ancient Chinese painting.

*Essential Aphorisms*

Whatever happened to you was whatever was meant to happen;
And if the opposite happened, then that too was just as meant.

If I thought every day was a new start, I would kill myself.
I would do so over and over again for as long as might prove necessary.

Some things change for the better, Marcus. Some things change for the worse.
And some things change, apparently, for the mere sake of change.

Alas, the great old stories are being forgotten.
And, what's worse, the terrible new ones are being made up.

The universe has farted immensely in all our faces;
And we try to ignore the huge stink as best we can.

Make your next move from where you actually are.

Art is the perfume sprinkled on a privy.

Another flaw of old age is that it does not last long enough.

**LAUB, GABRIEL** (Poland, 1928–1998) Laub grew up near Krakow, Poland, but in 1939 he and his family fled the Nazi persecution of the Jews, eventually ending up in the Soviet Union. Laub escaped one set of persecutors only to fall into the hands of another; he and his family were interned in the Urals by the Soviets for sixteen months. After World War II, Laub settled in Prague, where he worked as an author and journalist and translated the plays of Václav Havel. But when the Soviets crushed the Prague Spring democracy movement in 1968, Laub fled again, this time to Hamburg, where he began writing and publishing his politically pungent aphorisms. Laub's aphorisms have the same shrewd humor and wicked political sting as those of his fellow countryman Stanislaw Jerzy Lec.

*Essential Aphorisms*

In a totalitarian regime, idiots gain power through violence and intrigue; in a democracy, through free elections.

Theory should never forget that it is nothing but applied practice.

When everyone is courageous that's reason enough to worry.

Crown: A headgear that makes the head superfluous.

Man: an ape that has gotten past the censor.

Political parties with strong wings develop weak legs.

Courageousness is a way of death, not a way of life.

Negation is the stronger faith.

Dogma: the attempt to create a one-ended stick.

Why isn't there any punishment for the rape of muses?

Imagination is something some people cannot imagine.

The battle of the sexes is quite a pleasant one.

With its first attempt to think humankind began to live beyond its means.

Dogmatists are strange hyenas. They feed on the carrion of those thoughts they killed themselves.

Objectivity and courage increase in direct proportion to the square of distance.

Why shouldn't the egg feel wiser than the chicken? After all, it knows the chicken's darkest side.

Thus speaks the career: "Thou shall have no other gods before Me . . ."

All power comes from the people and never returns there.

Who will save the world from the saviors?

Collections of aphorisms: the cheapest clearance sale.

### Parallel Lines: Aphorisms

Men appreciate aphorisms because, among other reasons, they contain half-truths. That is an unusually high percentage.          —LAUB

When you wish to instruct, be brief; that men's minds take in quickly what you say, learn its lesson, and retain it faithfully. Every word that is unnecessary only pours over the side of a brimming mind.          —CICERO

Do not be a bore. The person obsessed with one activity or one topic is apt to be tiresome. Brevity is flattering and gets more accomplished—it gains by courtesy what it loses by curtness. Good things, when short, are twice as good. Well said is soon said.          —BALTASAR GRACIÁN

An aphorism is the last link in a long chain of thought.
          —MARIE VON EBNER-ESCHENBACH

There's a great power in words, if you don't hitch too many of them together.          —JOSH BILLINGS

The shortest aphorism that makes you think the longest is the best.
          —JULIEN DE VALCKENAERE

Bite-sized knowledge is not always easy to swallow.          —JACK GARDNER

**LEC, STANISLAW JERZY** (Poland, 1909–1966) "Life is too short to write long things," Lec once remarked. Born in Lvov, a city that in 1909 was in southeastern Poland but is now part of Ukraine, Lec came from a wealthy and aristocratic family. With the dismantling of the Austro-Hungarian Empire after World War I, he and his family lost most of their money and privileges. When World War II broke out, Lec was sent to a concentration camp in Tarnopol. He survived there for two years, until he managed to escape by donning a stolen German uniform. Back in Warsaw, he joined the communist resistance, first as an editor of underground periodicals and then as part of the guerrilla movement. After the war, Lec remained affiliated with the communists, serving as the press attaché at the Polish consulate in Vienna from 1946 to 1950. But he gradually grew disillusioned with communism. In his aphorisms, Lec parodied the feel-good platitudes and propaganda put out by the communist party machine. "Why do I write these short apho-risms?" he once asked. "Because words fail me!" Lec loved Vienna, partly because it was once the seat of his beloved Austro-Hungarian Empire and partly because it was the city where Karl Kraus, his literary idol and role model, used to live. Like Kraus, Lec was a satirist. While Kraus targeted the bourgeois values of Europe, Lec targeted the totalitarian state.

*Essential Aphorisms*

Stupidity is the mother of crime. But the fathers are frequently geniuses.

All is in the hands of man. Therefore wash them often.

When myth meets myth, the collision is very real.

You have to climb to reach a deep thought.

Never saw on the branch you are sitting on, unless they are trying to hang you from it.

Some people's thoughts are so shallow they don't even reach their heads.

Transparent aims cast a shadow.

It is easy to form a chain from a string of zeroes.

Many of those who were ahead of their time had to wait for it in not too comfortable quarters.

The weakest link in the chain is also the strongest. It can break the chain.

When everybody sings the same tune, the words are unimportant.

When Right goes before Might, it risks a shot in the back.

Pity the man who only sees stars when he is struck in the face.

The constitution of a country should not violate the constitution of its citizens.

When they blow the horn of plenty this loud, it must be empty.

I prefer the sign NO ENTRY to the one that says NO EXIT.

Tired rebels rest in the armchairs of power.

The strongest brakes fail on the path of least resistance.

Politics: a Trojan horse race.

There are those who reach great depths only to release little bubbles.

The mob shouts with one big mouth and eats with a thousand little ones.

The window on the world can be covered by a newspaper.

No snowflake in an avalanche ever feels responsible.

In the beginning was the Word—at the end just the Cliché.

### Parallel Lines: Stanislaw Jerzy Lec and Karl Kraus

It is amazingly difficult to raise an echo in empty heads.  —LEC

Lots of knowledge fits into a hollow head.  —KRAUS

Mud sometimes gives the illusion of depth.  —LEC

An illusion of depth often occurs if a blockhead is a muddlehead at the same time.  —KRAUS

An apt aphorism half kills, half immortalizes.  —LEC

Aphorisms are never congruent with the truth; they are either half-truths or one-and-a-half truths.  —KRAUS

**MENCKEN, H. L.** (United States, 1880–1956) Mencken always boasted of his great ability to resist temptation, proudly declaring, for example, that he didn't start smoking cigars until he was nine years old. That is more of an achievement than it might seem, since Mencken's father was the proprietor of the Mencken Cigar Company in Baltimore. The young Mencken's first job was at his father's factory, but he had his heart set on a career in journalism, going on to become the most controversial journalist and political commentator of his day. He is famous for his coverage in 1925 of the Scopes trial, in which lawyers William Jennings Bryan and Clarence Darrow clashed over a Tennessee law that forbade the teaching of evolution in public schools. Mencken dubbed it the "Monkey trial." He is also still renowned for "the bathtub hoax," an article in which Mencken credited U.S. president Millard Fillmore with popularizing the bathtub by having one installed in the White House in 1850. In fact, Mencken fabricated all the "facts" in the piece, but for years it was cited as a legitimate reference. As a satirist, Mencken attacked all forms of what he considered quackery (especially fundamentalist Christianity) and conformity (especially among the middle class), famously saying, "No one ever went broke underestimating the intelligence of the American middle class." Mencken was an aphorism collector, too; he compiled and edited *A New Dictionary of Quotations* in 1942. Mencken followed Friedrich Nietzsche in his rejection of middle-class morality and was deeply influenced by the great American aphorist-humorists like Mark Twain and especially Ambrose Bierce. Mencken once attended a funeral with Bierce, recalling how his role model unleashed a fusillade of gruesome but highly amusing witticisms all the way to the crematorium. During the drive, Bierce told Mencken that he kept the ashes of his deceased son on his writing desk. Mencken mumbled that the urn must be a "formidable ornament." "Urn hell!" Bierce thundered back. "I keep him in a cigar-box."

*Essential Aphorisms*

A politician is an animal which can sit on a fence and yet keep both ears to the ground.

As the arteries grow hard, the heart grows soft.

Conscience is the inner voice that warns us that someone might be looking.

Criticism is prejudice made plausible.

Democracy is a pathetic belief in the collective wisdom of individual ignorance.

For centuries, theologians have been explaining the unknowable in terms of the not-worth-knowing.

For every complex problem there is an answer that is clear, simple and wrong.

In war the heroes always outnumber the soldiers ten to one.

It is hard to believe that a man is telling the truth when you know that you would lie if you were in his place.

Love is the triumph of imagination over intelligence.

The whole aim of practical politics is to keep the populace alarmed (and hence clamorous to be led to safety) by menacing it with an endless series of hobgoblins, all of them imaginary.

We are here and it is now. Further than that, all human knowledge is moonshine.

When women kiss it always reminds one of prizefighters shaking hands.

Whenever a husband and wife begin to discuss their marriage they are giving evidence at a coroner's inquest.

**MESTRUM, THEO** (The Netherlands, 1956–  ) The Dutch language is rich in proverbs and proverbial expressions, many of which deal with the sea and are scattered liberally throughout everyday speech and in magazines and newspapers. Mestrum first began experimenting with these expressions—changing them around, subverting their original meanings—when he was in high school. He discovered aphorisms proper at university, when he bought one of those appointment diaries that sports a saying on every page. "Why couldn't I write these myself?" he wondered at the time. So he did.

*Essential Aphorisms*

Forced companionship makes you even lonelier.

An ideal is a blueprint for failure.

The biggest disagreements appear where the differences are least.

Whoever shouts is heard from far away but is not understood from close up.

Travel is for people who don't know the way home.

At least people who hide their heads in the sand don't run away.

The winner and the loser have a lost dream in common.

Death is unavoidable, life can pass you by.

### Parallel Lines: The Next Step

The second step in the right direction is the most difficult.  —MESTRUM

The great difficulty which history records is not that of the first step, but that of the second step.  —WALTER BAGEHOT

**MORGENSTERN, CHRISTIAN** (Germany, 1871–1914) The title of Morgenstern's most popular work, *Songs of the Gallows*, is typical of his black humor. Inspired by English nonsense rhymes, Morgenstern parodied all types of people from all social classes, though his verse and aphorisms are always tinged with a hint of darkness.

### Essential Aphorisms

If you do not want to conquer the world anew every single day, you will lose more of it day by day.

Why do you look left and right and get angry with your neighbor? You'd do better to get angry with yourself.

Enthusiasm is the most beautiful word in the world.

He who wants to remain true to himself cannot always remain true to others.

Modern man overheats too easily. He lacks too much of the oil of love.

For countless people there is only one remedy: the catastrophe.

**PARONEN, SAMULI** (Finland, 1917–1974) Paronen is Finland's quintessential anti-literary figure. He worked on farms and in the forestry industry for years before publishing a series of novels and a collection of short stories, all of which are written from the perspective of society's outcasts and underdogs. He was a relentless critic of consumer culture and the market economy. In the early 1970s, Paronen came up with the idea of "independence money," a government subsidy designed to provide a basic income to all Finns "without any quid pro quo except being a human being." His best-known work is his collection of aphorisms, *Maailma on Sana* ("The World Is a Word"). The Samuli Paronen Prize is awarded every year—on May 23, Paronen's birthday—to the best Finnish writer of aphorisms.

*Essential Aphorisms*

The most intelligence is wasted on the greatest foolishness.

Occupations used to be left to the children when the parents died; now the occupations die first, and people go looking for new ones.

More and more people have to work harder and harder to earn the right to do something else.

Guilt turns anyone into a prosecutor.

When they don't want to defend people they put them in uniforms and start defending the country.

When a person breaks the law, he has committed a crime. When the law breaks a person, it has fulfilled its task.

Power also ruins those who have none at all.

Real winners do not compete.

**POPE, ALEXANDER** (United Kingdom, 1688–1744) When Pope was about eight, he contracted spinal tuberculosis from infected milk. The disease stunted his growth—as an adult, he stood just four feet six inches tall—and caused a progressive curvature of his spine. He was prone to severe headaches, spasmodic fits, and respiratory problems. Toward the end of his life, he was unable to dress himself and had to wear an iron corset just to sit upright. Pope's illness did not blunt his satirical wit or his poetic output, though. In addition to his major works—*An Essay on Criticism*, *An Essay on Man*, and *The Dunciad*—he earned a modest fortune from his popular translation of the *Iliad*. Pope embraced the "grin and bear it" philosophy of the Stoics, particularly bringing up to date Epictetus's distinction between things we can and cannot control. Michel de Montaigne and Erasmus also influenced Pope; like them, he was a humanist thinker who rejected all forms of religious and moral dogmatism and believed that human failings should be treated with a modicum of mirth.

## Essential Aphorisms

They who say our thoughts are not our own, because they resemble the ancients, may as well say our faces are not our own, because they are like our fathers.

Wit and fine writing doth not consist so much in advancing things that are new, as in giving things that are known an agreeable turn.

Party is the madness of many for the gain of a few.

Some people will never learn anything for this reason, because they understand everything too soon.

A little learning is a dangerous thing.

To err is human, to forgive divine.

Fools rush in where angels fear to tread.

Hope springs eternal in the human breast.

'Tis with our judgements as our watches, none
Go just alike, yet each believes his own.

All Nature is but Art, unknown to thee;
All Chance, Direction, which thou canst not see;
All Discord, Harmony, not understood;
All partial Evil, universal Good:
And, spite of Pride, in erring Reason's spite,
One truth is clear, "Whatever is, is right."

In Parts superior what advantage lies?
Tell (for You can) what is it to be wise?
'Tis but to know how little can be known;
To see all others faults, and feel our own.

Know then thyself, presume not God to scan;
The proper study of mankind is man.

**RANEVSKAYA, FAINA** (Russia, 1896–1984) Ranevskaya was born in the small provincial town of Taganrog, on the Azov Sea in southern Russia. At the age of fourteen, she went to the theater for the first time; the play was Chekhov's *Cherry Orchard*. From that moment on, she was determined to become an actor. She may have even taken her stage name Ranevskaya (her real surname was Feldman) from one of the characters in the play. When she was nineteen, Ranevskaya ran away to Moscow to study acting, but the city's theater schools rejected her. Short of money, she returned to Taganrog and began performing with provincial troupes—and soon won local and then national renown, going on to become one of Russia's most beloved actors. She never wrote a book. Her aphorisms are collected from the extensive correspondence she conducted with many of her fans as well as the scraps of paper on which she quickly jotted down her thoughts. "When I don't act or work on a role," she once wrote, "I feel like a pianist whose hands have been amputated."

*Essential Aphorisms*

One should live his life in such a way that even bastards remember him.

Life is a short walk before an eternal dream.

Acting in a bad film is like spitting into eternity.

Optimism is lack of information.

Women are much smarter than men. No one has ever heard of a woman who lost her head only because a man had slender legs.

Health is when every day it hurts in a different place.

Doctors are powerless if a patient longs to live.

Baldness is the gradual transformation of the head into an ass, first in shape and then in content.

**ROGERS, WILL** (United States, 1879–1935) Rogers is remembered as a storyteller and humorist, but he got his start as a cowboy on his family's ranch in Oklahoma. At one point he made it into *The Guinness Book of Records* for his roping skills. He could throw three lassos at the same time: one around the neck of a galloping horse, another around the rider, and the third around the horse's legs. He demonstrated his lariat abilities in Wild West shows and on vaudeville stages, where he eventually began telling jokes and stories. One of his most famous lines, and the epitome of his homely philosophy, is: "I never met a man I didn't like."

*Essential Aphorisms*

Everybody is ignorant. Only on different subjects.

People don't change under governments. Governments change. People remain the same.

Diplomats are just as essential to starting a war as soldiers are for finishing it.

No man is great if he thinks he is.

Live your life so that whenever you lose, you are ahead.

If you live life right, death is a joke as far as fear is concerned.

**SCUTENAIRE, LOUIS** (Belgium, 1905–1987) Throughout his life, Scutenaire managed to straddle seemingly incompatible worlds: he was both a leading surrealist and a practicing criminal lawyer, an anarchist and a civil servant in the Belgian Ministry of the Interior. Along with his close friend René Magritte, who often asked Scutenaire to give titles to his paintings, he was a key member of Belgium's surrealist movement. Scutenaire's first collection of aphorisms, *Mes Inscriptions*, was published in 1945, containing "thoughts that everyone has, but does not write," he said. He produced a second volume, but Gallimard, his French publisher, wanted several lines cut. Scutenaire refused, and the book wasn't published until thirteen years later in Brussels. He died twenty years to the hour after Magritte, just after watching a television program about the painter.

*Essential Aphorisms*

Unique splendor of passion, trivial ugliness of its playing out.

A secret only exists when someone knows it.

He who understands, invents.

The biggest enemies of a regime are the agents of its propaganda.

Of course there are sometimes great signs in the sky: the clouds.

The real does not have an opposite.

To have neither faith nor hope but a correct knowledge of the play of probabilities.

I am talking to you about another world, yours.

What exists must be created.

To build Paradise with bricks baked in Hell.

**SHENDEROVICH, VICTOR** (Russia, 1958–   ) Between 1997 and 2002, Shenderovich was a familiar presence on Russian television, the host of his own current affairs chat show. He was instantly recognizable to millions of viewers by his neatly trimmed black beard, which he shaved off between each series. Shenderovich's wit and barbed critiques of the government won him a wide following, but they may have also prompted the authorities to cancel his show in 2002 as ownership of the country's main television stations shifted increasingly toward the state. Now Shenderovich sticks to radio, and he says he won't regrow his beard until there is a new, more democratic government in Russia.

*Essential Aphorisms*

In the state of metronomes, syncopation is illegal.

Several generations may fall into the gap between two epochs.

Those who talk of unity sometimes mean a communal grave.

A state is as easy to ride as a bicycle: handles at the top, chains below . . .

The guard is forced to follow in the footsteps of the prisoner.

There is no drumstick that doesn't dream of becoming a baton.

**SWIFT, JONATHAN** (Ireland, 1667–1745) The author of *Gulliver's Travels* was born in Dublin to English immigrant parents and spent much of his adult life shuttling between Ireland and England in pursuit of positions and preferment. Swift was ordained a priest in the Church of Ireland in the 1690s and was eventually appointed dean of St. Patrick's, Dublin. In addition to performing his duties as a cleric, Swift began writing satirical pamphlets that both chastised and championed his countrymen, including *A Modest Proposal*, in which Swift suggested that the Irish could free themselves from poverty by selling their children to the rich as food. Citing statistical evidence to support his scheme, and even offering a selection of recipes, he argued that cannibalism was the only way to address the country's problems of overpopulation and chronic unemployment. Not everyone took Swift's broadsides in the satirical spirit in which they were intended. After the publication of *A Modest Proposal*, Swift was widely condemned for his apparent barbarism. As his reputation as an author grew, Swift founded the Martinus Scriblerus Club with close friends like John Arbuthnot, John Gay, and fellow aphorist Alexander Pope. The goal of this informal group was to debunk intellectual pretense in politics, religion, and morality. Swift accomplished this with particular glee, in his books and pamphlets as well as a short collection of aphorisms called *Thoughts on Various Subjects*. The dean of St. Patrick's held few things sacred, least of all the vanity and venality of men.

## Essential Aphorisms

How is it possible to expect that mankind will take advice, when they will not so much as take warning?

When a true genius appears in the world you may know him by this sign; that the dunces are all in confederacy against him.

Ambition often puts men upon doing the meanest offices; so climbing is performed in the same posture with creeping.

Men are never so serious, thoughtful, and intent, as when they are at stool.

Men who possess all the advantages of life are in a state where there are many accidents to disorder and discompose, but few to please them.

It is in disputes as in armies, where the weaker side sets up false lights and makes great noise to make the enemy believe them more numerous and strong than they really are.

If a man would register all his opinions upon love, politics, religion, learning, etc., beginning from his youth and so go on to old age, what a bundle of inconsistencies and contradictions would appear at last!

Complaint is the largest tribute heaven receives, and the sincerest part of our devotion.

Small causes are sufficient to make a man uneasy when great ones are not in the way. For want of a block he will stumble at a straw.

Most sorts of diversion in men, children and other animals are an imitation of fighting.

Satire is a sort of glass, wherein beholders do generally discover everybody's face but their own.

Although men are accused for not knowing their weakness, yet perhaps as few know their own strength.

**TUCHOLSKY, KURT** (Germany, 1890–1935) One of the Weimar Republic's most influential journalists, Tucholsky was among the first to spot the threat posed by the rise of Hitler and National Socialism. When the Nazis finally did come to power in 1933, Tucholsky's books were burned and his German citizenship was revoked. By that time, though, he was already living in exile in Sweden and struggling with the recurrent health problems that would lead to his death two years later. Tucholsky got an early start as a political satirist. While still at university, his first piece was published in *Ulk* ("Prank"), a weekly satirical magazine. For the rest of his life, Tucholsky held editorial positions on publications with strong left-wing, pro-democratic and anti-militaristic views. In addition to aphorisms, which he always referred to as "snippets," Tucholsky composed politically irreverent songs and jokey couplets for cabaret. In 1929, when a close friend and colleague was imprisoned for treason after publishing an article on German rearmament, Tucholsky decided never to return to Germany.

*Essential Aphorisms*

A hole is there where something isn't.

You should always pay attention to quality. A coffin, for instance, should last a lifetime.

Every glorification of a person killed in war means three dead in the next war.

When someone hasn't learned anything, he organizes. When someone hasn't learned anything and has nothing to do, however, he makes propaganda.

I prefer a skeptical Catholic to a devout atheist.

The pessimist. "I'm going to die one day. Just my luck, naturally!"

The nicest thing about intoxication is the moment when it begins, and the memory of it.

In marriage one person is usually the dupe. Only when two dupes get married—that may work well.

If elections changed anything, they would be forbidden.

No one holds up a red card to an ocean.

Experiences are not hereditary—you have to make them yourself.

Nothing is harder and nothing requires a stronger character than being in opposition to your time and to say loudly: No.

Language is a weapon, keep it honed!

Life can sometimes be hard for women. But we men have to shave.

Most people's cruelty is a lack of imagination and their brutality ignorance.

Expect nothing. Today: that is your life.

Experience means nothing. You can bungle something for thirty-five years.

Apart from other matter, man also excretes words. One shouldn't take that too seriously.

**TWAIN, MARK** (United States, 1835–1910) Samuel Langhorne Clemens was born in Florida, Missouri, and moved to Hannibal—home of Huck Finn and Tom Sawyer—when he was four. At the beginning of the Civil War, he briefly joined a ragtag Confederate militia but didn't see any action. In 1861, he became a reporter for a variety of Nevada newspapers, writing satirical sketches and short pieces of fiction that were parodies of real events and people. When the recipients of Clemens's satire started getting upset, and litigious, his editor suggested he might want to consider a pseudonym. Thus, Mark Twain was born. Twain's biggest influence was Benjamin Franklin, a man whose rough, homespun persona

Twain adopted but whose philosophy he relentlessly parodied. Both men were once printer's apprentices; both were seasoned travelers; both loved technology; and both had a love for moneymaking schemes. But Twain wanted to be the anti-Franklin in everything, deliberately setting out to overturn Franklin's friendly, avuncular sayings with his own darker, more ornery aphorisms.

### Essential Aphorisms

The trouble ain't that there is too many fools, but that the lightning ain't distributed right.

It is more trouble to make a maxim than it is to do right.

Prosperity is the best protector of principle.

No narrative that tells the facts of a man's life in the man's own words can be uninteresting.

Spending one's capital is feeding a dog on his own tail.

The best way to cheer yourself up is to try to cheer somebody else up.

Unexpected money is a delight. The same sum is a bitterness when you expected more.

If you pick up a starving dog and make him prosperous, he will not bite you. This is the principal difference between a dog and a man.

If we had less statesmanship we could get along with fewer battleships.

An uneasy conscience is a hair in the mouth.

Civilization is a limitless multiplication of unnecessary necessaries.

Do your duty today and repent tomorrow.

Good friends, good books and a sleepy conscience: this is the ideal life.

It is better to take what does not belong to you than to let it lie around neglected.

The altar-cloth of one aeon is the doormat of the next.

Few slanders can stand the wear of silence.

Courage is resistance to fear, mastery of fear—not absence of fear.

To promise not to do a thing is the surest way in the world to make a body want to go and do that very thing.

Why is it that we rejoice at a birth and grieve at a funeral? It is because we are not the person involved.

Be good and you will be lonesome.

The truth is the most valuable thing we have. Let us economize it.

It is easier to stay out than to get out.

Hunger is the handmaid of genius.

Grief can take care of itself; but to get the full value of a joy you must have somebody to divide it with.

Irreverence is the champion of liberty, and its only sure defense.

### Parallel Lines: Money

The lack of money is the root of all evil.                              —TWAIN

If money go before, all ways do lie open.          —WILLIAM SHAKESPEARE

Money is like muck, not good except it be spread.          —FRANCIS BACON

They who are of the opinion that money will do everything may very well be suspected to do everything for money.
                          —GEORGE SAVILE, FIRST MARQUIS OF HALIFAX

Money, which represents the prose of life, and which is hardly spoken of in parlors without an apology, is, in its effects and laws, as beautiful as roses.
                                    —RALPH WALDO EMERSON

The fundamental evil of the world arose from the fact that the good Lord has not created money enough.                    —HEINRICH HEINE

*Money* is human happiness *in abstracto*; consequently he who is no longer capable of happiness *in concreto* sets his whole heart on money.

—ARTHUR SCHOPENHAUER

If the love of money is the root of all evil, the want of it is so quite as truly.

—SAMUEL BUTLER

**VALCKENAERE, JULIEN DE** (Belgium, 1898–1958) Born in Ghent, De Valckenaere was a teacher and chief inspector of schools in Belgium. He published a book of poems in the late 1920s, but then published nothing else until his first collection of aphorisms appeared more than twenty years later, in 1949. Like Ambrose Bierce, De Valckenaere presents many of his aphorisms as definitions. He shares a fatalistic, mordant humor with Bierce and Mark Twain.

*Essential Aphorisms*

A world in which a better one can be dreamed of is not the worst.

Wise man: someone who lands on his feet even when wisdom has been turned on its head.

Charity: the only way that some people can bring themselves to part with their old clothes and shoes.

Definition: the little one knows about something presented as if he knows everything about it.

Don't say anything good about yourself, people won't believe you; don't say anything bad about yourself, people will do it as soon as you're gone.

Reflex: as soon as someone is slapped on the wrist he makes a fist.

Love makes two hearts one in order to more easily break them in two.

You must know more than you say in order to occasionally say more than you know.

It is reassuring to know that so many species became extinct before man had a hand in it.

There would be fewer false prophets if there were more Doubting Thomases willing to put their finger in the wound.

You never know what someone thinks of you until you have stepped on his toes.

When everyone praises you your funeral has begun.

It is easier to approve of what men do than to do what men approve of.

A pessimist: a sundial that only tells the time on cloudy days.

### Parallel Lines: Julien de Valckenaere and Mark Twain

Man: the only animal that is ashamed to be one.    —DE VALCKENAERE

Man is the only animal that blushes. Or needs to.    —TWAIN

April 1: the day on which we don't mind being treated the same as the other 364.    —DE VALCKENAERE

April 1: This is the day upon which we are reminded of what we are on the other three hundred and sixty-four.    —TWAIN

**VERHOEVEN, TOON** (The Netherlands, 1941–   ) *Terzijde*, the title of Verhoeven's collection of aphorisms, is also the name of the column in the weekly magazine *Vrij Nederland* that the Dutch author wrote for more than twenty-five years. In Dutch, *terzijde* means an aside, something mentioned in passing. But Verhoeven's passing remarks—on politics, modern manners, the environment—have incredible staying power.

### Essential Aphorisms

Better one butterfly in your stomach than ten in the air.

Ethics: Do good and let evil be done.

Man is by nature good, but his fellow man isn't.

Rich enough for a calorie-poor diet.

We eat too salty and live too bland.

When did the march of history start breaking into a sprint?

Politics is the art of the affordable.

The earth is round but we'll flatten it yet.

The biggest environmental disaster of all time is described in Genesis.

Heaven is a punishment for Calvinists because there they must enjoy themselves.

*Parallel Lines: Hair Pieces*

Honesty is a toupee of pubic hair.                    —VERHOEVEN

In spiritual matters young people often wear wigs, but of their
own hair.                              —HUGO VON HOFMANNSTHAL

Arrogance is a hairpiece for covering up an intellectual bald spot.

—JAN WERICH

**VOLTAIRE** (France, 1694–1778) Writing under the pseudonym Voltaire, François-Marie Arouet excoriated the Catholic Church and those French institutions he believed held back individual human rights and civil liberties. His sharp satirical and polemical wit led his works to be included in the Vatican's *Index of Forbidden Books*, forced him into several temporary exiles, and saw him locked up in the Bastille. He used his newfound leisure in prison to write his first play, *Oedipe*, the success of which brought him fame in Parisian aristocratic circles. After offending a nobleman, Voltaire found himself the subject of a secret warrant that permitted punishment without a crime or trial. Voltaire's sentence was exile in England, where he was greatly influenced by the country's embrace of freedom of speech and religion. He returned three years later to Paris, where copies of his account of the ideas he had encountered in England, *Philosophical Letters*, were burned because of their implicit criticism of the French monarchy. He was not a democrat, however. He was convinced that only an enlightened monarch, advised by a philosopher like himself, was fit to govern. Voltaire also picked up an interest in science in England, particularly in the theories of Isaac Newton, and conducted his own experiments at the Château de Cirey in the Champagne region of France, where he retreated after his books were burned in Paris. Voltaire was a pronounced enemy of religion throughout his life and a firm believer in the separation of church and state. On his deathbed, when asked to renounce Satan and accept God, he replied: "Now is no time to be making new enemies."

*Essential Aphorisms*

Common sense is not so common.

Those who can make you believe absurdities can make you commit atrocities.

Paradise is where I am.

Use, do not abuse. Neither abstinence nor excess ever renders man happy.

To hold a pen is to be at war.

If God did not exist, it would be necessary to invent him.

If God has made us in his image, we have returned him the favor.

It is dangerous to be right in matters where established men are wrong.

We must cultivate our garden.

When we hear news, we should always wait for the sacrament of confirmation.

Prejudice is an opinion without judgment.

It is forbidden to kill; therefore all murderers are punished unless they kill in large numbers and to the sound of trumpets.

All is for the best in the best of all possible worlds.

The best is the enemy of the good.

God is a comedian playing to an audience too afraid to laugh.

History is the lie commonly agreed upon.

Love truth, but pardon error.

A witty saying proves nothing.

*Parallel Lines: Doubt*

Doubt is not an agreeable condition, but certainty is an absurd one.

—VOLTAIRE

If a man will begin with certainties, he shall end in doubts; but if he will be content to begin with doubts he shall end in certainties. —FRANCIS BACON

You really only know when you know little; doubt grows with knowledge.

—JOHANN WOLFGANG VON GOETHE

The search for truth is more precious than its possession.

—ALBERT EINSTEIN

All firm belief is a sickness.

—FRANCIS PICABIA

Believe those who are seeking the truth; doubt those who find it.

—ANDRÉ GIDE

Doubt is the yeast of cognition.        —ALESSANDRO MORANDOTTI

**WELLER, MIKHAIL** (Russia, 1948–   ) Weller feigned mental illness so he could drop out of college and avoid the obligatory military service in the Soviet army that would have ensued upon leaving school. He thoroughly enjoyed the two months of enforced leisure that followed. He was a brilliant student of philology at Leningrad University, but he gave up academia for a life of manual labor and odd jobs. At various times during his life, he's been a cattleman in Siberia, a lumberjack, railroad worker, and primary school teacher. Throughout these occupations, though, he continued to write, penning the novels and short stories in which his aphorisms can be found.

*Essential Aphorisms*

An unlucky person is not someone who has little of something, but someone who suffers and is miserable because of the need to have more.

Love is the instinct for reproduction triumphing over the instinct for self-preservation.

The more energetic and talented a man is the less he can be restrained at any stage.

It's easy to be kind when somebody else's needs don't infringe upon yours.

**WERICH, JAN** (Czech Republic, 1905–1980) Werich was one of Czechoslovakia's most beloved clowns. Between the two world wars, he collaborated with actor Jiří Voskovec and jazz musician Jaroslav Ježek on a series of absurdist political satires. Inspired by Dada, the troupe had a strong socialist bent, taking aim at militarism, totalitarianism, and conventional bourgeois values. Werich went into exile in the United States in 1938 but returned to Czechoslovakia after the war. Despite the communist takeover of 1948 and frequent run-ins with state censors, Werich remained committed to living in the country for the rest of his life. He enjoyed widespread popularity both on TV and in film. In 1968 he emerged as an outspoken supporter of the Prague Spring pro-democracy movement. But after the Soviet invasion in August of that year, he was rarely permitted to perform in public.

*Essential Aphorisms*

Memory is the domain of the dumb. The smart have no time to remember. The smart must invent.

One woman can sometimes see farther than five men with binoculars.

God created man but did not have it patented, and so now any nitwit can copy him.

There is nothing that undermines a man's self-confidence more than an uncertainty as to the number of his own children.

The world is set up in a way that a great number of nitwits pretend to be smart. Of those smart people, who are scarce in the world, only the smartest ones play dumb.

Laughter heals smart people and offends only nitwits.

**WRIGHT, STEVEN** (United States, 1955–   ) Wright's autobiography, as published on his Web site, makes compelling reading and is worth quoting in full: "I was born. When I was twenty-three I started telling jokes. Then I started going on television and doing films. That's still what I am doing. The end."

*Essential Aphorisms*

The early bird gets the worm, but the second mouse gets the cheese.

If everything seems to be going well, you have obviously overlooked something.

Dancing is a perpendicular expression of a horizontal desire.

A conclusion is the place where you got tired of thinking.

A clear conscience is usually the sign of a bad memory.

Experience is something you don't get until just after you need it.

The sooner you fall behind, the more time you'll have to catch up.

A conscience is what hurts when all your other parts feel so good.

**ZAKIĆ, RASTKO** (Serbia, 1942–  ) In 1984, Zakić was prosecuted and imprisoned for writing aphorisms like this: "Only when our Father [a reference to the late Yugoslav president Josip Broz, known as Marshal Tito] died did we realize he had abused us." A year later, he published the same aphorisms again, only this time with a slightly different, presumably more acceptable meaning: "When our Father died, the court found he actually didn't abuse us." He was arrested and sent to jail once more, after unsuccessfully arguing that he shouldn't be convicted twice for saying two opposed things. He is the author of some thirty books of satirical aphorisms and poetry, many of which end with the sarcastic statement: "All the characters in this book are completely invented, even the author."

*Essential Aphorisms*

Those who crawl cannot be brought down.

One should forgive one's enemies, and then destroy them as friends.

The distance from here to a brighter future can only be measured in light years.

He who is ahead of his time is closer to his grave.

# ICONS AND ICONOCLASTS

**I**CONS and iconoclasts are a nomadic species. They can be found just as readily in the fields of sport and entertainment as in religion, science, or politics. They tend to congregate around social and psychological fault lines, often opening up the first cracks in the status quo. Although their words and actions inspire trends, movements, and even revolutions, they tend to travel mostly on their own. And even when they are part of a group, they somehow manage to remain above and beyond it, too. Someone once described Winston Churchill as a pillar of society. "No," Churchill said, "I'm more of a flying buttress." That's true of all icons and iconoclasts. They stand alone, and they often bear the heaviest loads.

**ALI, MUHAMMAD** (United States, 1942–　) Ali has a bicycle thief to thank for his start in boxing. When the twelve-year-old Cassius Clay (as he was then called) came out of an auditorium in Louisville, Kentucky, to find his bike stolen, he reported the theft to a police officer who coached the local boxing team, adding that he wouldn't mind punishing the perpetrator himself. The officer suggested Clay first learn how to fight before administering justice. Clay started training the next day. As a professional, Ali was as famous for his wit as for his exploits in the ring. But he could always take as well as he could give. When asked to fasten his seatbelt on a flight, he told the attendant: "Superman don't need no seatbelt." "Superman don't need no airplane, either," the attendant hit back.

*Essential Aphorisms*

> If they can make penicillin out of moldy bread, they can sure make something out of you.

> It isn't the mountains ahead to climb that wear you out, it's the pebble in your shoe.

It's not bragging if you can back it up.

Service to others is the rent you pay for your room here on earth.

The man who views the world at fifty the same as he did at twenty has wasted thirty years of his life.

To be a great champion you must believe you are the best. If you're not, pretend you are.

Wisdom is knowing when you can't be wise.

Float like a butterfly
Sting like a bee.
Your hands can't hit
What your eyes can't see.

**BAGEHOT, WALTER** (United Kingdom, 1826–1877) As editor of the *Economist* from 1861 until his death, Bagehot tried to make the English newspaper's style "conversational, to put things in the most direct and picturesque manner, as people would talk to each other in common speech." That is certainly the style of Bagehot's aphorisms, which are strewn among his journalistic writings; literary criticism; and books on economics, banking, politics, and the constitution of the United Kingdom. The *Economist*'s weekly column on British politics is named in his honor.

*Essential Aphorisms*

One of the greatest pains to human nature is the pain of a new idea.

The greatest pleasure in life is doing what people say you cannot do.

The reason why so few good books are written is that so few people who can write know anything.

The whole history of civilization is strewn with creeds and institutions which were invaluable at first, and deadly afterward.

It is good to be without vices, but it is not good to be without temptations.

Honor sinks where commerce long prevails.

So long as there are earnest believers in the world, they will always wish to punish opinions.

When great questions end, little parties begin.

**BARUCH, BERNARD** (United States, 1870–1965) Baruch made himself a millionaire before he was thirty. He also had some great nicknames. In the early 1900s, the young financier was known as "the lone wolf of Wall Street" because of his insistence on staying with his own brokerage firm instead of joining up with a larger financial group. And during his days as a democratic presidential adviser (he was a key confidant of Woodrow Wilson and Franklin D. Roosevelt during World Wars I and II, respectively), he was dubbed "the park bench statesman" because of his habit of discussing economic affairs while seated on a bench in Washington, D.C.'s, Lafayette Park, just across from the White House. He was the first person to describe the struggle between the United States and the Soviet Union after World War II as a "cold war." A bench in Lafayette Park is dedicated to him.

*Essential Aphorisms*

Always do one thing less than you think you can do.

If all you have is a hammer, everything looks like a nail.

Never follow the crowd.

The art of living lies not in eliminating but in growing with troubles.

The ability to express an idea is well nigh as important as the idea itself.

Two things are bad for the heart—running up stairs and running down people.

Vote for the man who promises least; he'll be the least disappointing.

We did not all come over on the same ship, but we are all in the same boat.

**BURKE, EDMUND** (United Kingdom, 1729–1797) Burke's nickname in the British House of Commons was "Dinner Bell" because his fellow Members of Parliament routinely left the chamber to get something to eat as soon as he took the floor to speak. Burke may not have been much of an orator, but his political ideas did have a profound influence on Great Britain. An MP for almost thirty years, he supported the American colonies in their dispute with King George III and argued that elected politicians should serve as a restraint on royal power. He was also a fervent opponent of the persecution of Catholics in Ireland. His *Reflections on the Revolution in France* accurately predicted the violence and political chaos that followed the 1789 revolt. Burke was also a close friend of fellow English aphorist Samuel Johnson.

*Essential Aphorisms*

A state without the means of some change is without the means of its conservation.

All that is necessary for the triumph of evil is that good men do nothing.

Ambition can creep as well as soar.

Applause is the spur of noble minds, the end and aim of weak ones.

Custom reconciles us to everything.

He that wrestles with us strengthens our nerves and sharpens our skill. Our antagonist is our helper.

If we command our wealth, we shall be rich and free; if our wealth commands us, we are poor indeed.

Laws, like houses, lean on one another.

Our patience will achieve more than our force.

Society can overlook murder, adultery or swindling; it never forgives preaching of a new gospel.

Never despair, but if you do, work on in despair.

Nobody made a greater mistake than he who did nothing because he could do only a little.

**CHURCHILL, WINSTON** (United Kingdom, 1874–1965) Every Thursday evening, Churchill would leave 10 Downing Street for Chartwell, his family home in

Kent. When his driver reached Crystal Palace, Churchill always signaled him to stop at the same roadside newspaper vendor so he could pick up the late editions. The Prime Minister rolled down his window and the vendor handed him his papers. "In exchange," says Jane Williams, Churchill's personal secretary during his second stint as British Prime Minister, from 1951 to 1955, "he would hand the vendor the end of his cigar, which by that time was totally sodden." Williams often traveled with Churchill to Chartwell, all the while taking dictation. "He was always talking," she recalls. "After we passed Crystal Palace, he would start reciting poetry—Kipling, Tennyson, Hardy, and the whole of the *Ancient Mariner*—with tears streaming down his face. He was a great weeper." Churchill was also a brilliant spontaneous aphorist, and he recommended aphorisms as a way to keep the mind sharp. "It is a good thing for an uneducated man to read books of quotations," he wrote in one of his autobiographical works. "*Bartlett's Familiar Quotations* is an admirable work, and I studied it intently. The quotations when engraved upon the memory give you good thoughts. They also make you anxious to read the authors and look for more." After he left politics for good in 1955, Churchill's health began to decline. During a party to celebrate his seventy-fifth birthday, he quipped: "I am ready to meet my Maker. Whether my Maker is prepared for the ordeal of meeting me is another matter."

*Essential Aphorisms*

Success is the ability to go from failure to failure with no loss of enthusiasm.

It is better to be making the news than taking it, to be an actor rather than a critic.

Never give in—never, never, never, never, in nothing great or small, large or petty, never give in except to convictions of honor and good sense.

Now this is not the end. It is not even the beginning of the end. But it is, perhaps, the end of the beginning.

The empires of the future are the empires of the mind.

Democracy is the worst form of government except all those other forms that have been tried from time to time.

In war: resolution. In defeat: defiance. In victory: magnanimity. In peace: good will.

For myself, I am an optimist—it does not seem to be much use being anything else.

In time of war, when truth is so precious, it must be attended by a bodyguard of lies.

I have always felt that a politician is to be judged by the animosities he excites among his opponents.

Men occasionally stumble over the truth, but most of them pick themselves up and hurry off as if nothing ever happened.

It is a mistake to try to look too far ahead. The chain of destiny can only be grasped one link at a time.

The biggest argument against democracy is a five-minute discussion with the average voter.

Without tradition, art is a flock of sheep without a shepherd. Without innovation, it is a corpse.

The inherent vice of capitalism is the unequal sharing of blessings; the inherent virtue of socialism is the equal sharing of misery.

To improve is to change. To be perfect is to change often.

To jaw-jaw is always better than to war-war.

When you have to kill a man it costs nothing to be polite.

Withhold no sacrifice, begrudge no toil, seek no sordid gain, fear no foe, all will be well.

You have enemies? Good. That means you've stood up for something, sometime in your life.

*Parallel Lines: When the Tough Get Going*

If you're going through hell, keep going.                    —CHURCHILL

Life is thickly sown with thorns, and I know no other remedy than to pass quickly through them. The longer we dwell on our misfortunes, the greater is their power to harm us.

—VOLTAIRE

**CICERO, MARCUS TULLIUS** (Rome, 106–43 BCE) Cicero's eloquence won him great political influence in Rome, but it also proved his undoing. After Caesar's assassination, Cicero urged the Senate to declare Mark Antony a public enemy. He excoriated Antony in a series of impassioned speeches known as the Philippics. So, when Octavian, Caesar's heir, struck an alliance with Mark Antony and seized power, Cicero was hunted down by Antony's troops and decapitated. His head and hands were carried back to Rome and nailed to the podium from which he had delivered his speeches. Antony's wife, Fulvia, ripped Cicero's tongue from his skull and repeatedly stabbed it with a hairpin.

*Essential Aphorisms*

While there's life, there's hope.

Let the punishment match the offense.

If a man aspires to the highest place, it is no dishonor to him to halt at the second, or even at the third.

To be ignorant of the past is to forever be a child.

To each his own.

A room without books is like a body without a soul.

All action is of the mind and the mirror of the mind is the face, its index the eyes.

Politicians are not born; they are excreted.

The wise are instructed by reason; ordinary minds by experience; the stupid by necessity; and brutes by instinct.

A man's own manner and character is what most becomes him.

Advice in old age is foolish; for what can be more absurd than to increase our provisions for the road the nearer we approach to our journey's end.

I criticize by creation, not by finding fault.

If we are not ashamed to think it, we should not be ashamed to say it.

If you have a garden and a library, you have everything you need.

The greater the difficulty, the greater the glory.

The higher we are placed, the more humbly we should walk.

What one has, one ought to use; and whatever one does one should do with all one's might.

You will be as much value to others as you have been to yourself.

### Parallel Lines: Tears

A tear dries quickly when it is shed for the troubles of others.    —CICERO

Nothing dries sooner than a tear.    —BENJAMIN FRANKLIN

Tears dry the quickest when someone adds their own.
—JULIEN DE VALCKENAERE

The sea of tears is small.    —BERT HELLINGER

**CLAUSEWITZ, CARL VON** (Germany, 1780–1831) Clausewitz spent most of his career in the Prussian army fighting Napoleon. After the Napoleonic Wars were over, he became director of the Kriegsakademie in Berlin and began writing his treatise on military theory *On War*, the book that has given us the phrases "total war," "center of gravity," and "fog of war." Clausewitz's fame as a military theorist is surpassed only by that of Sun Tzu, an ancient Chinese warrior-philosopher whose *Art of War* is still used as a leadership manual today.

### Essential Aphorisms

War is not merely a political act, but also a real political instrument, a continuation of political commerce, a carrying out of the same by other means.

Intelligence alone is not courage. We often see that the most intelligent people are irresolute. Since in the rush of events a man is governed by feelings rather than by thought, the intellect needs to arouse the quality of courage, which then supports and sustains it in action.

In war the result is never final.

Politics is the womb in which war develops, where its outlines already exist in their hidden rudimentary form, like the characteristics of living creatures in their embryos.

War is such a dangerous business that the mistakes that come from kindness are the very worst.

War is very simple, but in war the simplest things become very difficult.

**CRUIJFF, JOHAN** (The Netherlands, 1947–   ) Clausewitz may have developed the concept of "total war," but Cruijff was the greatest exponent of the concept of "total football." Total football (soccer) was pioneered by Dutch coach Rinus Michels in the 1970s and involved an aggressive, swirling style of play in which various positions on the field were filled depending on which configuration best suited an offensive push. Cruijff's speed, agility, and ball-handling skills made him a natural at total football. In the Netherlands, the soccer star's distinctive sayings have been given their own name: Cruijffisms. Like American sportsmen Muhammad Ali and Yogi Berra, Cruijff is one of the relatively few athletes with a gift for coining aphorisms. Like Berra, he's also an inadvertent aphorist; his philosophical non sequiturs are spontaneous rather than deliberate.

*Essential Aphorisms*

Football is simple, but the most difficult is simple footballing.

You are as valuable as the time you are on TV.

Without the ball, you can't win.

Before I make a mistake, I do not make that mistake.

Every disadvantage gots its advantage.

Coincidence is logical.

**DISRAELI, BENJAMIN** (United Kingdom, 1804–1881) Disraeli twice served as prime minister and helped create the modern British Conservative Party, but politics was really his third career choice. As a young man, he speculated on the stock market, investing in the South American mining boom. When that boom went bust, so did Disraeli; he struggled with debts for the rest of his life. He then turned to literature, cranking out a series of moderately successful romantic novels. He was elected to Parliament in 1837, and served in the House of Commons until his death. On becoming prime minister, he observed, "I have climbed to the top of the greasy pole." His standard reply upon receiving complimentary copies of other people's publications is a masterpiece of wicked etiquette: "Dear Sir, I thank you for sending me a copy of your book, which I shall waste no time in reading."

*Essential Aphorisms*

Read no history: nothing but biography, for that is life without theory.

The magic of first love is our ignorance that it can ever end.

A precedent embalms a principle.

Justice is truth in action.

What is earnest is not always true; on the contrary, error is often more earnest than truth.

The secret of success is constancy to purpose.

Apologies only account for that which they do not alter.

Youth is a blunder; manhood a struggle; old age a regret.

Little things affect little minds.

If it is not necessary to change, it is necessary not to change.

Amusement to an observing mind is study.

Grief is the agony of an instant; the indulgence of grief the blunder of a life.

His shortcoming is his long staying.

Life is too short to be small.

Like all great travelers, I have seen more than I remember, and remember more than I have seen.

Never complain and never explain.

Next to knowing when to seize an opportunity, the most important thing in life is to know when to forgo an advantage.

The secret of success is to be ready when your opportunity comes.

The best way to become acquainted with a subject is to write a book about it.

The greatest good you can do for another is not just share your riches, but to reveal to him his own.

The palace is not safe when the cottage is not happy.

The world is governed by very different personages from what is imagined by those who are not behind the scenes.

The more extensive a man's knowledge of what has been done, the greater will be his power of knowing what to do.

Where knowledge ends, religion begins.

## Parallel Lines: The Law

When men are pure, laws are useless; when men are corrupt, laws are broken.
　　　　　　　　　　　　　　　　　　　　　　—DISRAELI

The strictest law often causes the most serious wrong.　　　—CICERO

The more corrupt the state, the more numerous the laws.　　—TACITUS

Bad laws are the worst sort of tyranny.　　　—EDMUND BURKE

When the people are good the government is good for nothing.
　　　　　　　　　　　　　　　—JOHANN GEORG ZIMMERMAN

**DYLAN, BOB** (United States, 1941–   ) In the first volume of his autobiography, *Chronicles: Volume One*, Dylan describes a trip to California during the early years of his fame, when it seemed like every 1960s pop star was covering one of his songs. Adjusting to adulation wasn't easy. "I needed to learn how to telescope things, ideas," he writes. "Things were too big to see all at once, like all the books in the library—everything laying around on all the tables. You might be able to put it all into one paragraph or into one verse of a song if you could get it right." Dylan gets it right a lot.

*Essential Aphorisms*

Don't trust me to show you love
When my love may be only lust.
If you want somebody you can trust
Trust yourself.

When you got nothing, you got nothing to lose.

He not busy being born is busy dying.

You don't need a weatherman to know which way the wind blows.

**EDISON, THOMAS ALVA** (United States, 1847–1931) There are more than 1,000 patents in Edison's name. One of the few things he invented but did not patent, though, is what has come to be known as the research and development laboratory. His company in Menlo Park, New Jersey, was the first to dedicate itself wholly to inventing things and then making money from selling those inventions. When he died at the age of eighty-four, Edison is reported to have said to his wife, "It is very beautiful over there." His last breath has been preserved along with his last words. Henry Ford, a lifelong friend of Edison's, supposedly asked the inventor's son Charles to bring him a test tube of air from the room in which the "Wizard of Menlo Park" died. The test tube and its contents, sealed inside with a cork, are on display at the Henry Ford Museum in Dearborn, Michigan.

*Essential Aphorisms*

Genius is one percent inspiration, ninety-nine percent perspiration.

All Bibles are man-made.

Everything comes to him who hustles while he waits.

I have not failed. I've just found ten thousand ways that won't work.

If we did all the things we are capable of doing, we would literally astound ourselves.

Just because something doesn't do what you planned it to do doesn't mean it's useless.

Many of life's failures are people who did not realize how close they were to success when they gave up.

Opportunity is missed by most people because it is dressed in overalls and looks like work.

Restless is discontent and discontent is the first necessity of progress.

There is no expedient to which a man will not go to avoid the labor of thinking.

**EINSTEIN, ALBERT** (Germany, 1879–1955) In accordance with his own instructions, Einstein was cremated on the day he died and his ashes were scattered at an undisclosed location. His brain, however, was preserved for scientific study. In 1999, analysis of Einstein's brain revealed that his inferior parietal lobe—the region responsible for, among other things, mathematical thought—was 15 percent larger than average and that he had upward of 70 percent more glial cells, which support and protect neurons, than average brains. In Einstein's case, a bigger brain certainly turned out to be a better one. He showed extraordinary intellectual talent from a very young age. As an adult, he recalled how at the age of five his father showed him a compass and he was mesmerized by how the invisible force of magnetism acted on the needle. But Einstein was not an outstanding student, often clashing with school authorities because of his dislike of routine and memorization. He was an employee of the Swiss Patent Office in Bern, Switzerland, in 1905 when the papers explaining his most important scientific discoveries, including special relativity, were published. When Hitler came to power in Germany in 1933, Einstein decided to remain in the United States, where he was visiting Princeton University. He was an ardent pacifist, socialist, and civil rights campaigner—passions that are reflected in his aphorisms. The FBI kept an extensive file on his activities and suggested that he be prevented from immigrating to the United States. Einstein cited Arthur

Schopenhauer's aphorism, "A man can do as he will, but not will as he will," as "an inspiration to me since my youth up, and a continual consolation and unfailing well-spring of patience in the face of the hardships of life, my own and others." But his own sayings are much more benevolent and funnier than those of Schopenhauer. Einstein's humor and suspicion of institutionalized religion are reminiscent of Mark Twain, while his interest in spirituality evokes the sayings of Gandhi.

## Essential Aphorisms

Imagination is more important than knowledge. For knowledge is limited, whereas imagination embraces the entire world, stimulating progress, giving birth to evolution.

Before God we are relatively all equally wise—equally foolish.

Nationalism is an infantile disease. It is the measles of mankind.

I do not know with what weapons World War Three will be fought, but World War Four will be fought with sticks and stones.

Science without religion is lame, religion without science is blind.

Falling in love is not at all the most stupid thing that people do—but gravitation cannot be held responsible for it.

Computers are incredibly fast, accurate and stupid. Human beings are incredibly slow, inaccurate and brilliant. Together they are powerful beyond imagination.

You do not really understand something unless you can explain it to your grandmother.

A clever person solves a problem. A wise person avoids it.

A person starts to live when he can live outside himself.

Anyone who has never made a mistake has never tried anything new.

As our circle of knowledge expands, so does the circumference of darkness surrounding it.

Common sense is the collection of prejudices acquired by age eighteen.

Ethical axioms are found and tested not very differently from the axioms of science. Truth is what stands the test of experience.

Few are those who see with their own eyes and feel with their own hearts.

Once you can accept the universe as matter expanding into nothing that is something, wearing stripes with plaid comes easy.

Insanity: doing the same thing over and over again and expecting different results.

It is harder to crack a prejudice than an atom.

Not everything that counts can be counted, and not everything that can be counted counts.

Never lose a holy curiosity.

The secret to creativity is knowing how to hide your sources.

You cannot simultaneously prevent and prepare for war.

Reality is merely an illusion, albeit a very persistent one.

The difference between genius and stupidity is that genius has its limits.

### Parallel Lines: School Days

Education is what remains after one has forgotten everything he learned in school.                                                —EINSTEIN

I never let school interfere with my education.          —MARK TWAIN

Men are born ignorant, not stupid. They are made stupid by education.
                                                —BERTRAND RUSSELL

A child educated only at school is an uneducated child.
                                                —GEORGE SANTAYANA

**EMERSON, RALPH WALDO** (United States, 1803–1882) Mary Moody Emerson had a decisive influence on the intellectual development of her young nephew, Ralph Waldo. She was a small, frail woman with a macabre sense of her own mortality: she slept in a bed shaped like a coffin and wore a burial shroud when traveling. For all her eccentricities, though, she was a fiercely intelligent and deeply religious person who, until her death in 1863, was Emerson's most important spiritual confidante and philosophical sparring partner. "Always do what you are afraid to do," she once advised him. Emerson took that counsel to heart, becoming the most iconoclastic thinker in nineteenth-century America. Emerson always wanted to confront life—and death—face to face, but he found that independence of mind was not always so sweet. Like his father before him, he entered the ministry and became widely known for the eloquence and power of his sermons. But in his late twenties, he began to question his faith. The death of his first wife prompted the final break with conventional Christianity. Realizing he no longer believed that Jesus' death offered human beings any redemption from sin, Emerson abandoned his vocation and quit the church. Yet his ministry continued. He stopped writing sermons and started writing essays, which he read aloud to large and enraptured audiences around the country. Emerson loved the Stoics, especially Seneca and Marcus Aurelius, and was among the first Americans to read Confucius in English. He was also deeply influenced by Michel de Montaigne and Francis Bacon, the two great essayist-aphorists whom he consciously set out to imitate.

*Essential Aphorisms*

Whoso would be a man must be a non-conformist.

A sect or party is an elegant incognito devised to save a man from the vexation of thinking.

Nothing great was ever achieved without enthusiasm.

Every poem must be made up of lines that are poems.

Language is fossil poetry.

Life is wasted in the necessary preparation of finding what is the true way, and we die just as we enter it.

After thirty a man wakes up sad every morning.

When it is darkest, men see the stars.

Every man's condition is a solution in hieroglyphic to those inquiries he would put.

The purpose of life seems to be to acquaint a man with himself. The highest revelation is that God is in every man.

We are always getting ready to live, but never living.

Insist on yourself; never imitate.

What is a weed? A plant whose virtues have yet to be discovered.

A man is a god in ruins.

In every work of genius we recognize our own rejected thoughts: they come back to us with a certain alienated majesty.

For it is not meters, but a meter-making argument, that makes a poem—a thought so passionate and alive, that, like the spirit of a plant or an animal, it has an architecture of its own, and adorns nature with a new thing.

The reward of a thing well done is to have done it.

We boil at different degrees.

In skating over thin ice our safety is in our speed.

A hero is no braver than an ordinary man, but he is braver five minutes longer.

A foolish consistency is the hobgoblin of little minds, adored by little statesmen and philosophers and divines. With consistency a great soul has simply nothing to do. He may as well concern himself with his shadow on the wall. Speak what you think now in hard words, and tomorrow speak what tomorrow thinks in hard words again, though it contradict every thing you said to-day.—"Ah, so you shall be sure to be misunderstood."—Is it so bad, then, to be misunderstood? Pythagoras was misunderstood, and Socrates, and Jesus, and Luther, and Copernicus, and Galileo, and Newton, and every pure and wise spirit that ever took flesh. To be great is to be misunderstood.

Look sharply after your thoughts. They come unlooked for, like a new bird seen on your trees, and, if you turn to your usual task, disappear; and you shall never find that perception again; never, I say,—but perhaps years, ages, and I know not what events and worlds may lie between you and its return!

What lies behind us and what lies before us are small matters compared to what lies within us.

Be an opener of doors for such as come after thee, and do not try to make the universe a blind alley.

### Parallel Lines: Living and Thinking

Life consists of what a man is thinking of all day. —EMERSON

What one does and what he thinks, that he becomes. —UPANISHADS

Life in the true sense is perceiving or thinking. —ARISTOTLE

To live is to think. CICERO

A person attains similarity to that which he thinks of. —SOMADEVA

Man is what he believes. —ANTON CHEKHOV

Thought is life. —WALLACE STEVENS

**FORD, HENRY** (United States, 1863–1947) Ford made a fortune from his innovations in the manufacture and sale of automobiles. But he was also fascinated by another industry, one he found so promising that he can almost be imagined whispering the word, the one word, vouchsafed to the Dustin Hoffman character in the 1967 film *The Graduate*: "Plastics." During the 1930s and early 1940s, the Ford Motor Company produced automobiles made almost entirely from soybean-based plastics. The cars ran on ethanol rather than gasoline. They never caught on. Ford got his start in business working for the Edison Illuminating Company, one of the companies owned by his friend Thomas Alva Edison. The Edison Illuminating Company was also one of the early investors in Ford's first car firm. Ironically, there was a blackout on the night Ford passed away; he died by candlelight.

*Essential Aphorisms*

History is more or less bunk. It's tradition. We don't want tradition. We want to live in the present and the only history that is worth a tinker's damn is the history we make today.

Failure is simply the opportunity to begin again, this time more intelligently.

A bore is a person who opens his mouth and puts his feats in it.

Don't find fault, find a remedy.

A business that makes nothing but money is a poor business.

Anyone who stops learning is old, whether at twenty or eighty. Anyone who keeps learning stays young. The greatest thing in life is to keep your mind young.

Before everything else, getting ready is the secret of success.

Before every minute of action, there should be an hour of thought.

Chop your own wood, and it will warm you twice.

It has been my observation that most people get ahead during the time that others waste.

Whether you believe you can do a thing or not, you are right.

You can't build a reputation on what you are going to do.

**GANDHI, MOHANDAS KARAMCHAND** (India, 1869–1948) When a South African magistrate asked Gandhi to remove his turban in court, Gandhi refused. When he was asked to move from the first-class coach in a train (for which he had a valid ticket) to a third-class compartment, he also refused. These experiences of racism and discrimination in South Africa transformed Gandhi from a shy, apolitical young lawyer into a courageous, outspoken activist. His activism moved from campaigning for civil rights for black people and Indians in South Africa to improving the economic lot of his countrymen to the struggle for India's independence from Britain. Gandhi's mother was a devout Hindu and instilled in him the core beliefs of her religion: respect for all living beings, vegetarianism, and tolerance toward members of other creeds and sects. Gandhi was a mediocre student and barely passed the exam to get into the University of Bombay in 1887. He went on to study in England, where he was eventually admitted to the bar of England and Wales. Unable to set up a law practice in Bombay, Gandhi took a job with an Indian firm in Natal, South Africa, in 1893. A year later, when his contract was due to expire, Gandhi prepared to return to India. But at a farewell party in his honor in Durban, he happened to glance at a newspaper and read that the Natal Legislative Assembly was considering a bill to deny the right to vote to Indians. Gandhi decided to stay and help oppose the bill. That campaign failed, but supporters convinced him to remain in Durban to fight discrimination against Indians in South Africa. At a rally in Johannesburg, Gandhi put his tactic of non-violent protest into practice for the first time. Henry David Thoreau's essay *Civil Disobedience*, written after he was imprisoned for a night for refusing to pay his poll tax, provided Gandhi with both a template for his activism and an eloquent philosophical defense of his beliefs. Gandhi was also deeply influenced by Leo Tolstoy, with whom he corresponded during the last year of the Russian author's life. In his autobiography, Gandhi described Tolstoy as "the greatest apostle of nonviolence that the present age has produced."

## Essential Aphorisms

The truth is far more powerful than any weapon of mass destruction.

An eye for an eye makes the whole world blind.

There are many causes that I am prepared to die for but no causes that I am prepared to kill for.

A convert's enthusiasm for his new religion is greater than that of a person who is born in it.

It is better in prayer to have a heart without words, than words without heart.

Trivialities possess deadly potentialities.

Strength does not come from physical capacity. It comes from an indomitable will.

The best and most solid work was done in the wilderness of minority.

Strength in numbers is the delight of the timid. The valiant of spirit glory in fighting alone.

We win justice quickest by rendering justice to the other party.

More is always expected from those who give much.

If one takes care of the means, the end will take care of itself.

Passive resistance blesses him who uses it and him against whom it is used.

Violence is suicide.

A civilization is to be judged by its treatment of minorities.

For the poor, the economic is the spiritual.

The teacher's work lies more outside than inside the lecture room.

He who perishes sword in hand is no doubt brave; but he who faces death without raising his little finger is braver.

To lose patience is to lose the battle.

If we develop the force of will, we shall find that we do not need the force of arms.

The chains of a slave are broken the moment he considers himself a free man.

Hate the sin and love the sinner.

## Parallel Lines: Change Yourself

You must be the change you wish to see in the world.        —GANDHI

God does not change what is in people until they change what is in themselves.        —MUHAMMAD

Everyone thinks of changing the world, but no one thinks of changing himself.        —LEO TOLSTOY

When we are no longer able to change a situation we are challenged to
change ourselves.                                          —VIKTOR FRANKL

**HIPPOCRATES** (Greece, c. 450–c. 380 BCE) The Greek physician Hippocrates
was a prolific aphorist. He composed hundreds of terse, prosaic maxims to instruct his students in the diagnosis and treatment of disease. Most of his sayings
are straightforward tips on how to spot various illnesses or what it means when
patients display specific symptoms. But he occasionally waxed philosophical. His
aphorisms are a crucial source of information about ancient biomedicine, and
they still serve as the basis for the medical profession's code of ethics. Hippocrates founded the art of the medical or scientific aphorism, a tradition that continues unbroken from his own time until today. Other notable practitioners
include the early medical pioneer Galen, the eighteenth-century Dutch scientist
Herman Boerhaave, and the Jewish physician and philosopher Moses Maimon-
ides, who also wrote a commentary on Hippocrates' aphorisms. More recent collections of medical maxims have to do with specialized fields like pediatrics and
gynecology.

*Essential Aphorisms*

Neither repletion, nor fasting, nor anything else, is good when more than
natural.

Diseases which arise from repletion are cured by depletion; and those that
arise from depletion are cured by repletion; and in general, diseases are
cured by their contraries.

Those diseases which medicines do not cure, iron cures; those which iron
cannot cure, fire cures; and those which fire cannot cure, are to be reckoned
wholly incurable.

Life is short, and art long; the crisis fleeting; experience perilous, and
decision difficult. The physician must not only be prepared to do what is
right himself, but also to make the patient, the attendants, and externals
cooperate.

**HOLMES, OLIVER WENDELL, JR.** (United States, 1841–1935) Holmes was
the son of New England physician and "Fireside Poet" Oliver Wendell Holmes
Sr., from whom he inherited his aphoristic talent. While Holmes Sr. expressed his
aphorisms in poems and novels, Holmes Jr. couched his in the (often dissenting)
opinions he wrote as a Supreme Court Justice from 1902 to 1932. Holmes remained

spry and thoughtful up until his death at the age of ninety-four. Once, while in his nineties, he passed a beautiful young woman on the street and sighed to his companion, "Oh, to be seventy again!"

*Essential Aphorisms*

To be seventy years young is sometimes far more cheerful and hopeful than to be forty years old.

Most people think mostly what they want to think the majority of the time.

Eloquence may set fire to reason.

A child's education should begin at least one hundred years before he is born.

A man's mind, stretched by a new idea, never goes back to its original dimensions.

The mind of a bigot is like the pupil of the eye. The more light you shine on it, the more it will contract.

To have doubted one's own first principles is the mark of a civilized man.

The right to swing my fist ends where the other man's nose begins.

**KENNEDY, JOHN FITZGERALD** (United States, 1917–1963) Kennedy is among the few U.S. presidents to have written a best-selling nonfiction book. In 1940, he completed his thesis at Harvard University on the British government's policy of appeasement before the outbreak of World War II. Kennedy's father, Joseph, arranged to have the dissertation published later that same year under the title *Why England Slept*, a reference to Winston Churchill's 1938 book *While England Slept*, which also examined the buildup of German power. During recuperation from back surgery between 1954 and 1955, Kennedy wrote (or perhaps had ghostwritten for him) *Profiles in Courage*, portraits of eight U.S. senators whom Kennedy believed displayed conspicuous heroism by standing up for their personal beliefs. The book won a Pulitzer Prize in 1957. Kennedy emulated Winston Churchill, both in his career as an author and as a public speaker, striving for the same rhetorical elegance and eloquence.

*Essential Aphorisms*

Forgive your enemies, but never forget their names.

Ask not what your country can do for you, but what you can do for your country.

The time to repair the roof is when the sun is shining.

Those who make peaceful revolution impossible will make violent revolution inevitable.

Liberty without learning is always in peril; learning without liberty is always in vain.

Of those to whom much is given, much is required.

Mankind must put an end to war or war will put an end to mankind.

Let us never negotiate out of fear. But let us never fear to negotiate.

**KING, MARTIN LUTHER, JR.** (United States, 1929–1968) When he delivered his "I Have a Dream" speech from the steps of the Lincoln Memorial in Washington, D.C., King deliberately echoed Abraham Lincoln's rhetoric. Lincoln began the Gettysburg Address with the words "Four score and seven years ago"; King began his with "Five score years ago," a reference to the president's signing of the Emancipation Proclamation a century earlier. The occasion of Lincoln's speech was the consecration of a cemetery for Civil War dead, but he used his oration to rally the divided country behind "a new birth of freedom." King's objective was the same, urging all Americans to bring about the day when "this nation will rise up and live out the true meaning of its creed: 'We hold these truths to be self-evident: that all men are created equal.' "

*Essential Aphorisms*

The time is always right to do what is right.

Our lives begin to end the day we become silent about things that matter.

In the end, we will remember not the words of our enemies but the silence of our friends.

Only when it is dark enough can you see the stars.

In the process of gaining our rightful place we must not be guilty of wrongful deeds.

Injustice anywhere is a threat to justice everywhere.

I submit to you that if a man has not discovered something that he will die for, he isn't fit to live.

A riot is the language of the unheard.

**LINCOLN, ABRAHAM** (United States, 1809–1865) Lincoln's son Robert Todd once fell onto the tracks while waiting for a train to Washington, D.C. Another passenger pulled him back onto the platform, out of the way of an oncoming train. That passenger was Edwin Booth, one of the most famous actors in America and the brother of John Wilkes Booth, who on April 14, 1865, would assassinate Abraham Lincoln. Lincoln suffered from nightmares throughout his life, one of which seems to have prefigured his murder. Lincoln dreamed that he was part of a crowd that had gathered around a train; he asked a woman what was going on. "The president has been shot," she replied.

*Essential Aphorisms*

A house divided against itself cannot stand.

With public sentiment, nothing can fail; without it nothing can succeed.

Let us have faith that right makes might, and in that faith, let us, to the end, dare to do our duty as we understand it.

I shall try to correct errors when shown to be errors; and I shall adopt new views so fast as they shall appear to be true views.

Be sure you put your feet in the right place, then stand firm.

No matter how much cats fight, there always seems to be plenty of kittens.

Ballots are the rightful and peaceful successors to bullets.

Determine that the thing can and shall be done, and then we shall find the way.

Give me six hours to chop down a tree and I will spend the first four sharpening the axe.

He has the right to criticize who has the heart to help.

I am a slow walker, but I never walk backwards.

I am not concerned that you have fallen; I am concerned that you arise.

It is better to stay silent and let people think you are an idiot than to open your mouth and remove all doubt.

Nearly all men can stand adversity, but if you want to test a man's character, give him power.

The best way to get a bad law repealed is to enforce it strictly.

Things may come to those who wait, but only the things left behind by those who hustle.

The only person who is a worse liar than a faith healer is his patient.

You have to do your own growing no matter how tall your grandfather was.

When I do good, I feel good. When I do bad, I feel bad. That's my religion.

I have often been forced to my knees by the overwhelming conviction that there was no place else to go.

**MONTESQUIEU, CHARLES-LOUIS DE SECONDAT, BARON DE** (France, 1689–1755) Montesquieu came from a wealthy and well-connected family in the Bordeaux region of France. Like his father before him, he served as a councillor in the Bordeaux Parliament. But Montesquieu much preferred writing about the law to practicing it. After stepping down from the bench, he retired to his family's estate to work on his magnum opus, *The Spirit of the Laws*, in which he set out key principles like the separation of government powers. He also put forward the theory that climate influences the kinds of governments societies devise for themselves: hot climates produce hot-tempered people, cold climates produce cooler, more reasonable folk. The temperate climate of France was, of course, the best. Montesquieu was an enormous influence on the American Founding Fathers, who incorporated many of his ideas into the U.S. Constitution.

*Essential Aphorisms*

Not to be loved is a misfortune, but it is an insult to be loved no longer.

A man should be mourned at his birth, not at his death.

Republics end through luxury, monarchies through poverty.

The deterioration of a government begins almost always by the decay of its principles.

The success of most things depends upon knowing how long it will take to succeed.

You have to study a great deal to know a little.

Power ought to serve as a check to power.

The less men think, the more they talk.

Peace is a natural effect of trade.

There is no crueler tyranny than that which is perpetuated under the shield of law and in the name of justice.

Friendship is an arrangement by which we undertake to exchange small favors for big ones.

A nation may lose its liberties in a day and not miss them in a century.

If triangles made a god, they would give him three sides.

Liberty is the right to do what the law permits.

**NAPOLEON** (France, 1769–1821) In 1798, when Napoleon Bonaparte invaded Egypt, he took a contingent of scientists and archaeologists with him. Their assignment: to discover and investigate Egyptian antiquities as the French army swept across the country. The campaign didn't go quite as planned; Napoleon fled Egypt to restore order in France, leaving his troops to fend for themselves against the British. The French army eventually capitulated and the soldiers were transported back to Europe—along with their Egyptian plunder, including the Rosetta Stone—in British ships. The Egyptian campaign is one example of Napoleon's interest in culture. Another is his composition of aphorisms, which cover everything from military matters to matters of the heart.

*Essential Aphorisms*

Fanaticism must be first lulled in order that it may be eradicated.

Nothing is done while anything yet remains to be done.

He who fears being conquered is certain of defeat.

Great men are like meteors, which shine and consume themselves to enlighten the earth.

We should wash our dirty linen at home.

We walk faster when we walk alone.

Nothing is more arrogant than the weakness that feels itself propped up by force.

Sufficient for the day is the evil thereof.

There is but one step from the sublime to the ridiculous.

Power is founded upon opinion.

Men are led by trifles.

Better to have a known enemy than a forced ally.

There is neither subordination nor fear in empty bellies.

To have a right estimate of a man's character, we must see him in adversity.

**PAINE, THOMAS** (United States, 1737–1809) Paine's life and ideas are inextricably bound up with those of a handful of other aphorists. Like Benjamin Franklin, he was an inventor; he developed the single-span iron bridge and the smokeless candle while also tinkering with improvements to early steam engines. In 1774, Paine met Franklin by chance on a London street, and Franklin convinced him to immigrate to the American colonies. In America, Paine's books and pamphlets helped inspire the Revolution. George Washington's troops were read Paine's pamphlet *The Crisis* before crossing the Delaware River on December 25, 1776. Paine wrote *The Rights of Man*, which supported the French Revolution, in reply to Edmund Burke's condemnation of that revolt in *Reflections on the Revolution in France*. Napoleon claimed he slept with a copy of *The Rights of Man* under his pillow. A century after Paine's death, another inventor-aphorist, Thomas Alva Edison, helped rehabilitate the great pamphleteer's reputation, writing of Paine, "I have always regarded Paine as one of the greatest of all Americans. Never have we had a sounder intelligence in this republic."

*Essential Aphorisms*

The blunders of one man often serve to suggest right ideas to another man.

It is impossible to be a hypocrite and to be brave at the same instant.

Want of consistency is the natural consequence of want of principle.

Where there is no danger, cowards are bold.

The nearer any disease approaches to a crisis, the nearer it is to a cure.

Danger and deliverance make their advances together, and it is only in the last push that one or the other takes the lead.

Time makes more converts than reason.

Death is not the monarch of the dead, but the dying. The moment he obtains a conquest he loses a subject.

Mutual fear is a principal link in the chain of mutual love.

If I do not believe as you believe, it proves that you do not believe as I believe, and this is all that it proves.

As in absolute governments, the king is law, so in free countries the law ought to be king.

A thing, moderately good, is not as good as it ought to be. Moderation in temper is always a virtue; but moderation in principle is always a vice.

Every religion is good that teaches man to be good.

Individuals are often the last to hear what it concerns themselves the most to know.

When we are planning for posterity, we ought to remember that virtue is not hereditary.

My own mind is my own church.

**RALEIGH, SIR WALTER** (United Kingdom, c. 1554–1618) Raleigh seems to have taken literally Shakespeare's line from *Hamlet*: "I could be bounded in a nutshell and count myself king of infinite space." During his imprisonment for sedition in the Tower of London, he composed a little tome called *A Historie of the World*. Raleigh was a poet and explorer as well as a historian. After he was beheaded for sacking a Spanish outpost while searching for El Dorado in South America, his wife is said to have had Raleigh's head embalmed.

*Essential Aphorisms*

Hatreds are the cinders of affection.

If the heart be right, it matters not which way the head lies.

Speaking much is a sign of vanity, for he that is lavish with words is a niggard in deed.

Prevention is the daughter of intelligence.

Passions are likened best to floods and streams,
The shallow murmur, but the deep are dumb.

Divine is Love and scorneth worldly pelf,
And can be bought with nothing but with self.

**ROOSEVELT, ELEANOR** (United States, 1884–1962) Born in New York City, Eleanor was the niece of President Theodore Roosevelt. After Eleanor's parents died, President Roosevelt became something of a surrogate father to her, giving her away when she married her distant cousin, Franklin Delano Roosevelt, in 1905. Starting in 1935, Roosevelt wrote a daily newspaper column, "My Day," in which she took up the various liberal causes—among them, civil rights, human rights, and women's rights—that made her one of the most outspoken and influential first ladies in American history.

*Essential Aphorisms*

No one can make you feel inferior without your consent.

The most important thing in any relationship is not what you get but what you give.

One should always sleep in all of one's guest beds, to make sure that they are comfortable.

A woman is like a teabag—only in hot water do you realize how strong she is.

Do what you feel in your heart to be right—for you'll be criticized anyway. You'll be damned if you do, and damned if you don't.

Great minds discuss ideas; average minds discuss events; small minds discuss people.

You gain strength, courage and confidence by every experience in which you really stop to look fear in the face. You are able to say to yourself, "I have lived through this horror. I can take the next thing that comes along." You must do the thing you think you cannot do.

If someone betrays you once, it's their fault; if they betray you twice, it's your fault.

**ROOSEVELT, FRANKLIN DELANO** (United States, 1882–1945) Roosevelt contracted polio in 1921, resulting in his paralysis below the waist. He founded a hydrotherapy center for the treatment of polio patients in Georgia and helped establish the National Foundation for Infantile Paralysis, now known as the March of Dimes. This is why his portrait appears on the U.S. dime.

*Essential Aphorisms*

It is common sense to take a method and try it. If it fails, admit it frankly and try another. But above all, try something.

Yours is not the task of making your way in the world, but the task of remaking the world which you will find before you.

The only thing we have to fear is fear itself.

Better the occasional faults of a government that lives in a spirit of charity than the consistent omissions of a government frozen in the ice of its own indifference.

A radical is a man with both feet firmly planted—in the air. A conservative is a man with two perfectly good legs who, however, has never learned to walk forward. A reactionary is a somnambulist walking backwards. A liberal is a man who uses his legs and his hands at the behest of his head.

Judge me by the enemies I have made.

It is an unfortunate human failing that a full pocketbook often groans more loudly than an empty stomach.

Men are not prisoners of fate, but only prisoners of their own minds.

**ROOSEVELT, THEODORE** (United States, 1858–1919) Roosevelt became president after William McKinley was assassinated by an anarchist in 1901. McKinley did not die immediately from his wounds. When it appeared that the president would recover, Roosevelt made the somewhat bizarre decision to go hiking. He was quickly tracked down and returned to Buffalo, New York, where he took the oath of office to become the twenty-sixth president of the United States. Before becoming president, Roosevelt was a widely respected historian and naturalist. He wrote thirty-five books, including works on outdoor life, natural history, U.S. Western and political history, and an autobiography. Roosevelt was one of the most physically active presidents, yet as a child he was frail and frequently ill. In the 1880s, he lived for a time in North Dakota, where he learned to ride and rope. On his honeymoon in 1886, he climbed Mont Blanc in France, leading only the third expedition to reach the summit. He had a photographic memory and developed a lifelong habit of devouring books, memorizing every detail. Roosevelt was the first American president to prioritize the environment. He set aside more land for national parks and nature preserves than all of his predecessors combined. In 1912, while Roosevelt was campaigning in Milwaukee, Wisconsin, for a return to the White House, saloon keeper John Schrank shot him. With the bullet still lodged in his chest, Roosevelt delivered his scheduled speech.

## Essential Aphorisms

Great thoughts speak only to the thoughtful mind, but great actions speak to all mankind.

Do what you can, with what you have, where you are.

I think there is only one quality worse than hardness of heart and that is softness of head.

If you could kick the person in the pants responsible for most of your trouble, you wouldn't sit for a month.

It is hard to fail, but it is worse never to have tried to succeed.

Nine-tenths of wisdom consists in being wise in time.

Nobody cares how much you know, until they know how much you care.

People ask the difference between a leader and a boss. The leader leads, and the boss drives.

The most successful politician is he who says what everybody is thinking most often and in the loudest voice.

The only time you really live fully is from thirty to sixty. The young are slaves to dreams; the old servants of regrets. Only the middle-aged have all their five senses in the keeping of their wits.

In a moment of decision the best thing you can do is the right thing. The worst thing you can do is nothing.

Pray not for lighter burdens but for stronger backs.

*Parallel Lines: Stargazing*

Keep your eyes on the stars, and your feet on the ground.　　—ROOSEVELT

Hitch your wagon to a star.　　—RALPH WALDO EMERSON

**SCHREINER, OLIVE** (South Africa, 1855–1920) In 1881, Schreiner traveled from her native South Africa to England to find a publisher for her novels. George Meredith, a novelist, aphorist, and reader for the publishers Chapman and Hall, accepted the manuscript of what became known as *The Story of an African Farm*. Schreiner had to publish the novel under a male pseudonym because of widespread prejudice against female authors. The book's progressive stance on feminism and religion caused quite a stir. Schreiner subsequently became an ardent social activist, speaking out against colonialism and World War I and in favor of women's rights.

*Essential Aphorisms*

The surest sign of fitness is success.

A train is better than an ox-wagon only when it carries better men.

Sin looks much more terrible to those who look at it than to those who do it.

Men are like the earth and we are the moon; we turn always one side to them, and they think there is no other, because they don't see it—but there is.

There was never a great man who had not a great mother.

All that is buried is not dead.

Wisdom never kicks at the iron walls it can't bring down.

On the path to truth, at every step you set your foot down on your heart.

**SUN TZU** (China, c. sixth century BCE) If he lived at all—as with so many ancient Chinese sages, Sun Tzu may not have been an actual historical figure—he was a contemporary of Confucius. The book that bears Sun Tzu's name, however, was most likely written in the fourth century BCE. While Confucius focused on moral probity and good governance, Sun Tzu focused on victory on the battlefield, preferably without the necessity to fight. Though Sun Tzu was concerned primarily with the clash of arms, his strategies and tactics can be applied to many situations from office politics to family dynamics.

*Essential Aphorisms*

The best victory is when the opponent surrenders of its own accord before there are any actual hostilities. It is best to win without fighting.

A military operation involves deception. Even though you are competent, appear to be incompetent. Though effective, appear to be ineffective.

Victorious warriors win first and then go to war, while defeated warriors go to war first and then seek to win.

To win one hundred victories in one hundred battles is not the acme of skill. To subdue the enemy without fighting is the acme of skill.

He who knows when he can fight and when he cannot will be victorious.

Opportunities multiply as they are seized.

There is no instance of a nation benefiting from prolonged warfare.

When the enemy is at ease, be able to weary him; when well fed, to starve him; when at rest, to make him move. Appear at places to which he must hasten; move swiftly where he does not expect you.

To a surrounded enemy, you must leave a way of escape.

Build your enemy a golden bridge across which to retreat.

A leader leads by example not by force.

A skilled commander seeks victory from the situation and does not demand it of his subordinates.

**THOREAU, HENRY DAVID** (United States, 1817–1862) Thoreau was twenty-eight when he moved into his one-room cabin near Walden Pond. The date was July 4, 1845; he called it his independence day. He went to live in the woods not because he wanted to be a hermit—Thoreau often walked into town to visit his family, he dined every Sunday with Ralph Waldo Emerson and his family, and often had friends out to visit—but because he wanted to get back to nature. He started with the most basic thing of all: building a place to live. The cabin at Walden Pond was the most eloquent statement of Thoreau's do-it-yourself spirit, proof of his view that even the loftiest thoughts mean little unless they're applied in daily life. What Thoreau never acknowledged in *Walden* was that the land on which he built, along with the very idea of living out by the pond in the first place, were borrowed from Emerson. The two men had a close relationship, alternating between warm friendship and intense rivalry. In addition to lending him the land and the idea of moving to the woods, Emerson was also the one who counseled Thoreau to keep the journal of his sojourn at the pond that eventually became *Walden*.

## Essential Aphorisms

If a man does not keep pace with his companions, perhaps it is because he hears a different drummer. Let him step to the music which he hears, however measured or far away.

If you have built castles in the air, your work need not be lost; that is where they should be. Now put the foundations under them.

The mass of men lead lives of quiet desperation. What is called resignation is confirmed desperation.

Say what you have to say, not what you ought.

Morning is when I am awake and there is dawn in me.

The youth gets together his materials to build a bridge to the moon, or perchance a palace or temple on the earth, and at length the middle-aged man concludes to build a wood shed with them.

It is never too late to give up our prejudices. No way of thinking or doing, however ancient, can be trusted without proof.

Beware of all enterprises that require new clothes, and not rather a new wearer of clothes.

Every generation laughs at the old fashions, but follows religiously the new.

I would rather sit on a pumpkin and have it all to myself than be crowded on a velvet cushion.

No man ever followed his genius till it misled him.

Under a government which imprisons any unjustly, the true place for a just man is also a prison.

It is difficult to begin without borrowing.

I went to the woods because I wished to live deliberately, to front only the essential facts of life, and see if I could not learn what it had to teach, and not, when I came to die, discover that I had not lived.

## Parallel Lines: Setting Sail

Be a Columbus to whole new continents and worlds within you, opening new channels, not of trade, but of thought.    —THOREAU

The secret for harvesting from existence the greatest fruitfulness and the greatest enjoyment is—to live dangerously! Build your cities on the slopes of Vesuvius! Send your ships into uncharted seas! Live at war with your peers and yourselves!    —FRIEDRICH NIETZSCHE

**TOCQUEVILLE, ALEXIS DE** (France, 1805–1859) De Tocqueville, a twenty-five-year-old French aristocrat, visited the United States in 1831 to study the American prison system. He spent nine months in the United States, traveling almost constantly and meeting with some of the country's most prominent politicians and thinkers. The result is *Democracy in America*, an astute analysis of the young nation. De Tocqueville also fulfilled the original mission behind his trip. Together with his colleague Gustave de Beaumont, he wrote *The U.S. Penitentiary System and Its Application in France.*

## Essential Aphorisms

In politics shared hatreds are almost always the basis of friendships.

History is a gallery of pictures in which there are few originals and many copies.

A democratic government is the only one in which those who vote for a tax can escape the obligation to pay it.

No protracted war can fail to endanger the freedom of a democratic country.

We succeed in enterprises that demand the positive qualities we possess, but we excel in those which can also make use of our defects.

What is not yet done is only what we have not yet attempted to do.

In a revolution, as in a novel, the most difficult part to invent is the end.

The most dangerous moment for a bad government is when it begins to reform.

**TRUMAN, HARRY S.** (United States, 1884–1972) Like Theodore Roosevelt, Truman succeeded to the presidency on the death of the incumbent, then went on to win election as president himself. When Franklin Delano Roosevelt died on April 12, 1945, Truman asked Eleanor Roosevelt, the former first lady, if there was anything he could do for her. "Is there anything we can do for you?" she replied. "For you are the one in trouble now." Truman later told journalists that he "felt like the moon, the stars and all the planets fell on me" when he got the news that FDR had died and he was now president. Also like Theodore Roosevelt, he had a blunt, homely way of speaking that often resulted in memorable phrases, such as "The buck stops here."

*Essential Aphorisms*

A politician is a man who understands government. A statesman is a politician who's been dead for fifteen years.

Always be sincere, even if you don't mean it.

I have found the best way to give advice to your children is to find out what they want and then advise them to do it.

If you can't convince 'em, confuse 'em.

If you can't stand the heat, get out of the kitchen.

Never kick a fresh turd on a hot day.

Intense feeling too often obscures the truth.

It's a recession when your neighbor loses his job; it's a depression when you lose yours.

It is amazing what you can accomplish if you do not care who gets the credit.

The only thing new in the world is the history you don't know.

**TUTU, DESMOND** (South Africa, 1931–   ) Tutu, the Anglican Archbishop Emeritus of Cape Town, was one of South Africa's most prominent opponents of apartheid. After the country's first multiracial elections in 1994, Tutu chaired the Truth and Reconciliation Commission, which investigated the human rights violations of the apartheid regime. Tutu is also credited with coining the phrase "rainbow nation" to describe South Africa's ethnic and racial mix.

*Essential Aphorisms*

To be impartial is to have taken sides already with the status quo.

If you are neutral in situations of injustice, you have chosen the side of the oppressor.

History, like beauty, depends largely on the beholder.

A person is a person because he recognizes others as persons.

When the missionaries came to Africa they had the Bible and we had the land. They said, "Let us pray." We closed our eyes. When we opened them we had the Bible and they had the land.

God is not a Christian.

**WARHOL, ANDY** (United States, 1928–1987) Warhol was an obsessive collector and chronicler of his own life. For a time, he carried a tape recorder with him wherever he went, recording in full every conversation he had. He also kept all the memorabilia associated with his fame, from fan mail to newspaper and magazine clippings, and stored them in hundreds of boxes in his home. By the time he died, he had so much stuff that it took nine days to auction off his estate. Warhol was born in Pittsburgh, Pennsylvania, where his father worked as a coal miner. As a painter, he was looking for a distinctive subject matter. Friends suggested he simply paint what he loved. So he started painting his favorite things: money, celebrities, and cans of Campbell's soup, which his mother served him as a child when he was sick and which he had for lunch almost every day of his adult life. Warhol was in many ways a twentieth-century version of Sébastien-Roch-Nicolas Chamfort—someone who managed to ridicule and critique high society from a prominent position within it. Like Chamfort, he was fascinated by fame, what it meant and how to get it.

*Essential Aphorisms*

An artist is someone who produces things that people don't need to have but that he, for some reason, thinks it would be a good idea to give them.

Being born is like being kidnapped. And then sold into slavery.

Don't pay any attention to what they write about you. Just measure it in inches.

I am a deeply superficial person.

In the future everyone will be world-famous for fifteen minutes.

In fifteen minutes everybody will be famous.

**WASHINGTON, GEORGE** (United States, 1732–1799) As a teenager, Washington copied down 110 rules of etiquette and gentlemanly deportment into a notebook. He kept the notebook and referred to the precepts—based on a primer called *The Rules of Civility & Decent Behavior in Company and Conversation*, first compiled by French Jesuits in 1595—for the rest of his life. These 110 rules guided Washington's actions in both statesmanship and social life.

*Essential Aphorisms*

Undertake not what you cannot perform but be careful to keep your promise.

Be not apt to relate news if you know not the truth thereof. In discoursing of things you have heard name not your author. Always a secret discover not.

Associate yourself with men of good quality if you esteem your own reputation; for 'tis better to be alone than in bad company.

Wherein you reprove another be unblameable yourself, for example is more prevalent than precepts.

**WEST, MAE** (United States, 1893–1980) West was tough and beautiful, qualities she may have inherited from her parents. Her father was Battlin' Jack West, a policeman and former boxer, and her mother was a fashion model. West needed to be tough to fight the constant battles with censors that her risqué stage plays occasioned. She started out in vaudeville at the age of five and had already acquired the moniker "the baby vamp" by the time she was twelve. Throughout her career, West wrote her own screenplays and often inserted bawdy double entendres into the lines written for her by others. Her first Broadway production was called *Sex*. The reviews were bad but the publicity was good; West and the rest of the cast were arrested for obscenity. West herself ended up serving eight days in jail. Her early brush with the law didn't stop her from coming up with her sexy one-liners, though, such as the classic from the 1933 film *She Done Him Wrong*: "Is that a gun in your pocket, or are you just happy to see me?"

*Essential Aphorisms*

Between two evils, I always pick the one I never tried before.

A man in the house is worth two in the street.

When women go wrong, men go right after them.

An orgasm a day keeps the doctor away.

I generally avoid temptation unless I can't resist it.

Sex is an emotion in motion.

Sex with love is the greatest thing in life. But sex without love—that's not so bad either.

Too much of a good thing can be simply wonderful.

# MORALISTS, MAJOR AND MINOR

**THE** moralists are the oldest species of aphorist in existence. The earliest aphorisms, which originated in Egypt circa 3500 BCE, are simple moral lessons passed on from father to son. Our moral dilemmas really haven't changed much over the past five thousand years. That perhaps explains why so many moralists—both the major ones, who are among the greatest practitioners of the form, and the minor ones, their somewhat less illustrious fellows—are preachers. Yet this species counts just as many poets, soldiers, diplomats, and activists, plus a few downright scoundrels, among its number. That's because moralists don't moralize. They outline the stark ethical choices we all face; most leave God to one side. Then, for better and for worse, they insist it's up to each of us alone to decide. "If you mean to know yourself," Johann Kaspar Lavater once wrote, "interline such of these aphorisms as affected you agreeably in reading, and set a mark to such as left a sense of uneasiness with you; and then show your copy to whom you please."

## THE MAJOR MORALISTS

**AMENEMOPE** (Egypt, c. 1100 BCE) Amenemope lived in the Egyptian town of Akhim on the east bank of the Nile. His moral instructions are part of an ancient Egyptian tradition, begun some two millennia earlier by rulers like Ptah-Hotep. These aphoristic handbooks usually take the form of brief dicta in which a father passes on moral lessons to his son. Along with the Chinese book *I Ching* (c. 3000 BCE), these examples of Egyptian wisdom literature are the oldest aphorisms, as well as the oldest examples of written literature, in existence.

*Essential Aphorisms*

> Don't raise an outcry against one who attacks you,
> Nor answer him yourself.

He who does evil, the shore rejects him,
Its floodwater carries him away.

Do not set your heart on wealth,
There is no ignoring Fate and Destiny;
Do not let your heart go straying,
Every man comes to his hour.
Do not strain to seek increase,
What you have, let it suffice you.
If riches come to you by theft,
They will not stay the night with you.
They made themselves wings like geese,
And flew away to the sky.

Better is praise with the love of men
Than wealth in the storehouse;
Better is bread with a happy heart
Than wealth with vexation.

The arm is not hurt by being bared,
The back is not broken by bending it.
A man does not lose by speaking sweetly,
Nor does he gain if his speech bristles.
The pilot who sees from afar,
He will not wreck his boat.

**BACON, FRANCIS** (United Kingdom, 1561–1626) Bacon was a great believer in the didactic power of aphorisms, considering them the best form for both scientific and literary compositions. Indeed, part of *The New Organon*, Bacon's attempt to create a new philosophy of science, is written as a series of interconnected aphorisms. "Aphorisms, except they should be ridiculous, cannot be made but of the pith and heart of sciences," Bacon wrote, "for discourse of illustration is cut off; recitals of examples are cut off; discourse of connection and order are cut off; descriptions of practice are cut off. So there remaineth nothing to fill the aphorisms but some good quantity of observation: and therefore no man can suffice, nor in reason will attempt to write aphorisms, but he that is sound and grounded." Bacon's theories about the aphorism, and his mastery of the form, were an enormous influence on the aphorists who came after him. Bacon himself may have inherited his love of aphorisms from his father, who had quotations from the classics carved into the columns of the family estate in Gorhambury in Hertfordshire, just north of London.

*Essential Aphorisms*

It would be an unsound fancy and self-contradictory to expect that things which have never yet been done can be done except by means which have never yet been tried.

The last thing anyone would be likely to entertain is an unfamiliar thought.

Nature to be commanded must be obeyed.

Children sweeten labors; but they make misfortunes more bitter.

He that hath wife and children hath given hostages to fortune.

There is nothing makes a man suspect much more than to know little.

Seek not proud riches, but such as thou mayest get justly, use soberly, distribute cheerfully, and leave contentedly.

It breeds great perfection, if the practice be harder than the use.

A wise man will make more opportunities than he finds.

In the youth of a state, arms do flourish; in the middle age of a state, learning, and then both of them together for a time; in the declining age of a state, mechanical arts and merchandise.

He of whom many are afraid ought himself to fear many.

There is surely no greater wisdom than well to time the beginnings and onsets of things.

It is not possible to run a course aright when the goal itself has not been rightly placed.

Hope is a good breakfast but it is a bad supper.

A little philosophy inclineth man's mind to atheism, but depth in philosophy bringeth men's minds about to religion.

He that will not apply new remedies must expect new evils; for time is the greatest innovator.

Choose the life that is most useful and habit will make it the most agreeable.

Imagination was given to man to compensate for what he is not, and a sense of humor to console him for what he is.

### Parallel Lines: Imitations of Bacon

Even a single hair casts a shadow.                           —BACON

The smallest hair casts its shadow.    —JOHANN WOLFGANG VON GOETHE

Laws are like cobwebs, where the small flies are caught, and the great break through.                                                —BACON

Laws are like cobwebs, which may catch small flies, but let wasps and hornets break through.                       —JONATHAN SWIFT

He conquers twice who restrains himself in victory.          —BACON

Moderate your desire of victory over your adversary, and be pleased with the one over yourself.                      —BENJAMIN FRANKLIN

**BRUYÈRE, JEAN DE LA** (France, 1645–1696) In 1684, La Bruyère was appointed tutor to the young duke of Bourbon in Paris. He was a close observer of court life—"I am opening my eyes and looking, opening my ears and listening," he once wrote—and all the pageantry, pettiness, and political intrigue provided him with ample material for his *Characters*, a collection of thinly disguised sketches, or "portraits," of the Parisian elite. When the book appeared in 1688, an acquaintance of the author predicted it would bring him "many readers and many enemies." Indeed, the book sold briskly; La Bruyère produced four editions, each time adding new and even more scathing portraits. As a result, his enemies were many, too. When he died suddenly, poison was suspected, though evidence of foul play was never discovered. In his aphoristic character sketches, La Bruyère sought to combine Michel de Montaigne's storytelling skills with François de la Rochefoucauld's cynical, clinical eye for vanity and personal weaknesses.

*Essential Aphorisms*

Liberality consists less in giving a great deal than in gifts well timed.

Time, which strengthens friendship, weakens love.

We must laugh before we are happy, for fear we die before we laugh at all.

To laugh at men of sense is the privilege of fools.

There are but three events in a man's life: birth, life and death. He is not conscious of being born, he dies in pain, and he forgets to live.

Most men make use of the first part of their life to render the last part miserable.

Eminent posts make great men greater, and little men less.

The flatterer has not a sufficiently good opinion either of himself or of others.

All confidence is dangerous, unless it is complete: there are few circumstances in which it is not best either to hide all or to tell all.

When the people are in a state of agitation, we do not see how quiet is to return; and when it is tranquil, we do not see how the quiet is to be disturbed.

It is not so easy to make a name by an excellent work, as to make an indifferent work valued through the name already acquired.

It is a weakness to love; it is sometimes another weakness to be cured of it.

The things we most desire never happen, or if they happen, it is neither at the time nor under the circumstances when they would have given most pleasure.

If life be miserable, to live is painful; if happy, to die is terrible. Both come to the same thing.

**BUNSCH, KAROL** (Poland, 1898–1987) Bunsch is one of Poland's greatest aphorists. Outside of his own country, he is primarily known as the author of a series of historical novels about the Piast dynasty, the first kings of Poland. Piast, the legendary founder of the Polish state, was said to have lived in the ninth century. The rule of the last Piast monarch came to an end in 1370.

## Essential Aphorisms

Honest conceit is better than false modesty.

If people talked only of reasonable things, many would forget how to speak.

You can only believe when you cannot ascertain.

It is easier to rebuild a destroyed city than a destroyed confidence.

The tidal wave lifts and drowns.

The root of materialism is poverty; the well-fed remain idealists.

One cannot slap the faces of the beheaded.

The patient and parsimonious man buys another cow with what he's milked from the first one.

There are no shoes that fit great people.

Those who fear death do not live forever either.

The more laws, the more criminals.

Ideas are kindled through friction.

He who is fearful has already lost.

He who accepts slavery once will never be free.

The chip gets off the old block only once.

Thoughts illuminate the ways of action, but go their own ways.

Man would grow accustomed even to death, if he died several times.

The ends of war might be justified, but never the means.

Borders are established so there is something to fight about.

We feel only the limb that hurts.

Those adopt new manners most easily who have none.

Roads endure longer than pyramids.

It is unreasonable always to follow only reason.

The blossom withers, the thorn remains.

**CHESTERTON, GILBERT KEITH** (United Kingdom, 1874–1936) Alfred Kessler, an avid collector of the works of G. K. Chesterton, recounts a classic Chesterton anecdote first told by David Magee, an Englishman who ran a bookshop in San Francisco. Magee's parents had been neighbors and friends of the Chestertons in Beaconsfield, England, and as a boy David was an acquaintance of the young Chesterton. As an adult, Chesterton stood six feet, four inches tall and weighed close to 300 pounds. So whenever Chesterton visited the Magees for tea, he was served at a table with a concavity cut out of it to accommodate his enormous girth. His appetite was not the only prodigious thing about Chesterton. He was vastly well read and incredibly productive, writing short stories, novels, plays, poems, thousands of essays, and close to 100 books. Like Samuel Johnson, for a time he published his own periodical, *G.K.'s Weekly*. He was devout, erudite, witty, and absentminded. He was notoriously inept at keeping appointments and was in the habit of sending telegrams from the road to his wife to discover what was next on his schedule. One of the most famous reads: "Am at Market Harborough. Where ought I to be?"

*Essential Aphorisms*

A dead thing can go with the stream, but only a living thing can go against it.

Fallacies do not cease to be fallacies because they become fashions.

An inconvenience is only an adventure wrongly considered; an adventure is an inconvenience rightly considered.

He is a [sane] man who can have tragedy in his heart and comedy in his head.

To have a right to do a thing is not at all the same as to be right in doing it.

The reformer is always right about what is wrong. He is generally wrong about what is right.

The past is not what it was.

The only defensible war is a war of defense.

The true soldier fights not because he hates what is in front of him, but because he loves what is behind him.

For fear of the newspapers politicians are dull, and at last they are too dull even for the newspapers.

When a politician is in opposition he is an expert on the means to some end; and when he is in office he is an expert on the obstacles to it.

The Bible tells us to love our neighbors, and also to love our enemies; probably because they are generally the same people.

The riddles of God are more satisfying than the solutions of man.

There is no such thing on earth as an uninteresting subject; the only thing that can exist is an uninterested person.

The Christian ideal has not been tried and found wanting; it has been found difficult and left untried.

In the struggle for existence, it is only on those who hang on for ten minutes after all is hopeless, that hope begins to dawn.

**EBNER-ESCHENBACH, MARIE VON** (Austria, 1830–1916) The literary life was considered an unseemly profession for someone of Von Ebner-Eschenbach's gender and noble lineage. Yet even as a child the Austrian countess devoted herself to writing, and while still a teenager she impressed some of the Hapsburg Empire's most famous authors with her poetry and prose. Among her admirers was the playwright and fellow aphorist Franz Grillparzer, who was instrumental in getting Von Ebner-Eschenbach's works published. Her carefully researched short stories and novels focus on the morals and manners of Austria's nobility and petite bourgeoisie, but Von Ebner-Eschenbach was surprisingly free from the prejudices typical of her class. She sympathized with the Empire's peasants, and to a large extent blamed the nobility for their impoverishment. Though she lived a conventional life as the wife of a minor aristocrat, she held liberal views about the role of women in society and advocated moderate political reforms that would have deprived the aristocracy of some of its privileges. It was not until 1880, when Von Ebner-Eschenbach was fifty, that she published her first collection of aphorisms.

## Essential Aphorisms

You can sink so fast that you think you're flying.

An intelligent woman has millions of born enemies . . . all the stupid men.

No nation sinks to greater depths than when its government is obliged to listen silently to moral sermons preached by obvious scoundrels.

Think once before you give, twice before you accept, and a thousand times before you ask.

Just rise up again from every fall from a great height! Either you'll fall to your death or you'll grow wings.

In misfortune we usually regain the peace that we were robbed of through the fear of that very misfortune.

Nothing is so often and so irrevocably missed as the opportunity that crops up daily.

We generally learn how to wait when there is nothing more to wait for.

If there is a faith that can move mountains, then it is faith in one's own strength.

To have and not to give is in some cases worse than stealing.

People who read only the classics are sure to remain up-to-date.

It's not those who argue who are to be feared but those who evade argument.

You can buy many things that are priceless.

To be satisfied with little is hard, to be satisfied with a lot impossible.

There is only one proof of ability: doing it.

Nothing alienates two people who have nothing in common more than living together.

A gradual retreat is often worse than a sudden fall.

Between being able to and actually doing something lies an ocean and on its bottom rests all too often the wreck of willpower.

Think about what has to be accomplished; forget what you have already accomplished.

Deep learning doesn't shine.

Those who were carried to a goal should not think they've reached it.

Freedom stretches as far as your self-control.

It takes less courage to be the only one to find fault than to be the only one to find favor.

A defeat borne with pride is also a victory.

## Parallel Lines: Helping Hands

Better be struck rather than stroked by the hand we'd just as soon not shake.                                    —VON EBNER-ESCHENBACH

A blow from your friend is better than a kiss from your enemy.
                                                              —PYTHAGORAS

People who bite the hand that feeds them usually lick the boot that kicks them.                                              —ERIC HOFFER

**FRANKLIN, BENJAMIN** (United States, 1706–1790) In his autobiography, Franklin recounts how in 1734, at the age of twenty-eight, he compiled a list of the thirteen essential virtues he considered "necessary or desirable, and annexed to each a short maxim, which fully expressed the extent I gave to its meaning." Franklin's thirteen commandments include the usual suspects—temperance, cleanliness, humility—and his familiar exhortations to industry and frugality. Beginning in 1732, Franklin came into his own as America's first homegrown aphorist with the premiere edition of *Poor Richard's Almanack*. Franklin penned his almanac under the pseudonym of Richard Saunders, an impoverished, absentminded astrologer who took up writing to make ends meet. In addition to the standard horoscopes, weather predictions, and lists of everything from county fairs to solar eclipses, "Poor Richard" offered his own common-sense musings about how to live a virtuous life and how to earn a living. He intended the almanac to "inculcate industry and frugality as the means of procuring wealth, and thereby securing virtue." Franklin often borrowed, adapted, or simply condensed old English proverbs, or plundered Bacon, Dryden, Swift, Sterne, and Pope, to come up with Poor Richard's encomiums to self-improvement. He was also very much like his great German contemporary, Georg Christoph Lichtenberg. Both were renowned as scientists and wits; both edited almanacs; both won fame for their experiments with electricity; and neither could abide dogmatism in morality or religion.

*Essential Aphorisms*

Work as if you were to live 100 years, pray as if you were to die tomorrow.

There are no gains without pains.

Eat to live, and not live to eat.

He that drinks fast pays slow.

He that lieth down with dogs shall rise up with fleas.

It is hard for an empty sack to stand upright.

Little strokes fell great oaks.

Take counsel in wine, but resolve afterwards in water.

Resolve to perform what you ought; perform without fail what you resolve.

We must all hang together, or assuredly we shall all hang separately.

Early to bed, and early to rise, makes a man healthy, wealthy and wise.

Content and riches seldom meet together.

The use of money is all the advantage there is in having money.

He's a fool that cannot conceal his wisdom.

There's a time to wink as well as to see.

Search others for their virtues, thy self for thy vices.

Wise men learn by others' harms; fools by their own.

Having been poor is no shame, but being ashamed of it is.

He that would live in peace and at ease must not speak all he knows nor judge all he sees.

Better slip with foot than tongue.

Would you persuade speak of Interest not of Reason.

Gifts burst rocks.

He that can compose himself is wiser than he that composes books.

The way to be safe is never to be secure.

### Parallel Lines: Good and Bad Examples

A good example is the best sermon.                    —FRANKLIN

Errors are good examples.   —JOHANN GEORG RITTER VON ZIMMERMAN

Few things are harder to put up with than the annoyance of a good example.                    —MARK TWAIN

Bad examples are often the best.                    —MARCEL MARIËN

**GRACIÁN, BALTASAR** (Spain, 1601–1658) Gracián entered the Society of Jesus when he was eighteen, but he always maintained interests outside the monastery, one of which was writing books. His first book, *El Héroe*, was a disquisition on the qualities of the ideal leader. *El Criticón* was an allegorical novel that criticized and parodied some of his contemporaries, including a few fellow Jesuits. The Society of Jesus was less than pleased with the secular tone and subject matter of these works, to say nothing of the criticism of its own members. Retribution was swift. Gracián was denounced for publishing frivolous books unworthy of a priest and, as penance, was sentenced to a fast of bread and water. He was kept under surveillance, his rooms were searched, and he wasn't permitted to keep anything under lock and key. He was even deprived of pen, ink, and paper.

*Essential Aphorisms*

Life is a warfare against the malice of others.

Avoid outshining your superiors. All victories breed hate, and that over your superior is foolish or fatal. Pre-eminence is always detested, especially over those in high positions. Caution can gloss over common advantages. For example, good looks may be cloaked by careless attire. There are some that will grant you superiority in good luck or good temper, but none in good sense, least of all a prince—for good sense is a royal prerogative and any claim of superiority in that is a crime against majesty. They are princes, and wish to be so in that most princely of qualities. They will allow someone to help them but not to surpass them. So make any advice given to them appear like a recollection of something they have only forgotten rather than as a guide to something they cannot find. The stars teach us this finesse with happy tact: though they are his children and brilliant like him, they never rival the brilliance of the sun.

Know how to use evasion. That is how smart people get out of difficulties. They extricate themselves from the most intricate labyrinth by some witty application of a bright remark. They get out of a serious contention by an airy nothing or by raising a smile. Most of the great leaders are well grounded in this art. When you have to refuse something, often the most courteous way is to just change the subject. And sometimes it proves the highest understanding to act like you do not understand.

Leave your luck while still winning.

Make people depend on you. It is not he that adorns but he that adores that makes a divinity. The wise person would rather see others needing him than thanking him. To keep them on the threshold of hope is diplomatic, to trust to their gratitude is boorish; hope has a good memory, gratitude a bad one. More is to be got from dependence than from courtesy. He that has satisfied his thirst turns his back on the well, and the orange once squeezed falls from the golden platter into the wastebasket.

Do pleasant things yourself, unpleasant things through others.

Push advantages. Strike down your quarry, if you are wise—do not be content merely to flush it out.

First be master over yourself if you would be master over others.

Do not affect what you have not effected.

When you hear anything favorable, keep a tight rein on your credulity; if unfavorable, give it the spur.

A fountain gets muddy with but little stirring up, and does not get clear by our meddling with it but by our leaving it alone. The best remedy for disturbances is to let them run their course, for so they quiet down.

Display startling novelty—rise afresh like the sun every day. Change too the scene on which you shine, so that your loss may be felt in the old scenes of your triumph, while the novelty of your powers wins applause in the new.

Evil news carries farther than any applause. Many people are not known to the world till they have left it.

The greatest foresight consists in determining beforehand the time of trouble.

It is better to sleep on things beforehand than lie awake about them afterwards.

A wise prince must never take things easy in times of peace, but rather use the latter assiduously, in order to be able to reap the profit in times of adversity. Then, when his fortunes change, he will be found ready to resist adversity.

Keep matters for a time in suspense. Admiration of their novelty heightens the value of your achievements. It is both useless and insipid to play with your cards on the table. If you do not declare yourself immediately, you arouse expectation, especially when the importance of your position makes you the object of general attention. Mix a little mystery with everything, and the very mystery arouses veneration. And when you explain, do not be too explicit, just as you do not expose your inmost thoughts in ordinary conversation. Cautious silence is the sacred sanctuary of worldly wisdom. A resolution declared is never highly thought of—it only leaves room for criticism. And if it happens to fail, you are doubly unfortunate. Besides, you imitate the divine way when you inspire people to wonder and watch.

To be occupied in what does not concern you is worse than doing nothing. It is not enough for a careful person not to interfere with others, he must see that they do not interfere with him.

A shot foreseen always misses the mark.

A fine retreat is as good as a gallant attack.

Fortune pays you sometimes for the intensity of her favors by the shortness of their duration. She soon tires of carrying anyone long on her shoulders.

Keep expectation alive. Keep stirring it up. Let much promise more, and great deeds herald greater.

## Parallel Lines: Baltasar Gracián and Confucius

Be more careful not to miss once than to hit a hundred times. No one looks at the blazing sun, but all gaze when it is eclipsed.          —GRACIÁN

The faults of the superior man are like the eclipses of the sun and moon. He has his faults, and all men see them; he changes again, and all men look up to him.          —CONFUCIUS

Be slow and sure. Things are done quickly enough if done well. If just quickly done they can be quickly undone. To last an eternity requires an eternity of preparation.          —GRACIÁN

Do not be desirous to have things done quickly; do not look at small advantages. Desire to have things done quickly prevents their being done thoroughly. Looking at small advantages prevents great affairs from being accomplished.                                          —CONFUCIUS

**JOHNSON, SAMUEL** (United Kingdom, 1709–1784) In 1764, when Johnson was fifty-five and a celebrated author, his biographer, James Boswell, recorded a visit Johnson made to friends in the Lincolnshire countryside. "Johnson and [his friends] walked to the top of a steep hill," Boswell wrote, "and Johnson decided that he would like to roll down it. He said that he had not had a roll for a long time. Emptying his pockets, he lay down and rolled all the way to the bottom." The anecdote perfectly illustrates Johnson's boisterous, fun-loving character. His writing is charged with the same sense of energy and mischief. He was incredibly prolific. For two years while he was compiling his famous *Dictionary*, Johnson cranked out a couple of essays a week—on subjects ranging from "The invalidity of all excuses for betraying secrets" to "The nature and remedies of bashfulness"— for his self-published periodical the *Rambler*. Starting in 1758, he wrote weekly essays for the *Idler*. This was in addition to his steady output of biographies, essays, pamphlets, and poetry. His essays and conversation are the sources for some of his greatest aphorisms. For a time, he even wrote fictional parliamentary reports. In the late 1730s, when Parliament outlawed verbatim reports of its debates, Johnson got around the prohibition by making up the parliamentary speeches himself and inserting them into the mouths of thinly disguised versions of contemporary politicians.

*Essential Aphorisms*

Life is a pill which none of us can bear to swallow without gilding.

To build is to be robbed.

The only end of writing is to enable the readers better to enjoy life or better to endure it.

The advice that is wanted is commonly unwelcome, and that which is not wanted is evidently impertinent.

The men who can be charged with fewest failings are generally most ready to allow them.

The chains of habit are too weak to be felt until they are too strong to be broken.

What is written without effort is generally read without pleasure.

Curiosity is one of the permanent and certain characteristics of a vigorous mind.

If you are idle, be not solitary; if you are solitary, be not idle.

It is better to live rich than to die rich.

It is better to suffer wrong than to do it, and happier to be sometimes cheated than not to trust.

Self-confidence is the first requisite to great undertakings.

Silence propagates itself, and the longer talk has been suspended, the more difficult it is to find anything to say.

Pleasure is very seldom found where it is sought. Our brightest blazes of gladness are commonly kindled by unexpected sparks.

Human life is everywhere a state in which much is to be endured and little to be enjoyed.

We are more pained by ignorance than delighted by instruction.

Men more frequently require to be reminded than informed.

Many need no other provocation to enmity than that they find themselves excelled.

The vanity of being known to be entrusted with a secret is generally one of the chief motives to disclose it.

The safe and general antidote against sorrow is employment.

Few things are impossible to diligence and skill. Great works are performed not by strength, but perseverance.

No place affords a more striking conviction of the vanity of human hopes than a public library.

*Parallel Lines: Patriotism*

Patriotism is the last refuge of a scoundrel.                    —JOHNSON

Patriotism, n. Combustible rubbish ready to the torch of anyone ambitious to illuminate his name. In Dr. Johnson's famous dictionary patriotism is defined as the last refuge of a scoundrel. With all due respect to an enlightened but inferior lexicographer I beg to submit that it is the first.

—AMBROSE BIERCE

Patriotism is an ephemeral motive that scarcely ever outlasts the particular threat to society that aroused it.                    —DENIS DIDEROT

**LAVATER, JOHANN KASPAR** (Switzerland, 1741–1801) Lavater was a Swiss poet, priest, and theologian, but he is remembered chiefly for popularizing physiognomy, the practice of deducing personality traits and character from an individual's facial features. Lavater's *Essays on Physiognomy, Calculated to Extend the Knowledge and Love of Mankind* was a sensation when it was first published in 1775. During the end of the eighteenth and much of the nineteenth century, physiognomy—and the related practice of phrenology, the deduction of an individual's character from the shape of his or her skull—were simultaneously considered serious scientific disciplines and popular parlor games.

*Essential Aphorisms*

He submits to be seen through a microscope who suffers himself to be caught in a fit of passion.

The glad gladdens—who gladdens not is not glad. Who is fatal to others is so to himself—to him, heaven, earth, wisdom, folly, virtue, vice are equal—to such a one tell neither good nor bad of yourself.

Man is forever the same, the same under every form, in all situations and relations that admit of free and unrestrained exertion. The same regard that you have for yourself, you have for others, for nature, for the invisible *Numen*, which you call God. Who has witnessed one free and unconstrained act of yours has witnessed all.

The freer you feel yourself in the presence of another, the more free is he: who is free makes free.

Who cuts is easily wounded; the readier you are to offend the sooner you are offended.

As you treat your body, so your house, your domestics, your enemies, your friends—dress is a table of your contents.

Say not that you know another entirely till you have divided an inheritance with him.

The manner of giving shows the character of the giver more than the gift itself. There is a princely manner of giving, and a royal manner of accepting.

He who goes round about in his requests wants commonly more than he chooses to appear to want.

Too much gravity argues a shallow mind.

The more one speaks of himself the less he likes to hear another talked of.

Who can conceal his joys is greater than he who can hide his griefs.

We see more when others converse among themselves than when they speak to us.

Who can subdue his own anger is more than strong; who can allay another is more than wise; hold fast on him who can do both.

He whose pride oppresses the humble may perhaps be humbled, but will never be humble.

Who, in receiving a benefit, estimates its value more closely than in conferring one shall be a citizen of a better world.

Who can act or perform as if each work or action were the first, the last, and the only one in his life is great in his sphere.

Who finds the clearest not clear thinks the darkest not obscure.

Who will not see where he should or could shall not see when he would.

Search carefully if one patiently finishes what he boldly began.

He alone is an acute observer who can observe minutely without being observed.

Who seizes too rapidly drops as hastily.

Three days of uninterrupted company in a vehicle will make you better acquainted with another than one hour's conversation with him every day for three years.

He surely is most in want of another's patience who has none of his own.

**MONTAIGNE, MICHEL DE** (France, 1533–1592) Montaigne was thirty-eight when he began composing the *Essays*, his homely reflections on life and literature. He had already studied to be a lawyer and served thirteen years as a magistrate in the Bordeaux parliament. But he was tired of the intrigues of law and politics, occupations he never relished in the first place. So he quit his seat and retired to his ancestral home, a stern medieval chateau perched on a wooded hillside surrounded by vineyards above the banks of the Dordogne, about thirty miles east of Bordeaux. "Finding myself quite empty, with nothing to write about, I offered my self to myself as theme and subject matter," is how he described his new literary venture in one of his essays. Montaigne was steeped in the classics as a child. His father insisted that his son hear nothing but Latin spoken in the family home, and to aid his mental development had the boy awakened each morning by chamber music. Montaigne was an aphorism collector, too, carving his favorites on the bare wooden beams of the ceiling in his study. On that ceiling can be found the classical authors of Greece and Rome as well as Stoics like Epictetus. But by far the most citations, thirteen, come from Ecclesiastes, Montaigne's favorite book of the Bible.

*Essential Aphorisms*

I want Death to find me planting my cabbages.

The man who is happy is not he who is believed to be so but he who believes he is so.

Truth for us nowadays is not what is, but what others can be brought to accept.

We are constantly beginning our lives all over again. We already have one foot in the grave yet our tastes and our pursuits are always just being born.

To judge a man properly we must principally look at his routine activities and surprise him in his everyday dress.

If I can, I will prevent my death from saying anything not first said by my life.

The world is nothing but chatter.

My business, my art, is to live my life.

It is difficulty that makes us prize things.

What a stupid nation we are. We are not content with letting the world know of our vices and follies by repute, we go to foreign nations in order to show them to them by our presence!

Faults seen through anger are like objects seen through a mist: They appear larger.

There is in truth no greater silliness, none more enduring, than to be provoked and enraged by the silliness of this world.

If we had sound nostrils our shit ought to stink all the more for its being our own.

We must lend ourselves to others but give ourselves to ourselves alone.

We can never control well any business that obsesses and controls us.

Upon the highest throne in the world, we are seated, still, upon our arses.

## Parallel Lines: The Word

Our understanding is conducted solely by means of the word: anyone who falsifies it betrays public society. It is the only tool by which we communicate our wishes and our thoughts; it is our soul's interpreter: if we lack that, we can no longer hold together; we can no longer know each other. When words deceive us, it breaks all intercourse and loosens the bonds of our polity.
—MONTAIGNE

With the falsification of the word everything else is betrayed.

—EZRA POUND

**PTAH-HOTEP** (Egypt, c. 3550–2300 BCE) Ptah-Hotep was an Egyptian governor who set down a collection of aphorisms to be used as a kind of moral instruction manual for his sons. In the preface to this ancient papyrus, Ptah-Hotep is quoted as saying, "Old age descends [upon me]; feebleness comes, and childishness is renewed . . . Let me speak unto [my son] the words of them that hearken to the counsel of the men of old time, those that hearkened unto the gods . . . that sin may be banished from among persons of understanding . . . If you obey these things that I have said unto you, all your demeanor shall be of the best." More recently, the tradition of writing aphoristic instructions for offspring was practiced in the United Kingdom. George Savile, First Marquis of Halifax, practiced it, as did his grandson, Philip Stanhope, Fourth Earl of Chesterfield. Rudyard Kipling's poem-aphorism "If" is also part of the tradition of passing on moral instruction to children.

*Essential Aphorisms*

If you be powerful, make yourself to be honored for knowledge and for gentleness. Speak with authority, that is, not as if following injunctions, for he that is humble when highly placed falls into errors. Exalt not your heart, that it be not brought low. Be not silent, but beware of interruption and of answering words with heat. Put it far from you; control yourself. The wrathful heart speaks fiery words; it darts out at the man of peace who approaches, stopping his path.

Let your face be bright during the time you live. That which goes into the storehouse must come out therefrom; and bread is to be shared.

He that is grasping in entertainment shall himself have an empty belly; he that causes strife comes himself to sorrow. Take not such a one for your companion.

He that obeys becomes one obeyed.

Be not proud because you are learned; but converse with the ignorant man as with the sage. For no limit can be set to skill, neither is there any craftsman who possesses full advantages. Fair speech is more rare than the emerald that is found by slave-maidens on the pebbles.

Follow your heart during your lifetime; do not more than is commanded of you. Diminish not the time of following the heart; it is abhorred of the soul that its time of ease be taken away. Shorten not the daytime more than is needful to maintain your house. When riches are gained, follow the heart; for riches are of no avail if one be weary.

**ROCHEFOUCAULD, FRANÇOIS, DUC DE LA** (France, 1613–1680) La Rochefoucauld was a broken and bitter middle-aged man when he began writing maxims in the 1650s. In his youth, he had been a wealthy and influential courtier. But he emerged a big loser from the series of civil wars known as the Fronde. La Rochefoucauld paid a heavy price for his insurgency. He was financially ruined, his family was driven from their ancestral home, and his other properties were seized and ransacked. His career prospects were obliterated; he was stripped of his titles and banished from Paris. He was a physical wreck; he'd been badly wounded in battle and nearly lost his eyesight, and he never fully recovered his health. This was a remarkable reversal of fortune for La Rochefoucauld. Born in Paris, eldest son of the fifth count François of the ancient line of La Rochefoucauld, one of the noblest families in France, the young duke was a swashbuckling rogue fired by romantic ideals of heroism and gallantry. He excelled in skulduggery and quickly became embroiled in court intrigue. He was suave, witty, and ambitious, a born plotter. But he was also strangely irresolute, prone to melancholy, and possessed of an uncanny ability to pick the losing side in any battle. When La Rochefoucauld published his *Maxims* in 1665, the public was scandalized by their cynicism. After the debacle of the Fronde, La Rochefoucauld retired to a relative's country estate, where he read Seneca and the other Greek and Roman Stoics. La Rochefoucauld become close friends with another aphorist, Madeleine de Souvré, Marquise de Sablé, and came to rely on her conversation and criticism during the composition of his aphorisms.

*Essential Aphorisms*

Absence lessens moderate passions and intensifies great ones, as the wind blows out a candle but fans up a fire.

The cleverest subtlety of all is knowing how to appear to fall into traps set for us; people are never caught so easily as when they are out to catch others.

Neither the sun nor death can be looked at steadily.

Virtue would not go so far without vanity to bear it company.

We never praise except for profit.

Before strongly desiring anything we should look carefully into the happiness of its present owner.

How comes it that our memories are good enough to retain even the minutest details of what has befallen us, but not to recollect how many times we have recounted them to the same person?

We only blame ourselves in order to be praised.

We all have strength enough to endure the troubles of others.

The scorn for riches displayed by the philosophers was a secret desire to recompense their own merit for the injustice of Fortune by scorning those very benefits she had denied them; it was a private way of remaining unsullied by poverty, a devious path toward the high respect they could not command by wealth.

It is easier to appear worthy of positions one does not occupy than of those one does.

When the vices give us up we flatter ourselves that we are giving up them.

The man who thinks he can find enough in himself to be able to dispense with everybody else makes a great mistake, but the man who thinks he is indispensable to others makes an even greater.

Pride refuses to owe, self-love to pay.

Youth is one long intoxication; it is reason in a fever.

The reason why lovers never tire of each other's company is that the conversation is always about themselves.

We try to make virtues out of the faults we have no wish to correct.

It is less trouble for the right-thinking to let the wrong-headed have their way than it is to put them right.

We are never as unhappy as we think, nor as happy as we had hoped.

When you cannot find your peace in yourself it is useless to look for it elsewhere.

We seldom praise except to get praise back.

We find few guilty of ingratitude while we are still in a position to help them.

Moderation in times of good fortune is merely dread of the humiliating aftermath of excess, or fear of losing what one has.

Perfect valor consists in doing without witnesses what one would be capable of doing before the world at large.

### Parallel Lines: Enemies

Our enemies are nearer the truth in their opinion of us than we are ourselves.                                    —LA ROCHEFOUCAULD

The noblest kind of retribution is not to become like your enemy.
—MARCUS AURELIUS

A prudent enemy is better than a foolish friend.
—MUHAMMAD SHEMS AL-DEEN

Love your enemies, for they will tell you your faults.
—BENJAMIN FRANKLIN

It is from our enemies that we often gain excellent maxims, and are frequently surprised into reason by their mistakes.
—THOMAS PAINE

'Tis good to have enemies if only to hear our faults.
—JOHANN GEORG RITTER VON ZIMMERMAN

Every admirer is a potential enemy.            —CYRIL CONNOLLY

I owe much to my friends; but, all things considered, it strikes me that I owe even more to my enemies. The real person springs to life under a sting even better than under a caress.

—ANDRÉ GIDE

Mowst enummeez get yu with a wepun that yu hav givun them.

—JACK GARDNER

**SABLÉ, MADELEINE DE SOUVRÉ, MARQUISE DE** (France, 1599–1678) Madame de Sablé had two great loves in life: fine food and fine writing. At De Sablé's famous salon, where guests came to discuss life, love, and literature, France's sharpest minds partook of her exquisite cakes, jellies, and pastries. François, duc de la Rochefoucauld, was a regular, as was the scientist and inventor Blaise Pascal. But De Sablé could do far more than just cook. She was intelligent, well read, an accomplished aphorist, and long accustomed to living by her wits. She was married at fifteen to a man who quickly squandered his own considerable fortune and much of his young wife's as well. When he died in 1640, De Sablé sold most of her remaining property to support herself and her children. By the mid-1650s, she was financially and socially secure enough to launch her own salon. Guests passed the time listening to music, playing literary parlor games, and even indulging in the occasional scientific experiments. Often they competed to come up with the most concise and elegant maxims based on the evening's discussions. For most of the latter half of her life, De Sablé lived and held court in the Cistercian monastery of Port-Royal on the outskirts of Paris. The nuns of Port-Royal were devotees of Jansenism, a Catholic fundamentalist sect that emphasized mankind's depravity, a faith De Sablé embraced after a lover was killed in a duel. At Port-Royal, De Sablé enjoyed the best of both worlds: the scintillating intellectual and sensual life of the Parisian salons as well as the pious, gently ascetic seclusion of the convent. The great lady was terribly afraid of death, and she often took elaborate precautions to avoid suspected infections. Toward the end of her life, she often refused to see even her closest friends. She died as she had lived her final days, quietly, among the nuns. It is difficult to say who influenced whom in the literary relationship between Madame de Sablé and La Rochefoucauld. The two were very close friends and confidants, and shared a somewhat jaundiced view of human nature. Both came to aphorisms in middle age, in the aftermath of personal tragedy: La Rochefoucauld after he lost his health, money, and reputation for siding with the losers in France's civil wars; De Sablé after she lost her husband, her fortune, and her favorite son in battle. Many of their aphorisms are strikingly similar in both content and construction. La Rochefoucauld is consistently sharper and shorter; De Sablé is always more gracious and gentle. La Rochefoucauld acknowledged their creative collaboration when he wrote to De Sablé: "You know well that my sentences are not complete until you have approved them."

*Essential Aphorisms*

Instead of taking care to acquaint ourselves with others, we only think of making ourselves known to them. It would be better to listen to other people in order to become enlightened rather than to speak so as to shine in front of them.

It is sometimes useful to pretend we are deceived, because when we show a deceiving man that we see through his artifices, we only encourage him to increase his deceptions.

To be too dissatisfied with ourselves is a weakness. To be too satisfied with ourselves is a stupidity.

Wealth does not teach us to transcend the desire for wealth. The possession of many goods does not bring the repose of not desiring them.

Sometimes we praise the way things used to be in order to blame the present, and we esteem what is no longer in order to scorn what is.

To know how to unveil the inner workings of others, and how to hide one's own, is the great mark of the superior intellect.

Often the desire to appear competent impedes our ability to become competent, because we are more anxious to display our knowledge than to learn what we do not know.

It is neither a great praise nor a great blame when people say a tendency is in or out of fashion. If a tendency is as it should be at one time, it is always as it should be.

The foolish acts of others ought to serve more as a lesson to us than an occasion to laugh at those who commit them.

There is a certain manner of self-absorption in speaking that always renders the speaker disagreeable. For it is as great a folly to listen only to ourselves while we are carrying on a conversation with others as it is to talk to ourselves while we are alone.

It is a very common failing, never to be pleased with our fortune nor displeased with our character.

It is a singular characteristic of love that we cannot hide it where it exists, or pretend it where it does not exist.

## Parallel Lines: Madeleine de Souvré, Marquise de Sablé, and François, Duc de la Rochefoucauld

If we took as much trouble to be what we should be as we take to deceive others by disguising what we are, we could appear as we really are without having the trouble of disguising ourselves.    —DE SABLÉ

It is as easy to deceive ourselves without noticing it as it is hard to deceive others without their noticing.    —LA ROCHEFOUCAULD

We so love all new and unusual things that we even derive a secret pleasure from the saddest and most tragic events, both because of their novelty and because of the natural malignity that exists within us.    —DE SABLÉ

In the adversity of even our best friends we always find something not wholly displeasing.    —LA ROCHEFOUCAULD

Social intercourse, even friendship among most people, is merely a business arrangement that lasts only so long as there is need.    —DE SABLÉ

Pity is often feeling our own sufferings in those of others, a shrewd precaution against misfortunes that may befall us. We give help to others so that they have to do the same for us on similar occasions, and these kindnesses we do them are, to put it plainly, gifts we bestow on ourselves in advance.    —LA ROCHEFOUCAULD

It is such a great fault to talk too much that, in business and conversation, if what is good is also brief, it is doubly good, and one gains by brevity what one often loses by an excess of words.    —DE SABLÉ

True eloquence consists in saying all that is required and only what is required.    —LA ROCHEFOUCAULD

**SENECA** (Rome, c. 4 BCE–65 CE) Seneca was among the richest men in Rome, having amassed a considerable fortune during his career as one of the most influential and eloquent speakers in the Senate. Born in what is now Spain, Seneca won fame as a playwright and philosopher. Emperor Claudius feared Seneca's powers of persuasion so much that he exiled him to Corsica. Claudius's wife recalled him from exile and appointed him to tutor her twelve-year-old son, Nero. When Claudius died, Seneca ruled for a time as regent until Nero came of age. But Seneca's adversaries turned the young emperor against him. In AD 65, a plot against Nero's life was uncovered and Seneca was falsely implicated. It was diplomatically suggested to him that he might like to take his own life. He slit his wrists, but he did not die quickly. His circulation was slow, so when his wrist wounds didn't do the trick he opened up the veins in his ankles and behind his knees as well. But still he did not die. So he drank poison. When that failed to kill him he was placed in a vapor bath, where he eventually suffocated.

## Essential Aphorisms

Misfortune has a way of choosing some unprecedented means or other of impressing its power on those who might be said to have forgotten it.

Would you say that anyone who took the view that a lamp was worse off when it was put out than it was before it was lit was an utter idiot? We, too, are lit and put out. We suffer somewhat in the intervening period, but at either end of it there is a deep tranquility.

You have buried someone you loved. Now look for someone to love. It is better to make good the loss of a friend than to cry over him.

To be everywhere is to be nowhere.

Each man has a character of his own choosing; it is chance or fate that decides his choice of a job.

If you really want to escape the things that harass you, what you're needing is not to be in a different place but to be a different person.

You will only achieve [riches] in one way, by convincing yourself that you can live a happy life even without them, and by always regarding them as being on the point of vanishing.

Do not regard as valuable anything that can be taken away.

Whatever can happen at any time can happen today.

Cling tooth and nail to the following rule: not to give in to adversity, never to trust prosperity, and always take full note of fortune's habit of behaving just as she pleases, treating her as if she were actually going to do everything it is in her power to do. Whatever you have been expecting for some time comes as less of a shock.

There is nothing the wise man does reluctantly. He escapes necessity because he wills what necessity is going to force on him.

It is in no man's power to have whatever he wants; but he has it in his power not to wish for what he hasn't got, and cheerfully make the most of the things that do come his way.

*Parallel Lines: Contentment*

Only the wise man is content with what is his. All foolishness suffers the burden of dissatisfaction with itself.    —SENECA

Contentment is natural wealth; luxury is artificial poverty.    —SOCRATES

Nought's had, all's spent, where our desire is got without content.

—WILLIAM SHAKESPEARE

**STAËL-HOLSTEIN, ANNE-LOUISE-GERMAINE NECKER, BARONESS DE** (France, 1766–1817) Like Madeleine de Souvré, Marquise de Sablé, Madame de Staël was the presiding genius of her own salon. Unlike Madame de Sablé, however, De Staël did not avoid the subject of politics. She addressed it head on, and her glittering evenings became focal points for opponents of Napoleon Bonaparte's regime. Napoleon was so incensed by her support for political and religious freedoms, and so threatened by her influence, that he temporarily exiled her in the mid-1790s and in 1803 ordered her to remain at least 150 miles outside Paris for the next seven years. De Staël's love life was as radical as her politics. She had a string of famous lovers, including opposition leader Benjamin Constant and diplomat Charles Maurice de Talleyrand. De Staël was a novelist as well as a political theorist. Her books *Delphine* and *Corinne*—both tales of intelligent, independent women whose intelligence and independence gets them into trouble—are among the earliest romantic novels to be published in France. De Staël fled to Germany in 1808, after her outspoken political views prompted death threats against her. In Germany, she met and corresponded with Goethe, Friedrich Schiller, and Friedrich von Schlegel, all of whom influenced her with their theories about and practice of the aphoristic form.

*Essential Aphorisms*

A man must know how to fly in the face of opinion, a woman to submit to it.

The more I see of men the more I like dogs.

In matters of the heart, nothing is true except the improbable.

We cease loving ourselves if no one loves us.

Search for the truth is the noblest occupation of man; its publication is a duty.

The human mind always makes progress, but it is a progress in spirals.

To be totally understanding makes one very indulgent.

Wit lies in recognizing the resemblance among things that differ and the difference between things that are alike.

The greatest happiness is to transform one's feelings into action.

Politeness is the art of choosing among your thoughts.

**TOLSTOY, LEO** (Russia, 1828–1910) Tolstoy was born into the Russian nobility, to an extremely wealthy family that owned a vast estate in Tula, in the southwest of the country. But by the end of his life, Tolstoy had come to reject his noble lineage, believing that inherited wealth and social and political conventions kept the upper classes elevated and the peasants down. Tolstoy's political views were profoundly influenced by a tour through Europe in the early 1860s. In Brussels, he met the French anarchist Pierre-Joseph Proudhon, whose most famous saying is "Property is theft." The encounter inspired Tolstoy to set up a number of schools for the children of the serfs who lived on his family's estate, Yasnaya Polyana. His experiences as a member of an artillery regiment during the Crimean War led him to become an ardent pacifist. His radical political views, as well as his rejection of organized religion as the final arbiter of spiritual truth, resulted in his excommunication from the Orthodox Church in 1901. At the age of eighty-two, he abandoned his family, assigned the copyright to all of his books to his serfs, and left Yasnaya Polyana to live the life of an itinerant ascetic. He didn't get very far. He died of pneumonia at the railway station in the town of Astapovo, just a few days after his journey had begun. In his will, Tolstoy asked to be buried in the Zakaz forest near the place where, as part of a childhood game more than seventy years earlier, his brother Nikolai claimed to have hidden a green stick. Written on the stick, Nikolai told his younger brother Leo, was the secret to everlasting happiness. In later life, Tolstoy considered himself more of a sage and moral reformer than a novelist. He found the spiritual basis of his anarchism, altruism, and pacifism in the preaching of Jesus, particularly in the ethical instructions of the Sermon on the Mount.

## Essential Aphorisms

When the connection between this life and the other is established, everything becomes easy and joyous.

I am not afraid of a candle that is not burning, but of one that is, and not because its fire is not the real one, but because it is the property of fire to flame up and go out.

I do not say that they, or anyone else, ought to travel on the same path with me. The point is not how I arrived but what I arrived at.

Boredom—the desire for desires.

You have just had time to think, "I have conquered!" and are triumphant, when you are ready to fall into the ditch.

The struggle with evil by means of violence is the same as an attempt to stop a cloud in order that there may be no rain.

The seed recognizes its integument as its real ego, and is worried and weeps because it will perish. But it grew out of a seed, fell out of an ear, and again, perishing and throwing up its integument produces an ear, which is full of seeds. "The seed shall not come to life unless it perish."

Dissatisfaction is a sign of people who are walking on the road and not standing still, as we should like to. A joyous sensation!

Happy families are all alike; every unhappy family is unhappy in its own way.

In the name of God, stop a moment, cease your work, look around you.

**VAUVENARGUES, LUC DE CLAPIERS, MARQUIS DE** (France, 1715–1747)
Born in Aix-en-Provence in southern France, the eldest son of a family of minor
nobility, Vauvenargues was a sickly child who had defective eyesight. His poor
vision and even poorer general health often kept him home from school—and
thwarted his ambition for a life of action. He did see some action, though, during
the War of the Austrian Succession, when Vauvenargues' regiment marched all the
way to Prague. But the French were forced to retreat through one of the fiercest
cold spells on record. During the long, ignominious march Vauvenargues' legs became frostbitten, disabling him for the rest of his life, and he contracted the pul-
monary disease that killed him four years later. In 1746, the year before he died,
Vauvenargues published a little book containing some essays and a selection of his
maxims. Vauvenargues agreed with François de la Rochefoucauld about the
power of aphorisms to lay bare the human heart, but that's about the only thing
on which these two aphorists agreed. La Rochefoucauld saw deceit, betrayal, and
crass opportunism in the heart laid bare; Vauvenargues saw heroism, virtue, and
glory there. The two men are opposites in many ways: Vauvenargues was shy, un-
worldly, and introspective; La Rochefoucauld was smooth, urbane, and rakish.
Yet their lives had many parallels: both had lackluster military careers; both were
vexed by their failure to win favor at court; and both ultimately concluded that
society was a vicious, demeaning charade.

*Essential Aphorisms*

Opinion only rules the weak, but hope misleads the noblest souls.

There are none so sour as those who are sweet to order.

The perfection of a clock is not to go fast, but to be accurate.

Prosperity makes new friends.

Few maxims are true in every respect.

The common excuse of those who bring misfortune on others is that they
desire their good.

It is good to be firm by temperament and pliant by reflection.

The shortness of life can neither dissuade us from its pleasures, nor console
us for its pains.

The things we know best are those we have not learned.

We discover in ourselves what others hide from us, and we recognize in others what we hide from ourselves.

When a man is always trying to say something astonishing, he says little that is worth saying.

One who imposes on himself can impose on others.

Writers steal what is ours, and mask it, to give us the joy of finding it again.

To accomplish great things we must live as though we had never to die.

Clearness is the ornament of deep thought.

The maxims of men reveal their hearts.

The greatest evil that fortune can bring to men is to endow them with feeble resources and yet to make them ambitious.

Necessity saves us the trouble of choosing.

He who knows how to suffer everything can dare everything.

Consciousness of our strength increases it.

Men of parts seldom think of questioning anything else but what other people hold beyond question.

Most men grow old in a little groove of notions which they have not originated: perhaps there are fewer crooked minds than barren ones.

## Parallel Lines: Appearances

Before you can write you must have thought; before you can excite emotion in others you must have felt it yourself; before you can convince you must know with certainty. Every effort made to seem what you are not, only serves to prove more clearly what you are.          —VAUVENARGUES

We ought to be such as we intend to appear.    —BENJAMIN WHICHCOTE

There are hardly two creatures of a more differing species than the same man when he is pretending to a place and when he is in possession of it.
—GEORGE SAVILE, FIRST MARQUIS OF HALIFAX

To make clever people believe we are what we are not is in most instances harder than really to become what we want to seem to be.
—GEORG CHRISTOPH LICHTENBERG

We are not always that which we appear to be most often.
—MARIE VON EBNER-ESCHENBACH

## THE MINOR MORALISTS

**AL-SIQILLI, MUHAMMAD IBN ZAFAR** (Italy, 1104–c. 1172) Al-Siqilli was known in his lifetime as the "Sicilian Wanderer" because he left his native Sicily to roam the Maghreb, searching for an Arab prince who would put his political teachings into practice. He didn't have much luck. After traveling back and forth between Sicily and northern Africa, al-Siqilli finally settled in Syria, where he died in poverty and without an official position. Al-Siqilli's story has much in common with those of Confucius and Machiavelli. All three men sought and failed to achieve influential positions at court, and both al-Siqilli and Confucius lived the latter parts of their lives as itinerant sages in search of like-minded monarchs.

*Essential Aphorisms*

Counsel is the mirror of the intellect. If, therefore, you would like to know the capacity of anyone, ask for their advice.

Wealth is like water. He who does not open up a gate to carry off its overflow drowns in it.

Fortitude is misfortune's heaven, the virtue of noble men.

Ignorance of your faults is a greater evil than the fault itself.

Even as the iron cleaves to the magnet, so does success to patience. Endure, therefore, and you shall conquer.

Incline yourself to contentment before you are compelled to it by necessity.

**BEAUSACQ, MARIE-JOSEPHINE DE SUIN DE** (France, 1829–1899) In her own day, Madame de Beausacq was ranked among the great French aphorists, alongside La Bruyère, La Rochefoucauld, Chamfort, and Vauvenargues. Under the pseudonym Comtesse Diane, she wrote two books of aphorisms and presided over her own prestigious salon. Francis Grierson, an Englishman who met Madame de Beausacq several times toward the end of her life, painted this fascinating if not entirely flattering portrait of her: "Madame de Beausacq herself made me think of a mauve orchid tipped with yellow, that had withered on the wall of some neglected hot-house . . . Her hair, which she wore anyhow, fell here and there in straggling bits, giving her the appearance of one who had been confined in an asylum, had dressed up as Ophelia and escaped through the back door at the cry of fire . . . But her face bore an indubitable expression of power and distinction."

*Essential Aphorisms*

Light-hearted people take serious things lightly and light things seriously.

Doubt poisons everything and kills nothing.

You have to be very religious to change your religion.

The deceiver's punishment is to be obliged to deceive again.

Conscience warns us before it reproaches us.

It is a great boldness to dare to simplify oneself.

To make a good enemy, take a friend: he knows where to strike.

Young, we are hard to please in happiness; later, we become less exacting, because we know the cruelties of life. It is audacious to attempt to render happy he who has not yet suffered.

We penetrate to the bottom of things by a long and difficult road; then, when we announce the truth at which we have arrived, we are astonished to find that we are not always understood: this is because a truth is not rendered evident save by the souvenir of the road which led to it.

Only a born artist can endure the labor of becoming one.

**BURDIN, FRANCESCO** (Italy, 1916–2003) Burdin was a novelist as well as an aphorist. Born in Trieste, once part of the Habsburg Empire, he retained a Central European sensibility: a devilish sense of irony, black humor, and a taste for the macabre.

*Essential Aphorisms*

Too many ideas, no idea.

All of us are intelligent enough to know when we harm others. It requires an intelligence of a higher order to know when we harm ourselves.

Today's youth: forced to live in a world in which they don't believe. Yesterday's youth: forced to die for a world in which they didn't believe.

The human shadow is discreet: it doesn't reveal one's age.

Good, like evil, is a question of habit.

Disorder, anarchy, uneasiness, incomprehension, discomfort, impotence, disintegration, indifference, delusion, immorality: the world we live in is built on negations.

*Parallel Lines: Age and Youth*

The main satisfaction of old people is deluding themselves that young people aren't happy.
                                                                —BURDIN

Youth lasts much longer than young people think.
                        —MARIE-JOSEPHINE DE SUIN DE BEAUSACQ

Old age and youth have the same appetites but not the same teeth.
                              —MAGDALENA SAMOZWANIEC

You do not die as easily in old age as in youth.   —GERTRUD VON LE FORT

**COLLINS, JOHN CHURTON** (United Kingdom, 1848–1908) Collins was an English critic, essayist, and university lecturer who possessed an abiding fascination with the Whitechapel murders, a series of eleven killings that took place between 1888 and 1891 in London's East End. For a time, at least, each murder was believed to have been committed by Jack the Ripper. The victims were all prostitutes whose throats were cut; in some cases, their bodies were mutilated and internal organs removed. In 1905, Collins took a stroll through the streets of Whitechapel, visiting the scenes of the crimes in the company of Sir Arthur Conan Doyle, author of the Sherlock Holmes stories, and a gaggle of others with a professional or personal interest in the murders. In his memoirs, published by his son in 1912, Collins describes the theory of Dr. Gordon Browne, who did autopsies on most of the victims, that the murderer had been a medical student and also probably a butcher, basing his opinion on the slashes and incisions found on the bodies. But the murders have never been solved, and the identity of Jack the Ripper remains unknown.

### Essential Aphorisms

To ask for advice is in nine cases out of ten to ask for flattery.

In prosperity our friends know us; in adversity we know our friends.

Never trust a man who speaks well of everybody.

A wise man, like the moon, only shows his bright side to the world.

There can only be one end to marriage without love, and that is love without marriage.

To profit from good advice requires more wisdom than to give it.

A fool often fails because he thinks what is difficult is easy.

A wise man thinks what is easy is difficult.

Never claim as a right what you can ask as a favor.

The world, like an accomplished hostess, pays most attention to those whom it will soonest forget.

**ECCLESIASTICUS** (Israel, c. 180 BCE) The author of *Ecclesiasticus* identifies himself as "Jesus the son of Sirach of Jerusalem." Hence, this collection of moral precepts is also known as "The Wisdom of Ben Sirach." Ben Sirach was said to have been a well-traveled scribe who believed God had delivered him from many dangers. His ethical teachings emphasize the power and wisdom of the Lord and the duty of the individual to his or her family, community, and God. Ben Sirach concludes his admonitions with these words: "Jesus the son of Sirach of Jerusalem hath written in this book the instruction of understanding and knowledge . . . He that layeth them up in his heart shall become wise." *Ecclesiasticus* is part of the tradition of wisdom writing that began with ancient Egyptian texts like *The Instruction of Amenemope* and *The Instruction of Ptah-Hotep* and sought to provide handy moral maxims for the proper conduct of life.

*Essential Aphorisms*

To fear the Lord is the beginning of wisdom.

The greater thou art, the more humble thyself.

Force not the course of the river.

Let not thine hand be stretched out to receive,
And shut when thou shouldest repay.

A man may be known by his look.

Blame not before thou hast examined the truth:
Understand first, and then rebuke.

A friend cannot be known in prosperity:
And an enemy cannot be hidden in adversity.

The heart of fools is in their mouth:
But the mouth of the wise is in their heart.

**ECKERMANN, JOHANN PETER** (Germany, 1792–1854) When Eckermann was in his early thirties, he sent Johann Wolfgang von Goethe the manuscript of some of his essays on poetry. Goethe must have liked what he read, because the two men struck up an intimate friendship. Eckermann's *Conversations with Goethe* is filled with sayings and insights by and about the great German poet and aphorist.

*Essential Aphorisms*

It doesn't only take a great mind to make a great man, but a great character as well.

Diversity is not a law but a result. The law is unity.

You can have so much experience that you lose all appetite for more.

It often takes centuries for a people to get through the shell of a single idea.

The idea is your own work but the conditions are the work of God.

It's a good thing that man doesn't always recognize his errors.

To ignore what has already been found and to keep wanting to create something new is an entirely mistaken endeavor.

Courtesy: To avoid inflicting on your inferiors what your betters have inflicted on you.

## Parallel Lines: Proper Execution

Invention requires an excited mind; execution, a calm one.  —ECKERMANN

Boldness is blind: whereof 'tis ill in counsel, but good in execution. For in counsel it is good to see dangers, in execution not to see them, except they be very great.                                                    —FRANCIS BACON

Good results are sometimes owing to a failure of judgement, because the faculty of judgement often hinders us from undertaking many things that would succeed if carried through without thinking.

—MADELEINE DE SOUVRÉ, MARQUISE DE SABLÉ

**FORT, GERTRUD VON LE** (Germany, 1876–1971) Von le Fort was a German Protestant of Huguenot descent who converted to Catholicism as a young woman. She is better known for her poetry and prose than for her aphorisms. Her novel, *Die Letzte am Schafott* ("The Last at the Scaffold"), inspired the opera *Dialogues of the Carmelites* by Francis Poulenc. Set during the French Revolution, the novel is based on the experiences of a group of Carmelite nuns who were evicted from their convent and eventually executed.

## Essential Aphorisms

A woman's tears mean little and neither does her mercifulness. But when a man becomes merciful, the world moves.

Patience is strength in the highest degree.

Suffering, too, is nothing but love—wait a little while and you will experience it.

When faith in God ceases to exist, the world will no longer be afraid of anything.

Evil really has no other power than the impotence of the good.

Everything that is commonly called the past is merely a kind of present that has become quieter and darker.

**FULLER, THOMAS** (United Kingdom, 1608–1661) According to John Aubrey, author of *Brief Lives*, a collection of gossipy biographies of prominent late-seventeenth-century Englishmen, Fuller was even in his youth "a boy of pregnant wit." He grew up to become a vicar and historian. His reputation as a speaker was such that the crowds attending his sermons would often spill out the front door of the church and into the churchyard.

*Essential Aphorisms*

It is always darkest just before the day dawneth.

He knows little who will tell his wife all he knows.

Fame sometimes hath created something of nothing.

Learning hath gained most by those books by which the printers have lost.

Some men, like a tiled house, are long before they take fire, but once on flame there is no coming near to quench them.

Do not in an instant what an age cannot recompense.

**FULLER, THOMAS** (United Kingdom, 1654–1734) This Thomas Fuller was a physician and preacher, though no relation of the above-mentioned Thomas Fuller. He is famous for *Gnomologia: Adagies and Proverbs, Wise Sentences and Witty Sayings, Ancient and Modern, Foreign and British*, a massive compilation of proverbs and aphorisms published in 1732. Benjamin Franklin is said to have used *Gnomologia* as a source for some of the sayings he printed in *Poor Richard's*

*Almanack.* Fuller claimed to have amassed the most extensive collection of sayings ever compiled by an Englishman. He explained his method like this: "All of us forget more than we remember, and therefore it has been my constant custom to note down and record whatever I thought of myself, or received from men, or books worth preserving."

*Essential Aphorisms*

All things are difficult before they are easy.

Let not thy will roar, when thy power can but whisper.

A conservative believes nothing should be done for the first time.

A good garden may have some weeds.

A small demerit extinguishes a long service.

Great hopes make great men.

Charity begins at home, but should not end there.

Bad excuses are worse than none.

Better break your word than do worse in keeping it.

Choose a wife rather by your ear than your eye.

Contentment consists not in adding more fuel, but in taking away some fire.

He that hopes no good fears no ill.

A wise man turns chance into good fortune.

Better be alone than in bad company.

The patient is not likely to recover who makes the doctor his heir.

'Tis not every question that deserves an answer.

**HAMMARSKJÖLD, DAG** (Sweden, 1905–1961) Hammarskjöld came from a long line of Swedish civil servants. His family had been involved in politics and diplomacy since the seventeenth century, and his father was prime minister from 1914 to 1917. Hammarskjöld held a variety of prominent posts in Sweden before becoming secretary-general of the United Nations in 1953. His aphorisms come from the book *Markings*, a selection of excerpts from the diaries Hammarskjöld began keeping when he was twenty years old. *Markings* is remarkable, among other reasons, because it contains very little about Hammarskjöld's political and diplomatic doings. Instead, he writes about his deeply held spiritual and aesthetic beliefs, very much like his fellow Swedish aphorist Vilhelm Ekelund.

*Essential Aphorisms*

Life yields only to the conqueror. Never accept what can be gained by giving in. You will be living off stolen goods, and your muscles will atrophy.

Never measure the height of a mountain, until you have reached the top. Then you will see how low it was.

Life only demands from you the strength you possess. Only one feat is possible—not to have run away.

The devils enter uninvited when the house stands empty. For other kinds of guests, you have first to open the door.

Time goes by: reputation increases, ability declines.

There is a profound causal relation between the height of a man's ambition and the depth of his possible fall.

How humble the tool when praised for what the hand has done.

Praise those of your critics for whom nothing is up to standard.

**HAZLITT, WILLIAM** (United Kingdom, 1778–1830) Hazlitt knew all the leading literary and political rebels of his time—Jeremy Bentham, Lord Byron, Samuel Taylor Coleridge, William Wordsworth—yet always remained something of an outsider. His father was a Unitarian minister from Kent who was forced to immigrate to Ireland for a time because of his public support for the American

Revolution. Hazlitt himself studied for the ministry, but he gave it up to pursue his first love, painting. When he couldn't make a living at that, he turned to journalism, mostly for the *Times* (London). He also wrote political pamphlets on topics like official corruption and the need for electoral reform. He had a lifelong interest in aphorisms and proverbs, publishing an important anthology of the latter. He died penniless. Hazlitt subtitled *Characteristics*, his collection of aphorisms, "in the Manner of Rochefoucauld's *Maxims*." "Struck with the force and beauty of the style and matter [of the *Maxims*]," he wrote, "I felt an earnest ambition to embody some occasional thoughts of my own in the same form."

*Essential Aphorisms*

Leave something to wish for. That way you will not be miserable from too much happiness. Even in knowledge there should be always something left to know in order to arouse curiosity and excite hope.

There is nothing truly contemptible, but that which is always tacking and veering before the breath of power.

The greatest proof of superiority is to bear with impertinences.

Abuse is an indirect species of homage.

The greatest crime in the eye of the world is to endeavor to instruct or amend it.

We are never so much disposed to quarrel with others as when we are dissatisfied with ourselves.

We talk little if we do not talk about ourselves.

I have thought and suffered too much to have thought and suffered in vain.

**HERBERT, GEORGE** (United Kingdom, 1593–1633) Herbert came from a wealthy and cultured family. One of his mother's best friends was the poet and dean of Saint Paul's Cathedral in London, John Donne. Herbert himself went on to become one of England's greatest metaphysical poets. Like his friend Francis Bacon, he was also a connoisseur of proverbs and aphorisms. Aphorisms are scattered throughout Herbert's devotional verse. *Jacula Prudentum* ("Outlandish Proverbs"), his compilation of English proverbs published in 1651, juxtaposes serious, spiritual sayings with funny, cynical ones.

*Essential Aphorisms*

A verse may find him, who a sermon flies.

Wit's an unruly engine, wildly striking
Sometimes a friend, sometimes the engineer.

When a dog is drowning, everyone offers him drink.

Love, and a cough, cannot be hid.

Love your neighbor, yet pull not down your hedge.

The best mirror is an old friend.

Trust not one night's ice.

Living well is the best revenge.

Life is half spent before we know what it is.

When you finish the house, leave it.

**HIDDEMA, FRANS** (The Netherlands, 1923–1997) Hiddema was a Dutch psy-
choanalyst and poet. He was also a sculptor, and in his aphorisms he takes old
Dutch proverbial expressions and carves them into new meanings.

*Essential Aphorisms*

Many who are called are never heard from again.

Pioneers have left many people behind.

To broaden your horizon, take a step forward.

With the wind in your sails you can calm storms.

He who leaves the door open a crack stands in the draught.

Blind spots don't want to be seen.

Working yourself to death is a highly regarded form of suicide.

The lonely form the biggest group.

More is swallowed than is spit up.

He who is locked up in himself has the best-guarded cell.

He who is always climbing sees less and less of more and more.

The right track takes detours.

What you find far away you overlook at home.

A buried past lives underground.

### Parallel Lines: On the Road, I

Crossroads in life are created through collisions.                    —HIDDEMA

The best path through life is the highway.     —HENRI FRÉDÉRIC AMIEL

Road, n. A strip of land along which one may pass from where it is too tiresome to be to where it is futile to go.          —AMBROSE BIERCE

The road runs in both directions. That's why it stands still.
                                                        —MALCOLM DE CHAZAL

After a certain age every milestone on our road is a gravestone, and the rest of life seems a continuance of our own funeral procession.
                                                        —F. H. BRADLEY

Never look down to test the ground before taking your next step: only he who keeps his eye fixed on the far horizon will find his right road.
                                                        —DAG HAMMARSKJÖLD

Most people stay on the right path only on the way to their grave.
                                                        —THEO MESTRUM

If you are not sure where you are going, it is possible you are on the right road.                                           —LES COLEMAN

**HOFFER, ERIC** (United States, 1902–1983) Hoffer was a precociously early reader. But when he was seven, he inexplicably went blind and remained so until he was fifteen, when his sight just as inexplicably returned. For the rest of his life, fear of going blind again made him an even more voracious reader. Hoffer is often called "the longshoreman philosopher" because for most of his adult life he worked as a stevedore, educating himself by methodically reading in public libraries. His most famous book is *The True Believer* (1951), an insightful analysis of how lack of self-esteem leads people to join fanatical mass movements. Hoffer was deeply influenced by his reading of Michel de Montaigne's *Essays*, and he incorporated Montaigne's humanity and praise of the individual into his own writing.

*Essential Aphorisms*

Add a few drops of malice to a half-truth and you have an absolute truth.

The uncompromising attitude is more indicative of an inner uncertainty than of deep conviction. The implacable stand is directed more against the doubt within than the assailant without.

In running away from ourselves we either fall on our neighbor's shoulder or fly at his throat.

Belief passes, but to have believed never passes.

When grubbing for necessities man is still an animal. He becomes uniquely human when he reaches out for the superfluous and extravagant.

Nonconformists travel as a rule in bunches. You rarely find a nonconformist who goes it alone. And woe to him inside a nonconformist clique who does not conform with nonconformity.

How frighteningly few are the persons whose death would spoil our appetite and make the world seem empty.

There are no chaste minds. Minds copulate wherever they meet.

A man's heart is a grave long before he is buried. Youth dies, and beauty, and hope, and desire. A grave is buried within a grave when a man is buried.

The feeling of being hurried is not usually the result of living a full life and having no time. It is on the contrary born of a vague fear that we are wasting our life. When we do not do the one thing we ought to do, we have no time for anything else—we are the busiest people in the world.

The hardest arithmetic to master is that which enables us to count our blessings.

Doing nothing is harmless, but being busy doing nothing is not.

Our greatest weariness comes from work not done.

A society that refuses to strive for superfluities is likely to end up lacking in necessities.

It is not actual suffering but a taste of better things which excites people to revolt.

The technique of a mass movement aims to infect people with a malady and then offer the movement as a cure.

## Parallel Lines: Rats

It is cheering to see the rats are still around—the ship is not sinking.

—HOFFER

The rats that have left the ship resent its not sinking.

—WIESLAW BRUDZINSKI

**INGE, WILLIAM RALPH** (United Kingdom, 1860–1954) Inge served as dean of Saint Paul's Cathedral in London from 1911 until his death. He was nicknamed "the gloomy dean" because of his dark views on culture and civilization, which he eloquently expressed in a column for the *Evening Standard* newspaper from 1921 to 1946.

## Essential Aphorisms

Worry is interest paid on trouble before it comes due.

A man may build himself a throne of bayonets, but he can't sit on it.

A nation is a society united by a delusion about its ancestry and by common hatred of its neighbors.

There are no rewards or punishments—only consequences.

Prayer gives a man the opportunity of getting to know a gentleman he hardly ever meets. I do not mean his maker, but himself.

It is useless for the sheep to pass resolutions in favor of vegetarianism, while the wolf remains of a different opinion.

Nobody is bored when he is trying to make something that is beautiful or to discover something that is true.

Originality is undetected plagiarism.

Every institution not only carries within it the seeds of its own dissolution but prepares the way for its most hated rival.

To become a popular religion, it is only necessary for a superstition to enslave a philosophy.

**JÜNGER, ERNST** (Germany, 1895–1998) Jünger did what most people only ever read about in adventure stories: he ran away to join the French Foreign Legion at the age of eighteen. He had a less than glorious career. Within a year, his father had tracked him down in Morocco and taken him back home. But with the outbreak of World War I, Jünger immediately enlisted in the German army. And this time he really did become a war hero. In the 1920 and '30s, he became a nationalist and socialist, envisioning a new kind of worker's utopia. He briefly flirted with Nazism, but he steadfastly refused to join the party. He remained an adventurer to the last, becoming an early experimenter with hallucinogenic drugs like LSD, mescaline, and psilocybin. Jünger's physical heroism was matched by his philosophical heroism. Like Nietzsche, he believed that whatever didn't kill him only made him stronger.

*Essential Aphorisms*

Man's dignity must be even holier to us than life.

The age of humanity is the age in which humans have become rare.

The true leaders of the world are at home in the graves.

When you're surrounded, with no way out, you have to show your colors, like a man-o'-war that raises its flag.

Popularity is like a disease that threatens to become all the more chronic the later in life it starts to afflict the patient.

The hierarchy of friendships corresponds to a hierarchy of secrets. To share what cannot be shared, you must be united.

**JÜNGER, FRIEDRICH GEORG** (Germany, 1898–1977) Aphorisms ran in the Jünger family; both Friedrich Georg and his elder brother Ernst became famous writers and aphorists. Friedrich Georg would not have survived World War I without his brother. In 1917, Jünger was badly wounded in the battle of Langemarck, in which the British fought to displace the Germans from Belgium. Ernst rescued his brother from the front and took him to a field hospital, where surgeons saved his life.

*Essential Aphorisms*

Language is thought, and art is turning thought into language.

When you move from one extreme to the other, you haven't learned anything. You don't even move.

Complete equality of those who govern and those who are governed is a breeding ground for all despotism.

Science doesn't make eyes but spectacles.

Death seems unbearable to many people because it grants leisure.

The cork is not afraid of even the greatest depth.

Voices become louder when understanding diminishes.

A drop of mercy weighs more than a barrel of knowledge.

**KUDSZUS, HANS** (Germany, 1901–1977) Kudszus never managed to gain much popularity as an author. Another German aphorist, Theodor Adorno, was a fan, though, and through Adorno's influence Kudszus was awarded an honorary doctorate from Berlin's Freie Universität. Only one volume of aphorisms was published in Kudszus's lifetime, but an additional thousand sayings were discovered among his papers after his death.

## Essential Aphorisms

When we lower the last mask, we lose our face.

No bridge reduces the distance between two shores.

Paths do not change when night falls; only the wanderer does.

Birth is being issued with a return ticket.

Death by natural causes is a successful escape from suicide.

Tradition is the most sublime form of necrophilia.

No paradise is complete without a serpent.

Ideas do not "mature"; only our courage to think them does.

Routine is an early stage of decay.

If we could say what we think, we would also be able to think what we say.

Where there's no way, there's still a goal.

Where there's a will, there's a wrong way.

## Parallel Lines: Mirrors

Envy is a creation of the mirror.                                    —KUDSZUS

The world is a mirror in which everyone sees only their own soul.

                                                        —ISOLDE KURZ

Mirrors would do well to reflect a little more before sending back images.

                                                        —JEAN COCTEAU

**KURZ, ISOLDE** (Germany, 1853–1944) Kurz's father abandoned his calling as a Lutheran minister to become a writer, but German society looked less kindly on women with a vocation for literature. So Kurz took encouragement from the Italian renaissance, a period when women were recognized for their artistic gifts. She made the most of her talents, achieving popular success with her aphorisms, poetry, and short stories.

### Essential Aphorisms

There are three things that make those who are obsessed by them lonely: madness—guilt—genius.

Sometimes a cruel punishment awaits foolish wishes: their fulfillment.

Time isn't measured by length but by depth.

The only people who have a completely untroubled conscience are the great criminals.

Woman's frailty! Yes, it is inexpressible. There is only one creature that is even weaker—man.

I love what loves me, says the little person. I don't, I only love what is lovable, says the great person. So do I, the little person eagerly responds, but what loves me is lovable, is it not.

We call "mystical" a connection that we feel without understanding it.

Human prejudices are like nasty dogs that only attack the fearful.

Shallowness with an impenetrable surface is often regarded as unfathomable.

Nothing characterizes man more than that for which he never finds the time.

### Parallel Lines: Marriage

Man and wife are two nations that never fraternize, least of all when they shake hands for the great alliance.

—KURZ

Marriage must perforce fight against the all-devouring monster of habit.
—HONORÉ DE BALZAC

Marriage resembles a pair of shears, so joined that they cannot be separated; often moving in opposite directions, yet always punishing anyone who comes between them.    —SYDNEY SMITH

The most happy marriage I can picture or imagine to myself would be the union of a deaf man to a blind woman.    —SAMUEL TAYLOR COLERIDGE

Each one of an affectionate couple may be willing, as we say, to die for the other, yet unwilling to utter the agreeable word at the right moment.
—GEORGE MEREDITH

Marriage is one long conversation, checkered by disputes.
—ROBERT LOUIS STEVENSON

Marriages are made in heaven, but whether they prosper is of no concern there.    —MARIE VON EBNER-ESCHENBACH

Marriages made in heaven are not exported.
A fool and his money are soon courted.    —SAMUEL HOFFENSTEIN

**MARCUSE, LUDWIG** (Germany, 1894–1971) Marcuse worked as a biographer, essayist, and theater critic in Germany before being forced to flee the Nazis in 1933. He returned to Germany in the 1960s, after publishing his best-known book, *Obscene: The History of an Indignation*, a study of some of literature's most famous obscenity trials.

*Essential Aphorisms*

Academic: It is in the nature of the academic to consider only that which is dead; you are only completely sure of what can no longer move.

Thinking and Believing: Thinking is an effort, believing is a comfort.

The Luck of the Hopeless: Freedom from all illusions is the luck of the hopeless.

Mercy: Those who sell potatoes or clean the paintbrush or do finger exercises or endure a faculty meeting or haul garbage or knit another loop are mercifully prevented from thinking about the futility of human thoughts and actions.

Criteria: Usefulness weighs more than talent; perhaps not before God, but before the personnel manager.

Boredom: Better to be bored alone than in company. You can yawn with more abandon.

Lack of Truth: The truths we find are not of ultimate importance; and the truths that are of ultimate importance we do not find.

Revolutions 1: The thought of death, combined with the thought of happiness, is the strongest dynamite of Being, the deepest root of all revolutions.

**MORANDOTTI, ALESSANDRO** (Italy, 1909–1979) Morandotti was an art collector and dealer, managing the firm Antiquaria in Rome for many years. During World War II, some suspected him of selling paintings to the Nazis. Morandotti is also said to have hidden Jews in his gallery in Rome, which was across the street from Gestapo headquarters.

*Essential Aphorisms*

Cherishing an idea can become so compromising that you have to marry it.

There's a difference between forgetting and not recalling.

Those who do not believe in coincidence lose it.

Only those are faithful who do not have the opportunity to be otherwise.

The virtue of vices is that they make those happy who practice them and those rich who encourage them.

The kiss is an ingenious invention that prevents lovers from uttering too many inanities.

You recognize a true friend by how he lies to you.

Love is a divine gift that can easily transform into a divine punishment.

Love is born through appetite, lives through hunger, and dies through surfeit.

The most widespread beliefs draw their power from the fact that they cannot be verified.

The only way to explain away a lie is another lie.

Only those who aren't hungry are able to judge the quality of a meal.

Things would be much simpler if we were born with an instruction manual and a sell-by date.

Humans and melons have one thing in common: You can't tell from their looks whether they are ripe.

*Parallel Lines: Optimists and Pessimists*

An optimist is he who believes that things can get no worse than they are.
—MORANDOTTI

Optimists and pessimists differ only on the date of the end of the world.
—STANISLAW JERZY LEC

**MULTATULI** (The Netherlands, 1820–1887) Multatuli was the pseudonym of Eduard Douwes Dekker, the son of a Dutch sea captain. Dekker seemed destined for a career as an obscure colonial bureaucrat until he uncovered corruption in Dutch-administered Java and decided to expose it. When Dekker brought the exploitation of local labor to the attention of his superiors, they fired him. He returned to Europe and roamed around the Continent for a while, trying to earn enough money gambling to survive. He believed he had invented a foolproof system for winning at casinos, but he always lost. In 1860, he published *Max Havelaar*, a fictionalized account of the colonial abuses he had witnessed in the Dutch East Indies. The book caused a sensation throughout Europe, though it initially did nothing to stop the exploitation of the Javanese. After the success of *Max Havelaar*, Dekker made a career out of polemical writing, becoming an early supporter of women's rights, an impassioned lobbyist for educational reform, and a fierce critic of religion. His pseudonym is Latin and means, "I have suffered much."

*Essential Aphorisms*

Faith is the voluntary incarceration of the mind.

If a grain could speak, it would complain that there is pain in germination.

A horseman fell off his horse, and since that time anyone who fell off his horse has called himself a horseman.

He who is satisfied with his labor has reason to be dissatisfied with his satisfaction.

The most intense expression of grief is sarcasm.

There is not a single individual who would not be accused of being a criminal if he permitted himself what the state permits itself.

No one has a high enough estimation of what he could be, nor a low enough one of what he is.

To doubt nothing is the surest way of never knowing anything.

It is just as impossible to produce something good by following models as it is to feed oneself with the food someone else has eaten.

It is easier to imagine floating above a far distant mountain than it is to pick up one's foot to step over a pebble in reality.

The worst trials are visited upon us by trivial things. They attack us daily, incessantly and tenaciously, and usually find us unprepared. Furthermore, there is no honor to be gained in such a battle. Moses and the "Lord" knew what they were doing. They didn't plague Egypt with tigers but with grasshoppers.

Nothing is less often applied than a generally accepted truth.

A standpoint reached as the result of an ascent has a different meaning from the same standpoint reached as the result of a fall.

One does not advance the swimming abilities of ducks by throwing the eggs in the water.

*Parallel Lines: Standing Firm*

He who has never fallen has no true appreciation of what's needed to stand firm.                                    —MULTATULI

Don't learn to do, but learn in doing. Let your falls not be on a prepared ground, but let them be bona fide falls in the rough and tumble of the world; only, of course, let them be on a small scale in the first instance till you feel your feet safe under you. Act more and rehearse less.

—SAMUEL BUTLER

**MUSIL, ROBERT** (Austria, 1880–1942) In his diaries, which he began keeping from around the age of seventeen, Musil mused that he had acquired regular working habits from his experience of science and inspiration from his experience of literature. Musil was nothing if not a hard worker. He abandoned an academic career in engineering to devote himself entirely to writing. He only managed to scrape together enough money to survive thanks to the generosity of friends and literary admirers. He labored over his unfinished novel, *The Man Without Qualities*, from 1921 right up until his death. Musil once described the influence of Friedrich Nietzsche on his work as "decisive." He was attracted to the unsystematic nature of Nietzsche's philosophy, the way his ideas posed new questions rather than resolved old ones. "To me [Nietzsche] seems to be someone who opened hundreds of new possible ways and has realized none," Musil wrote in his diary. "That is the reason why people to whom new ways are a necessity love him, and those who cannot do without mathematically calculated results call him unphilosophical . . . Nietzsche is like a park, open to the public—but nobody enters!"

*Essential Aphorisms*

*Cruelty* arises through domestication. The drive no longer serves its native purpose.

Desire is will that doesn't take itself quite seriously; why may that be?

*Definition.* Modern man is a coward but likes to be forced to heroism.

*Poetry.* You have light and let it cast a shadow; you don't create (draw) light.

*A difference.* It's not the genius who is 100 years ahead of his time but average man who is 100 years behind it.

Why do old people sleep less? Because it's easier to move downhill than uphill.

*Culture and politics.* Culture: Grass which is trampled down again and again but always straightens up.

You do what you are. You become what you do.

**PAASILINNA, ERNO** (Finland, 1935–2000) In Finland, Paasilinna is known as the "national cynic laureate" and the "official dissident" for his dour view of human nature and relentless critique of the state. He was a journalist and essayist as well as an aphorist, and he also wrote a comprehensive history of his native region, Petsamo.

*Essential Aphorisms*

Nothing will change until everything changes.

Millions of common solutions do not exist for all the millions of private problems.

The self-taught are the only ones who have learned. The rest have been taught.

There would not be a lot to laugh about in this world if nothing was serious.

We are instructed in life by those whose company we should avoid.

It is also a victory to know when to retreat.

Those with the fewest connections are the most tied up.

It is necessary to train oneself to think wrongly, otherwise it is impossible to understand the order of things.

**PENN, WILLIAM** (United Kingdom, 1644–1718) When Penn founded the province of Sylvania in North America, later to become the state of Pennsylvania, he set up a democratic system of government that guaranteed freedom of religion; trial by jury; and the separation of executive, judicial, and legislative powers—all innovations that would later be incorporated into the Constitution of the United States of America. (Thomas Paine, Penn's fellow aphorist, was the first to suggest the new country's name: the United States of America.) Penn developed his passion for democracy back in England, where he was persecuted and repeatedly jailed because of his Quaker faith.

*Essential Aphorisms*

Time is what we want most, but what, alas! few use worse.

For disappointments that come not by our own folly, they are the trials or correction of heaven. And it is our own fault if they prove not our advantage.

Nor can we fall below the arms of God, how low soever it be we fall.

They have a right to censure that have a heart to help.

Choose a friend as thou dost a wife, till death separate you.

If thou thinkest twice before thou speakest once thou wilt speak twice the better for it.

Where thou art obliged to speak, be sure to speak the truth. For equivocation is half way to lying; as lying, the whole way to hell.

Believe nothing against another but upon good authority. Nor report what may hurt another, unless it be a greater hurt to others to conceal it.

Never give out while there is hope; but hope not beyond reason, for that shows more desire than judgment.

Do good with what thou hast, or it will do thee no good.

We should not be troubled for what we cannot help. But if it was our fault let it be so no more. Amendment is repentance if not reparation.

If I am even with my enemy, the debt is paid; but if I forgive it I oblige him forever.

**PRESCOTT, JOSEPH** (United States, 1913–2001) Prescott was an early and prolific James Joyce scholar, skilled in ferreting out the intellectual origins of Joyce's novels *Ulysses* and *Finnegans Wake*. He privately printed several volumes of his own aphorisms.

*Essential Aphorisms*

A common assumption: if you don't know what I know, you don't know anything.

To profess to be doing God's will is a form of megalomania.

Old age begins when you realize that forever is not as long as it used to be.

The child prodigy often remains a prodigious child.

**RIVAROL, ANTOINE DE** (France, 1753–1801) Rivarol specialized in epigrammatic attacks on his rivals among the Parisian literati. But he himself may not have been all that he seemed. His critics said he invented his allegedly noble Italian lineage. Nevertheless, Rivarol consistently managed to make his sayings both cutting and eloquent.

*Essential Aphorisms*

Vanity is forgetting our faults.

The eyes. Where the body ends and the spirit begins.

Talent is nothing but the spirit to use spirit.

The biggest obstacles to virtue are listlessness and impatience.

Love is a petty theft that the state of nature commits against the state of civilization.

When everybody is wrong, everybody is right.

Man's unhappiness is that he often mistakes means for ends. What am I saying! He thinks he is himself an end.

Brambles cover the way of friendship when one doesn't often pass by.

**SAINTE-BEUVE, CHARLES-AUGUSTIN** (France, 1804–1869) Sainte-Beuve held some unusual views for a Frenchman and a literary critic. He counseled young people to learn English, not because it was swiftly becoming the language of business but because in his opinion English poets were the best. He also had a pronounced disdain for the "literary." "Literary opinions occupy very little place in my life and in my thoughts," he wrote. "What does occupy me seriously is life itself and the object of it."

### Essential Aphorisms

There's no point in giving up society if society doesn't realize it.

There are people whose watch stops at a certain hour and who remain permanently at that age.

A skeptic is not one who doubts but one who examines.

It is rare that, after having given the key to her heart, a woman does not change the lock the day after.

There is nothing in love but what we imagine.

In most men there is a dead poet whom the man survives.

**SAMOZWANIEC, MAGDALENA** (Poland, 1894–1972) Samozwaniec came from an illustrious family of artists and authors. Her grandfather (Juliusz Kossak) and father (Wojciech Kossak) were famous for their paintings of military leaders and historical battles. Her sister, Maria Pawlikowska-Jasnorzewska, was known in her lifetime as "the Polish Sappho." Samozwaniec's comic writing first became popular in Poland in the 1920s. Like her compatriot Wieslaw Brudzinski, she published many of her aphorisms in the satirical weekly *Szpilki* ("Needles").

### Essential Aphorisms

Until a certain age, life consists of our own sorrows and our own joys; then, after a certain age, of our own sorrows and others' joys.

In old age a man resembles a retired actor who sits in the auditorium glumly watching others playing his favorite roles.

Love is that short period of time when a person of the opposite sex holds the same opinion of us as we do of ourselves.

Haughtiness is sometimes the self-defense of those whom no one praises.

There are no incomprehensible women—only ignorant men.

Laughter is the habitual crying of the wise.

People of small caliber like to sit on high horses.

In marriage, it is important to choose each other not only on the basis of merits but also of faults.

We are good to others to like ourselves more.

Hell is paved with male indiscretions.

Words are often the gossip of our thoughts.

Curiosity—the first step to betrayal.

Every man thinks himself a great actor who deserves a wider audience—one woman is not enough.

The kiss was invented by men to finally shut women up.

**SAVILE, GEORGE, FIRST MARQUIS OF HALIFAX** (United Kingdom, 1633–1695) Savile was among the most influential and eloquent statesmen of his day. During one famous seven-hour debate in the House of Lords in 1680, he outargued his uncle, Lord Shaftesbury, to successfully defeat the Exclusion Bill, which was designed to prevent James, the brother of King Charles II and a Catholic, from succeeding to the throne. Savile's wit and brilliant repartee were well known outside the debating chamber as well. He is credited with originating the phrase "kicked upstairs," which he first used in reference to a former favorite of the king who had fallen out of favor and was appointed to a loftier though far less important position.

*Essential Aphorisms*

The man that despiseth slander deserves it.

Nothing has an uglier look to us than reason when it is not on our side.

He who thinks his place below him will certainly be below his place.

Many men swallow the being cheated, but no man could ever endure to chew it.

An old man concludeth from his knowing mankind that they know him, too, and that maketh him very wary.

All are apt to shrink from those who lean upon them.

Hope is generally a wrong guide, though it is very good company by the way.

The more we deserve jests the less we bear them.

**SCHNITZLER, ARTHUR** (Austria, 1862–1931) Schnitzler was often labeled a pornographer, since nearly all of his novels, plays, and short stories deal with sex in an extremely candid manner. Indeed, he meticulously kept a diary from the age of seventeen until just before his death in which for a period of several years he faithfully recorded each of his orgasms. The Stanley Kubrick film *Eyes Wide Shut* is based on Schnitzler's *Traumnovelle* (*Dream Story*).

*Essential Aphorisms*

The path from religious feeling to dogma is infinitely longer than the one from dogma to religious mania.

Heaven save us from "understanding." It robs our anger of power, our hatred of dignity, our revenge of lust and our memory of bliss.

When you are inclined toward forgiveness, ask yourself in particular what it is that makes you feel so mild: a bad conscience, laziness, or cowardice.

In a diseased relationship, as in a diseased organism, we must interpret even the apparently most insignificant thing as a symptom of the disease.

To *confess some things* is usually more perfidiously deceitful than to *conceal everything*.

As senseless as the world may seem to you, never forget that you contribute a fair share to this senselessness by what you do as well as what you don't do.

**SELDEN, JOHN** (United Kingdom, 1584–1654) Selden, an English scholar and jurist, was a frequent guest at the Tower of London, imprisoned for what the church and the monarchy regarded as seditious remarks. In his *History of Tithes*, published in 1618, Selden suggested that the clergy's practice of collecting tithes—in which the church could claim up to 10 percent of a person's income—was not ordained by God. The argument was an implicit criticism of the divine right of kings, which incensed King James I. In 1621, Selden argued that the House of Commons derived its power from the people and not from the Crown. These views made Selden distinctly unpopular at court. But he was very popular in Parliament, to which he was elected several times. His aphorisms are not in his many books on political and legal history but in *Table Talk*, a record of his conversations kept by his secretary, Richard Milward.

### Essential Aphorisms

Syllables govern the world.

*Scrutamini scripturas*. [Let us look at the scriptures.] These two words have undone the world.

Humility is a virtue all preach, none practice; and yet everybody is content to hear.

Ignorance of the law excuses no man; not that all men know the law, but because 'tis an excuse every man will plead, and no man can tell how to refute him.

No man is the wiser for his learning.

Take a straw and throw it up into the air—you may see by that which way the wind is.

Philosophy is nothing but discretion.

They that govern the most make the least noise.

Never tell your resolution beforehand.

Wise men say nothing in dangerous times.

**SEUME, JOHANN GOTTFRIED** (Germany, 1763–1810) Seume was a reluctant adventurer and an enthusiastic pedestrian. While traveling to Paris, he was kidnapped by Hessian recruiting officers and sold to the English, who sent him to fight in Canada. On his return to Germany in 1783, he repeatedly tried to desert the army, finally succeeding after several failed attempts. In December of 1801, he began walking to Sicily, a nine-month trek he memorialized in *Spaziergang nach Syrakus.*

## Essential Aphorisms

The noble and the nobility are usually at odds with one another.

The word body politic has been very aptly chosen; after all, until the present moment, little thought has been given to imbuing it with soul.

All you can do for your character in this day and age is to document the fact that you are not part of this day and age.

History is usually the disgrace of mankind.

What appears to be evil usually is evil, but what appears to be good isn't always good.

Idleness is the stupidity of the body, and stupidity the idleness of the mind.

Man ought always to have something that he prefers to life; otherwise life itself will appear to him tiresome and void.

Tear man out of his outward circumstances and what he then is, that only is he.

**SMITH, LOGAN PEARSALL** (United States, 1865–1946) Smith's father was an evangelical Quaker and his mother a best-selling author of inspirational literature, so it's no wonder the young Logan Pearsall became an obsessive collector of aphorisms. He specialized in English-language aphorists, compiling an important anthology and writing monographs about unjustly neglected practitioners of the form. Although an American, Smith lived almost his entire adult life in London, where he became known as an essayist and critic.

## Essential Aphorisms

There are few sorrows, however poignant, in which a good income is of no avail.

There are people who, like houses, are beautiful in dilapidation.

Those who set out to serve both God and Mammon soon discover that there is no God.

Most people sell their souls, and live with a good conscience on the proceeds.

Hearts that are delicate and kind and tongues that are neither—these make the finest company in the world.

The test of a vocation is the love of the drudgery it involves.

Aphorisms are salted and not sugared almonds at Reason's feast.

People say that life is the thing, but I prefer reading.

**SMITH, SYDNEY** (United Kingdom, 1771–1845) Smith was a writer and clergyman renowned for the verve of his sermons—and his progressive politics. He defended Catholics at a time when they were persecuted in England, and he supported the education of women and called for the abolition of slavery. Smith was known for his levity as well as for his moral leverage, composing this rhyming recipe for salad dressing that is still in use today: "Let onion atoms lurk within the bowl / And, scarce suspected, animate the whole." In 1802, Smith was one of the founders of the *Edinburgh Review*, which is still published today. He and the other editors chose an aphorism by the Latin author Publilius Syrus as the publication's motto: "The judge is condemned when the guilty is acquitted."

*Essential Aphorisms*

We know nothing of tomorrow; our business is to be good and happy today.

A great deal of talent is lost to the world for want of a little courage. Every day sends to their graves obscure men whose timidity prevented them from making a first effort.

It is the greatest of all mistakes to do nothing because you can only do little.

Have the courage to be ignorant of a great number of things, in order to avoid the calamity of being ignorant of everything.

Whatever you are by nature, keep to it; never desert your line of talent. Be what nature intended you for, and you will succeed.

Some men have only one book in them; others, a library.

Live always in the best company when you read.

What you don't know would make a great book.

**STANHOPE, PHILIP, FOURTH EARL OF CHESTERFIELD** (United Kingdom, 1694–1773) Beginning in 1737, when he was forty-three, Stanhope composed regular letters to his son, advising him on the practical and ethical necessities of life. The letters mix earnest moral instruction with Machiavellian machination. Stanhope presses on his son, who was illegitimate, the virtues of industry, independence, and education. But he also urges him to start affairs with married women if the relationships might advance his standing or improve his manners. In 1761, Stanhope began writing similarly didactic and aphoristic letters to his godson, who was four years old at the time. When his son died in 1768, Stanhope discovered that he had been secretly married for years and had two young sons of his own. The tradition of composing aphoristic letters of advice goes at least as far back as the ancient Egyptians. The Stoics were especially good at it, and Seneca is probably the most famous correspondent. His best aphorisms can be found in the friendly and avuncular letters he wrote to the aspiring young philosopher Lucilius. The epistolary tradition clearly ran in Stanhope's family, too. In 1688, George Savile, First Marquis of Halifax, wrote *Advice to a Daughter* for his daughter Elizabeth, who was Stanhope's mother.

*Essential Aphorisms*

Whatever is worth doing at all is worth doing well.

The knowledge of the world is only to be acquired in the world, and not in a closet.

Advice is seldom welcome; and those who want it the most always like it the least.

Wear your learning, like your watch, in a private pocket: and do not pull it out and strike it merely to show that you have one.

Without some dissimulation no business can be carried on at all.

Dispatch is the soul of business.

Knowledge may give weight, but accomplishments give luster, and many more people see than weigh.

Let blockheads read what blockheads write.

Take the tone of the company you are in.

Learn to shrink yourself to the size of the company you are in.

A wise man will live as much within his wit as his income.

As fathers commonly go, it is seldom a misfortune to be fatherless; and considering the general run of sons, so seldom a misfortune to be childless.

**WAGENSBERG, JORGE** (Spain, 1948–   ) Wagensberg teaches the "theory of irreversible processes" at Barcelona University and has published scientific papers in fields as diverse as biophysics, microbiology, palaeontology, and entomology. He is director of Barcelona's La Caixa Foundation Science Museum.

*Essential Aphorisms*

Ethics is the aesthetics of conduct.

Civilization is culture that is universally useful.

The brain keeps the body between two extreme illusions: a minimal one, survival, and a maximal one, happiness.

The difference between the hunter and the hunted is that the former can allow himself a mistake.

Life after death can't be much worse than life before birth.

If not for the occurrence of improbable events, we would all be bacteria today.

**WHICHCOTE, BENJAMIN** (United Kingdom, 1609–1683) As a vicar in the Anglican church, responsible for parishes in London and Cambridge, Whichcote was in the habit of preaching from brief written notes, which he embellished as he spoke. Partly as a result of his preference for extemporaneous composition, nearly all of his books—collections of sermons, "notions," and aphorisms—were published after his death. During his time at Cambridge, Whichcote was among the most prominent of the Cambridge Platonists, a group of English philosophers and divines who argued for the compatibility of reason and faith and took a keen interest in scientific advances. In his sermons and aphorisms, Whichcote tried to provide rational and practical arguments for religious and moral beliefs.

*Essential Aphorisms*

Using and enjoying is the true having.

Many use themselves so as to lessen themselves.

He that is full of himself goes out of company as wise as he came in.

Whoever suspects thinks himself suspected.

We find it easier to go on than to go back.

They that force things often break themselves, but things return to their course again.

He that knows most thinks he has most still to learn.

He knows most who does best.

None so empty as those that are full of themselves.

A good word costs as little as a bad one and is worth more, is more to the purpose.

A good man's life is all of a piece.

It is not good to live in jest since we must die in earnest.

Yesterday we were not; today we are but little; tomorrow we may be nothing.

Some make their last understanding the first thing they do.

### Parallel Lines: Conscience

We never do anything so secretly but that it is in the presence of two witnesses: God and our own conscience.   —WHICHCOTE

The voice of conscience is so delicate that it is easy to stifle it; but it is also so clear that it is impossible to mistake it.
   —ANNE-LOUISE-GERMAINE NECKER, BARONESS DE STAËL-HOLSTEIN

Be master of your will and servant to your conscience.
   —MARIE VON EBNER-ESCHENBACH

**WOTTON, SIR HENRY** (United Kingdom, 1568–1639) For most of his adult life, Wotton was a diplomat in Florence and Venice, but today we would call him a spy. His main task was to gather intelligence on England's allies and neighbors. In 1602, he learned of a plot to murder James VI of Scotland and traveled incognito from Italy to warn the king. He also brought along some Italian antidotes for poison, just in case. Wotton's diplomatic skills momentarily deserted him when he penned his famous definition of an ambassador: "an honest man, sent to lie abroad for the good of his country." The quip caused Wotton some discomfort at home, but he eventually managed to restore his reputation at court. Tiring of diplomacy, Wotton ended his career back in England as provost of Eton College.

### Essential Aphorisms

He seldom speeds well in his course that stumbles at his setting forth.

Discretion is the most universal art, and hath more professors than students.

They who travel far easily miss their way.

Books and friends are better received by weight than number.

Few men thrive by one only art, fewer by many.

Felicity shows the ground where industry builds a fortune.

**ZIMMERMAN, JOHANN GEORG RITTER VON** (Switzerland, 1728–1795) Zimmerman was a doctor to kings, serving as the private physician to both George III and Frederick the Great. He attended to the maladies of the soul as well, winning widespread renown for tomes like *On Loneliness*, first published in 1756. Born in Brugg, Switzerland, he studied medicine at Göttingen and eventually settled in Hanover. Before his death, Zimmerman entrusted his aphorisms to a friend, who ensured their publication. Their swift translation into English, in 1800, is a measure of Zimmerman's popularity at the time.

### Essential Aphorisms

We are the last to acknowledge but the first to worship our own picture.

If virtue is its own reward, as the adage pronounces it, who should be surprised at their own poverty?

Good friends are safe enemies, and good enemies may become safe friends.

Appear to be a dupe if you want dupes.

What scholars and artists borrow they should make their own.

Report is a quick traveler but an unsafe guide.

The instant our successor is fixed we look upon him with secret, in-felt detestation.

Laugh as loud as you please at your companion's wit; do not even smile at his folly.

Let the captious know that the best way to get rid of a quarrel is not always the quickest way of getting out of it.

Before good sense, or a good dress, is a good address.

'Tis difficult to walk your own pace amidst observers.

The best advice is not always that which is, or can, but which ought to be abided by.

A good name will wear out; a bad one may be turned; a nickname lasts forever.

Fools cherish what the sage despises: the value of what we love is the amount of our own value.

When the first opportunity is irretrievable contrive to take double advantage of the second.

The most successful juggler keeps his spectators most in the dark.

# NOVELISTS AND PLAYWRIGHTS

**N**OVELISTS and playwrights can best be described as accidental aphorists; most do not deliberately set out to write aphorisms. Instead, their sayings are stylistic spin-offs. Embedded in narrative passages or stretches of dialogue, they are part of the larger work yet completely self-contained, like literary fossils. They glitter like specks of gold in a character's stream of consciousness. Stumbling across an aphorism in a novel or a play is always a provocative delight. "How many of us have been attracted to reason; first learned to think, to draw conclusions, to extract a moral from the follies of life, by some dazzling aphorism," as Edward Bulwer-Lytton so aptly put it.

### NOVELISTS

**BACH, RICHARD** (United States, 1936– ) Bach's 1972 novel *Jonathan Livingston Seagull* sold a million copies in its first year of publication alone. He followed it up in 1977 with *Illusions: The Adventures of a Reluctant Messiah*, the story of two pilots—one of whom is a miracle-working, aphorism-uttering sage—who meet by accident in a field in the American Midwest. Bach compiled his antihero's sayings into a fictional scripture called the *Messiah's Handbook*.

*Essential Aphorisms*

Shop for security over happiness and you buy it, at that price.

No one does anything uncharacteristic of who they are.

Before you'll change, something important must be at risk.

You learn most when you play against an opponent who can beat you.

Learn what the magician knows and it's not magic anymore.

Rarely do members of one family grow up under the same roof.

Argue for your limitations and sure enough, they're yours.

Everything in this book may be wrong.

**BÉALU, MARCEL** (France, 1908–1993) In addition to writing slightly sinister, surrealistic novels, Béalu was the proprietor of a renowned antiquarian bookshop in Paris called Le Pont Traversé. In 1937, he met and became close friends with the French poet and critic Max Jacob, a Jew who died in a Nazi deportation camp in 1944. But Jacob's influence stayed with Béalu, who followed the recommendation his friend gave in the 1941 book *Advice to a Young Poet*: "Love words. Love a word. Repeat it, gargle with it."

*Essential Aphorisms*

By refusing everything in life that is not the best, one soon risks finding nothing but the worst.

A miserable childhood provides the comforting reassurance of never falling any lower than your starting point.

We live in a closed world not knowing that a door exists and that it may be enough to knock at this door to have it opened.

Obstacles never come from below but from those who never managed to reach the top and are blocking the way.

**BIBESCO, ELIZABETH** (United Kingdom, 1897–1945) Bibesco was the daughter of Herbert Asquith, British prime minister from 1908 to 1916. In 1919, she married a Romanian prince and moved with him to Paris, where she began writing novels, short stories, and poetry. In Paris, Bibesco became close friends with Marcel Proust, who described her as "probably unsurpassed in intelligence by any of her contemporaries."

*Essential Aphorisms*

We go through life expecting to be tasted while we are being swallowed.

It is better to be made unhappy by your own love than bored by someone else's.

The problem of life is the problem of knowing what to do with our second times.

Of all the disguises truth assumes, fact is the most misleading.

With some people anything out of the picture is out of the question.

The only true monument is a gap.

Greed is a perpetual demand for hunger.

Life is a series of discoveries of what we were born knowing.

**BOWEN, ELIZABETH** (Ireland, 1899–1973) Bowen was born in Dublin but lived most of her life in England, where she hovered on the periphery of the Bloomsbury group of writers. During World War II, she was an air-raid warden in London, an experience vividly recalled in her novels. She also edited Elizabeth Bibesco's last book, a collection of short stories, poems, and aphorisms.

*Essential Aphorisms*

We are minor in everything but our passions.

The heart may think it knows better: the senses know that absence blots people out. We really have no absent friends.

Experience isn't interesting until it begins to repeat itself. In fact, till it does that, it hardly is experience.

No object is mysterious. The mystery is your eye.

Art is one thing that can go on mattering once it has stopped hurting.

Intimacies between women often go backward, beginning in revelations and ending in small talk.

**BULGAKOV, MIKHAIL** (Russia, 1891–1940) In 1930, Bulgakov was desperate. His plays and short stories had been banned from publication because the Soviet censors thought he paid too little attention to the lives of peasants. The author was broke and despondent. So he wrote a letter to Stalin, pleading for the dictator's intercession. "I ask the Soviet government to order me to leave the USSR immediately," the letter reads in part. "I appeal to the humanity of the Soviet regime and ask it to generously set me free, the writer who is useless in his own country." If emigration was not an option, Bulgakov helpfully provided Stalin with another alternative: employment in the Russian theater, in practically any capacity whatsoever. Such an impetuous letter could have gotten Bulgakov sent to a Siberian work camp at best; at worst, it could have cost him his life. Instead, he got a phone call from Stalin himself, who arranged a job at the Moscow Art Theater for him. (More than a century before Bulgakov's plea to Stalin, Alexander Pushkin made a similar request of Tsar Nicholas I. In 1825, Pushkin was implicated in the Decembrist Uprising, a failed coup by a group of Russian officers who wanted to see more democracy and human rights in Russia. After a year in internal exile in the provinces, Pushkin petitioned the tsar for his release. Nicholas I summoned him to Moscow and granted the request, throwing in a minor court appointment for good measure.) Bulgakov got his theater job, but his masterpiece, *The Master and Margarita*, was not published until twenty-five years after his death. Just before he died, Bulgakov insisted on seeing the manuscript, which he had hidden in his house to prevent its confiscation, one last time. "Leaning on my arm, he walked through all the rooms, barefoot and in his dressing gown, to make sure the manuscript . . . was still there," his wife recalled.

*Essential Aphorisms*

Manuscripts don't burn.

The lover is destined to share the fate of the beloved.

A man without some inner surprise is dull and boring.

The writer will always remain in opposition to politics as long as politics remains in opposition to culture.

He who never hurries is always on time.

Not being able to write is like being buried alive.

**BULWER-LYTTON, EDWARD** (United Kingdom, 1803–1873) Bulwer-Lytton, an English novelist, playwright, and politician, is famous for composing what has come to be universally regarded as the most awful opening line of any novel ever written: "It was a dark and stormy night; the rain fell in torrents—except at occasional intervals, when it was checked by a violent gust of wind which swept up the streets (for it is in London that our scene lies), rattling along the housetops, and fiercely agitating the scanty flame of the lamps that struggled against the darkness." This is the opening of *Paul Clifford*, published in 1830, and the inspiration for the Bulwer-Lytton Fiction Contest, an annual competition organized by the English Department of San José State University to write "the opening sentence to the worst of all possible novels." Surprisingly, Bulwer-Lytton is also credited with composing some of the best lines in the English language, including "the pen is mightier than the sword," "the great unwashed," and the "pursuit of the almighty dollar."

## Essential Aphorisms

A fool flatters himself; a wise man flatters the fool.

If you wish to be loved, show more of your faults than your virtues.

One of the surest evidences of friendship that one individual can display to another is telling him gently of a fault. If any other can excel it, it is listening to such a disclosure with gratitude, and amending the error.

You believe that easily which you hope for earnestly.

Whatever our wandering our happiness will always be found within a narrow compass, and in the middle of the objects more immediately within our reach.

The easiest person to deceive is one's self.

## Parallel Lines: Genius

Talent does what it can; genius does what it must.     —BULWER-LYTTON

Genius is eternal patience.     —MICHELANGELO

Talent does whatever it wants to do; genius does only what it can.
     —EUGÈNE DELACROIX

Doing easily what others find difficult is talent; doing what is impossible for talent is genius.     —HENRI FRÉDÉRIC AMIEL

As it must not, so genius cannot be lawless; for it is even that which constitutes its genius—the power of acting creatively under laws of its own origination.     —SAMUEL TAYLOR COLERIDGE

Genius is an infinite capacity for taking pains.        —THOMAS CARLYLE

Genius, in truth, means little more than the faculty of perceiving in an
unhabitual way.        —WILLIAM JAMES

**CERVANTES, MIGUEL DE** (Spain, 1547–1616) Cervantes led a life every bit as
eventful as that of his most famous character, Don Quixote de la Mancha. He
was born in the town of Alcalá de Henares outside Madrid. In the early 1570s he
was a soldier, fighting (and being wounded) in several naval battles. After Turks
captured his ship, Cervantes was sold into slavery in Algiers. He spent five years in
captivity before being released in exchange for a ransom. Back in Madrid, he
worked a series of odd jobs, was imprisoned for embezzlement, and went bankrupt before publishing the first part of *Don Quixote*. Cervantes is said to have died
on April 23, 1616, the same day on which Shakespeare passed away.

*Essential Aphorisms*

Keep your mouth shut and your eyes open.

Many go out for wool and return shorn.

Fortune always leaves some door open in misfortune.

Sometimes we look for one thing and find another.

Self-praise depreciates.

Fear hath many eyes.

Who sings in grief procures relief.

Let everyone turn himself around, and look at home, and he will find
enough to do.

He who gives freely gives twice.

He must be blind, indeed, who cannot see through a sieve.

He that covers, discovers.

He that's coy when fortune's kind may after seek but never find.

By the streets of "by-and-by" one arrives at the house of "never."

So much thou art worth as thou hast, and so much thou hast as thou art worth.

Length begets loathing.

Cheats are always at the mercy of their accomplices.

There is a remedy for all things except death.

The heart will not grieve for what the eye doth not perceive.

Delay breeds danger.

Patience, and shuffle the cards.

**CHATEAUBRIAND, FRANÇOIS-RENÉ, VICOMTE DE** (France, 1768–1848) Chateaubriand was France's answer to Lord Byron. Like that of his flamboyant British counterpart, Chateaubriand's life was just as famous as his art. Born in Brittany in 1768, he fled the chaos that followed the Revolution and went to America, where he traveled around what is now known as the Midwest and wrote exotic descriptions of the natural world and fictionalized encounters with Native Americans. The novels based on these excursions are credited with introducing Romanticism to France. Chateaubriand had a long career as a government official as well, serving variously as secretary to the embassy at Rome, ambassador to London, and eventually minister of foreign affairs.

*Essential Aphorisms*

An original writer is not one who imitates nobody, but one whom nobody can imitate.

As long as the heart preserves desire, the mind preserves illusion.

The heart is like the tree that gives balm for the wounds of man, only when the iron has wounded it.

Poets are like birds: the least thing makes them sing.

Justice is the bread of nations: they are always famishing for it.

There are two sorts of ruins: one is the work of time, the other of men.

**DOUGLAS, NORMAN** (Scotland, 1868–1952) After working for the British Foreign Office in the United Kingdom and Russia, Douglas devoted himself to writing full time. His first and still best-known novel, *South Wind*, was co-written with his cousin and ex-wife, Elsa Fitzgibbon, and published under the pseudonym Normyx.

*Essential Aphorisms*

You can tell the ideals of a nation by its advertisements.

You can construct the character of a man and his age not only from what he does and says, but from what he fails to say and do.

Distrust of authority should be the first civic duty.

The longer one lives, the more one realizes that nothing is a dish for every day.

They who are all things to their neighbors cease to be anything to themselves.

What is all wisdom save a collection of platitudes?

**ELIOT, GEORGE** (United Kingdom, 1819–1880) Mary Ann Evans took the pseudonym George Eliot to avoid the bias against female authors that was prevalent in her time. Women were seen as writers of harmless romances, but Eliot's work was far more provocative. As a young woman, she rejected Christianity and lived with a married man—George Henry Lewes, her colleague at the *Westminster Review*—who was not able to obtain a divorce from his wife. Her novels, in which her aphorisms can be found, depict the personal and psychological struggles of people who don't quite conform to society. Many of her sayings are actually spoken by the characters in her books, and many are spelled phonetically to capture the local vernacular.

*Essential Aphorisms*

There are many victories worse than a defeat.

It's them as take advantage that gets advantage i' this world.

It's but little good you'll do a-watering the last year's crop.

Our deeds determine us, as much as we determine our deeds.

If you could make a pudding wi' thinking o' the batter, it 'ud be easy getting dinner.

Love has a way of cheating itself consciously, like a child who plays at solitary hide-and-seek; it is pleased with assurances that it all the while disbelieves.

People who love downy peaches are apt not to think of the stone, and sometimes jar their teeth terribly against it.

There's folks 'ud hold a sieve under the pump and expect to carry away the water.

A man never lies with more delicious languor under the influence of a passion than when he has persuaded himself that he shall subdue it tomorrow.

Anger and jealousy can no more bear to lose sight of their objects than love.

Better spend an extra hundred or two on your son's education than leave it him in your will.

The best augury of a man's success in his profession is that he thinks it the finest in the world.

A difference of taste in jokes is a great strain on the affections.

Vanity is as ill at ease under indifference as tenderness is under a love which it cannot return.

Ignorance gives one a large range of probabilities.

A maggot must be born in rotten cheese to like it.

**FRANCE, ANATOLE** (France, 1844–1924) Anatole France was the pseudonym of Jacques-Anatole-François Thibault, whose father was a bookseller. Anatole took his nom de plume from the name of his father's shop, the Librairie de France. Thanks to his father's profession, France grew up surrounded by books, eventually being appointed as a librarian for the French Senate. In the 1920s, his skeptical, satirical stance earned his novels a place on the Vatican's Index of Prohibited Books. He was awarded the Noble Prize for literature in 1921.

*Essential Aphorisms*

Lovers who love truly do not write down their happiness.

Religion has done love a great service by making it a sin.

Man is so made that he can only find relaxation from one kind of labor by taking up another.

An education isn't how much you have committed to memory, or even how much you know. It's being able to differentiate between what you do know and what you don't.

I prefer the folly of enthusiasm to the indifference of wisdom.

It is better to understand little than to misunderstand a lot.

To imagine is everything, to know is nothing at all.

Chance is perhaps the pseudonym of God when He did not want to sign.

**GICGIER, TADEUSZ** (Poland, 1927–2005) Gicgier published poetry and short stories as well as novels. Though he was a master of the written word, he made his living by the spoken word: as an editor for Polish radio.

*Essential Aphorisms*

Nothing is as ridiculous as the fear of being ridiculous.

Man's smallness is great.

Some do a lot of work; others are a lot of work.

Those who build castles on ice often slip up.

Love is blind; therefore, it loves the dark.

Some find their balance only through instability.

**GIDE, ANDRÉ** (France, 1869–1951) Gide was part hedonist, part holy man. Even as a boy, he was hypersensitive to sensual beauty. Natural scenes, of woodlands and flowers, would send him into raptures, and he experimented with sex at an early age, usually with other boys. As a young man, he became something of a mystic, sleeping on a board and always carrying a copy of the New Testament in his pocket. Born in Paris, Gide used his inherited wealth to fund a life of literature and travel, mostly to central and northern Africa. His novels and autobiographical works explore the tension between the impulses of the spirit and society's moral and ethical constraints. In the 1920s, his books became a touchstone for French existentialist writers like Albert Camus and Jean-Paul Sartre. He was awarded the Nobel Prize for literature in 1947.

*Essential Aphorisms*

Art is a collaboration between God and the artist, and the less the artist does the better.

Dare to be yourself.

In hell there is no other punishment than to begin over and over again the tasks left unfinished in your lifetime.

It is better to be hated for what you are than loved for what you are not.

It is easier to lead men to combat, stirring up their passion, than to restrain them and direct them toward the patient labors of peace.

It is good to follow one's own bent, so long as it leads upward.

Nothing prevents happiness like the memory of happiness.

One doesn't discover new lands without consenting to lose sight of the shore for a very long time.

Sin is whatever obscures the soul.

Welcome anything that comes to you, but do not long for anything else.

What another would have done as well as you, do not do it. What another would have said as well as you, do not say it. What another would have written as well, do not write it. Be faithful to that which exists nowhere but in yourself—and thus make yourself indispensable.

Work and struggle and never accept an evil that you can change.

## Parallel Lines: Say It Again

Everything has been said before, but since nobody listens we have to keep going back and beginning all over again.                    —GIDE

We come too late to say anything that has not been said already.
                                              —JEAN DE LA BRUYÈRE

It is important to say all the great thoughts again, without knowing that they have already been said.                    —ELIAS CANETTI

**GOMBROWICZ, WITOLD** (Poland, 1904–1969) Just days before the outbreak of World War II, Gombrowicz boarded an ocean liner bound for Argentina. He impulsively signed on as a newspaper correspondent on the ship's maiden voyage. When Germany invaded his native Poland, Gombrowicz decided to remain in Argentina, settling in Buenos Aires. He lived there in obscurity and penury for more than twenty years, reportedly attending the funerals of strangers in order to eat the free food. His novels, short stories, and dramas only achieved critical recognition in Europe in the 1950s and '60s.

## Essential Aphorisms

Man does not fear death, only the suffering.

The difference between Western and Eastern intellectuals is that the former have not been kicked in the ass enough.

The world owes its existence only to the fact that it's always too late to step back.

Normality is a tightrope walker above the abyss of the abnormal.

Suicide is not worth the effort since death comes anyway.

Anyone who loves only the beautiful and the pure, loves barely half of life.

Everyone consumes his life like a beefsteak—on a separate plate, at a separate table.

Mankind turns everything into money and returns what is left over as change.

Pain creates reality.

We choose the first chord, all the others just follow.

**HUXLEY, ALDOUS** (United Kingdom, 1894–1963) In *Crome Yellow*, Huxley caricatures a certain type of New Age aphorist through the character of Mr. Barbecue-Smith, an author of inspirational books (with titles like *Humble Heroisms*) who claims he can help readers access their subconscious springs of creativity. "When I have to do my aphorisms," Mr. Barbecue-Smith says in the novel, "I prelude my trance by turning over the pages of any Dictionary of Quotations or Shakespeare Calendar that comes to hand. That sets the key, so to speak; that ensures that the Universe shall come flowing in, not in a continuous rush, but in aphorismic drops." Some of Mr. Barbecue-Smith's aphorisms include: "The things that really matter happen in the heart" and "The flame of the candle gives light, but it also burns." Huxley's own aphorisms are more scientifically precise than those of Mr. Barbecue-Smith, but he did have some New Age interests of his own, particularly spirituality and psychic research. Huxley also experimented avidly with the psychoactive drug mescaline. On his deathbed, he asked his wife to give him LSD just hours before he died, which she did by administering two injections. Huxley was the grandson of Thomas Henry Huxley, the famous nineteenth-century aphorist, scientist, and promoter of Darwin's theory of evolution. Like his grandfather, Huxley believed scientific progress should challenge, and eventually overturn, prevailing social conventions.

*Essential Aphorisms*

Facts do not cease to exist because they are ignored.

Experience is not what happens to a man; it is what a man does with what happens to him.

The propagandist's purpose is to make one set of people forget that certain other sets of people are human.

Several excuses are always less convincing than one.

Technological progress has merely provided us with more efficient means for going backward.

There's only one corner of the universe you can be certain of improving, and that's your own self.

Most human beings have an almost infinite capacity for taking things for granted.

The course of every intellectual, if he pursues his journey long and unflinchingly enough, ends in the obvious, from which the non-intellectuals have never stirred.

**IRZYKOWSKI, KAROL** (Poland, 1873–1944) Irzykowski studied German philosophy at university, and his first published work was a monograph on German playwright and aphorist Friedrich Hebbel. In his fiction, Irzykowski explored the hidden psychological motivations of his characters, a technique that would later prove very influential on fellow Pole Witold Gombrowicz.

*Essential Aphorisms*

Man is a horse that gives itself the spur.

Ten wise men cannot move a stone that one fool has thrown into the garden.

You cannot avoid a decision, because even the avoidance is a concealed decision.

He who climbs onto the roof should not push away the ladder.

The kiss is where the play of souls ends and the play of flesh begins.

God made the world, then stopped bothering.

The poet writes the bill. He leaves it to the reader to add it up.

The aphorism enlightens and deceives by its brevity.

**KOUROUMA, AHMADOU** (Côte d'Ivoire, 1927–2003) All of Kourouma's novels deal in one form or another with post-colonial Africa's struggles with dictatorships, poverty, and war. His criticism of the government of his native Côte d'Ivoire forced him to live in exile for almost thirty years.

*Essential Aphorisms*

Don't gather birds together if you fear the sound of wings.

When a fool shakes his rattle, it should always be another fool who dances.

It's always those whose earlobes aren't strong enough for heavy earrings who find gold.

Misfortune is sometimes just good fortune well wrapped up; when the wrapping wears away, good fortune tumbles out.

The deepest buried secret always gives off a faint smell.

Chat between panther and hyena honors the latter but lowers the former.

The truth may redden your eyes, but it won't blind you.

If you pretend, out of discretion, not to notice a shameless man's fart, he'll just assume you've no sense of smell.

**LERMONTOV, MIKHAIL** (Russia, 1814–1841) Lermontov was a rebellious, extremely gifted youth. He spoke French and German; painted; and played the flute, piano, and violin, in addition to writing novels and poetry. But he had trouble holding his tongue. His impertinence got him kicked out of Moscow University and he ended up in a military academy instead. In 1837, when Alexander Pushkin was killed in a duel, Lermontov wrote the poem "On the Death of a Poet," which brought him fame throughout Russia. Four years later, Lermontov himself was challenged to a duel. He had been teasing a fellow soldier by writing wicked epigrams about him. But the soldier failed to see the joke and challenged him to fight. When the two men faced off, Lermontov refused to fire. But his opponent did, fatally wounding the poet.

*Essential Aphorisms*

We tend to always excuse what is beyond our understanding.

Of two friends, one is always the slave of the other, although often neither one confesses the truth to himself.

With all the sweets fed to people for so long, the stomach is spoiled; sour medicine and bitter truth are badly needed nowadays.

Women love only those they know not.

When love has brought no joy or gladness
Parting shall have little sadness.

God knows why backward folks advance so far around here.

**LI AO** (Taiwan, 1935–   ) Born in the Manchurian city of Harbin, Li fled with his family to Taiwan in 1949. In the 1960s, he edited a pro-democracy journal critical of Chiang Kai-shek's rule. During the late 1970s and early '80s, he spent five years in prison for helping a pro-independence figure escape the island. Li has written novels and nonfiction, and since 2005 he has been a renegade member of Taiwan's Legislative Yuan. In a bid to cut off debate about buying American submarines during a 2006 National Defense Committee meeting, he donned a gas mask and doused the room with pepper spray, forcing the evacuation of the building.

*Essential Aphorisms*

An iron pestle can be ground into a needle, but when you grind down a wooden pestle you can make at best a false tooth. It doesn't matter how much energy you put into something, if you're working with the wrong material.

To feel close together even when miles apart is like a religious experience; to feel far apart even when stuck close together is an art.

Successful people seek out their futures from the present; failures seek out their futures from the past.

Often there's no need for an explanation: your enemies won't believe it, and your friends don't need to hear it.

Optimists seek to increase good fortune; pessimists seek to avoid disaster.

Without some start-up capital you can't do much. Just to steal a chicken, you need to lure it with a handful of rice.

**LU XUN** (China, 1881–1936) Lu is known as the "father of modern Chinese literature" in large part because he wrote in the vernacular, a radical break from the tradition of using only the classical language, which is all but unreadable to most Chinese. His stories and essays attacked China's feudalistic social practices, which led Chairman Mao to give him another honorary title: "commander of China's cultural revolution." But while Lu was undoubtedly left-leaning, he was also an independent freethinker who never joined the Communist Party.

*Essential Aphorisms*

The first man to eat a crab deserves our respect. Who save a courageous person would have dared to try?

Dissatisfaction is the wheel pushing progress.

One good way to extend one's lifespan is to not waste time.

The most important thing for a person is the act of living; only when we live is there space for love to attach itself.

**MEREDITH, GEORGE** (United Kingdom, 1828–1909) Meredith worked as a reader for the publishers Chapman and Hall. His talent-spotting record is, well, spotty. He recommended publication for Thomas Hardy but rejected George Bernard Shaw. His own literary reputation is similarly mixed. His poetry is largely forgotten now, but his novel *The Ordeal of Richard Feverel*, from which his aphorisms are drawn, is still considered a classic.

*Essential Aphorisms*

Who rises from prayer a better man, his prayer is answered.

Kissing don't last; cookery do!

Speech is the small change of silence.

Always imitate the behavior of the winners when you lose.

Memoirs are the backstairs of history.

Caricature is rough truth.

The man of science is nothing if not a poet gone wrong.

Don't just count your years, make your years count.

**NATSUME, SOSEKI** (Japan, 1867–1916) Soseki in many ways typifies a Japanese generation confronted with the challenges and contradictions of a rapidly modernizing country. He studied English literature at Tokyo University and spent two years in England, but he gave up academic life on his return to Japan and took a job with one of the major Tokyo dailies, which published his fiction in serial form. His novels are classics in Japan and are widely available in English translation.

*Essential Aphorisms*

If you use your knowledge, you will offend. If you ride your emotions, you will be swept away. If you insist on having your way, you will feel cramped. In any case, it is hard to live in this world.

Modern society is nothing more than a collection of isolated human beings. The earth is still filled with nature, but once you build a house in it, it is immediately broken. And the people inside the house are also broken. Civilization isolates us.

All adventures begin with drink. And all end with women.

Freedom without great ideals is nothing but decadence.

I prefer living people to dead gods.

Just as you can't tell the size of your own nose, it is rather difficult to figure things out about yourself.

**PAVESE, CESARE** (Italy, 1908–1950) In the years leading up to World War II, Pavese was a leftist dissident. He was arrested in 1935 and sent into internal exile in southern Italy. When the Germans arrived, he went into hiding in the countryside, but he did not fight alongside the partisans. After the war, he joined the Italian Communist Party and continued to write novels and poetry, also working as a literary critic and translator. He committed suicide by taking an overdose of barbiturates. His aphorisms can be found in his diaries, which he kept from 1935 until his death.

*Essential Aphorisms*

We get the things we want when we no longer want them.

No one ever lacks a good reason for suicide.

Life is pain and the enjoyment of love is an anesthetic.

The only joy in the world is to begin.

One stops being a child when one realizes that telling one's trouble does not make it any better.

One must look for one thing only to find many.

*Parallel Lines: Lies, Damned Lies*

The art of living is the art of knowing how to believe lies.     —PAVESE

Life is the art of being well deceived.     —WILLIAM HAZLITT

**RENARD, JULES** (France, 1864–1910) Renard's best-known novel is *Poil de Carotte* ("Carrot Top"), his autobiographical account of an unhappy childhood in central France. Many of his aphorisms can be found in the journal he kept from 1897 until his death.

*Essential Aphorisms*

Failure is not our only punishment for laziness; there is also the success of others.

It is not how old you are, but how you are old.

Laziness is nothing more than the habit of resting before you get tired.

Love is like an hourglass, with the heart filling up as the brain empties.

The only man who is really free is the one who can turn down an invitation to dinner without giving an excuse.

Writing is the only profession where no one considers you ridiculous if you earn no money.

Culture is what's left after you have forgotten everything.

There are good and bad times, but our mood changes more often than our fortune.

If one were to build the house of happiness, the largest space would be the waiting room.

Words are the small change of thought.

**RICHTER, JEAN PAUL** (Germany, 1763–1825) Richter's writing is lyrical and grotesque, romantic and satiric. The son of a poor village pastor, he originally studied to take up his father's vocation but abandoned theology for literature. He turned to tutoring to make a living, but gave that up when his books started selling well enough for him to live off the proceeds. In his novel *Siebenkäs*, the tale of a man who fakes his own death to escape an unhappy marriage, Richter developed the idea of the doppelgänger, an individual's ghostly counterpart or evil alter ego.

*Essential Aphorisms*

A man never discloses his own character so clearly as when he describes another's.

A timid person is frightened before a danger, a coward during the time, and a courageous person afterward.

Age does not matter if the matter does not age.

As winter strips the leaves from around us, so that we may see the distant regions they formerly concealed, so old age takes away our enjoyments only to enlarge the prospect of the coming eternity.

Be great in act, as you have been in thought.

Courage consists not in blindly overlooking danger, but in seeing it and conquering it.

Do not wait for extraordinary circumstances to do good action; try to use ordinary situations.

Every friend is to the other a sun, and a sunflower also. He attracts and follows.

Every man has a rainy corner of his life whence comes foul weather that follows him.

Every man regards his own life as the New Year's Eve of time.

For sleep, riches and health to be truly enjoyed, they must be interrupted.

It is simpler and easier to flatter people than to praise them.

Men, like bullets, go farthest when they are smoothest.

Poverty is the only load that is the heavier the more loved ones there are to assist in bearing it.

Recollection is the only paradise from which we cannot be turned out.

There is a joy in sorrow which none but a mourner can know.

What makes old age so sad is not that our joys but our hopes cease.

You prove your worth with your actions, not with your mouth.

**ROA BASTOS, AUGUSTO** (Paraguay, 1917–2005) Roa Bastos's opposition to the Paraguayan military dictatorship in the 1970s forced him to flee to France, where he taught literature at the University of Toulouse. He did not return to Paraguay until 1989. His most famous novel is *I, the Supreme*, based on the life and career of José Gaspar Rodríguez de Francia, the nineteenth-century Paraguayan dictator. Francia, Paraguay's first leader after independence from Spain, cut the country off from the rest of the world and imposed increasingly peculiar dictates on the populace. Only he, for example, was permitted to perform marriage ceremonies. And he ordered that all dogs in the country be shot.

*Essential Aphorisms*

There is always time to take more time.

In the majority of cases, the essential is rooted in what is most simple.

To have everything one must give everything.

In desperate situations, the truth affords as much support as a falsehood.

All the heroes of just causes died young. The antiheroes are condemned to longevity.

Things are not as we see and sense them but as we wish they were seen and sensed.

**SHIMAZAKI, TOSON** (Japan, 1872–1943) Toson drew from his often complicated personal life—his unrequited love for one of his pupils at the girls' school where he taught; his relationship with his niece, which resulted in her pregnancy—for material for his novels. As a young man, Toson was heavily influenced by the Christian missionaries active in Japan, but he ultimately rejected the faith because of its moral restrictions.

*Essential Aphorisms*

It is a waste of time to try to destroy old things. If you are truly able to become new, the old has already been destroyed.

I keep thinking tomorrow, tomorrow, tomorrow, but today I seem to be living in a dream.

Why is it that academics and art, romance between a man and a woman, are so incompatible?

It is always the man who, standing on the stage of love, plays the part of the fool.

**STEVENSON, ROBERT LOUIS** (Scotland, 1850–1894) On his father's side, Stevenson was descended from a line of Scottish seaman and lighthouse keepers. His maternal grandfather was a minister. Stevenson combined both these professions in his own life. He loved sailing, traveling widely in the South Pacific, and he eventually settled in the Samoan Islands. His aphorisms also abound with moral instruction, especially lessons intended to be useful during times of adversity.

*Essential Aphorisms*

To travel hopefully is a better thing than to arrive.

The obscurest epoch is today.

If your morals make you dreary, depend upon it they are wrong.

Our business in this world is not to succeed, but to continue to fail, in good spirits.

The price we pay for money is paid in liberty.

It is perhaps a more fortunate destiny to have a taste for collecting shells than to be born a millionaire.

All natural talk is a festival of ostentation.

To be what we are, and to become what we are capable of becoming, is the only end of life.

In every part and corner of our life, to lose oneself is to be a gainer; to forget oneself is to be happy.

Perpetual devotion to what a man calls his business is only to be sustained by perpetual neglect of many other things.

So long as we love to serve, so long as we are loved by others, I would almost say that we are indispensable; and no man is useless while he has a friend.

You cannot run away from a weakness; you must sometimes fight it out or perish. And if that be so, why not now, and where you stand?

**TOOMER, JEAN** (United States, 1894–1967) Toomer was of mixed racial descent and as a child attended both all-white and all-black schools. His most famous book is *Cane*, a series of poems and stories about African Americans and the experience of racism in the United States. In the mid-1920s, Toomer traveled to the Institute for the Harmonious Development of Man in Fountainebleau, France, to study with the Greek-Armenian mystic George Ivanovitch Gurdjieff. Gurdjieff was in the habit of inscribing his aphorisms on the walls of the institute, and it is there that Toomer came across this saying: "Remember you come here having already understood the necessity of struggling with yourself—only with yourself. Therefore thank everyone who gives you the opportunity." "The saying took hold of me," Toomer wrote afterward, "found purchase in my very roots . . . Thank everyone who calls out your faults, your anger, your impatience, your egotism; do this consciously, voluntarily."

*Essential Aphorisms*

Meet life's terms but never accept them.

We must know a force greater than our weaknesses.

We are tired of not being intense.

Success often means increase of the illusion that we can make things happen.

Man is a nerve of the cosmos, dislocated, trying to quiver into place.

People mistake their limitations for high standards.

To understand a new idea break an old habit.

Aim to encounter unknown difficulties that you may gain unexpected results.

**ZOMEREN, KOOS VAN** (The Netherlands, 1946–   ) Van Zomeren is a novelist and columnist for the Dutch daily *NRC Handelsblad*. He is also a committed environmentalist and advocate of animal rights. A journalist who interviewed Van Zomeren at his home remarked on how nearly every painting in the house depicted cows.

*Essential Aphorisms*

Whatever happens, there will always be people who say: It's all completely awful, and others who say: It's all a complete joke.

We don't want memories that tell the truth, we want memories that make us happy.

Ah, it's like that: We learn from our mistakes so that we don't lose the courage to make new ones.

We read about decline and experience beauty. We read about grief and experience comfort. Language is always busy easing the pain of the hurt it describes.

You always see beauty for the first time. Ugliness begins where surprise ends.

In fact, reproduction is a roundabout way of self-destruction.

Talking is searching, writing is finding.

Because you really know so little, and it makes so little difference that you know so little.

People say time heals all wounds. They forget to say that time also inflicts all wounds.

A happy ending is often a question of a timely departure.

## PLAYWRIGHTS

**BAHR, HERMANN** (Austria, 1863–1934) A "bearded, hearty, smiling tower of fine physical strength"; "some robust, giant gymnast" with "the beard of a Viking, of a Whitman." That's how Percival Pollard of the *New York Times* described Bahr in 1911. Bahr was certainly a giant among literary critics; he was the first person to apply the term "modernism" to the literature of his time. Born in Linz, Austria, he was also a theater director, novelist, playwright, and leading member of the Austrian avant-garde. He helped launch Hugo von Hofmannsthal's literary career, was responsible for the translation of George Bernard Shaw's plays into German, and was a contemporary of Austrian aphorist Karl Kraus, who frequently targeted him in his self-published journal *Die Fackel*. Kraus accused Bahr of writing favorable book and play reviews in exchange for financial kickbacks. Bahr sued him for libel and won, and Kraus had to pay extensive damages.

### Essential Aphorisms

He who has character can then dare the most difficult thing: to be nothing but an ordinary person; and then we would be redeemed.

Routine is creating without feeling. Where it starts, there is no more art.

Masterpieces don't even allow any thought of their "creator" to arise.

An artist is he who feels that the last word of creation hasn't been spoken yet: and that he was sent into the world to utter it.

It doesn't matter so much what kind of talent a person has as what he does with his talent.

The intellect can negate, but it cannot create.

Enthusiasm is always right, even in the wrong place.

Genius always consists of conceiving of the self-evident.

The mystical talent consists in not finding the mystical mystical.

We have to learn to endure what we cannot change. We have to learn to change what we don't want to endure.

**BRECHT, BERTOLT** (Germany, 1898–1956) Politically, Brecht just couldn't get a break. In the 1920s, his collaboration with Kurt Weill, *The Threepenny Opera*, was a sensation in Berlin, setting the stage for a string of theatrical successes. But when the Nazis came to power in 1933, his work fell swiftly out of favor. Then in the 1950s, after his emigration to America, Brecht's communist sympathies drew the ire of Senator Joseph McCarthy and the U.S. House Un-American Activities Committee. He was blacklisted by Hollywood, where he was trying to earn a living as a screenwriter. Brecht never let official opprobrium affect his political views or his work, though. And he retained his flair for drama to the last. In his will, he stipulated that a stiletto be driven through his heart.

*Essential Aphorisms*

First comes grub, then morality.

There is nothing so interesting on stage as a man trying to get a knot out of his shoelaces.

In the contradiction lies the hope.

War always finds a way.

Art is not a mirror with which to reflect reality, but a hammer with which to shape it.

Because things are the way they are, things will not stay the way they are.

When the leaders curse war the mobilization order is already written out.

He who laughs has not yet heard the terrible news.

**CHEKHOV, ANTON** (Russia, 1860–1904) Chekhov studied medicine at the University of Moscow. After obtaining his degree in 1884, he began working as a freelance journalist, specializing in short comic sketches. The plays for which Chekhov is famous—*The Seagull, Uncle Vanya, The Three Sisters,* and *The Cherry Orchard*—were all written or revised during the last few years of his life, when he was dying from tuberculosis.

*Essential Aphorisms*

Love, friendship and respect do not unite people as much as a common hatred for something.

Any idiot can face a crisis. It is this day-to-day living that wears you out.

If you are afraid of loneliness, do not marry.

Only entropy comes easy.

When a lot of remedies are suggested for a disease that means it can't be cured.

The person who wants nothing, hopes for nothing and fears nothing can never be an artist.

Solomon made a big mistake when he asked for wisdom.

They say that in the end truth will triumph, but it's a lie.

**GRILLPARZER, FRANZ** (Austria, 1791–1872) Almost all Grillparzer's professional career was spent as a minor bureaucrat in the Austrian exchequer. He had no real talent or interest in government administration, but the post provided him with the financial security he needed to write plays. He specialized in historical tragedies, which dramatized his rather grim view that life was made up of a series of disappointments and thwarted hopes.

*Essential Aphorisms*

It is the misfortune of the uneducated that they cannot understand the difficult; the educated, in contrast, often do not understand the simple, which is a much greater misfortune.

Religiousness is the wine fermentation of the developing and rotting of the disintegrating mind.

Morality, a muzzle for the will; logic, a stirrup for the mind.

The most dreadful remedy for tormenting thoughts is distraction; it leads to thoughtlessness.

What do you lose joyfully? A sick man his fever, a harassed husband his wife, a gambler his debt and a girl—her virginity.

We are never more intolerant of other people's faults than when they are a caricature of our own.

No one has ever paid any attention to the relationship between vengeance and love of justice.

Villains will always be more practically able than honest people because they don't care what means they use.

**HEBBEL, CHRISTIAN FRIEDRICH** (Germany, 1813–1863) Hebbel's life is a classic rags-to-riches tale. He was born in Wesselburen, Germany, to a bricklayer who was determined that his son should be a manual laborer, too. The family was desperately poor, but a local novelist spotted Hebbel's poetic gift and set up a fund to enable the boy to attend school. When Hebbel's father died, the fourteen-year-old was finally free to pursue his interests in poetry and theater. That pursuit was made possible by the intercession of Elise Lensing. Eight years older than Hebbel, Lensing fed, funded, and fawned over him while he was an impoverished student living in Munich, where he steeped himself in philosophy and literature. In the mid-1840s, Hebbel's tragic and taciturn plays became a success and he moved to Vienna, where he met and married a wealthy and beautiful actress, leaving Lensing behind. In Vienna, Hebbel was at last financially secure and devoted himself wholly to what he described in his diary as "the most powerful force within him, that which alone can give him happiness and be of service to the world"—writing.

## Essential Aphorisms

The world is God's Fall.

Beauty: the genius of matter.

In the end, the best thing about religion is that it produces heretics.

People: out-of-tune musical instruments.

Obstinacy is the cheapest substitute for character.

Remember: One lie does not cost you one truth but the truth.

Life is never something; it is merely the opportunity for something.

When life becomes heavy, death becomes light.

## Parallel Lines: A Hair in the Soup

There are some persons who always find a hair in their bowl of soup for the simple reason that, when they sit down before it, they shake their heads until one falls in.　　　　　　　　—HEBBEL

Whoever looks for the hair misses the soup.　　　　　—BERT HELLINGER

**IBSEN, HENRIK** (Norway, 1828–1906) Ibsen was an archetypal iconoclast. All of his greatest dramas—*A Doll's House, Ghosts, An Enemy of the People, Hedda Gabler, The Master Builder*—revolve around the battle of a lone individual against the values and morality of the majority. Ibsen left home at fifteen, ostensibly to study pharmacy but in reality to become a playwright. In 1864, he left his native Norway to live in Italy and Germany, where all of his major plays were composed. Ibsen's work was considered by many to be immoral and scandalous. And the man himself was angry and obstreperous to the last. During his final illness, when his nurse remarked that he was looking a little better, Ibsen retorted, "On the contrary." Then he died.

*Essential Aphorisms*

Open-mindedness is virtually the same as morality.

The minority is always right.

The most dangerous enemies of truth and freedom among us are the compact majority.

The strongest man in the world is he who is most alone.

The worst a human being can do to himself is to do wrong to others.

The state is the curse of the individual.

**JARDIEL PONCELA, ENRIQUE** (Spain, 1901–1952) Poncela got his start writing short stories for Spanish humor magazines. In the early 1930s, his witty dramatic comedies attracted the attention of the Fox Movietone Corporation and he was invited to Hollywood to work on the parallel English and Spanish film adaptations of his work. After World War II, though, his plays were far less popular, and toward the end of his life he only managed to get by thanks to the generosity of friends.

*Essential Aphorisms*

Dictatorship: a system of government in which whatever is not prohibited is obligatory.

Society is a decomposing organism that is preserved thanks to the ice of hypocrisy.

Youth is a defect that corrects itself with time.

From afar, everything looks smaller, except an intelligent person, who from afar looks larger.

Women, like swords, inspire the most respect when they are naked.

When something can be read without effort, great effort has gone into writing it.

**KAISER, GEORG** (Germany, 1878–1945) An early exponent of Expressionism in the German theater, Kaiser wrote more than sixty plays, many of which deal with what he considered the dehumanizing effects of modern society. One of his last works is *The Raft of the Medusa*, which relates the true story of how a group of children on a raft deliberately drown the youngest child because they believe it will protect them from bad luck.

*Essential Aphorisms*

Life lives us.

We must live from what we live for.

You must always conserve as much energy as it takes to decide against life.

There is no up—there is only a down. God is subterranean.

History as a warning of the future—that we shouldn't expect anything different or anything better than what was.

The larger a state, the smaller the individuals who make it up.

**MOLINA, TIRSO DE** (Spain, 1579–1648) De Molina is one of Spain's greatest dramatists—and its most prolific. By De Molina's own count, he wrote more than 400 plays, of which only about eighty survive, including *El Burlador de Sevilla*, which marks the first appearance of the Don Juan legend in written literature.

*Essential Aphorisms*

A secret insult demands secret satisfaction.

The bond of friendship makes one life out of two.

A love without equality will not last.

He who doesn't give, doesn't love.

Knowledge is the mother of prudence.

It is better to die fighting than to live dying.

**SCHILLER, FRIEDRICH VON** (Germany, 1759–1805) Schiller studied medicine and for a time served as a physician in the German military. Throughout his life he also treated himself for symptoms of the disease that eventually killed him at the age of forty-five: tuberculosis. His first play—*The Robbers*, the story of a group of political revolutionaries—won him widespread acclaim and the less welcome attention of the government, which prohibited him from publishing anything else. Schiller eventually became friends with Goethe, who convinced Schiller to start writing plays again. Together they founded the Weimar Theater. In a series of philosophical letters and essays, Schiller expounded his idea that an appreciation of and education in art was crucial to the development of individuals and society as a whole.

*Essential Aphorisms*

A merely fallen enemy may rise again, but the reconciled one is truly vanquished.

Against stupidity the very gods themselves contend in vain.

Appearance rules the world.

Dare to err and to dream. Deep meaning often lies in childish play.

Happy is he who learns to bear what he cannot change.

He who considers too much will perform little.

He who has done his best for his own time has lived for all times.

It does not prove a thing to be right because the majority say it is so.

It is base to filch a purse, daring to embezzle a million, but it is great beyond measure to steal a crown. The sin lessens as the guilt increases.

They would need to be already wise in order to love wisdom.

To save all we must risk all.

Keep true to the dreams of your youth.

*Parallel Lines: When to Speak*

It is often wise to reveal that which cannot be concealed for long.

—SCHILLER

Proclaim aloud what is on the eve of being discovered.

—JOHANN GEORG RITTER VON ZIMMERMAN

**SHAKESPEARE, WILLIAM** (United Kingdom, 1564–1616) "Therefore, since brevity is the soul of wit, and tediousness the limbs and outward flourishes, I will be brief." *Hamlet* II, 2. Enough said.

*Essential Aphorisms*

Suit the action to the word, the word to the action.

Lions make leopards tame.

It is a wise father that knows his own child.

Men must endure their going hence, even as their coming hither: Ripeness is all.

He that dies pays all debts.

In cases of defense 'tis best to weigh the enemy more might than he seems.

Our will and fates do so contrary run
That our devices still are overthrown.
What fates impose, that men must needs abide;
It boots not to resist both wind and tide.

Everyone can master a grief but he that hath it.

Wisely and slow; they stumble that run fast.

A light heart lives long.

Where joy most revels, grief doth most lament;
Grief joys, joy grieves, on slender accident.

Use every man after his desert, and who shall 'scape whipping.

We know what we are, but not what we may be.

Love is not love which alters when it alteration finds.

The worst is not so long as we can say, "This is the worst."

Misery acquaints a man with strange bedfellows.

Nothing emboldens sin so much as mercy.

Better a witty fool than a foolish wit.

The better part of valor is discretion.

**SHAW, GEORGE BERNARD** (Ireland, 1856–1950) Shaw started out in fiction, writing five unpublished novels before moving into journalism as a critic, first of music and then of drama for London's *Saturday Review*. He was active in politics, too. He was a committed pacifist, a socialist (an ardent supporter of Stalin), and a lifelong vegetarian.

*Essential Aphorisms*

Better keep yourself clean and bright: you are the window through which you must see the world.

Youth is wasted on the young.

You see things and you say, "Why?" But I see things that never were; and I say, "Why not?"

The golden rule is that there are no golden rules.

He who can, does. He who cannot, teaches.

No man can be a pure specialist without being in the strict sense an idiot.

Man is the only animal which esteems itself rich in proportion to the number and voracity of its parasites.

The most intolerable pain is produced by prolonging the keenest pleasure.

Hell is paved with good intentions, not with bad ones.

Take care to get what you like or you will be forced to like what you get.

Every man over forty is a scoundrel.

The reasonable man adapts himself to the world: the unreasonable one persists in trying to adapt the world to himself. Therefore all progress depends on the unreasonable man.

### Parallel Lines: Action Man

Activity is the only road to knowledge.                         —SHAW

The only man who never makes a mistake is the man who never does anything.                                  —THEODORE ROOSEVELT

**TERENCE** (Rome, c. 190–159 BCE) Terence is only known to have written six plays. His comedies were first performed when he was in his early twenties. He left Rome at the age of twenty-five and was never heard of again. Some ancient Roman historians speculate that he died in a shipwreck.

### Essential Aphorisms

Moderation in all things.

Obsequiousness begets friends, truth hatred.

Lovers' quarrels are the renewal of love.

Draw from others the lesson that may profit yourself.

There is nothing so easy but that it becomes difficult when you do it reluctantly.

While there's life, there's hope.

He is wise who tries everything before arms.

Fortune favors the brave.

Charity begins at home.

So many men, so many opinions: to each his own way.

**WILDE, OSCAR** (Ireland, 1854–1900) After his release from prison—where he served two years for "committing acts of gross indecency with other male persons," a reference to his relationship with Lord Alfred Douglas—Wilde moved to Paris. To avoid publicity, he lived under an assumed name and was largely impoverished, in self-imposed exile from society. Prison had seriously undermined his health and he spent his last few days in a hotel in Paris. But his wit, and his emphasis on esthetics, was undiminished. "My wallpaper and I are fighting a duel to the death," he is reported to have said of his lodgings. "One or other of us has got to go."

*Essential Aphorisms*

Bad art is a great deal worse than no art at all.

Life is much too important a thing ever to talk seriously about it.

The only form of fiction in which real characters do not seem out of place is history.

Life imitates Art far more than Art imitates Life.

To become a work of art is the object of living.

Man is least himself when he talks in his own person. Give him a mask, and he will tell you the truth.

All art is quite useless.

The only things one never regrets are one's mistakes.

When one is in love, one always begins by deceiving one's self, and one always ends by deceiving others.

Nothing looks so like innocence as an indiscretion.

What is a cynic? A man who knows the price of everything and the value of nothing.

Only the shallow know themselves.

# OLD SOULS AND ORACLES

**T**HE aphorism is the oldest form of written literature on the planet; old souls and oracles, along with the early moralists, are the original practitioners. People first consulted books of aphorisms—such as the *I Ching,* which was compiled around 3000 BCE—in order to foretell the future. Then the great sages, preachers, and prophets picked up on the aphorism as a way to memorably impart moral and spiritual counsel in the largely oral cultures of the ancient world. The tradition continues today, in the "Quote of the Day" sections of daily newspapers, on the multitude of quotation sites on the Internet, in the inspirational literature departments of bookshops. The motivation, too, is the same. People still look to words of wisdom for emotional and spiritual first aid, just as the author of the *Book of Proverbs* said: "A wise man will hear, and will increase learning; and a man of understanding shall attain unto wise counsels: to understand a proverb, and the interpretation; the words of the wise, and their dark sayings."

**AL-DEEN, MUHAMMAD SHEMS** (Middle East, c. sixteenth century) In 1515, Muhammad Shems al-Deen compiled a collection of Arabic aphorisms, some of which were possibly original to him but most of which were probably drawn from other sources. In an endearing introduction to the volume, al-Deen commends to the reader what he describes as "precious pearls which are falling fast to decay and perishing from age." He added to each aphorism a brief commentary in Persian verse, all of which was deftly translated by a man named Stephen Weston and published in London in 1805.

*Essential Aphorisms*

The best repentance is seldom to offend.

Do good to the evil doer.

The payment of debts is true religion.

He who is slow to offend is truly fortunate.

For relief from the distress of the mind or body, travel.

The best compliment is a short one.

A full purse makes an empty heart.

Friendship, though freckled, is preferable to the beauty of promise.

The separation of lovers is the renewing of love.

The last wish of the miser while life remains is covetous.

Solitude is better than a bad companion.

It is ruin to a man to be lost in admiration.

**AL-ISKANDARI, ABU AL-FADL IBN ATA'ALLAH** (Egypt, c. 650–709) For
more than 1,000 years, the tomb of Abu al-Fadl ibn Ata'Allah al-Iskandari in
Cairo has been the site of pilgrimages, prayers, and miracles. Visitors to the grave
have reported hearing the Sufi saint speak to them. Even when he was alive, Ibn
Ata'Allah was said to have performed wonders. One of his followers claimed to
have seen the sage three different times in Mecca, only to learn upon his return
to Egypt that Ibn Ata'Allah had never left the country. Born in Alexandria, Ibn
Ata'Allah came from a family of distinguished Islamic scholars. But like Saint Augustine, he was initially something of a skeptic, with a particular hostility toward
Sufism, the mystical strain of Islam. He had his conversion experience while listening to a lecture by the revered Sufi teacher Sheik Abu'l-Abbas al-Mursi. He
became a devoted student and disciple, whose renown eventually surpassed even
that of his master. His most famous work is *Kitab al-Hikam*, a collection of 264
spiritual aphorisms.

*Essential Aphorisms*

Your requesting Him is suspecting Him. Your seeking Him is due to
your absence from Him. Your seeking someone else is because of your
immodesty toward Him. Your requesting someone else is on account of
your distance from Him.

Among the signs of success at the end is the turning to God at the beginning.

No deed is more fruitful for the heart than the one you are not aware of and which is deemed paltry by you.

In your despairing, you are a free man; but in your coveting, you are a slave.

Whoever does not draw near to God as a result of the caresses of love is shackled to Him with the chains of misfortune.

The best that you can seek from Him is that which He seeks from you.

If you want a glory that does not vanish, then do not glory in a glory that vanishes.

Far be it for our Lord to recompense with credit the servant who deals with him in cash.

When the forgetful man gets up in the morning, he reflects on what he is going to do, whereas the intelligent man sees what God is doing with him.

The most ignorant of all people is the one who abandons the certitude he has for an opinion people have.

That part of your life that has gone by is irreplaceable, and that which has arrived is priceless.

States of need are gift-laden carpets.

### Parallel Lines: Little Joys

So that your sadness over something be little, let your joy in it be little.

—IBN ATA'ALLAH

The wind cannot shake a mountain. Neither praise nor blame moves the wise man. Happiness or sorrow—whatever befalls you, walk on untouched, unattached.                                                                —BUDDHA

Remember that there is nothing stable in human affairs; therefore avoid undue elation in prosperity, or undue depression in adversity.  —SOCRATES

**ANONYMOUS** (United Kingdom, c. fourteenth century) An anonymous English monk composed *The Cloud of Unknowing* as a spiritual guidebook in the latter half of the fourteenth century. Made up of seventy-five short chapters, the book is packed with contemplative aids and advice for young men just entering the monastic life. Each chapter is written in an unadorned, avuncular tone that's replete with tips on how monks can stay focused on the sacred during the most mundane daily chores. The book has been used as a spiritual instruction manual for centuries, often forming the basis for the practice of Christian meditation. The author of *The Cloud of Unknowing* was part of a contemplative tradition that stretches back to the ancient Jewish sages and early Christian ascetics who removed themselves from society in order to better experience and appreciate their relationship to the divine. These monks lived lives of hard work and deep prayer; their aphorisms are similarly spare.

*Essential Aphorisms*

Strain every nerve in every possible way to know and experience yourself as you really are.

Deeds may properly be judged whether they are good or bad, but not men.

Short prayer penetrates heaven.

Those who will not go the hard way to heaven will go the comfortable way to hell.

**AUGUSTINE** (North Africa, 354–430) Before becoming a saint, Augustine was a sinner. Born in the provincial Roman city of Tagaste in North Africa, he was a follower of Manichaeanism, a dualistic religion whose adherents believed that human beings were battlegrounds between good and evil. Augustine certainly felt himself to be such a battleground. As a young man, he had a fondness for wine and women and fathered a son by his longtime mistress. He was both a heretic and a hedonist. He was also a brilliant scholar and was appointed professor of rhetoric to the imperial court at Milan. But after hearing the voice of a girl telling him to pick up the Bible and read, Augustine converted to Christianity and returned to Africa, where he eventually became bishop of Hippo. Augustine was renowned as a theologian and preacher. His *Confessions* is both a moving autobiography and a brilliant work of philosophy. His thinking was crucial in the formation of early Church doctrine, and he made a specialty of combating heresies, specifically Manichaeanism.

*Essential Aphorisms*

Hope has two beautiful daughters. Their names are anger and courage; anger at the way things are, and courage to see that they do not remain the way they are.

Thou must be emptied of that wherewith thou art full, that thou mayest be filled with that whereof thou art empty.

The world is a book, and those who do not travel read only a page.

Seek not to understand that you may believe, but believe that you may understand.

Do you wish to rise? Begin by descending. You plan a tower that will pierce the clouds? Lay first the foundation of humility.

Pray as though everything depended on God. Work as though everything depended on you.

*Parallel Lines: Small Beginnings*

You aspire to great things? Begin with little ones.                    —AUGUSTINE

Put things in order before they have got into confusion. For the tree big as a man's embrace began as a tiny sprout, the tower nine stories high began with a heap of earth, the journey of a thousand leagues began with what was under the feet.                    —LAO TZU

Small beginnings, hardly worthy of notice, are often the cause of great misfortune or of great success. Thus, it is very wise to note and to weigh everything, no matter how tiny.                    —FRANCESCO GUICCIARDINI

**BERRA, YOGI (LAWRENCE PETER BERRA)** (United States, 1925–    ) Larry Berra got his nickname, Yogi, from a childhood friend who thought he looked like the Hindu sage in a film about an Indian snake charmer. Berra is as famous for his malapropisms and witticisms as he is for his exploits on the baseball field for the New York Yankees and New York Mets. Once in an Italian restaurant, for example, he was asked if he wanted his pizza cut into four or eight slices. "Four," he said. "I don't think I can eat eight." Berra's baseball career took off after World War II, in which he took part in the Omaha Beach landing during the Allies'

D-Day invasion of France. He played in fourteen World Series, managed both the Yankees and the Mets, and was elected to the Baseball Hall of Fame in 1972. His sayings, though they often sound like non sequiturs, contain real wisdom. Yogi's nickname was more apt than his childhood friend ever knew.

*Essential Aphorisms*

Always go to other people's funerals; otherwise they won't go to yours.

When you come to a fork in the road, take it.

It's déjà vu all over again.

Don't always follow the crowd, because nobody goes there anymore. It's too crowded.

Stay alert—you can observe a lot by watching.

Never give up, because it ain't over 'til it's over.

***BHAGAVAD GITA*** (India, c. 500–50 BCE) The *Bhagavad Gita* is part of the ancient Indian epic the *Mahabharata*, a massive tale of dynastic struggle that incorporates parables and other cosmological, mythological, and philosophical stories. The *Gita* itself (the title means "Song of the Divine One") consists of a conversation between the god Krishna and Arjuna, a famous warrior. Arjuna is paralyzed by moral doubt before a decisive battle, and the text relates Krishna's advice to him regarding everything from action and duty to the proper method of meditation and the nature of the self. In Hindu philosophy, the *Gita* is one of three primary sacred scriptures, alongside the *Upanishads* (a collection of philosophical sayings by ancient Indian sages) and the *Vedanta Sutras* (a series of spiritual axioms based on the *Upanishads*).

*Essential Aphorisms*

A man achieves perfection by contenting himself with his own work.

It is better to do one's own duty inadequately than another's well.

Knowledge is better than study, meditation is superior to knowledge, the abandonment of the fruit of actions is better than meditation, and after abandonment peace immediately follows.

A person is constructed by faith: whatever his faith is, so is he.

A man should raise up the self by the self, he should not drag the self down; for the self is the self's only ally, and the self is the self's only enemy.

For the Brahmin who knows, there is no more purpose in all the Vedas than in a water tank surrounded by a flood.

**BUDDHA** (Nepal, c. 563–483 BCE) As the son of a clan chieftain in the village of Lumbini, some 170 miles north of Benares in what is now Nepal, Siddhartha Gautama was born into a life of luxury, power, and sensual pleasure. But as a young man he gave it all up to live as a mendicant, traveling from teacher to teacher, from one ascetic discipline to another. After six years of fruitless searching, he realized he would never find what he was looking for in the spiritual regimens of any guru. So he sat down under a tree, in a place now known as Bodh Gaya, and resolved not to move from that spot until he had seen the light. It was here that Siddhartha Gautama became the Buddha, "the enlightened one," a term derived from the Pali word *budh*, which means "to be awake." After his experience at Bodh Gaya, the Buddha spent the next forty-five years as an itinerant preacher in northern India. The *Dhammapada* is a collection of the Buddha's aphorisms originally put together in northern India in the third century BCE.

*Essential Aphorisms*

We are what we think.

Your worst enemy cannot harm you as much as your own thoughts, unguarded. But once mastered, no one can help you as much.

The fool who knows he is a fool is that much wiser.

Like a broken gong be still, be silent. Know the stillness of freedom where there is no more striving.

It is not life and wealth and power that enslave men, but the cleaving to life and wealth and power.

To straighten the crooked you must first do a harder thing—straighten yourself.

You are your only master.

Hard it is to be born, hard it is to live, harder still to hear of the way, and hard to rise, follow and awake. Yet the teaching is simple. Do what is right. Be pure. At the end of the way is freedom. Till then, patience.

Like the Himalayas good men shine from afar. But bad men move unseen like arrows in the night.

Awake. Be the witness of your thoughts.

Wakefulness is the way to life.

O seeker! Rely on nothing until you want nothing.

Your work is to discover your work and then with all your heart to give yourself to it.

Be lamps unto yourselves.

## Parallel Lines: In and Of the World

It is hard to live in the world and it is hard to live out of it. It is hard to be one among many.                                                —BUDDHA

There are many who live in the mountains and behave as if they were in the town, and they are wasting their time. It is possible to be a solitary in one's own mind while living in a crowd, and it is possible for one who is a solitary to live in the crowd of his own thoughts.

—APOPHTHEGMATA PATRUM

It is easy in the world to live after the world's opinion; it is easy in solitude to live after our own; but the great man is he who in the midst of the crowd keeps with perfect sweetness the independence of solitude.

—RALPH WALDO EMERSON

**CHRISTIAN FATHERS** (Middle East, c. fourth–fifth century) During the early years of Christianity, a group of men (as well as a few women) withdrew from the world to live a life of prayer and contemplation in some of the most remote, in-hospitable regions of what is now Egypt, Palestine, and Syria. Some—like Simeon Stylites, who lived atop a fifty-foot pillar for forty years—practiced extreme forms of asceticism. But most led simple lives of quietude and manual labor. These small communities of monks cherished silent meditation. Often, the monks would visit each other in search of spiritual wisdom, of a "turning word" that would set them on the path toward enlightenment. These encounters are preserved in the *Apophthegmata Patrum*, or "Sayings of the Fathers," a collection of brief exchanges and admonitions recorded by the monks who witnessed them and passed them on from generation to generation.

*Essential Aphorisms*

Abba Arsenius used to say to himself: "Arsenius, why have you left the world? I have often repented of having spoken, but never of having been silent."

Abba Agathon also said, "I have never gone to sleep with a grievance against anyone, and, as far as I could, I never let anyone go to sleep with a grievance against me."

Abba Isaiah said, "Nothing is so useful to the beginner as insults. The beginner who bears insults is like a tree that is watered every day."

The same Abba Theophilus, the archbishop, came to Scetis one day. The brethren who were assembled said to Abba Pambo, "Say something to the archbishop, so that he may be edified." The old man said to them, "If he is not edified by my silence, he will not be edified by my speech."

Abba Isidore of Pelusia said, "To live without speaking is better than to speak without living. For the former who lives rightly does good even by his silence but the latter does no good even when he speaks. When words and life correspond to one another they are together the whole of philosophy."

Abba Moses asked Abba Silvanus, "Can a man lay a new foundation every day?" The old man said, "If he works hard, he can lay a new foundation at every moment."

**CHUANG TZU** (China, c. 370–c. 300 BCE) The sole historical fact about Chuang Tzu (also known as Chuang Chou) that can be verified with any certainty is that a book of fables and anecdotes bears his name. Together with Lao Tzu, Chuang Tzu is credited as a founder of the Taoist school of Chinese philosophy, though it is impossible to determine if either man ever really existed. What is indisputable, however, is that the book of Chuang Tzu is one of the most amazing and amusing collections of stories, parables, and aphorisms ever written. The work attributed to Chuang Tzu takes the form of a series of dialogues, strange encounters, and tall tales populated by bewildered acolytes, mythical heroes, and a menagerie of talking beasts. Chuang Tzu sometimes narrates these stories and sometimes appears in them as one of the characters. The point of Chuang Tzu's puns, paradoxes, and nonsequiturs is to guide or goad his listeners to insight by discarding conventional labels. For Chuang Tzu, wisdom meant living your life like an artist or athlete "in the zone"—in tune with the unconscious, instinctive part of your self that allows you to respond spontaneously and creatively to whatever fate throws your way. Chuang Tzu insisted that judgments like right and wrong, good and evil, fair and unfair were just mental habits, ideas that had gained currency through repeated use rather than through inherent truth. Apart from Lao Tzu, Chuang Tzu's predecessors are few. He has many descendants, though. The Greek and Roman Stoics advocated the same kind of enlightened resignation about the inevitable; the Zen masters practiced the same style of nonlinear thinking and storytelling in their *koans*; Baltasar Gracián wrote similar kinds of dense and highly imaginative aphorisms; and Ludwig Wittgenstein shared Chuang Tzu's suspicion of language as a means of communication.

*Essential Aphorisms*

Once Chuang Tzu dreamt he was a butterfly, a butterfly flitting and fluttering around, happy with himself and doing as he pleased. He didn't know he was Chuang Tzu. Suddenly he woke up and there he was, solid and unmistakable Chuang Tzu. But he didn't know if he was Chuang Tzu who had dreamt he was a butterfly, or a butterfly dreaming he was Chuang Tzu.

Just go along with things and let your mind move freely. Resign yourself to what cannot be avoided and nourish what is within you—this is best.

Good fortune is light as a feather, but nobody knows how to hold it up. Misfortune is heavy as the earth, but nobody knows how to stay out of its way.

When you're betting for tiles in an archery contest, you shoot with skill. When you're betting for fancy belt buckles, you worry about your aim. And when you're betting for real gold, you're a nervous wreck. Your skill is the same in all three cases—but because one prize means more to you than another, you let outside considerations weigh on your mind. He who looks too hard at the outside gets clumsy on the inside.

Once there was a man who was afraid of his shadow and who hated his footprints, and so he tried to get away from them by running. But the more he lifted his feet and put them down again, the more footprints he made. And no matter how fast he ran, his shadow never left him, and so, thinking that he was still going too slowly, he ran faster and faster without a stop until his strength gave out and he fell down dead. He didn't understand that by lolling in the shade he could have gotten rid of his shadow and by resting in quietude he could have put an end to his footprints.

The fish trap exists because of the fish; once you've gotten the fish, you can forget the trap. The rabbit snare exists because of the rabbit; once you've gotten the rabbit, you can forget the snare. Words exist because of the meaning; once you've gotten the meaning, you can forget the words. Where can I find a man who has forgotten words so I can have a word with him?

## Parallel Lines: Silence

Those who know do not speak; those who speak do not know.

—CHUANG TZU

A fool's voice is known by a multitude of words.        —ECCLESIASTES

Much silence and a good disposition, there are no two works better than those.                                                —MUHAMMAD

As the stamp of great minds is to suggest much in few words, so, contrariwise, little minds have the gift of talking a great deal and saying nothing.                                        —LA ROCHEFOUCAULD

Is it not in philosophy as in love? The more we have of it, and the less we talk about it, the better.              —WALTER SAVAGE LANDOR

What can be said at all can be said clearly, and what we cannot talk about we must pass over in silence.              —LUDWIG WITTGENSTEIN

The less we know, the longer our explanations.          —EZRA POUND

He who tells the truth says almost nothing.          —ANTONIO PORCHIA

**CONFUCIUS** (China, 551–479 BCE) The son of a noble family fallen on hard times, Confucius was orphaned as a young boy. Too poor to afford a formal education, he taught himself the Chinese classics and in his early twenties became a tutor to the sons of the local nobility. His brilliance was widely praised, but his relentless honesty and forthright manner made it hard for him to find a job as a minister at court, the usual career route for bright young men. When he was in his fifties, Confucius left his home and spent the next ten years wandering through China in search of a ruler who would put his ideas into practice. He traveled from court to court, from fiefdom to fiefdom, but never found one. It would be another 300 years before China's leaders began to seek out his teachings. Confucius is recorded as saying that if he had fifty years to devote exclusively to the study of the *I Ching*, then he might finally know something. He wrote an extensive commentary on the ancient Chinese classic; and the *Analects*, the collection of sayings by and stories about Confucius, clearly shows the influence of the *I Ching* on his thought.

## Essential Aphorisms

I am not concerned that I have no place, I am concerned how I may fit myself for one. I am not concerned that I am not known, I seek to be worthy to be known.

I will not be afflicted at men's not knowing me; I will be afflicted that I do not know men.

When a country is well governed, poverty and a mean condition are things to be ashamed of. When a country is ill governed, riches and honors are things to be ashamed of.

The wise man acts before he speaks, and afterward speaks according to his actions.

The commander of the forces of a large state may be carried off, but the will of even a common man cannot be taken from him.

Hold faithfulness and sincerity as first principles. Have no friends not equal to yourself. When you have faults, do not fear to abandon them.

If a man in the morning hear the right way, he may die in the evening without regret.

See what a man does. Mark his motives. Examine in what things he rests. How can a man conceal his character?

By nature, men are nearly alike; by practice, they get to be wide apart.

Learn as if you could not reach your object, and were always fearing also lest you should lose it.

To lead an uninstructed people to war is to throw them away.

There are only the wise of the highest class, and the stupid of the lowest class, who cannot be changed.

If a man take no thought of what is distant, he will find sorrow near at hand.

To go beyond is as wrong as to fall short.

### Parallel Lines: Do Unto Others?

Tsze-kung asked, saying, "Is there one word which may serve as a rule of practice for all one's life?" The Master said, "Is not reciprocity such a word? What you do not want done to yourself, do not do to others."

—CONFUCIUS

Do unto others as you would have them do to you.     —JESUS

Do as you would be done by is the surest method of pleasing.

—PHILIP STANHOPE, FOURTH EARL OF CHESTERFIELD

Enjoy and give pleasure, without doing harm to yourself or to anyone else—that, I think, is the whole of morality.

—SÉBASTIEN-ROCH-NICOLAS CHAMFORT

Do not do unto others as you would that they should do unto you. Their tastes may not be the same.     —GEORGE BERNARD SHAW

**ECCLESIASTES** (Israel, c. 450–c. 330 BCE) In Greek, the title of this book of the Old Testament means "The Preacher," or in Hebrew, "The Gatherer." The sayings gathered here have been attributed to Solomon, ancient sage of Israel. The wisdom of these aphorisms is dark and somber, with an encouragement to hedonism that is surprising in the Old Testament. There is no hope for salvation, deliverance, or redemption, just a grim acceptance of the inevitability of fate and the certainty of death. The book's bleak grandeur lies in its acceptance of these realities, and in the author's determination to enjoy the pleasures of life as long as they last.

*Essential Aphorisms*

All is vanity.

A living dog is better than a dead lion.

In much wisdom is much grief: and he that increaseth knowledge increaseth sorrow.

The words of the wise are as goads.

Of making many books there is no end; and much study is a weariness of the flesh.

The eye is not satisfied with seeing, nor the ear filled with hearing. The thing that hath been, it is that which shall be; and that which is done is that which shall be done: and there is no new thing under the sun.

All are of the dust, and all turn to dust again.

The heart of the wise is in the house of mourning; but the heart of fools is in the house of mirth. It is better to hear the rebuke of the wise, than for a man to hear the song of fools.

A man hath no better thing under the sun, than to eat, and to drink, and to be merry.

The dead know not any thing. No resurrection, afterlife, no cure for the human condition.

Whatsoever thy hand findeth to do, do it with thy might; for there is no work, nor device, nor knowledge, nor wisdom, in the grave, whither thou goest.

The race is not to the swift, nor the battle to the strong, neither yet bread to the wise, nor yet riches to men of understanding, nor yet favor to men of skill; but time and chance happeneth to them all.

**ECKHART, JOHANNES** (Germany, c. 1260–c. 1328) Meister Eckhart was a borderline heretic all his life. To this day, the Catholic Church has not made a final ruling on the orthodoxy of his teachings. Born near Erfurt in Germany, Eckhart was a Dominican priest and held a series of prominent positions within that order. He emphasized the individual's personal relationship to the divine rather than the efficacy of religious ceremonies and sacraments. He was unusual not only for his mystical views but because he expressed them in his sermons in the German vernacular rather than in the more customary Latin. Toward the end of his life, he was tried as a heretic. He fulsomely renounced any errors found in his teachings, but died before the Church reached a verdict.

## Essential Aphorisms

We shall find God in everything alike, and find God always alike in everything.

Only those who have dared to let go can dare to reenter.

To be full of things is to be empty of God. To be empty of things is to be full of God.

The more we have the less we own.

The outward work will never be puny if the inward work is great.

Only the hand that erases can write the true thing.

Jesus might have said, "I became man for you. If you do not become God for me, you wrong me."

God is at home, it's we who have gone out for a walk.

He who would be serene and pure needs but one thing, detachment.

The price of inaction is far greater than the cost of making a mistake.

Every creature is a word of God.

The outward man is the swinging door; the inner man is the still hinge.

When you are thwarted, it is your own attitude that is out of order.

If the only prayer you said in your whole life was, "Thank you," that would suffice.

**ENO, BRIAN** (United Kingdom, 1948–    ) and **Peter Schmidt** (United Kingdom, 1931–1980) In the 1970s, artists Peter Schmidt and Brian Eno created Oblique Strategies, a set of aphoristic playing cards containing what they described as "over one hundred worthwhile dilemmas." The sayings evolved from separate observations of the creative process. Eno began collecting his thoughts on cards, while Schmidt jotted his down in a notebook. When the two men discovered remarkable parallels among their thoughts, they decided to publish them as a pack of cards. The deck may have been devised as an aid to solving creative blocks, but it can also be used when confronted with other artistic or personal difficulties. Eno relates how a brain surgeon he once met boasted of playing Oblique Strategies all the time—hopefully, not while performing surgery. Simply pick a card and follow the instructions. Results may vary.

*Essential Aphorisms*

Make a blank valuable by putting it in an exquisite frame.

Cut a vital connection.

Slow preparation. Fast execution.

Honor thy error as a hidden intention.

Be less critical more often.

Just carry on.

**GABIROL, SOLOMON BEN JUDAH IBN** (Spain, c. 1021–c. 1069) Gabirol was born into the Jewish community of Málaga in southern Spain. He was known as a great poet, writing his verse in Arabic as was common for Spanish Jews at the time. He was also an avid collector of aphorisms, compiling some 650 sayings from the great Jewish sages. "I gather stray phrases into strings of thought, and from scattered words I collect pearls of wisdom," is how he described his aphorism habit in one poem. Gabirol's fame as a poet was such that a jealous rival is said to have murdered him and secretly buried the body beneath a fig tree. The tree went on to bear such luscious fruit in such abundance that people became suspicious. So they dug up the tree and found Gabirol's corpse.

*Essential Aphorisms*

Everything requires a fence.

Worry over what has not occurred is a serious malady.

There is a calamity which, when contrasted with another kind of calamity, appears fortunate. Sometimes a calamity becomes auspicious through patience.

Regard the whole world as loss. So that whatever a man does possess is gain.

The eye of a needle is not narrow for two friends, but the world is not wide enough for two enemies.

Whatever thou wouldst hide from thine enemy, do not disclose to thy friend.

The sage was asked, "How dost thou hide a secret?" He replied, "I make my heart its grave."

The bait by which a man is caught lies concealed beneath his tongue; a man's death is between his cheeks.

Beware of too frequent visits, because that is the cause of estrangement. It is like rain—men loathe it when it falls unceasingly, and pray for it when it is withheld.

It was told to a sage that a certain person had acquired great wealth. He said, "Has he also acquired the days in which to spend it?"

**GARDNER, JACK** (United Kingdom, 1946–  ) Gardner started out as a graphic designer and uses his design skills to play with the typography of his sayings: short words are printed tall; big thoughts are printed small. In *Wot Iz Lojik?* he uses eccentric phonetic spellings to force readers to linger over the phrases. Through his quirky typography and spellings, Gardner employs the old Zen technique of short-circuiting readers' expectations to give the mind a jolt. Gardner's sayings are also infused with Zen's mischievous sense of humor, while his phonetic spellings are reminiscent of American humorist Josh Billings.

*Essential Aphorisms*

If nothing else is available, clutch at straws.

One step is a complete journey.

We choose the morality that suits our ambitions.

When something is so familiar you can do it with your eyes shut, don't.

Preparation is an end in itself.

If it is gone and you are alive, you didn't need it.

Inuff iz awlweyz an unnown kwontitee.

Wylst thu tym bom iz ticking it iz sayf.

Seedz kan miss a yeer and stil gro.

Tu leev thingz az thay arr yu must furst now houw thingz arr.

*Parallel Lines: Hiding in Plain Sight*

Thu klowsur yu kan hyd tu yor huntur thu less lyklee they ar tu fynd yu.
—GARDNER

The fly that does not want to be swatted is safest if it sits on the fly-swatter.
—GEORG CHRISTOPH LICHTENBERG

**GURDJIEFF, GEORGE IVANOVITCH** (Armenia, c. 1866–1949) Gurdjieff founded the Institute for the Harmonious Development of Man in Fontainebleau, France, to disseminate his teachings about how to live a conscious life. One of his practices was to make his students freeze in place whenever he gave a specific signal. The idea was to focus their attention on the present moment—their thoughts, body language, habits—and so lead them to a more conscious awareness of themselves. Gurdjieff was also in the habit of inscribing his aphorisms on the walls of the institute.

*Essential Aphorisms*

Beware of someone who wants to teach you something.

Patience is the mother of will.

Like what "it" does not like.

The worse the conditions of life the more productive the work, always provided you remember the work.

**HÁVAMÁL** (Scandinavia, c. ninth century) The *Hávamál*, or "Sayings of the High One," is part of the *Edda*, the epic poems of the early Scandinavians. Purportedly written by the Norse god Odin, the collection provides practical and metaphysical guidelines for survival in a dangerous and often hostile world. The *Hávamál* is divided into several sections. One section is devoted to the importance of wisdom; another comprises maxims on how to comport and protect yourself while traveling. Odin himself was often depicted as a traveler. He was said to roam the world as an old man with a gray beard, wearing a wide-brimmed hat and carrying a staff—kind of like Walt Whitman with supernatural powers. He had only one eye; he gave the other to the goddess Mímir in exchange for a drink from the waters of wisdom in her well.

*Essential Aphorisms*

When passing a door post watch as you walk on, inspect as you enter. It is uncertain where enemies lurk or crouch in a dark corner.

No man should call himself clever but manage his mind. A sage visitor is a silent guest. The cautious evade evil. Never a friend more faithful, nor greater wealth, than wisdom.

Better weight than wisdom a traveler cannot carry. The poor man's strength in a strange place, worth more than wealth.

The cattle know when to come home from the grazing ground. A man of lean wisdom will never learn what his stomach can store.

Never walk away from home ahead of your axe and sword. You can't feel a battle in your bones or foresee a fight.

A log's flame leaps to another, fire kindles fire. A man listens, thus he learns. The shy stays shallow.

Wake early if you want another man's life or land. No lamb for the lazy wolf. No battles won in bed.

The lame rides a horse, the maimed drives the herd, the deaf is brave in battle. A man is better blind than buried. A dead man is deft at nothing.

**HELLINGER, BERT** (Germany, 1925–    ) Conscripted into the German army at the age of seventeen, Hellinger spent the latter part of World War II in a Belgian prisoner-of-war camp. When the war was over, he entered the Catholic seminary, eventually becoming a priest and working for sixteen years in South Africa as a missionary to the Zulus. After twenty-five years as a Catholic priest, he left the order and took up the study of psychoanalysis. He is renowned for his work with "family constellations," a form of therapy that explores an individual's psychological growth within the context of his or her family relationships.

*Essential Aphorisms*

Hope muddies seeing.

Skepticism is like faith: both are substitutes for seeing.

Growth always deviates a little bit.

The direct path sometimes takes longer.

The right thing is hard to find and easy to understand.

Some run after good fortune not realizing that good fortune is running after them, but never reaches them, because they are running.

With blinders on, one runs faster.

What we take in hand becomes small.

The wrong way is endless.

The optimum is a little bit less.

Some who make an objection are taking a single stone from the cathedral, and finding it is nothing special.

Rejection leads to resemblance.

Avoiding something brings it about.

Often the good thing comes about only through a transgression.

Whiteness attracts blemishes.

If one is content, one will have more of what one already has.

In dwindling, we become full.

The lesser power lasts longer.

### Parallel Lines: In the Distance

The farther away you push something, the larger it becomes. —HELLINGER

What seems large from a distance, close up ain't never that big.

—BOB DYLAN

*I CHING* (China, c. 3000 BCE) According to Chinese legend, the mythical folk hero Fu Hsi compiled the *I Ching*, or Book of Changes, some 5,000 years ago. Originally intended as a method of divination, the Book of Changes embodies the essence of ancient Chinese philosophy: all is flux and everything is in the process of becoming something else. These transformations are chronicled in a cycle of sixty-four scenarios that cover the full spectrum of human life. Each scenario represents a primal experience, a situation everyone has faced or will face in the future. And since change is inevitable, each situation is shadowed by its opposite. Each of the sixty-four scenarios is made up of six brief, aphoristic lines of text that both narrate and comment on the experience through a mix of blunt judgments and bewildering but often beautiful imagery.

### Essential Aphorisms

When there is hoarfrost underfoot, solid ice is not far off.

Whoever hunts deer without the forester only loses his way in the forest.

When ribbon grass is pulled up, the sod comes with it.

The finest clothes turn to rags. Be careful all day long.

Shock comes and makes one distraught. If shock spurs to action one remains free of misfortune.

Doubt not. You gather friends around you as a hair clasp gathers the hair.

### Parallel Lines: Ups and Downs

No plain not followed by a slope. No going not followed by a return. He who remains persevering in danger is without blame. Do not complain about this truth; enjoy the good fortune you still possess.        —*I CHING*

All growing ends in fading, all rising ends in falling, all meeting ends in parting; such indeed is the law of this world.        —*THE UPANISHADS*

We know health by illness, good by evil, satisfaction by hunger, leisure by fatigue.        —HERACLITUS

**JESUS** (Palestine, c. 4 BCE–33 CE) The New Testament tells just a small part of the story of Jesus. The Gnostic gospels—written around the same time as the canonical scriptures, roughly the end of the first and beginning of the second century—provide alternative accounts of Jesus's life and teachings that were rejected as heretical by the early Church leaders. These documents portray Jesus as a mischievous and vengeful little boy. He casually strikes down and then resurrects his playmates, and enjoys transforming clay pigeons into real pigeons for his friends. The Gospel of Thomas records nothing of Jesus's life—no virgin birth, no miracles, no crucifixion—just 114 of Jesus's most startling aphorisms. Muhammad also honored Jesus as a true prophet, and the Islamic tradition has a rich literature of Jesus's sayings as well as stories about him.

### Essential Aphorisms

Show me the stone that the builders rejected: that is the cornerstone.

You see the speck that is in your brother's eye, but you do not see the beam that is in your own eye. When you take the beam out of your own eye, then you will see clearly to take the speck out of your brother's eye.

If your leaders say to you, "Look, the kingdom is in heaven," then the birds of heaven will precede you. If they say to you, "It is in the sea," then the fish will precede you. Rather the kingdom is inside you and it is outside you. When you know yourselves, then you will be known, and you will understand that you are children of the living father.

Do not worry, from morning to evening and from evening to morning, about what you will wear.

If you bring forth what is within you, what you have will save you. If you do not have that within you, what you do not have within you will kill you.

If a blind person leads a blind person both of them will fall into a hole.

One who knows all but is lacking in oneself is utterly lacking.

If the flesh came into being because of spirit, it is a marvel, but if spirit came into being because of the body, it is a marvel of marvels. Yet I marvel at how this great wealth has come to dwell in this poverty.

I am the light that is over all things. I am all: from me all has come forth, and to me all has reached. Split a piece of wood; I am there. Lift up the stone, and you will find me there.

Be at ease with people and ill at ease with yourself.

Those who sorrow most in misfortune are the most attached to this world.

Jesus was asked, "Which of your deeds is the best?" He answered, "Leaving alone that which does not concern me."

Blessed is he who sees with his heart but whose heart is not in what he sees.

The world is a bridge. Cross this bridge but do not build upon it.

### Parallel Lines: Just Passing Through

Be passersby.

—JESUS

Never say about anything, "I have lost it," but instead, "I have given it back." Did your child die? It was given back. Did your wife die? She was given back. "My land was taken." So this too was given back. "But the person who took it was bad!" How does the way the giver asked for it back concern you? As long as he gives it, take care of it as something that is not your own, just as travelers treat an inn.          —EPICTETUS

Live your life without attracting attention.          —EPICURUS

He has not lived badly whose birth and death has been unnoticed by the world.          —HORACE

Be in the world as if you were a stranger or a traveler.          —MUHAMMAD

**JEWISH FATHERS** (Israel, c. 200 BCE–200 CE) Several centuries before the early Christian monks set up their first monastic communities, Jewish sages had opted for the same kind of quietude and contemplation. The *Pirke Avot*, or Sayings of the Fathers, is a compendium of their anecdotes and aphorisms focusing on practical ethics with a hint of mysticism. Since the collection took final form around the second century, these moral sayings have been used as an ethical instruction manual by the pious.

*Essential Aphorisms*

Hillel used to say, "If I am not for myself, who will be for me? But if I care for myself only, what am I? And if not now, when?"

Simeon said, "All my days I have grown up among the wise, and I have found nothing better for man than silence; not learning but doing is the chief thing; and whoso multiplies words causes sin."

R. Chanina, the vice–high priest, said, "Pray for the welfare of the government, since but for the fear thereof men would swallow each other alive."

Ben Azzai used to say, "Despise not any man, and carp not at any thing; for there is not a man that has not his hour, and there is not a thing that has not its place."

R. Jannia said, "It is not in our power to explain either the prosperity of the wicked or the afflictions of the righteous."

Ben Bag Bag said, "Turn it, and turn it over again, for everything is in it, and contemplate it, and wax gray and old over it, and stir not from it, for thou canst have no better rule than this."

## Parallel Lines: Increase and Decrease

Hillel used to say, "He who does not increase his knowledge decreases it."

—*PIRKE AVOT*

Love decreases when it ceases to increase.

—FRANÇOIS-RENÉ, VICOMTE DE CHATEAUBRIAND

**KANG HSI** (China, 1654–1722) Kang Hsi was a remarkable emperor of China. He was a student of Renaissance science and the Confucian classics and was trained in Christian theology by the Jesuits, who were proselytizing in China at the time. He was a poet, essayist, and great patron of the arts, commissioning a massive dictionary of Chinese that is still in use. He eventually allowed the Jesuits to work for him as astronomers and engineers, and he granted them the right to teach, preach, and convert throughout the empire. China prospered and enjoyed relative peace throughout his more than sixty-year reign. Kang Hsi's Sacred Edicts originally consisted of sixteen of the emperor's maxims, issued in 1670 and prominently displayed in courts of law. In 1724, Kang Hsi's son and successor republished the Edicts in an enlarged form, adding a commentary on his father's texts. Like Marcus Aurelius, Kang Hsi kept a diary in which he recorded his ruminations on the art of statecraft and his philosophical speculations.

## Essential Aphorisms

In every affair retire a step, and you have an advantage.

Seeing men in haste, do not seek to overtake them.

Covet not an empty name.

Each grass blade has its drop of dew. The wild birds lay up no stores; but heaven and earth are wide. Strange, indeed, if you cannot rest in the duties of your sphere.

**KEMPIS, THOMAS À** (Germany, 1380–1471) Thomas à Kempis was a German priest and scribe who spent most of his life in monasteries in the Netherlands. He was a follower of the "new devotion," a spiritual practice of manual labor and meditation that sought to recreate the piety of the early Christian monks. One portrait said to be of Thomas à Kempis is inscribed with the aphorism, "Everywhere I have sought rest and found it nowhere, save in little nooks with little books."

*Essential Aphorisms*

Of two evils we must always choose the least.

Remember that lost time does not return.

At the Day of Judgment we shall not be asked what we have read but what we have done; not how well we have spoken, but how holily we have lived.

Be not angry that you cannot make others as you wish them to be, since you cannot make yourself as you wish to be.

Man proposes, but God disposes.

No man ruleth safely but that he is willingly ruled.

First keep the peace within yourself, then you can also bring peace to others.

Great tranquility of heart is his who cares for neither praise nor blame.

We usually know what we can do, but temptation shows us who we are.

Would that we had spent one whole day well in this world!

**LAO TZU** (China, c. 604–531 BCE) As an old man, Lao Tzu decided to get away from it all. He was a historian of the Chou dynasty and, disgusted with the corruption and venality of the local aristocracy, left his home and his job to live alone in the mountains. Legend has it that a gatekeeper recognized Lao Tzu on the way to his solitary retreat and asked him to write down his teachings before departing. The result is the *Tao Te Ching*, the founding treatise of Taoism, a quietist philosophy in ancient China that stressed the importance of living in accord with nature. That's more or less all there is to Lao Tzu's biography, but the historical record on him is so sparse that it's impossible to say for sure whether he really existed. Like Confucius after him, Lao Tzu was a student of the *I Ching*. He adopted its homely aphoristic style and its philosophical stance: whenever one state of affairs reaches its peak, another opposing state of affairs is already taking shape to replace it.

*Essential Aphorisms*

Stretch a bow to the very full, and you will wish you had stopped in time; temper a sword-edge to its very sharpest, and you will find it soon grows dull. When bronze and jade fill your hall it can no longer be guarded. Wealth and place breed insolence that brings ruin in its train. When your work is done, then withdraw! Such is Heaven's Way.

We put thirty spokes together and call it a wheel; but it is on the empty space where there is nothing that the usefulness of the wheel depends. We turn clay to make a vessel; but it is on the space where there is nothing that the usefulness of the vessel depends. We pierce doors and windows to make a house; and it is on these spaces where there is nothing that the usefulness of the house depends. Therefore just as we take advantage of what is, we should recognize the usefulness of what is not.

Ruling a large kingdom is like cooking a small fish; the less handled the better.

The greatest carver does the least cutting.

He who stands on tiptoe does not stand firm; he who takes the longest strides does not walk the fastest.

To remain whole, be twisted! To become straight, let yourself be bent. To become full, be hollow. Be tattered, that you may be renewed.

No lure is greater than to possess what others want, no disaster greater than not to be content with what one has.

As good sight means seeing what is very small so strength means holding on to what is weak.

A hurricane never lasts a whole morning, nor a rainstorm all day.

To know when one does not know is best. To think one knows when one does not know is a dire disease.

Nothing under heaven is softer or more yielding than water; but when it attacks things hard and resistant there is not one of them that can prevail.

Too much strength overextends itself; overshooting the mark is just as bad as missing it altogether.

### Parallel Lines: Easy Does It

In the governance of empire everything difficult must be dealt with while it is still easy, everything great must be dealt with while it is still small. Therefore the sage never has to deal with the great; and so achieves greatness. But again, light assent inspires little confidence and many easies means many a hard. Therefore the sage knows too how to make the easy difficult, and by so doing avoid all difficulties.                    —LAO TZU

Attempt easy tasks as if they were difficult and difficult as if they were easy. In the one case so that confidence may not fall asleep, in the other so that it may not be dismayed. For a thing to remain undone nothing more is needed than to think it done.                    —BALTASAR GRACIÁN

**MARCUS AURELIUS** (Italy, 121–180) Marcus Aurelius was born into a distinguished Roman family and became a favorite of Emperor Hadrian, who arranged for his own adopted heir, Antoninus Pius, to adopt Marcus Aurelius, thus placing him in the imperial succession. When Marcus came to the throne in 161, the empire was besieged by constant threats on the frontier. So as emperor, he spent most of his career quelling revolts and fighting back invading hordes. It was in the midst of these military campaigns that he wrote his *Meditations*, the candid and confessional journal that contains his aphoristic reflections on being a man, an emperor, and a Stoic. The *Meditations* are in many ways restatements of the key principles of Stoicism. Marcus Aurelius was deeply influenced by Stoics like Epictetus and Seneca. His aphorisms record his attempts to put their ideas into practice in his life.

### Essential Aphorisms

To be always the same, in sharp attacks of pain, in the loss of a child, in long illnesses. To see clearly in a living example that a man can be at once very much in earnest and yet able to relax.

Perfection of character possesses this: to live each day as if the last, to be neither feverish nor apathetic, and not to act a part.

Philosophy is a way of life.

Give full attention and devotion to each act.

And among what is most ready to hand into which you will look have these two: the one, that things do not take hold upon the mind, but stand without unmoved, and that disturbances come only from the judgment within; the second, that all that your eyes behold will change in a moment and be no more.

The Universe is change; life is opinion.

At dawn of day, when you dislike being called, have this thought ready: "I am called to man's labor; why then do I make a difficulty if I am going out to do what I was born to do and what I was brought into the world for?"

Do not because a thing is hard for you yourself to accomplish, imagine that it is humanly impossible: but if a thing is humanly possible and appropriate, consider it also to be within your own reach.

Near at hand is your forgetting all; near, too, all forgetting you.

Leave the wrong done by another where the wrong arose.

If it is not right, don't do it: if it is not true, don't say it.

Every man is worth just so much as the worth of what he has set his heart upon.

Do each act as though it were your last, freed from every random aim, from willful turning away from the directing Reason, from pretense, self-love and displeasure with what is allotted to you.

Delve within; within is the fountain of good, and it is always ready to bubble up, if you always delve.

## Parallel Lines: Change

Repeatedly dwell on the swiftness of the passage and departure of things that are and of things that come to be. For substance is like a river in perpetual flux.                                                    —MARCUS AURELIUS

Everything flows; nothing remains.                                    —HERACLITUS

**MENCIUS** (China, c. 372–c. 289 BCE) Mencius lived during the Warring States period of Chinese history, a time when regional monarchs battled local feudal lords for dominance. Like Confucius, Mencius set out to define a set of precepts by which a moral ruler could govern a large, unwieldy kingdom. He and his disciples traveled around China looking for a monarch who might employ them to help administer his realm, thus giving the philosopher a chance to put his ideas into practice. It is ironic that this chaotic and brutal era produced the sophisticated ethical system of Confucius, which Mencius adapted and embellished in part by emphasizing that the political failings of a ruler were due to his personal failings. Mencius was said to have studied with Confucius's grandson. Though the historical accuracy of this is in doubt, there is no question that Mencius is the most illustrious philosophical descendant of Confucius.

### Essential Aphorisms

Dig your well before you are thirsty. Swim with one foot on the ground. Forbearance is the jewel of home.

The multitude can be said never to understand what they practice, to notice what they repeatedly do, or to be aware of the path they follow all their lives.

Only when a man will not do some things is he capable of doing great things.

A carpenter or a carriage-maker can pass on to another the rules of his craft, but he cannot make him skillful.

Think of the consequences before you speak of the shortcomings of others.

If others do not respond to your love with love, look into your own benevolence; if others fail to respond to your attempts to govern them with order, look into your own wisdom; if others do not return your courtesy, look into your own respect. In other words, look into yourself whenever you fail to achieve your purpose.

### Parallel Lines: The Child Is the Father of the Man

A great man is one who retains the heart of a newborn babe.    —MENCIUS

Genius is only childhood recovered at will, childhood now gifted to express itself with the faculties of manhood and with the analytic mind that allows him to give order to the heap of unwittingly hoarded material.

—CHARLES BAUDELAIRE

Maturity—to recover the seriousness one had as a child at play.

—FRIEDRICH NIETZSCHE

Maturity: among other things, the unclouded happiness of the child at play, who takes it for granted that he is at one with his playmates.

—DAG HAMMARSKJÖLD

The pursuit of truth and beauty is a sphere of activity in which we are permitted to remain children all our lives. —ALBERT EINSTEIN

**MUHAMMAD** (Arabia, c. 570–632) Muhammad was an unlikely prophet. Born in Mecca, he was an illiterate camel-driver who spent his youth and early manhood in the desert working the caravan trade routes between Yemen and the Levant. Then, when he was forty years old, he began having the revelations in which the angel Gabriel commanded him to recite the Koran. Muslims believe the Koran is the word of God, but the *Hadith* is a collection of aphorisms by and anecdotes about Muhammad himself. In the roughly 1,500 aphorisms in the *Hadith*, Muhammad speaks as a practical prophet, someone with deep spiritual instincts who integrates his revelations with the more mundane concerns of daily life. He preached a benevolent morality based on honesty, moderation, and charity. But Muhammad was a fighter, too. When the Meccan rulers in what is now Saudi Arabia resisted his message, he converted them to Islam by force.

*Essential Aphorisms*

The most excellent jihad is that for the conquest of self.

He who knoweth his own self, knoweth God.

No person hath drunk a better draught than that of anger which he hath swallowed for God's sake.

Riches are not from abundance of worldly goods, but from a contented mind.

The ink of the scholar is more holy than the blood of the martyr.

Trust in God, but tie your camel.

Everyone starts the day selling his soul, and either frees it or ruins it.

An hour's contemplation is better than a year's adoration.

The garden of Paradise is closer to you than your shoelace; and so is the fire of hell.

He who leaves home in search of knowledge walks in the path of God.

The Prophet said, "Help your brother, whether he be an oppressor or one of the oppressed." Some said, "O Messenger of God, we help him if he is oppressed; but how can we help him if he is an oppressor?" The Prophet said, "By stopping him."

The Prophet was asked, "What is the most blessed struggle?" He said, "Speaking truth to an oppressive ruler."

The world is a prison for the believer, a paradise for the atheist.

He dieth not who giveth life to learning.

**PROVERBS** (Israel, *c.* 715–686 BCE) The sayings contained in the Book of Proverbs have traditionally been attributed to Solomon, probably as a way to enhance their authority. There is no historical evidence to suggest that Solomon actually wrote them, though. It is more likely that the Book of Proverbs is itself an anthology of aphorisms collected from authors whose names are now forgotten. The authors seek to inculcate humility and righteousness in the hearts of their readers, starting from the principle that "fear of the Lord is the beginning of wisdom."

*Essential Aphorisms*

Surely in vain the net is spread in sight of any bird.

Whom the Lord loveth he correcteth.

Withhold not good from them to whom it is due, when it is in the power of thine hand to do it.

A soft answer turneth away wrath: But grievous words stir up anger.

Answer not a fool according to his folly, lest thou also be like unto him.

As a dog returneth to his vomit, so a fool returneth to his folly.

Whoso diggeth a pit shall fall therein: And he that rolleth a stone, it will return upon him.

Faithful are the wounds of a friend; but the kisses of an enemy are deceitful.

**PUBLILIUS SYRUS** (Syria, c. first century BCE) Publilius Syrus was a performer as well as an aphorist; he once received a prize for improvisation from Caesar himself. Born in Syria, he was taken as a slave to Italy, where he eventually won his freedom. His sole surviving work is called *Sententiae* ("Sentences").

*Essential Aphorisms*

Love may be produced by choice, but you cannot when you choose get free from it.

A lover knows what he would have, but not what he ought to have.

Fortune makes a fool of him whom she long caresses.

No fortune is so good as not to be complained of.

Danger cannot be avoided without danger.

What is not missed is not lost.

He is every day condemned who is always in fear.

Extension spoils a bow, relaxation the mind.

How miserable it is to be wronged by those of whom you dare not complain.

A seeming friend is the worst of enemies.

That ought to be long considered which can be done at once.

Other people's possessions please us, and ours please other people.

**PYTHAGORAS** (Greece, c. sixth century BCE) Other ancient Greek philosophers postulated that all things were made of earth, air, water, or fire; Pythagoras held that all things were numbers. Pythagoras was both a natural philosopher and an instinctive mystic. At his school in Kroton in southern Italy, he taught the numerical ratios of the musical scale and the transmigration of souls. Pythagoras wrote nothing—or at least nothing he wrote has survived—and his sayings were only preserved through records of his teachings made by others.

*Essential Aphorisms*

Philosophy is the medicine of the soul.

Not everything that is pleasurable is useful, but everything that is useful is pleasurable.

Sleep is a light death, and death is a long sleep.

Write in the sand the flaws of your friend.

The oldest, shortest words—"yes" and "no"—are those which require the most thought.

Let not sleep fall upon thy eyes till thou has thrice reviewed the transactions of the past day. Where have I turned aside from rectitude? What have I been doing? What have I left undone, which I ought to have done?

Educate the children and it won't be necessary to punish the men.

A thought is an idea in transit.

*Parallel Lines: Education*

Lack of education is a cause of every evil.                    —PYTHAGORAS

Ignorance, the root and the stem of every evil.                —PLATO

Education is an ornament in prosperity and a refuge in adversity.

—ARISTOTLE

Acquire knowledge. It enables its possessor to distinguish right from wrong; it lights the way to heaven; it is our friend in the desert, our society in solitude, our companion when friendless; it guides us to happiness; it sustains us in misery; it is an ornament among friends, and an armor against enemies.

—MUHAMMAD

**SOCRATES** (Greece, c. 470–399 BCE) Socrates liked to think of himself more as a midwife than as a philosopher. His role, he claimed, was to help other people's ideas to be born. (Apparently, Socrates' mother, Phaenarete, was an actual midwife.) Most of what we know about what Socrates said and did comes from the early dialogues of his most famous student, Plato. Without Plato's intellectual midwifery in the early dialogues, Socrates' sayings would have been lost forever. According to Plato's *Apology*, Socrates embarked on his career as an interrogator of other people's ideas after a friend asked the oracle at Delphi if anyone was wiser than Socrates. When the oracle said "No," Socrates set off to find someone wiser than himself. What he discovered was that people didn't really know what they thought they knew.

*Essential Aphorisms*

I know nothing except the fact of my ignorance.

Often when looking at a mass of things for sale, he would say to himself, "How many things I have no need of!"

There is only one good, knowledge, and one evil, ignorance.

Beauty is a short-lived tyranny.

Beware the barrenness of a busy life.

If all misfortunes were laid in one common heap whence everyone must take an equal portion, most people would be contented to take their own and depart.

Let him that would move the world first move himself.

Regard your good name as the richest jewel you can possibly be possessed of—for credit is like fire; when once you have kindled it you may easily preserve it, but if you once extinguish it, you will find it an arduous task to rekindle it again. The way to gain a good reputation is to endeavor to be what you desire to appear.

The highest form of human excellence is to question oneself and others.

The unexamined life is not worth living.

## Parallel Lines: Wonder

Philosophy begins with wonder.                                    —SOCRATES

Let one who seeks not stop seeking until one finds. When one finds, one will be troubled. When one is troubled, one will marvel and will rule over all.                                                            —JESUS

He who can no longer pause to wonder and stand rapt in awe, is as good as dead; his eyes are closed.                          —ALBERT EINSTEIN

To be surprised, to wonder, is to begin to understand.
                                              —JOSÉ ORTEGA Y GASSET

**SOMADEVA** (Kashmir, 1035–1085) Somadeva is the author of the *Katha-Sarit-Sagara* ("The Ocean of Story"), a compendium of ancient Indian legends, fairy tales, and folk stories. Originally from Kashmir, he composed the work (which is studded with wise Sanskrit sayings) for the amusement of Queen Suryamati, wife of King Ananta of Kashmir. Like all great fairy tales, the *Katha-Sarit-Sagara* is populated by dragons, demons, and damsels in distress. Daring knights fight pitched battles against wicked witches. The stories are filled with intrigue, magic, and treachery. Sadly, the royal couple experienced treachery at first hand. After agreeing to willingly surrender his throne to his eldest son in 1063, Ananta was attacked and overthrown by the new monarch's armies. Ananta killed himself in despair. Suryamati threw herself onto his funeral pyre.

## Essential Aphorisms

No one can escape from the shadow of his own head, or the course of destiny.

If destiny is adverse, it is not even possible to die.

Fate seems to take pleasure in perpetually creating new marvels.

The man who is not distracted in calamity obtains prosperity.

It is better that a little be given in time, than much when it is too late.

Those that have lost their wealth die daily, not so those that have lost their breath.

Often the harm that one wishes to do to another recoils on one's self, as a ball thrown against a wall rebounds frequently.

A fool never takes leave of his wealth until his wealth takes leave of him.

There is not wealth enough in the whole world to satisfy gamblers.

Mud thrown at heaven falls on the head of the thrower.

**TALIB, ALI IBN ABI** (Arabia, 599–661) Ali ibn Abi Talib was Muhammad's cousin and, after marrying one of the Prophet's daughters, his son-in-law. There are many legends surrounding Ali's birth, one of which is that he was born inside the Kaaba, the stone shrine in Mecca that Muslims face during prayer. Ali's mother is said to have emerged from the Kaaba holding the baby in her arms. Muhammad took the child from her and kissed him, so Ali's first nourishment was the saliva from Muhammad's lips. Ali grew up to be one of the Prophet's earliest and most devoted followers. When Muhammad died, Ali's followers believed that he was the Prophet's designated successor, while another group believed that Abu Bakr was next in line. Abu Bakr was duly elected caliph, prompting a doctrinal split that still exists to this day. Shi'a Muslims contend Ali was Muhammad's rightful heir; Sunni Muslims support Abu Bakr. Ali did eventually become caliph, after his predecessor, Uthman ibn Affan, was assassinated. But Ali himself was later assassinated, too, by a faction that believed he was implicated in Uthman's death.

*Essential Aphorisms*

Contradict thyself, and thou shalt find rest.

The covetous man's penny is a stone.

The restraining the soul from the appetite is the greatest holy war.

Riches are a damage to the owner, except that part of them which he sends before him.

Opportunity is swift of flight, slow of return.

A wise enemy is better than a foolish friend.

A man is hid under his tongue.

A man's affliction is the forerunner of his prosperity.

Despair is a freeman, hope is a slave.

Men, or mankind, is divided into two parts or sorts: the one seeketh and doth not find; another findeth and is not contented.

Adversity makes no impression upon a brave soul.

Impatience under an affliction is worse than the affliction.

**UPANISHADS** (India, c. 1500–500 BCE) The term *upanishad* is derived from Sanskrit words meaning "to sit down near," a phrase that evokes the image of a teacher speaking intimately with a group of disciples. The teachings contained in the *Upanishads* are part of ancient Indian sacred literature. The richly imagistic texts lay out the path to self-knowledge through yoga and meditation, while also exploring the doctrines of karma and reincarnation. The *Upanishads* record the sayings of sages like Manu, Narada, and Yajnavalkya.

*Essential Aphorisms*

You may drink the ocean dry; you may uproot from its base the mountain Meru; you may swallow fire. But more difficult than all these, Oh Good One, is control over the mind.

Where is the man who doubts the fact of his own existence? If such a one be found, he should be told that he himself who thus doubts is the Self he denies.

No other knowledge is necessary in knowing one's self, for the Self is all knowledge; the lamp requires not the light of another lamp for its own illumination.

As the statue preexists in the wood; and a statue exists again in every limb of that statue; and so on ad infinitum, so does this gigantic statue—the Cosmos—exist in the One.

Liberation is not on the other side of the sky, nor in the netherworld, nor on earth; liberation lies in the mind purified by proper spiritual knowing.

That which is naught at the beginning and end is naught in the present moment also; things though fully resembling unreality are said to be real by a kind of metaphor.

As the rope not understood as such is mistaken in the dark for a snake, so is Spirit mistaken for the variety of this world.

Experience, full of likes and dislikes, is verily a dream, real while it lasts, all unreal on being awake.

Formal objects of worship are devised for the use of those who have not yet realized the Essence; going by miles is devised for those who cannot go by leagues.

There is the greatest misery in hope; in hopelessness is the height of bliss. Everything that depends on Self is bliss, everything that depends on self is misery.

Relate thyself not with the future, not with what has gone by; live the present out with smiling heart.

He who sees all beings in the Self, and the Self in all beings, hates none.

### Parallel Lines: When the Shoe Fits

The mind being full, the whole universe is filled with the juice of nectar; the whole earth is covered with leather to him who has put his foot in the shoe.
                                                              —THE *UPANISHADS*

You forget your feet when the shoes are comfortable. You forget your waist when the belt is comfortable. Understanding forgets right and wrong when the mind is comfortable. There is no change in what is inside, no following what is outside, when the adjustment to events is comfortable. You begin with what is comfortable and never experience what is uncomfortable when you know the comfort of forgetting what is comfortable.  —CHUANG TZU

**ZEN MASTERS** (China, c. 960–1279) The Japanese word *koan* (a term derived from the Chinese word *kung-an*, which originally meant a government file or document) is a literary form developed by Buddhist monks in China between the tenth and thirteenth centuries. Koans are aphorisms disguised as riddles and usually take the form of terse, witty dialogues between a Zen master and his students. They often involve some slapstick element and—compiled into two great collections, the *Mumonkan* and the *Hekiganroku*—were used as case studies for aspiring monks. Koans often read like some kind of Punch and Judy show, with the monks trading blows and insults. Even the names of the monks have something slapstick about them; Seppo, for example, acts like he could well have been one of the Marx Brothers. The *Hekiganroku* ("Blue Cliff Records") consists of 100 koans and was composed by the Zen monk Setcho in the early eleventh century. The *Mumonkan* ("Gateless Gate") consists of 48 koans and was composed in 1228 by the Zen monk Mumon Ekai. In his postscript to the collection, Mumon avers that he's taken down the sayings of the Buddhas and patriarchs in their original form. "Nothing superfluous has been added by the author," he writes, "who has taken the lid off his head and exposed his eyeballs. Your direct realization is demanded; it should not be sought through others."

*Essential Aphorisms*

The wind was flapping a temple flag, and two monks started an argument. One said the flag moved, the other said the wind moved; they argued back and forth but could not reach a conclusion. The Sixth Patriarch said, "It is not the wind that moves, it is not the flag that moves; it is your mind that moves." The two monks were awe-struck.

As for those who try to understand through other people's words, they are striking at the moon with a stick; scratching a shoe, whereas it is the foot that itches.

Nansen one day saw the monks of the Eastern and Western halls quarreling over a cat. He held up the cat and said, "If you can give an answer, I will not kill it." No one could answer. Nansen cut the cat in two. Nansen told [the story about cutting the cat in two] to Joshu and asked his opinion. Joshu then took off his sandals and, putting them on his head, went away. Nansen said, "If you had been there, the cat would have been saved."

A monk asked Joshu, "I have heard that you closely follow Nansen. Is that true?" Joshu said, "Chinshu produces a big radish."

Basho Osho said to his disciples, "If you have a staff, I will give you a staff. If you have no staff, I will take it from you."

A monk said to Hogen, "My name is Echo. I ask you, what is the Buddha?" Hogen said, "You are Echo."

Seppo addressed the assembly and said, "All the great world, if I pick it up with my fingertips, is found to be like a grain of rice. I throw it in front of your face, but you do not see it. Beat the drum, telling the monks to come out to work, and search for it."

Whenever Gutei Osho was asked about Zen, he simply raised a finger. Once a visitor asked Gutei's boy attendant, "What does your master teach?" The boy too raised his finger. Hearing of this, Gutei cut off the boy's finger with a knife. The boy, screaming with pain, began to run away. Gutei called to him, and when he turned around, Gutei raised his finger. The boy suddenly became enlightened.

Tokusan asked Ryutan about Zen far into the night. At last Ryutan said, "The night is late. Why don't you retire?" Tokusan made his bows and lifted the blinds to withdraw, but he was met by darkness. Turning back to Ryutan, he said, "It is dark outside." Ryutan lit a paper candle and handed it to him. Tokusan was about to take it when Ryutan blew it out. At this, all of a sudden, Tokusan went through a deep experience and made bows.

Bodhidharma sat facing the wall. The Second Patriarch stood in the snow. He cut off his arm and presented it to the Bodhidharma, crying, "My mind has no peace as yet! I beg you, master, please pacify my mind!" "Bring your mind here and I will pacify it for you," replied Bodhidharma. "I have searched for my mind, and I cannot take hold of it," said the Second Patriarch. "Now your mind is pacified," said Bodhidharma.

# PAINTERS AND POETS

**S**AMUEL Taylor Coleridge was one of the most garrulous poets of his or any other age. He was renowned for the brilliance, and interminability, of his conversation. But he also had an acute appreciation for the shortest mode of communication: the aphorism, of course. "Exclusively of the abstract sciences, the largest and worthiest portion of our knowledge consists of aphorisms, and the greatest and best of men is but an aphorist," he wrote. "Truths, of all others the most awful and interesting, are too often considered as so true that they lose all the power of truth, and lie bed-ridden in the dormitory of the soul, side by side with the most despised and exploded errors. There is one way of giving freshness and importance to the most commonplace maxims—that of reflecting on them in direct reference to our own state and conduct, to our own past and future being." Painters and poets jolt our souls out of the dormitory of the ordinary. In quick verbal brushstrokes or single beautifully executed lines, they do more than just present old, half-forgotten truths in a new light; they give us new eyes.

## PAINTERS

**ALLSTON, WASHINGTON** (United States, 1779–1843) In his early twenties, after graduating from Harvard, Allston sold his share of his family's estate in Charleston, South Carolina, and used the proceeds to fund a trip to Europe, where he was determined to become an artist. In 1801, he began his studies at the Royal Academy in London; three years later he went to Italy, where he became friends with the English poet Samuel Taylor Coleridge in Rome. Allston returned to the United States for good in 1818. Toward the end of his life, he prepared a series of lectures on art, but he didn't live long enough to deliver them. After his death, his aphorisms—about fifty of them—were found painted on the walls of his studio.

*Essential Aphorisms*

Reverence is an ennobling sentiment; it is felt to be degrading only by the vulgar mind, which would escape the sense of its own littleness by elevating itself into an antagonist of what is above it. He that has no pleasure in looking up is not fit so much as to look down. Of such minds are mannerists in art; in the world, tyrants of all sorts.

Nothing is rarer than a solitary lie; for lies breed like Surinam toads; you cannot tell one but out it comes with a hundred young ones on its back.

It is a hard matter for a man to lie all over, Nature having provided king's evidence in almost every member. The hand will sometimes act as a vane to show which way the wind blows, when every feature is set the other way; the knees smite together, and sound the alarm of fear, under a fierce countenance; and the legs shake with anger, when all above is calm.

The phrenologists are right in placing the organ of self-love in the back of the head, it being there where a vain man carries his intellectual light; the consequence of which is, that every man he approaches is obscured by his own shadow.

The most common disguise of envy is in the praise of what is subordinate.

The painter who seeks popularity in art closes the door upon his own genius.

The painter who is content with the praise of the world in respect to what does not satisfy himself is not an artist but an artisan; for though his reward be only praise, his pay is that of a mechanic, for his time and not for his art.

There is an essential meanness in the wish to get the better of anyone. The only competition worthy of a wise man is with himself.

*Parallel Lines: Humility*

The only true independence is in humility; for the humble man exacts nothing, and cannot be mortified, expects nothing, and cannot be disappointed. Humility is also a healing virtue; it will cicatrize a thousand wounds, which pride would keep forever open. But humility is not the virtue of a fool; since it is not consequent upon any comparison between ourselves and others, but between what we are and what we ought to be—which no man ever was.                                    —ALLSTON

He who attributes humility to himself is really proud.

—ABU AL-FADL IBN ATA'ALLAH AL-ISKANDARI

To refuse to accept praise is to want to be praised twice over.

—LA ROCHEFOUCAULD

He who speaks humbly of himself becomes angry if you believe him and furious if you repeat what he says.                             —MULTATULI

**DELACROIX, EUGÈNE** (France, 1798–1863) Delacroix always had a flair for drama. Born in the Ardèche region of southern France, he achieved early recognition with dramatic paintings of dramatic events, such as the battles of the Greeks in their war of independence against the Turks. He created his most famous work, *Liberty Leading the People*, in 1830. This painting, which has become synonymous with France, was initially considered by King Louis-Philippe too controversial to display. It was only after the end of Louis-Philippe's reign in 1848 that the painting was shown.

*Essential Aphorisms*

The artist who aims at perfection in everything achieves it in nothing.

What moves those of genius, what inspires their work is not new ideas, but their obsession with the idea that what has already been said is still not enough.

Do all the work you can; that is the whole philosophy of the good way of life.

To be a poet at twenty is to be twenty; to be a poet at forty is to be a poet.

**LEONARDO DA VINCI** (Italy, 1452–1519) In 1550, Giorgio Vasari published *The Lives of the Most Excellent Italian Architects, Painters and Sculptors*, which contains the earliest known biography of Leonardo. The book is filled with anecdotes about Leonardo—including one account of his habit of buying caged birds just so he could release them—collected and compiled from the painter's contemporaries. "The greatest of all Andrea's pupils [referring to Andrea del Verrocchio, Leonardo's first painting instructor] was Leonardo da Vinci," Vasari writes, "in whom, besides a beauty of person never sufficiently admired and a wonderful grace in all his actions, there was such a power of intellect that whatever he turned his mind to he made himself master of with ease."

*Essential Aphorisms*

It had long since come to my attention that people of accomplishment rarely sat back and let things happen to them. They went out and happened to things.

Life well spent is long.

You do ill if you praise, but worse if you censure, what you do not understand.

Shun those studies in which the work that results dies with the worker.

Whoever in discussion adduces authority uses not intellect but rather memory.

He who does not punish evil commands it to be done.

It is easier to resist at the beginning than at the end.

The grave will fall in upon him who digs it.

**MARIËN, MARCEL** (Belgium, 1920–1993) Mariën was working as a photographer's apprentice when, at the age of fifteen, he saw the paintings of René Magritte for the first time. He decided on the spot to become an artist, and he eventually ended up as one of the most prominent of the Belgian surrealists, serving alternately as the group's chief publisher, polemicist, and *provocateur*. Mariën's visual art—a mix of collage, found objects, painting, and tableaux—is puzzling and playful, just like his aphorisms. One of his photographs is of an extended arm holding a charity tin printed with the words: HELP THE MISANTHROPES. Another is called "The Unfindable": a pair of spectacles with just a single lens, an object Mariën made in 1937 when his own glasses broke in half. His tombstone reads: "There is no merit being anything at all."

*Essential Aphorisms*

Vultures die last.

Strike the iron while you're hot.

You can't see the roots for the tree.

To set out is to arrive a little.

To confer a pathetic dimension on a football match, introduce a second ball.

Destiny exists only when accomplished.

Jam made of forbidden fruits.

The egoist is content with little.

Rare are the slaves who never feel the need, if not the pleasure, of polishing their chains.

On arrival, the journey begins.

**MICHELANGELO** (Italy, 1475–1564) Michelangelo's father used to beat his young son to dissuade him from becoming an artist. It didn't work. After the death of his mother, Michelangelo lived with a stonecutter's family in Settignano, a small town near Florence where the elder Michelangelo owned a marble quarry. "What good I have comes . . . because I sucked in chisels and hammers with my mother's milk," Michelangelo told Giorgio Vasari, the famous biographer of Renaissance artists.

*Essential Aphorisms*

Beauty is the purgation of superfluities.

My soul can find no staircase to Heaven unless it be through Earth's loveliness.

It is necessary to keep one's compass in one's eyes and not in the hand, for the hands execute, but the eye judges.

Trifles make perfection, and perfection is no trifle.

I hope that I may always desire more than I can accomplish.

The greater danger for most of us lies not in setting our aim too high and falling short; but in setting our aim too low, and achieving our mark.

**PICABIA, FRANCIS** (France, 1879–1953) Picabia was a serial trendsetter. He was involved in, and had a part in creating, most of the major movements of the first half of the twentieth century. Born in Paris, he started out as an Impressionist but quickly moved on to create his own mix of Fauvism and Cubism. Around the start of World War I, he became fascinated by machinery (he collected automobiles, at one point owning around 150 of them) and took up with the Dadaist movement in Zurich. He was also for a time associated with the Surrealists. But Picabia never stuck with one movement for very long. He inevitably ended up leaving these groups and later denouncing them for being behind the times. One constant throughout his career, though, was his interest in poetry and aphorisms, which he continued writing until his death.

*Essential Aphorisms*

Serious people have a slight odor of carrion.

Art is the cult of error.

Art is a pharmaceutical product for idiots.

If you want to have your own ideas, change them as often as you would a shirt.

Paralysis is the first stage of wisdom.

If you offer a helping hand your friends will chop it off.

Knowledge is ancient error reflecting on its youth.

Morality is out of place in a pair of pants.

The world is divided into two categories: failures and unknowns.

The only way to win a following is to run faster than the others.

Our heads are round so that thought can change direction.

My arse contemplates those who talk behind my back.

**ROSA, SALVATOR** (Italy, 1615–1673) Rosa was a pioneer in painting what became known as "romantic" landscapes—dark, wild scenes of untamed nature. He was something of a Renaissance man as well. In addition to painting, he wrote poems and satires, played music, and did a few turns as a comic actor.

*Essential Aphorisms*

The worst accident of our existence is dying.

Often there is no real middle ground between the best and the worst fortune.

Envy is an enemy you can conquer by flight.

As the body is made up of various members, so the heart is made up of many friends.

The silent madman is deemed wise.

The sycophant is like a shadow that doesn't love you but follows you anyway.

## POETS

**AL-MA'ARI, ABUL ALA** (Syria, 973–1057) Al-Ma'ari is considered among the greatest Arabic poets of all time. He was born in Syria and traveled widely in his youth, before smallpox rendered him blind. His travels perhaps helped make al-Ma'ari one of the earliest cultural relativists. He was tolerant of other cultures and religions and extremely skeptical about his own. He was a pronounced misanthrope, however. As a young man, he traveled to Baghdad, then the center of learning and culture in the Arab world. He was hoping to win fame as a scholar there but he returned to his hometown disappointed and lived in seclusion for the rest of his life. "I was made an abstainer from mankind by my acquaintance with them and my knowledge that created beings are dust," he wrote. In an age of absolutism, he was a pronounced atheist and critic of organized religion. He was extremely pessimistic as well. One of his poems warns couples against begetting children. If you must marry, he wrote, at least make sure you remain childless.

Al-Ma'ari practiced what he preached. On his tombstone was inscribed: "My father brought this on me, but I on none."

*Essential Aphorisms*

If ye unto your sons would prove
By act how dearly them ye love,
Then every voice of wisdom joins
To bid you leave them in your loins.

Had men wit, happy would they call
The kinsfolk at the funeral;
Nor messengers would run with joy
To greet the birthday of a boy.

Falsehood hath so corrupted all the world,
Ne'er deal as true friends they whom sects divide;
But were not hate Man's natural element,
Churches and mosques had risen side by side.

There are two kinds of people:
One with reason and without religion,
The other with religion and without reason.

O fools, awake! The rites ye sacred hold
Are but a cheat contrived by men of old,
Who lusted after wealth and gained their lust
And died in baseness—and their law is dust.

Age after age entirely dark hath run,
Nor any dawn led up a rising sun.

**AUDEN, W. H.** (United Kingdom, 1907–1973) Auden was an avid collector of aphorisms as well as an aphorist himself; with Louis Kronenberger, he edited *The Viking Book of Aphorisms* in 1964. While Auden's poems tend toward the aphoristic, he also specifically set out to write a book of *pensées*: *The Prolific and the Devourer*, which he began in the spring of 1939 just after immigrating to the United States only to abandon it in the autumn of that year. Inspired to take up the form by reading Pascal, Auden described the book as "a new Marriage of Heaven and Hell," referring to William Blake's collection of visionary sayings. The prolific and the devourer are two types of people Blake envisioned:

the former represents the farmer or the artist, anyone who creates, and the latter represents politicians and bureaucrats, people whom Blake believed fed off the labors of others. For Auden, the types represented the opposition between the poet and the social forces that prevented him from practicing his art. Like Søren Kierkegaard, Auden was intensely interested in the nature of sin and faith, and like William Blake he believed in the sanctity of the artist's spiritual calling.

*Essential Aphorisms*

Not only does Man create the world in his own image, but the different types of man create different kinds of worlds.

We are not free to will not to be free.

His penis never fully belongs to a man.

To be saved is to want only what one has.

It takes little talent to see clearly what lies under one's nose, a good deal of it to know in which direction to point that organ.

The greatest writer cannot see through a brick wall but, unlike the rest of us, he does not build one.

Some books are undeservedly forgotten; none are undeservedly remembered.

Knowledge may have its purposes, but guessing is always more fun than knowing.

**BAUDELAIRE, CHARLES** (France, 1821–1867) Baudelaire first made his name as an art critic rather than a poet, but in both genres he was equally controversial. He was an early proponent of the work of Édouard Manet, at a time when the Parisian salons regularly rejected the early Impressionist's canvases. When *Les Fleurs du Mal (The Flowers of Evil)* was published in 1857, Baudelaire, his publisher, and his printer were found guilty of obscenity.

*Essential Aphorisms*

Evil happens without effort, naturally, inevitably; good is always the product of skill.

It is necessary to work, if not from inclination, at least from despair. As it turns out, work is less boring than amusing oneself.

It is by universal misunderstanding that we agree with each other. If, by some misfortune, we understood each other, we would never agree.

The study of beauty is a duel in which the artist shrieks with terror before being overcome.

This life is a hospital where each patient is possessed by the desire to change his bed.

The finest trick of the devil is to persuade you that he does not exist.

**BERGAMÍN, JOSÉ** (Spain, 1895–1983) Bergamín was a staunch anticommunist, antifascist, and anti-Catholic. During the Spanish Civil War, he led the Alliance of Antifascist Intellectuals. When dictator Francisco Franco came to power, Bergamín fled to South America and, finally, to France. He only returned to Spain for good in 1970, eventually settling in the Basque Country. He was a close friend of fellow Spanish aphorist Miguel de Unamuno.

*Essential Aphorisms*

The woman who loves offers man a sweet enmity; the woman who doesn't love, a bitter friendship.

A faith that doesn't allow room for doubt is not a faith but a superstition.

See to create. Listen to doubt.

Searching for one's roots is a subterranean way of beating around the bush.

**BLAKE, WILLIAM** (United Kingdom, 1757–1827) Born above his father's hosier shop in London's Soho, Blake was a recalcitrant child who demonstrated an early aptitude for art, poetry, and religious studies. Recognizing his son's unusual talents, his father excused him from the family business. He also tried to encourage Blake's artistic ambitions by giving him money to purchase cheap prints and engravings for his studies. Blake had regular mystical experiences throughout his life. One of his earliest visions came when he was about eight. While walking in the country just outside London, Blake said he saw a tree draped with angels. As a young apprentice engraver, Blake had a job sketching the tombs at Westminster Abbey, where he regularly witnessed ghostly processions of medieval monks. As an adult, Blake held séances during which he executed quick portraits of some of the great historical figures who came to visit, including King Herod, Michelangelo, Paracelsus, Voltaire, and Socrates. Blake's thinking was influenced by Johann Kaspar Lavater, the Swiss scientist who popularized phys-iognomy. In 1787, Lavater published a book called *Aphorisms on Man*. Blake loved these shrewd reflections on everything from good manners to religious be-lief, and he scribbled enthusiastic replies to Lavater's aphorisms in his copy of the book.

*Essential Aphorisms*

Without Contraries is no progression.

Energy is Eternal Delight.

Eternity is in love with the productions of time.

What is now proved was once only imagined.

Exuberance is beauty.

Opposition is true friendship.

Everything that lives is Holy.

As none by traveling over known lands can find out the unknown, so from already acquired knowledge Man could not acquire more.

If the fool would persist in his folly he would become wise.

The road of excess leads to the palace of wisdom.

No bird soars too high if he soars with his own wings.

Joys impregnate. Sorrows bring forth.

Every thing possible to be believed is an image of truth.

One Law for the Lion and Ox is Oppression.

If the doors of perception were cleansed every thing would appear to man as it is, infinite.

## Parallel Lines: Fools

A fool sees not the same tree that a wise man sees.                          —BLAKE

The fool doth think he is wise, but the wise man knows himself to be a fool.                                    —WILLIAM SHAKESPEARE

Man's greatest wisdom consists in knowing his own follies.
                    —MADELEINE DE SOUVRÉ, MARQUISE DE SABLÉ

There is no greater joy for a fool than to find a greater fool.
                                            —ALEKSANDER FREDRO

The greatest of all fools is the proud fool, who is at the mercy of every fool he meets.                                    —WASHINGTON ALLSTON

**CHAR, RENÉ** (France, 1907–1988) In the early 1930s, Char was part of the French Surrealist movement and was friends with fellow poets Paul Eluard and André Breton. During World War II, he was a prominent member of the resistance in southern France. In the 1960s, he campaigned against the placement of nuclear weapons in his native Provence.

## Essential Aphorisms

That which comes into the world to disturb nothing deserves neither respect nor patience.

Many there are who wait till they are lifted by the reef, reached by the goal, before they take a stand.

Tears despise their sympathizer.

If we live in a lightning flash, it is the heart of eternity.

One borrows only what can be returned increased.

A poem is always married to someone.

**COCTEAU, JEAN** (France, 1889–1963) Cocteau always considered himself first and foremost a poet, but he was active in a bewildering range of disciplines, including as a designer, dramatist, filmmaker, novelist, memoirist, painter, screenwriter— and boxing manager. During the 1930s, he managed boxer Panama Al Brown, a black Panamanian who was the world bantamweight champion before going on to become a circus entertainer and jazz orchestra front man in France.

*Essential Aphorisms*

Art produces ugly things that frequently become more beautiful with time. Fashion, on the other hand, produces beautiful things that always become ugly with time.

A film is a petrified fountain of thought.

One must be a living man and a posthumous artist.

The joy of youth is to disobey, but the trouble is that there are no longer any orders.

The Louvre is a morgue; you go there to identify your friends.

The reward of art is not fame or success but intoxication: that is why so many bad artists are unable to give it up.

The trouble about the Académie is that by the time they get around to electing us to a seat, we really need a bed.

The worst tragedy for a poet is to be admired through being misunderstood.

What the public criticizes in you, cultivate. It is you.

When a work appears to be ahead of its time, it is only the time that is behind the work.

You've never seen death? Look in the mirror every day and you will see it like bees working in a glass hive.

True realism consists in revealing the surprising things which habit keeps covered and prevents us from seeing.

**COHEN, LEONARD** (Canada, 1934–    ) Cohen first won acclaim in his native Canada as a poet. His debut collection, *Let Us Compare Mythologies*, was published in 1956 while he was still a college student. Cohen's music career took off when he came to the attention of John H. Hammond, the record producer who also discovered Bob Dylan.

*Essential Aphorisms*

It's hard to hold the hand of anyone who is reaching for the sky just to surrender.

It is easy to display a wound, the proud scars of combat. It is hard to show a pimple.

Even damnation is poisoned with rainbows.

There is a crack in everything. It's how the light gets in.

**COLERIDGE, SAMUEL TAYLOR** (United Kingdom, 1772–1834) It seems only fitting that Coleridge should be credited with developing the "conversation poem"—brief, casual verse in colloquial language—since he was renowned for the power and eloquence of his own conversation. It was in conversation that Coleridge coined most of his aphorisms, and it was his conversation that John Keats remembered most of his first and only meeting with Coleridge on April 11, 1819, near London's Hampstead Heath. Coleridge was out for a stroll with a friend when he encountered Keats coming up the hill toward Highgate Village. Keats walked along for about two miles with the men, while Coleridge rattled on about everything from nightingales and mermaids to metaphysics and the different species of dreams. What Coleridge remembered was his parting handshake with Keats. "There is death in that hand," he later recalled. Keats died of tuberculosis two years later.

*Essential Aphorisms*

Common sense in an uncommon degree is what the world calls wisdom.

A great mind must be androgynous.

Advice is like snow—the softer it falls, the longer it dwells upon, and the deeper it sinks into the mind.

Prose is words in their best order; poetry is the best words in their best order.

If men could learn from history, what lessons it might teach us! But passion and party blind our eyes, and the light which experience gives is a lantern on the stern, which shines only on the waves behind us!

Every reform, however necessary, will by weak minds be carried to an excess that itself will need reforming.

Painting is the intermediate somewhat between a thought and a thing.

No one does anything from a single motive.

**CORN, ALFRED** (United States, 1943– ) Corn's interest in aphorisms began in childhood when he heard for the first time proverbial sayings (like "A stitch in time saves nine") and quotations from Proverbs, Job, and Ecclesiastes. "I didn't become aware of the aphorism as a literary form until studies in French literature brought me to La Rochefoucauld," he says, "who remains a kind of touchstone for me."

*Essential Aphorisms*

Laughter is the homage that reason pays to unreason.

Any mirror gazed at too long becomes stagnant.

Aphorisms are fictions, otherwise they would be no more striking than the morning paper. In fact, the best aphorisms are poems or novels in capsule form.

Metaphor sleeps around.

Why is it true that those who get on their high horse most often face in the wrong direction?

Life wounds everyone. Besides blood, though, the artist also sheds light.

**ENVALL, MARKKU** (Finland, 1944– ) Envall is a Finnish literary critic and historian as well as an author, with a long-standing interest in aphorisms. He wrote his doctoral dissertation in 1987 on the Finnish aphorism and edited an anthology of Finnish practitioners of the form, *A Century of Aphorisms*. One of his own collections is called *Pahojen Henkien Historia* ("The History of Evil Spirits"). For Envall, the most evil of all spirits are those economic, political, and social forces that suppress individuality. Literature is the only sure defense against them. "Censorship is a tribute to the importance of literature," Envall has written. "If the threat were a small one, no government would bother." But he fears freedom of speech may have unintended side effects: "To rejoice in complete freedom of speech is short-sighted. The more one is allowed to say, the fewer the people who will listen."

*Essential Aphorisms*

I go on, for my memory is shorter than the circle I go around.

An aphorism does not have to be the whole truth, but it is good if it contains a piece of it.

As long as you are able to cross an empty street against the lights, there is still hope.

Life gets easier and easier as the time goes by. There is so much less of it.

**FITZGERALD, EDWARD** (United Kingdom, 1809–1883) In his mid-forties, FitzGerald took up the study of Persian at the University of Oxford with Professor Edward Byles Cowell. In 1857, Cowell came across some Persian quatrains by a twelfth-century mystical poet named Omar Khayyám and sent them to FitzGerald, who set about translating them into English. On January 15, 1859, FitzGerald anonymously published a pamphlet called *The Rubaiyat of Omar Khayyam* containing seventy-five of his very freely translated versions. FitzGerald paid for the publication himself and the book received absolutely no notice whatsoever. It quickly ended up in the remaindered stacks of London's second-hand bookshops—where the poet and painter Dante Gabriel Rossetti found a copy in 1860, thus beginning the largely word-of-mouth process that gradually made the book a classic. FitzGerald was a great collector of aphorisms, too. In 1852, he published *Polonius: A Collection of Wise Saws and Modern Instances*, a selection of some of his original sayings but mostly a compendium of those of his favorite authors, who included Bacon, Goethe, Seneca, and Swift.

*Essential Aphorisms*

The higher the ape goes the more he shows his tail.

What can't be cured must be endured.

Any road leads to the end of the world.

Whatever a man delights in he will do best: and that he had best do.

God tempers the wind to the shorn lamb.

I am all for the short and merry life.

**FROST, ROBERT** (United States, 1874–1963) For a poet so indelibly associated with New England, it comes as a surprise to learn that Frost wrote and published his earliest poems in old England, while living in Beaconsfield, just outside London. Frost was discovered in 1912 by another American expatriate living in the United Kingdom, Ezra Pound, who wrote the first favorable notices of Frost's poetry. Frost returned to America in 1915, settling in New England. He is buried in the Old Bennington Cemetery in Bennington, Vermont. His epitaph reads: "I had a lover's quarrel with the world."

*Essential Aphorisms*

Something there is that doesn't love a wall.

A bank is a place where they lend you an umbrella in fair weather and ask for it back when it begins to rain.

Good fences make good neighbors.

A definite purpose, like blinders on a horse, inevitably narrows its possessor's point of view.

Home is the place where, when you have to go there, they have to take you in.

You can be a rank insider as well as a rank outsider.

Pressed into service means pressed out of shape.

Happiness makes up in height for what it lacks in length.

Poetry is a way of taking life by the throat.

The best way out is always through.

**GIBRAN, KAHLIL** (Lebanon, 1883–1931) My parents gave me a copy of Gibran's book *The Prophet* as a high school graduation present. I remember reading the book—a collection of brief, aphoristic essays purportedly delivered by a sage before returning to the "isle of his birth" on an ocean liner—with great excitement during "senior week," a seven-day period in early June when seemingly every high school senior in Pennsylvania travels to the New Jersey shore to celebrate graduation. I was entranced by Gibran's sermons on love, death, and friendship, written in the sonorous, archaic tones of the New Testament. Born in the Bsharri region of Lebanon to a Maronite Catholic family, from an early age Gibran was fascinated by prophets, especially Jesus. As a boy, he fell and dislocated his shoulder. To reset the shoulder in place, Gibran's family strapped a cross to his back for forty days, presumably because that's the amount of time Jesus spent fasting in the desert. Gibran immigrated to America in 1895 with his mother and three siblings. The family settled in Boston, where Gibran began selling his drawings for use on book covers. He studied with the sculptor Auguste Rodin in Paris for two years, and he gained a reputation as an artist before books like *The Prophet* made him famous. Gibran's art and aphorisms are very reminiscent of the work of William Blake. Like Blake, Gibran created lavish images of naked figures in dramatic or tortured poses. Also like Blake, he created prophetic personas through whom he delivered his sage sayings on religion and spirituality.

*Essential Aphorisms*

Even as love crowns you so shall he crucify you.

Your children are not your children. They are the sons and daughters of Life's longing for itself.

Is not dread of thirst when your well is full the thirst that is unquenchable?

Work is love made visible.

The lust for comfort murders the passion of the soul, and then walks grinning in the funeral.

Even those who limp go not backward.

**GOETHE, JOHANN WOLFGANG VON** (Germany, 1749–1832) Goethe considered himself a scientist as much as a poet. In addition to writing *Faust* and *The Sorrows of Young Werther* and almost single-handedly inventing German Romanticism, he independently proved the existence of the intermaxillary jawbone in humans, dabbled in alchemy, developed his own non-Newtonian theory of color ("Colors are the deeds and sufferings of light," he wrote), and claimed to have discovered that all plants are variations of the archetypal form of the leaf. Perhaps his alchemical interests led him to his fascination with mineralogy; goethite—an iron-bearing oxide mineral used since prehistoric times as a pigment, most notably in the cave paintings of Lascaux—is named after him. Goethe was also interested in folk customs, and he helped popularize many Western European traditions for celebrating Christmas. In his spare time, he was a member of the war commission, was director of roads and services, and managed the financial affairs and theaters of the court of Duke Karl August at Weimar. Goethe began writing aphorisms consistently when he was in his fifties. He got into the habit of quickly jotting down thoughts and ideas as they came to him, on any scrap of paper that was at hand. By the end of his life, he had composed 1,413 sayings, which he referred to variously as "shavings" or "gnomes." Goethe regarded his countryman Georg Christoph Lichtenberg as one of his guiding lights. Both men were scientists as well as aphorists. Though Goethe's own aphorisms can be tedious and overly didactic, he nevertheless appreciated Lichtenberg's lightning-like wit and humor. "We can use Lichtenberg's writings like a marvelous magic wand," Goethe wrote. "Wherever he cracks a joke, a problem lies hidden."

*Essential Aphorisms*

All beginnings are delightful. The threshold is the place to pause.

Hypotheses are scaffolding erected in front of a building and then dismantled when the building is finished. They are indispensable for the workman, but you mustn't mistake the scaffolding for the building.

A thinking man's greatest happiness is to have fathomed what can be fathomed and to revere in silence what cannot be fathomed.

We're only really thinking when we can't think out fully what we are thinking about!

If you miss the first buttonhole, you can't ever get fully buttoned up.

You never go farther than when you no longer know where you are going.

When two people are really happy about one another, one can generally assume that they are mistaken.

To do well you need talent, to do good you need means.

Duty: where one loves what one orders oneself to do.

It is better to do the most unimportant thing in the world than to look on half an hour as unimportant.

Nothing is more damaging to a new truth than an old error.

When one is old one has to do more than when one was young.

Begin by instructing yourself, then you will receive instruction from others.

It's really a person's mistakes that make him endearing.

A good man is always a beginner.

The world is a bell that is cracked: it clatters, but does not ring out clearly.

When a rainbow has lasted as long as a quarter of an hour we stop looking at it.

Dirt glitters when the sun happens to shine.

What you don't understand, you don't possess.

Anyone who doesn't know foreign languages knows nothing of his own.

We are never farther away from our desires than when we imagine we possess what we desire.

A mistaken idea is all very well as long as you are young; but it's no good dragging it on into old age.

As one grows older one must consciously, at some particular point, call a halt.

Young people are nature's new aperçus.

*Parallel Lines: Make It New*

The most original authors of the day are not rated as such because they produce something new, but only because they are capable of saying this kind of thing as though it had never been said before.    —GOETHE

Let no one say that I have said nothing new: the arrangement of the material is new. When playing tennis, both players hit the same ball, but one of them places it better.    —BLAISE PASCAL

Every thought is new when an author expresses it in a manner peculiar to himself.    —LUC DE CLAPIERS, MARQUIS DE VAUVENARGUES

I shall never repeat a conversation, but an idea often. I shall use the same types when I like, but not commonly the same stereotypes. A thought is often original, though you have uttered it a hundred times. It has come to you over a new route, by a new and express train of associations.

—OLIVER WENDELL HOLMES SR.

Literature is news that stays news.    —EZRA POUND

**GOURMONT, REMY DE** (France, 1858–1915) Gourmont was a leading French Symbolist poet, an influential and controversial critic, and one of the founders of the journal *Mercure de France*. He suffered from the disease lupus erythematosus, which left him with red rashes across his face. Gourmont believed that originality was an author's first and only duty; he wrote in the introduction to one of his collections of essays that the writer's "only excuse is to be original; he must speak of things not yet spoken of in a form not yet formulated. He must create his own aesthetics."

*Essential Aphorisms*

Art is the accomplice of love.

Women still remember the first kiss after men have forgotten the last.

A definition is a sack of flour compressed into a thimble.

All existence is a theft paid for by other existences; no life flowers except on a cemetery.

Each man must grant himself the emotions that he needs and the morality that suits him.

Most truths are nothing but prejudices.

Simple ideas lie within the reach only of complex minds.

The terrible thing about the quest for truth is that you find it.

**HEIN, PIET** (Denmark, 1905–1996) It is difficult to know which of Hein's occupations to list first. Born in Copenhagen, he was an author, designer, inventor, mathematician, and scientist. Among his most noteworthy inventions are the superellipse, a geometric shape widely used in architecture and interior design, and a series of mathematical strategy games such as Hex, Tangloids, and the Soma Cube. He also invented *gruks*, short, aphoristic poems that read something like philosophical limericks. Known in English as "grooks," the poems first appeared in the Danish daily newspaper *Politiken* in April 1940, just after the Nazi occupation of the country. At the time, Hein wrote under the pseudonym Kumbell Kumbell, which in English translates as "Tombstone Tombstone." The term *gruks* has no accepted definition. Some suggest it's a contraction of the Danish words *grin* and *suk* ("to laugh" and "to sigh"). Hein always maintained that he just made it up. Hein's jaunty rhythms and moralistic wit are reminiscent of the aphoristic poems of Dr. Seuss and Dorothy Parker.

*Essential Aphorisms*

Problems worthy of attack
Prove their worth by hitting back.

Put up in a place
Where it's easy to see
The cryptic admonishment
T. T. T.
When you feel how depressingly
Slowly you climb,
It's well to remember that
Things Take Time.

Knowing what
Thou knowest not
Is in a sense
Omniscience.

Our choicest plans have fallen through,
Our airiest castles tumbled over,
Because of lines we neatly drew
And later neatly stumbled over.

Living is a thing you do
Now or never—which do you?

He that lets the small things bind him
Leaves the great undone behind him.

To be brave is to behave
Bravely when your heart is faint.
So you can be really brave
Only when you really ain't.

A lifetime is more than sufficiently long
For people to get what there is of it wrong.

**HEINE, HEINRICH** (Germany, 1797–1856) From 1831 until his death, Heine lived
in Paris. What began as a voluntary exile—he traveled there to work as a journalist,
reporting on the political and economic development of France—became an enforced
one. Together with other German authors, including fellow aphorist Ludwig Börne,
Heine was part of the Young Germany movement, an attempt to export to Germany
the revolutionary ideas of France. The German government, annoyed by Heine's
criticism, banned his books. In 1847, Heine developed an illness, possibly syphilis,
multiple sclerosis, or what we know today as Lou Gehrig's disease, that left him partially paralyzed and bedridden for the rest of his life. From his "mattress grave," as he
described it, he still managed to compose poems and barbed critiques of politics and
religion. His last words were said to have been, "God will forgive me. It's his job."

*Essential Aphorisms*

Experience is a good school. But the fees are high.

Great genius takes shape by contact with another great genius, but less by
assimilation than by friction.

The weathercock on the church spire, though made of iron, would soon be
broken by the storm if it did not understand the noble art of turning with
every wind.

There are more fools in the world than there are people.

Whatever tears one may shed, in the end one always blows one's nose.

You cannot feed the hungry on statistics.

He only profits from praise who values criticism.

When the heroes go off the stage, the clowns come on.

Christ rode on an ass, but now asses ride on Christ.

Wherever they burn books they will also, in the end, burn human beings.

**HERBERT, ZBIGNIEW** (Poland, 1924–1998) During World War II, Herbert was active in the Polish resistance. Throughout the 1950s, he was forced to work at a series of low-paying jobs because he refused to toe the official Communist Party line in his writing. After his verse was translated into English in 1968, he became one of the most celebrated contemporary Polish poets.

*Essential Aphorisms*

Ignorance has an eagle's wings and an owl's gaze.

Talking without thinking is like shooting without aiming.

Hope is the bread of the poor.

A nation that loses its memory loses its conscience.

Study the world's skin before you set out to look for its heart.

The world wants to be nourished with false tears.

Wisdom adjusts itself to luck.

One always swims against the current to reach the source; it is trash that flows with the stream.

**HERNÁNDEZ, MIGUEL** (Spain, 1910–1942) Hernández was regularly arrested for his republican sympathies after the Spanish Civil War. As a result, most of his poems, known as *Songs and Ballads of Absence*, were written from his jail cell. He died in prison from tuberculosis.

*Essential Aphorisms*

If you analyze your happiness, you become sad.

I believe that humility is the virtue of the powerless: of oxen and lambs.

Motherhood: belly: first tomb.

Lowering your eyes, everything looks beautiful.

If it bit its tail, the serpent would be a collar.

Lovers tell each other secrets all the world knows.

**HOFFENSTEIN, SAMUEL** (United States, 1890–1947) Hoffenstein was among the most famous American light versifiers of the first half of the twentieth century, but today he is all but forgotten. Born in Lithuania, he immigrated to the United States when he was four years old and grew up in Wilkes-Barre, Pennsylvania, where he studied philosophy in college. In 1912, after a brief stint as the principal of a public school, he went to New York City, where he worked for a variety of newspapers as a reporter, drama critic, and columnist. After almost twenty years in journalism, Hoffenstein moved to Hollywood in 1931 to work as a screenwriter. There he wrote a clutch of moderately successful screenplays, including the adaptation of Theodore Dreiser's *An American Tragedy* (1931), *Dr. Jekyll and Mr. Hyde* (1931), and *Laura* (1944), for which he received one of his two Oscar nominations.

*Essential Aphorisms*

Wherever the worm turns, he is still a worm.
Power never serves too brief a term.
Where there are willing masters there are willing slaves.
Where there are mass men there are mass graves.

When I peruse the journals gray with strife
On earth, and hence assume distress above,
I must conclude, regretfully, that life
Seems (no reflection on the honest wife)
The occupational disease of love.

Fear not the atom in fission;
The cradle will outwit the hearse;
Man on this earth has a mission—
To survive and go on getting worse.

Babies haven't any hair;
Old men's heads are just as bare;—
Between the cradle and the grave
Lies a haircut and a shave.

**HOFMANNSTHAL, HUGO VON** (Austria, 1874–1929) Von Hofmannsthal made his debut on the Viennese literary scene at the age of sixteen, with the publication of his poem "Question." In no time he was part of a circle of artists that included fellow aphorists Hermann Bahr and Arthur Schnitzler as well as the sculptor Auguste Rodin and composer Johann Strauss. Von Hofmannsthal often wrote under pseudonyms. One of his most famous works is the *Lord Chandos Letter*, a fictional letter to Francis Bacon that Von Hofmannsthal ascribed to Philip, Lord Chandos, the younger son of the Earl of Bath, in which he apologizes for his total renunciation of literary activity.

*Essential Aphorisms*

It's not the doer who becomes unclean through the deed; only the deed through the doer.

Things experienced taste strangely and terribly like bilge water: a mix of death and life.

Depth has to be hidden. Where? On the surface.

Painting changes space into time; music time into space.

The genius creates harmony between the world in which he lives and the world that lives in him.

Man craves imagined experiences but refuses to recognize the experiences he has made himself.

**HOLMES, OLIVER WENDELL, SR.** (United States, 1809–1894) Along with William Cullen Bryant, Henry Wadsworth Longfellow, James Russell Lowell, and

John Greenleaf Whittier, Holmes was one of the "Fireside Poets," a group of nineteenth-century New England writers known for their genial, entertaining verse. Holmes was also a physician, and he is credited with coining the term "anesthesia" after witnessing the use of ether during a dental operation. His son, Oliver Wendell Holmes Jr., was an aphorist, too, as well as a Supreme Court Justice.

## Essential Aphorisms

The sound of a kiss is not so loud as that of a cannon, but its echo lasts a deal longer.

A moment's insight is sometimes worth a life's experience.

Most persons have died before they expire, died to all earthly longings, so that the last breath is only, as it were, the locking of the door of the already deserted mansion.

Insanity is often the logic of an accurate mind overtasked. Good mental machinery ought to break its own wheels and levers, if anything is thrust among them suddenly which tends to stop them or reverse their motion. A weak mind does not accumulate force enough to hurt itself; stupidity often saves a man from going mad.

Knowledge and timber shouldn't be much used till they are seasoned.

I find that the great thing in this world is not so much where we stand as in what direction we are moving: To reach the port of heaven, we must sail sometimes with the wind and sometimes against it—but we must sail, and not drift, nor lie at anchor.

Leverage is everything—don't begin to pry till you have got the long arm on your side.

Put not your trust in money, but put your money in trust.

**HORACE** (Rome, 65–8 BCE) After opposing the victorious Octavian (later to become Emperor Augustus) in the civil war, Horace returned to Rome broke—financially, politically, and spiritually. Then he struck up a friendship with Maecenas, a political adviser to Octavian, and his fortunes turned. Maecenas gave him a farm in the Sabine country near Tivoli. There Horace composed his epistles, odes, and satires, coining many expressions that are commonplace today, including "seize the day," a quintessentially Stoic sentiment. Horace carefully incorporated Stoic ideas into his poetry, once describing himself as "a true hog of Epicurus's herd."

## Essential Aphorisms

Adversity has the effect of eliciting talents, which in prosperous circumstances would have lain dormant.

He has the deed half done who has made a beginning.

He who postpones the hour of living is like the rustic who waits for the river to run out before he crosses.

Mingle some brief folly with your wisdom.

Nothing is beautiful from every point of view.

Subdue your passion or it will subdue you.

It is the mountaintop that the lightning strikes.

The covetous man is ever in want.

We are all driven into the same fold.

We rarely find anyone who can say he has lived a happy life, and who, content with his life, can retire from the world like a satisfied guest.

## Parallel Lines: Doing and Thinking

Don't think, just do.                                                —HORACE

Don't think—do.                                        —HOLBROOK JACKSON

Do think. Do!                                          —G. K. CHESTERTON

**KHAYYÁM, OMAR** (Persia, 1048–1131) Khayyám was born in the little town of Naishapur in what is now Iran. Few facts have been established about his life, but he might have followed his father into the tent-making business (the word *khayyám* means "tent maker") while also studying astronomy and mathematics. He wrote a number of important mathematical treatises, contributing to the development of non-Euclidean geometry, and eventually became the personal astronomer to Sultan Malik Shah, for whom he accurately calculated the length of the year. But Khayyám was also a poet, and his *Rubaiyat*, a collection of sensual and mystical hymns to life composed in rhymed quatrains, contain his aphorisms. Khayyám had a proclivity to wine, romance, and song, but the *Rubaiyat* is more than just a collection of songs in praise of drunkenness. Khayyám was a philosopher as well as a hedonist. He followed the Stoics in disdaining metaphysics and ridiculing any system of thought or belief that based itself solely on theoretical knowledge.

*Essential Aphorisms*

Here with a loaf of bread beneath the bough,
A flask of wine, a book of verse—and thou
Beside me singing in the wilderness—
And wilderness is paradise enow.

Myself when young did eagerly frequent
Doctor and saint, and heard great argument
About it and about: but evermore
Came out by the same door as in I went.

The moving finger writes; and, having writ,
Moves on: nor all thy piety nor wit
Shall lure it back to cancel half a line,
Nor all thy tears wash out a word of it.

There was a door to which I found no key:
There was a veil past which I could not see:
Some little talk awhile of me and thee
There seemed—and then no more of thee and me.

*Parallel Lines: For Tomorrow We Die*

But leave the wise to wrangle, and with me
The quarrel of the universe let be:
And, in some corner of the hubbub coucht,
Make game of that which makes as much of thee.      —KHAYYÁM

Drink and dance and laugh and lie,
Love, the reeling midnight through.

For tomorrow we shall die!
(But, alas, we never do.)

—DOROTHY PARKER

**KIPLING, RUDYARD** (United Kingdom, 1865–1936) Kipling originated many phrases—"East is East, and West is West, and never the twain shall meet," "A woman is only a woman, but a good cigar is a smoke," and "It's clever, but is it art?" to name just a few—that have entered common parlance in English. Perhaps only Alexander Pope and William Shakespeare have coined more terms that have gone on to become part of the language's proverbial resources. Kipling was born in India, the country from which he drew the inspiration for some of his most enduring children's stories, such as *The Jungle Book* and *Kim*. He was a journalist and travel writer before his fiction and poetry made him famous. His poem "If " consists of just one sentence, but at thirty-two lines it is one of the longest aphorisms in existence.

*Essential Aphorisms*

> If you can keep your head when all about you
> Are losing theirs and blaming it on you,
> If you can trust yourself when all men doubt you,
> But make allowance for their doubting too;
> If you can wait and not be tired by waiting,
> Or being lied about, don't deal in lies,
> Or being hated, don't give way to hating,
> And yet don't look too good, nor talk too wise;
> If you can dream—and not make dreams your master;
> If you can think—and not make thoughts your aim;
> If you can meet with Triumph and Disaster
> And treat those two imposters just the same;
> If you can bear to hear the truth you've spoken
> Twisted by knaves to make a trap for fools,
> Or watch the things you gave your life to, broken,
> And stoop and build 'em up with worn-out tools:

> If you can make one heap of all your winnings
> And risk it on one turn of pitch-and-toss,
> And lose, and start again at your beginnings
> And never breathe a word about your loss;
> If you can force your heart and nerve and sinew
> To serve your turn long after they are gone,
> And so hold on when there is nothing in you
> Except the Will which says to them: "Hold on!"

If you can talk with crowds and keep your virtue,
Or walk with Kings—nor lose the common touch,
If neither foes nor loving friends can hurt you,
If all men count with you, but none too much;
If you can fill the unforgiving minute
With sixty seconds' worth of distance run,
Yours is the Earth and everything that's in it,
And—which is more—you'll be a Man, my son!

As soon as you find you can do anything, do something you can't.

**LABABIDI, YAHIA** (Egypt, 1973– ) Lababidi, born in Cairo to Egyptian and Lebanese parents, describes his aphorisms as "the biography of my mental, spiritual, and emotional life." He started work on that biography as a teenager, after reading the aphoristic prose and bons mots of Friedrich Nietzsche and Oscar Wilde. He then moved on to existentialist authors like Franz Kafka, Søren Kierkegaard, and Blaise Pascal.

*Essential Aphorisms*

The thoughts we choose to act upon define us to others, the ones we do not define us to ourselves.

Impulses we attempt to strangle only develop stronger muscles.

Temptation: seeds we are forbidden to water, that are showered with rain.

A good listener helps us overhear ourselves.

The human animal is best revealed to others in their natural environment, yet best revealed to themselves outside it.

To hurry pain is to leave a classroom still in session. To prolong pain is to remain seated in a vacated classroom and miss the next lesson.

**LANDOR, WALTER SAVAGE** (United Kingdom, 1775–1864) "Savage" was certainly an appropriate middle name for Landor. He was a man of monumental tempers, easily given to apoplexy. He was kicked out of school several times as a youth—once for firing a gun at the home of a man with whom he had a political disagreement—and throughout his life was embroiled in bitter quarrels with family, friends, and fellow men of letters. Fortunately for him, he never needed a job.

He lived comfortably—first in Bath, England, and then in Florence, Italy—off an inheritance from his father. Surprisingly for a man of such towering rages, his aphorisms are not fulminations but sedate ruminations.

## Essential Aphorisms

Of the future we know nothing, of the past little, of the present less; the mirror is too close to our eyes, and our own breath dims it.

Goodness does not more certainly make men happy than happiness makes them good.

There being no pleasure in thinking ill, it is wonderful there should be any in speaking ill.

Everything is every man's over which his senses extend. What you can enjoy is yours; what you cannot, is not.

Superficial men have no absorbing passion: there are no whirlpools in a shallow.

There is often most love where there is the least acquaintance with the object beloved.

The happiest of pillows is not that which love first presses; it is that which Death has frowned on and passed over.

With most men, nothing seems to have happened so long ago as an affair of love.

Absence and death are the same—only that in death there is no suffering.

No thoroughly occupied person was ever found really miserable.

Consult duty not events.

A solitude is the audience-chamber of God.

## Parallel Lines: Roads to Ruin

Thrones are constructed on the petrification of the human heart.

—LANDOR

God builds his temple in the heart on the ruins of churches and religions.

—RALPH WALDO EMERSON

**LEÓN GONZÁLEZ, FRANCISCO** (Mexico, 1954–  ) Born in Mexico City, León González is a professor of classical languages and a translator from Greek and Latin. His aphorisms are tinged with Stoic pessimism.

*Essential Aphorisms*

Truth is a disillusioning illusion.

Nothing is so undesirable that we don't strive to possess it.

A person without fears cannot love anything.

Death is a truism.

**LEOPARDI, GIACOMO** (Italy, 1798–1837) Leopardi had a gift for languages. He once composed a long poem in ancient Greek that many scholars initially mistook for a previously unknown classic. Leopardi fed his love of languages and literature in the library of his father, a minor Italian nobleman who squandered his family's fortune in gambling. Starting in 1817, Leopardi began keeping the journals that contain his aphorisms, literary musings, moral reflections, and philosophical speculations. By the time he died in 1837, the journals, now known as *Pensieri*, consisted of more than 4,500 pages. Leopardi modeled his *Pensieri* on François de la Rochefoucauld's *Maxims*, and the Italian poet's thoughts are every bit as cynical as those of his French predecessor. Leopardi's pessimistic take on life is also similar to that of Arthur Schopenhauer.

*Essential Aphorisms*

Real misanthropes are not found in solitude, but in the world, since it is experience of life, and not philosophy, which produces real hatred of mankind.

Death is not evil, for it frees man from all ills and takes away his desires along with desire's rewards. Old age is the supreme evil, for it deprives man of all pleasures while allowing his appetites to remain, and it brings with it every possible sorrow. Yet men fear death and desire old age.

People are ridiculous only when they try or seem to be that which they are not.

No one is so completely disenchanted with the world, or knows it so thoroughly, or is so utterly disgusted with it, that when it begins to smile upon him he does not become partially reconciled to it.

No human trait deserves less tolerance in everyday life, and gets less, than intolerance.

There are some centuries that—apart from everything else—in the arts and other disciplines presume to remake everything because they know how to make nothing.

**LIEBERT, DANIEL** (United States, 1953–    ) Liebert grew up in St. Louis in what he describes as "a very verbal Jewish family." The table talk of his childhood was filled with proverbial expressions and Yiddishisms, echoes of which can be heard in his own aphorisms. "If grandma had a beard, she'd be grandpa," was an oft-cited explanation for why something happened to be the way that it was. Instead of going to college, Liebert embarked on a Whitmanesque wandering through Europe, Africa, and the Middle East, eventually settling in Cairo for several years during the 1970s. He's been a stand-up comedian and joke writer; now, he writes poems. Liebert came to aphorisms through humor; he once penned the sayings on bumper stickers and buttons for a living. His most famous line: JESUS IS COMING—LOOK BUSY. As a former stand-up comic, Liebert cites Stanislaw Jerzy Lec as his biggest influence. Lec is "the essential bridge between my comic sense and my philosophy," Liebert says.

*Essential Aphorisms*

Our most powerful emotion is indifference.

From fear of being used I become useless.

When lemons rot they become sweet.

Shallowness spreads.

In youth I ordered a feast that I've now no appetite for.

As we get older, truth becomes simpler, doubt more sophisticated.

In the belly of the beast—be indigestible.

The world is a million steps around and just one misstep down.

Those who claw to the top, seldom appreciate the view.

Even "too late" will come at its proper time.

**MACHADO, ANTONIO** (Spain, 1875–1939) Machado placed many of his aphorisms in the notebooks and classroom lectures of an apocryphal professor called Juan de Mairena. Mairena was more than just a pseudonym; Machado created an entire biography for him, including detailed references to completely fictional events, talks, and newspaper articles. After his wife's death in 1912, Machado became something of a recluse. But he made Mairena a busy, outgoing academic intent on popularizing difficult philosophical ideas.

*Essential Aphorisms*

In any duly constituted faculty of theology, a chair of blasphemy—in preparation for the doctorate, of course—would be indispensable; occupied by the Devil himself, if possible.

What is generally known by everybody is the province of nobody.

Those who have nothing to say to any man have nothing to say to mankind; and those who say nothing to mankind have no one to talk to at all.

Avoid pulpits, platforms, stages, and pedestals. Keep to the hard ground; it is the only way you can judge your approximate stature as a man.

In the last analysis, there will always be somebody face to face with a something: a something that seems to have no need of anyone—no one at all.

Walker, there is no path. The path is made by walking.

**MARTIAL** (Rome, c. 40–c. 100) Born in northeastern Spain, not far from present-day Saragossa, Martial went to Rome when he was twenty-four. There he found a sponsor in fellow Spaniard Seneca, who introduced him to the wealthy patrons who later supported Martial's career as a composer of epigrams. During Martial's time, the job of court poet was still a viable and lucrative one. Writers composed occasional verse to be read at dinner parties or during festivals, and in exchange they received cash, gifts, and access to the highest echelons of society. Martial wrote most of his verse to mock his rivals, ridicule his enemies, and wheedle more money from his patrons.

## Essential Aphorisms

You ask me what I get
Out of my country place.
The profit, gross or net,
Is never seeing your face.

Why did you cut out your slave's tongue,
Ponticus, and then have him hung
Crucified? Don't you realize, man,
Though he can't speak, the rest of us can?

Be pleased with what you are, keep hope
Within that self-appointed scope;
Neither uneasily apprehend
Nor morbidly desire the end.

It's easy to despise life when things go wrong:
The true hero endures much, and long.

**NAROSKY, JOSÉ** (Argentina, 1930–  ) In his native Argentina, Narosky is known as "the king of the brief thought." The title is well deserved; he has written more than 14,000 aphorisms and his collections have sold more than two million copies. He also writes poetry and short stories, but he began focusing on aphorisms after the death of a close friend. "My aphorisms are *my* reason," Narosky says, "because I can't make up my mind whether they are *the* reason."

## Essential Aphorisms

Few people die of love. But many of lovelessness.

It's preferable to be the victim rather than the executioner.

Cannibals devour the dead. Wars, the living.

Some people only feel at peace in war.

If it is necessary to kill for an ideal, the ideal dies.

Irony is gloved aggression.

In war, there are no unwounded soldiers.

We protest against unjust criticism, but we accept unearned applause.

**NASH, OGDEN** (United States, 1902–1971) While working as an editor and publicist at a New York City publishing firm, Nash threw his first comic poem—"Spring Comes to Murray Hill"—in the trash. On reflection, he thought better of it, picked it out of the wastepaper basket, and submitted it to the *New Yorker*, which accepted it in 1930—launching Nash's career as the most quoted light versifier of his time.

*Essential Aphorisms*

Candy is dandy
But liquor is quicker.

Purity is obscurity.

People who work sitting down get paid more than people who work
standing up.

Man is a victim of dope
In the incurable form of hope.

To keep your marriage brimming,
With love in the loving cup,
Whenever you're wrong, admit it;
Whenever you're right, shut up.

Oh, what a tangled web do parents weave
When they think that their children are naive.

The door of a bigoted mind opens outward so that the only result of the
pressure of facts upon it is to close it more snugly.

There is only one way to achieve happiness
On this terrestrial ball

And that is to have either a clear conscience
Or none at all.

**NOVALIS** (Germany, 1772–1801) Friedrich von Hardenberg took the pseudonym Novalis from "de Novali," one of his family's ancestral names. In the early 1790s, he studied law at the University of Jena, where he met Friedrich von Schlegel. Schlegel published Novalis's aphorisms in the *Athenaeum*, the literary journal he founded with his brother August Wilhelm. Schlegel and Novalis were fervent believers in the fragment as the highest form of literary art. They believed that fragmented philosophizing more accurately reflected the shifting, scattershot nature of thinking—and the experience of life itself. Like so many romantic poets, Novalis died of tuberculosis.

## Essential Aphorisms

Philosophy, too, has its blossoms. They are the thoughts we don't know whether to call beautiful or comical.

Every beloved object is the center of a paradise.

Humanity is a humorous role.

Where there are children, there is a golden age.

Nothing is more refreshing than to talk about our wishes when they are already coming true.

Every specific fact is a source for a special science.

Language is for philosophy what it is for music and painting, not the right medium for description.

The true poet is omniscient; he is a real world in miniature.

**PARKER, DOROTHY** (United States, 1893–1967) From 1919 to 1932, some of America's most famous men and women of letters met regularly for lunch at the Algonquin Hotel in New York City. This coterie of wags and wits consisted of playwrights George S. Kaufman and Robert Sherwood, columnists Franklin Pierce Adams and Heywood Broun, and authors Robert Benchley, Ring Lardner, and Edna Ferber, among others. Occasionally, people like Harold Ross of the *New Yorker*, Hollywood producer Herman Mankiewicz, and Harpo Marx would drop by. The critic and gourmand Alexander Woollcott was the group's founder and presiding genius. The gang's long, drunken lunches became such a fixture that the hotel's owner installed a large round table in the Rose Room specifically for their use. Soon, this loose collection of colleagues, friends, and rivals became known as the Algonquin Round Table. In their heyday in the early 1920s, they were among New York's biggest celebrities, filling the gossip columns with their barbed bons mots. Parker, who worked as a journalist for *Vanity Fair* and *Vogue*, was the wittiest of the bunch, notorious for the acidity of her wisecracks and ripostes. Parker's verse is just as filled with bile and derision as Martial's, with her own added touch of fatalistic philosophy.

*Essential Aphorisms*

Men seldom make passes
At girls who wear glasses.

Every love's the love before
In a duller dress.
That's the measure of my lore—
Here's my bitterness:
Would I knew a little more,
Or very much less!

Should they whisper false of you,
Never trouble to deny;
Should the words they say be true,
Weep and storm and say they lie.

My land is bare of chattering folk;
The clouds are low along the ridges,
And sweet's the air with curly smoke
From all my burning bridges.

**PATERSON, DON** (Scotland, 1963–   ) Paterson is a Scottish poet, playwright, and jazz guitarist. He describes the aphorism as "a *brief* waste of time." But other literary forms fare even worse, in his view. Paterson defines the poem as "a *complete* waste of time" and the novel as "a *monumental* waste of time." Like E. M. Cioran, Paterson tends toward the *pensée*, a languid meditation, with a strong inflection of Buddhism. In his collection of aphorisms, *The Book of Shadows*, Paterson himself acknowledges the resemblance: "Sometimes I am aware of just wittering on in Cioran's name, his shade, like those talentless spirit-channels of Chopin and Liszt."

## Essential Aphorisms

We lie down because the length of our shadows becomes intolerable.

We turn from the light to see.

Gravity fluctuates.

Less is pretty much the same.

Hell is an enforced solitude, heaven a voluntary one.

A book of aphorisms is a lexicon of disappointments.

**PÉGUY, CHARLES** (France, 1873–1914) In 1900, Péguy founded *Cahiers de la Quinzaine*, a fortnightly political and literary journal that he edited until his death and in which many of his own poems and aphorisms first appeared. Péguy was an ardent socialist, so the review did not accept advertising. Subscriptions were priced according to the subscriber's ability to pay. Péguy's editorial policy was simple—"A review only continues to have life if each issue annoys at least one fifth of its readers"—but, he added, it must not always be the same fifth that is offended. He died during World War I after being shot in the head in battle.

## Essential Aphorisms

One is never unwillingly ordered around. When one is ordered around, it is always willingly.

Those who increase their stature in the world by debasing the world do not rise.

Surrender is essentially an operation by means of which we set about explaining instead of acting.

He who does not bellow the truth when he knows the truth makes himself the accomplice of liars and forgers.

Tyranny is always better organized than freedom.

We must always tell what we see. Above all, and this is more difficult, we must always see what we see.

There is nothing so unforeseen as an event.

Everything begins in mysticism and ends in politics.

**PESSÕA, FERNANDO** (Portugal, 1888–1935) In the preface to *The Book of Disquietude*, a collection of aphorisms and ruminations, Pessõa describes how he met Bernardo Soares in a Lisbon restaurant. The two men were regulars there for years, but they only struck up a friendship after witnessing a fistfight in the street. Soares, a loner with no family or friends, left the manuscript of *The Book of Disquietude* in Pessõa's care after his death. And that is how, Pessõa tells us, it eventually came to be published. But Soares did not exist; he was one of Pessõa's many heteronyms, literary alter egos, to whom the Portuguese poet ascribed his works. Pessõa had more than seventy heteronyms, including Álvaro Campos (an engineer), Ricardo Reis (a physician), and Alberto Caeiro (a shepherd). "Be plural like the universe," he once wrote. Pessõa began inventing these fictional characters as a boy, when he composed regular letters to an imaginary friend he called Le Chevalier de Pas. Pessõa's own life was as solitary as that of Soares. He lived alone, had few friends, and worked as a commercial translator while he wrote his distinctively modernist poetry. After his death, a trunk was discovered with 27,543 individual documents inside it, among which was the manuscript of *The Book of Disquietude* as well as works by Pessõa's other heteronyms. In Portuguese, the name Pessõa means "person" or "persona." Pessõa and his contemporary Antonio Machado were both recluses who created elaborate biographies for their heteronyms. Søren Kierkegaard also ascribed some of his philosophical works to heteronyms.

*Essential Aphorisms*

To give good advice is to insult the faculty of erring that God gave to others.

Nature is the difference between the soul and God.

Some have a great dream in life and fall short of it. Others have no dream, and also fall short of it.

Never read a book to the end, nor even in sequence and without skipping.

To need to dominate others is to need others. The man in charge is dependent.

Life is the hesitation between an exclamation and a question. Doubt is resolved by a period.

Live your life. Don't be lived by it.

We never know self-realization. We are two abysses—a well staring at the Sky.

**PUSHKIN, ALEXANDER** (Russia, 1799–1837) From the time he published his first poem at the age of fifteen, Pushkin was a figure of controversy. His work made waves because of its style (he was the first to introduce everyday language into Russian verse) and its substance (Pushkin was sympathetic to Russia's liberal reformers who wanted more human rights and representative government). Pushkin's radical sympathies led to his periodic exile from Moscow, where he had become the country's leading literary celebrity. In December 1825, the autocratic Tsar Nicholas I put down the Decembrist Uprising, a revolt by a group of reform-minded officers. Pushkin's poems were found among the rebels' papers, leading to another spell in exile and a publication ban. The next year Pushkin successfully petitioned Nicholas I for his release from exile. Though his freedom to publish was still severely curtailed, he resumed his literary life and became a minor functionary at the tsar's Moscow court. In 1837, Pushkin challenged his wife's lover, Georges d'Anthès, to a duel. He was fatally wounded. His last words to his wife are said to have been: "Try to be forgotten. Go live in the country. Stay in mourning for two years, then remarry, but choose somebody decent."

## Essential Aphorisms

But sad to feel, when youth has left us,
That it was given us in vain,
That its unnoticed flight bereft us
And brought no harvest in its train.

Where Love is, Satan likes to play.

O idle seeker, phantom-breeder,
Lest thwarted ever be your quest,
Love your own self, I would suggest,
Respected and deserving reader!
A worthy object: surely none
Could possibly be greater fun.

What foes he had, what friends he had
(Same thing, perhaps, on close inspection.)

Habit is Heaven's own redress;
It takes the place of happiness.

Friends are made (I'm guilty, too)
For lack of something else to do.

Constant inconstancy turns dreary.

One can be capable and moral
With manicure upon one's mind:
Why vainly chide one's age and quarrel?
Custom is lord of all mankind.

He who has lived and thought can never
Look on mankind without disdain;
He who has felt is haunted ever
By days that will not come again.

The illusion that exalts us is dearer to us than ten thousand truths.

**QUEVEDO, FRANCISCO DE** (Spain, 1580–1645) Quevedo was a poet, duelist, and spy. He's considered the greatest poet of Spain's Golden Age, despite the fact that only a handful of his verses were published in his lifetime. He was also known as something of a lady's man, sporting fashionable pince-nez spectacles and flashing his accomplished swordsmanship. In his spare time, he tried and failed to help the Spanish duke Pedro Téllez-Girón bring down the republican government of Venice.

*Essential Aphorisms*

Deceit, the natural disease of lovers and the ambitious.

Where there is little justice, it is dangerous to be right.

A woman's caress is no less dangerous a weapon than a man's sword.

Fortune rarely turns its back on the prudent.

For our covetousness, much is little; for our neediness, little is much.

When there is less fear, there is less danger.

Only he who commands with love is served with fidelity. .

Patriotism always harms the individual.

**RICHARDSON, JAMES** (United States, 1950–  ) Back in 1993, Richardson was reading Michel de Montaigne as part of his research for an essay-in-progress. A footnote referred him to François de la Rochefoucauld's *Maxims*, an encounter that both delighted and provoked him. Soon he began scribbling ripostes and revisions to La Rochefoucauld's cynical sayings—and thus his affection for aphorisms was born. Richardson calls his maxims "literary Doritos, a vaguely guilty pleasure, like playing video games or eating corn chips." He likens aphorisms to wisecracks: "They give you the turn without the long straightaway, the takeoff without the mile of runway." Richardson shares a mystical streak with Antonio Porchia. Both men chronicle their spirituality through small domestic natural wonders. And both men's aphorisms have the knack of revealing the marvelous in the mundane. Richardson's sayings, published in his books of poetry, can also often be read as compact morality tales, like those of Marie von Ebner-Eschenbach.

### Essential Aphorisms

Growth is barely controlled damage.

Priceless things cannot be bought, though they are often sold.

Water deepens where it has to wait.

Some things, like faith, cheer, courage, you can give when you do not have them.

The best disguise is the one everyone else is wearing.

The knife disappears with sharpening.

You can't smell what the guests smell.

There is no misstep till you put your foot down.

The worst helplessness is forgetting there is help.

Patience is not very different from courage. It just takes longer.

Easier to keep changing your life than to live it.

Fewer regret wasting a year than never having wasted one.

The man who sticks to his plan will become what he used to want to be.

We like believing the best because nothing needs to be done about it, and the worst, because nothing can.

### Parallel Lines: On The Road, II

The ruts are deepest in the middle of the road.  —RICHARDSON

A man who is determined never to move out of the beaten road cannot lose his way.  —WILLIAM HAZLITT

Do not go where the path may lead, go instead where there is no path and leave a trail.  —RALPH WALDO EMERSON

If you walk down a well-trodden path long enough, you will eventually end up alone.  —MARIE VON EBNER-ESCHENBACH

You won't skid if you stay in a rut.  —FRANK MCKINNEY HUBBARD

They will say you are on the wrong road, if it is your own.
  —ANTONIO PORCHIA

**ROBINSON, PETER** (United Kingdom, 1953– ) Robinson did not begin writing aphorisms until the late 1990s. Part of the motivation to take up the form may have been a by-product of teaching in English at a Japanese university. "Because of the students' difficulties with listening composition, it had been my practice to formulate ideas in short, simple sentences that could be copied from the blackboard," Robinson says. "Naturally, these sentences did not tend to include puns or joking paradoxes, but this takeoff into aphoristic form might explain how these jottings started to come and then accelerated so unexpectedly."

*Essential Aphorisms*

People who always expect the worst can get a reputation for sagacity without having any real foresight: the odds are in their favor. Yet all life's important decisions are bets against the odds.

The point of no return is precisely the place from which you will have to find a way home.

In poetry the best way to fly is to be well grounded.

Understanding ourselves is like reaching an itch in the small of the back—more easily done with the help of someone else.

Death, after all, is not the end of the world.

A politically correct culture is an imitation fur coat—inhabited by real fleas.

**ROY, CLAUDE** (France, 1915–1997) During World War II, Roy was captured by the Germans but managed to escape. He joined the French resistance and, in 1943, the Communist Party. But like so many other postwar European intellectuals, he turned against communism when he actually saw its effects in Russia and China. In addition to poems and novels, he also wrote a series of what he called "log books" that recorded his aphorisms and observations.

*Essential Aphorisms*

To prepare yourself so well to die one day that you forget to live.

You are always somebody's fool. You get a head start being the first to laugh at yourself.

Acknowledgment provides the illusion of knowing yourself.

Even if our choices aren't free, we aren't free not to choose.

Lying is sometimes restful, but lying to yourself is tiring.

The danger of happiness is the same as that of unhappiness: to believe it is deserved.

**RUSTAVELI, SHOTA** (Georgia, c. twelfth century) The name Rustaveli means "the man from Rustavi," referring to a city in southern Georgia. Rustaveli is the author of *The Knight in the Panther's Skin*, a tale of love, heroism, and war that is sprinkled with aphorisms about fate and love. The epic is Georgia's official national poem and one of the centerpieces of medieval literature.

*Essential Aphorisms*

Spending on feasting and wine is better than hoarding our substance. That which we give makes us richer, that which is hoarded is lost.

What you've hidden is lost. What you've given away is all yours.

Since God forgives the sinner, be you also merciful to him whose might is brought to nought.

Each imagines himself the strategist as he observes the battle from the sidelines.

**SAAVEDRA WEISE, CARLOS** (Bolivia, 1945–   ) When he's not writing aphorisms, Saavedra Weise is a dentist in Bolivia, specializing in oral and maxillofacial surgery. When friends ask why write a book of aphorisms, he simply says, "It is a way of expressing myself, of feeling the human condition that surrounds me."

*Essential Aphorisms*

Life is crueler than death.

Solitude is a perfect vice.

A single line can contain many lives.

In the forest of the imagination, illusions get lost.

Being mortal implies a cruel compromise.

Human life is an unfinished round-trip.

**SABA, UMBERTO** (Italy, 1883–1957) Umberto Poli adopted the pseudonym Umberto Saba for his first book of poetry, published in 1911. In 1919, he opened the Ancient and Modern Bookstore in his hometown of Trieste and ran it—except during World War II, when his Jewish ancestry forced him to go into hiding from the Nazis—for the rest of his life.

## Essential Aphorisms

I have nothing to say to philosophers; they have nothing to say to me. As I approach them they turn fluid, expand to the universal so as not to be touched on a single nerve. All their systems are "patches" to hide a "puncture in reality." Poets promise less and keep more.

Chance doesn't exist; the famous roof-slate on the head does not exist. There are connections—and decisions that make themselves—that we don't know.

"Daddy," said one little girl to another, "is a child with lots of means at his disposal."

Facts exist in advance. We discover them by living them.

**SCHRÖDER, RUDOLF A.** (Germany, 1878–1962) A deeply religious man, Schröder was a successful architect before becoming a writer. He spent the Nazi period and World War II in Germany in relative obscurity, but in 1950 one of his poems, "Hymn to Germany," was unsuccessfully put forward as an alternative to "*Deutschland, Deutschland Über Alles*" as the country's national anthem.

## Essential Aphorisms

Man would devour the stars if only he could.

Psychology is philosophy after the Fall.

There is only one antidote to all the poison in the world: Faith.

Too close an understanding of sin is one of the greatest dangers for moral life.

When God says, "Your sins have been forgiven," he issues a death sentence.

Courage and innocence, fear and guilt are siblings. The most tender combination of courage and guilt is valor, the most violent is temerity, the most degenerate is effrontery.

A balled fist cannot accept a gift.

It's terrible how insolubly everything is entwined and entangled. We are serpent, fish, insect, worm, plant all in one!

**SEUSS, DR.** (United States, 1904–1991) Theodor Seuss Geisel, better known as Dr. Seuss, enjoyed a successful career in advertising before becoming a children's author. In the 1930s, his campaign for the manufacturer of a pesticide called Flit was a huge hit. He produced a series of amusing cartoons that featured a suburban couple who fearlessly dispatched swarms of pesky insects with a squirt from their trusty can of Flit. As a result, "Quick, Henry, the Flit" briefly entered the lexicon of American catchphrases. When he started writing books, Dr. Seuss (Seuss was his mother's maiden name) merged the techniques of the aphorism and advertising—arresting images combined with fresh, unforgettable jingles.

*Essential Aphorisms*

It's a troublesome world. All the people who're in it
Are troubled with troubles almost every minute.
You ought to be thankful, a whole heaping lot,
For the places and people you're lucky you're not.

You have brains in your head.
You have feet in your shoes.
You can steer yourself
Any direction you choose.

You're off to Great Places!
Today is your day!
Your mountain is waiting.
So . . . get on your way!

From there to here,
From here to there,
Funny things are everywhere.

**SIDNEY, SIR PHILIP** (United Kingdom, 1554–1586) Sidney was known more as a soldier than as a poet in his own day; none of his poems was published during his lifetime. He was, however, the first person to write a sonnet sequence in English. He was also a well-traveled and highly cultured aristocrat, the ideal English courtier. During the battle of Zutphen in the Netherlands, Sidney was shot in the thigh. He died from the wound three weeks later. As he lay dying, Sidney is reported to have given his water bottle to another wounded soldier, saying, "Thy need is greater than mine." In "The Defence of Poesie," Sidney defines poetry as an art of imitation: "a representing, counterfeiting, or figuring forth—so to speak metaphorically, a speaking picture—with this end, to teach and delight." Sidney derived this theory in part from the dramatic maxims of Horace, who believed that every play should instruct and entertain: "Mix pleasure and profit, and you are safe."

## Essential Aphorisms

Great is not great to the greater.

Remember, that in all miseries, lamenting becomes fools, and action, wise folk.

A noble heart, like the sun, showeth its greatest countenance in its lowest estate.

Whosoever in great things will think to prevent all objections must be still and do nothing.

The fall is greater from the first rank to the second, than from the second to the undermost.

Who only sees ill is worse than blind.

Who will adhere to him that abandons himself!

Commonly they use their feet for defense, whose tongue is their weapon.

**SPAZIANI, MARIA LUISA** (Italy, 1924–  ) In 1943, at the age of nineteen, Spaziani founded the literary journal *Il Dado*. In addition to writing poetry, she has translated dramatists such as Racine and Shakespeare into Italian.

## Essential Aphorisms

Too many hammers for very few nails.

Success when old: the climb up downhill.

Indispensable men are decidedly unbearable.

You have to feel like a free woman, somebody told me. I give you permission.

You're marrying him for sexual attraction? Do you want to build a house by starting from the roof?

If you've stuck a knife into someone's back, have the good taste not to report him to the police for unlawful possession of a weapon.

**STEVENS, WALLACE** (United States, 1879–1955) Stevens was a businessman all his life. After working for several New York law firms in the early 1900s, he became a lawyer for various insurance companies based in New York City. In 1916, he moved to Hartford, Connecticut, to join the Hartford Accident and Indemnity Company. In 1934, he was named vice president of the firm. Throughout his life, he composed poems on his way to and from the office. Florence Berkman, a Hartford neighbor, remembered him taking his walks like clockwork every morning. "If it was summer or good weather, I'd be outdoors with some of the neighbors' children," she recalled in *Parts of a World: Wallace Stevens Remembered*. "I'd make them stop and look at him, and I'd say, 'I want you to remember this is a great poet.'"

*Essential Aphorisms*

Poetry is a pheasant disappearing in the brush.

The tongue is an eye.

The poet makes silk dresses out of worms.

After one has abandoned a belief in god, poetry is that essence which takes its place as life's redemption.

Accuracy of observation is the equivalent of accuracy of thinking.

A poem is a meteor.

An evening's thought is like a day of clear weather.

There is nothing in life except what one thinks of it.

Sentimentality is a failure of feeling.

To read a poem should be an experience, like experiencing an act.

Money is a kind of poetry.

The death of one god is the death of all.

It is necessary to any originality to have the courage to be an amateur.

Metaphor creates a new reality from which the original appears to be unreal.

The poet comes to words as nature comes to dry sticks.

Loss of faith is growth.

To be at the end of fact is not to be at the beginning of imagination but it is to be at the end of both.

Poetry is a response to the daily necessity of getting the world right.

### Parallel Lines: Cliché

Reality is a cliché from which we escape by metaphor.        —STEVENS

Beauty is a brief gasp between one cliché and another.        —EZRA POUND

**TAGORE, RABINDRANATH** (Bangladesh, 1861–1941) Tagore was both precocious and prolific. He started writing poems when he was eight; by the time he was sixteen, he had published poetry, dramas, and short stories. He was also a visual artist, musician, and songwriter. His compositions serve as the national anthems of both India and his native Bangladesh. Like Gandhi, whom he befriended and supported in the campaign for Indian independence, Tagore went to England to study law. But he ended up pursuing a career as an artist instead. His writing first came to prominence in the West in 1912, when he returned to England, this time with a collection of his works translated into English. William Butler Yeats and Ezra Pound were among his boosters. Tagore's artistic and political views (he was a fierce opponent of Indian nationalism) won him enemies as well as friends. After a failed assassination attempt against him, he decided to found his own school where students and teachers could live in a self-sustaining community and provide a "connecting thread between India and the world." The school, called Visva-Bharati, is now part of India's university system.

*Essential Aphorisms*

It is the tears of the earth that keep her smiles in bloom.

Do not seat your love upon a precipice because it is high.

What you are you do not see, what you see is your shadow.

The dry riverbed finds no thanks for its past.

We read the world wrong and say that it deceives us.

Every child comes with the message that God is not yet discouraged of man.

In death the many becomes one; in life the one becomes many. Religion will be one when God is dead.

The scabbard is content to be dull when it protects the keenness of the sword.

Man goes into the noisy crowd to drown his own clamor of silence.

Truth in her dress finds facts too tight. In fiction she moves with ease.

Kicks only raise dust and not crops from the earth.

We live in this world when we love it.

**TAYLOR, HENRY** (United Kingdom, 1800–1886) Taylor was a poet and playwright, a friend of William Wordsworth, and, for almost fifty years, a British civil servant. His essay *The Statesman* satirizes those whose vocation is government service.

*Essential Aphorisms*

Shy and unready men are great betrayers of secrets; for there are few wants more urgent for the moment than the want of something to say.

The hope, and not the fact, of advancement is the spur to industry.

The world knows nothing of its greatest men.

Conscience is, in most men, an anticipation of the opinion of others.

The world will commonly end by making men that which it thinks them.

One who would thrive by seeking favors from the great should never trouble them for small ones.

An imaginative man is apt to see, in his life, the story of his life; and is thereby led to conduct himself in life in such a manner as to make a good story rather than a good life.

It sometimes happens that he who would not hurt a fly will hurt a nation.

**THEOGNIS OF MEGARA** (Greece, c. sixth century BCE) The 1,400 lines of poetry attributed to Theognis are collectively known as the "Theognidea." Many of the poems are addressed to Cyrnus, Theognis's young pupil and lover, to whom he tries to impart some of his wisdom of life.

*Essential Aphorisms*

One finds many companions for food and drink, but in a serious business a man's companions are very few.

Surfeit begets insolence, when prosperity comes to a bad man.

Adopt the character of the twisting octopus, which takes on the appearance of the nearby rock. Now follow in this direction, now turn a different hue.

Bright youth passes swiftly as a thought.

**VALÉRY, PAUL** (France, 1871–1945) Every morning just before dawn, in what Valéry described as that "pure and pregnant hour of daybreak," the French poet and essayist woke up and jotted down in his notebook anything and everything that came into his mind. Valéry believed that the creative process, the actual act of writing, was the most important thing, not the final product. "Nothing gives more boldness to the pen than the feeling that one can defer ad infinitum the time of recasting a phrase in its final form," he wrote. These notebooks contain Valéry's best aphorisms on mathematics, science, history, morality, and the art of poetry and thinking. Valéry shared Johann Wolfgang von Goethe's fascination with science, and like Goethe devoted much of his aphoristic writing to explorations of art and poetry.

*Essential Aphorisms*

The greatness of poets is that they grasp with their words what they only glimpse with their minds.

For a poet, it is never a matter of saying *it is raining*. It's a matter of . . . making rain.

Poetry aims to *express* by means of language precisely that which language is powerless to express.

Nothing is more "original," nothing more "oneself " than to feed on others. But one has to digest them. A lion is made of assimilated sheep.

We should be light as a bird, not as a feather.

One never finishes a work of art; one abandons it.

Man preens himself on his strokes of luck.

A very dangerous state of mind: thinking one understands.

Every man has his back to his death, like the talker leaning against the mantelpiece.

One should, after a fashion, welcome and esteem the difficulties one encounters. A difficulty is a lamp. An insuperable difficulty, a sun.

The brain is a place in which the Universe pricks and pinches itself so as to make sure it exists.

Man is absurd in what he seeks, great through what he finds.

God created man and, finding that he was not lonely enough, gave him a wife, so as to make him feel his solitude more keenly.

Growing old means experiencing the alterations of the permanent.

All we should ask of Heaven is euphoria, and an ability to make the most of it.

What's best in the new is what answers to an old desire.

Politics is the art of preventing people from minding their own business.

Beware of what you do best; it's bound to be a trap.

Consciousness abhors a vacuum.

Sometimes it is stupidity—but sometimes it is strength of mind—that makes one refuse to accept the facts.

Optimists write badly.

Eternity is a hobby for people who have time to burn; a form of leisure.

What resembles nothing does not exist.

A painter should not paint what he sees, but what will be seen.

### *Parallel Lines: Blame the Weather*

A cyclone can raze a city, yet not even open a letter or untie the knot in this piece of string.                                    —VALÉRY

A tornado can't stack two dimes.                                    —JAMES RICHARDSON

# PHILOSOPHERS AND THEORISTS

**T**HE first step toward philosophy," Denis Diderot wrote, "is incredulity." One of the distinguishing characteristics of aphorisms is that they sow doubt rather than certainty. In the nineteenth century, potassium bromide was used as a sedative; literary bromides still have the same effect. The word *nostrums* originally described medicines prescribed by a quack; literary nostrums are still peddled by psychic snake-oil salesmen. Platitudes of all kinds are merely placebos for the mind; aphorisms are defibrillators for the brain. Philosophers and theorists administer the electric shock.

**ADORNO, THEODOR** (Germany, 1903–1969) Adorno was one of the earliest critics of what's come to be known—largely thanks to him—as the "culture industry." He and other members of the Frankfurt School, a group of German thinkers critical of capitalism, believed pop culture anaesthetized the population, allowing governments and corporations to manipulate behavior. Adorno also saw mass entertainment as a danger to the "higher" arts, such as literature and music, which he thought were the only true sources of freedom and happiness. Ironically, his most famous saying is not actually an aphorism: "After Auschwitz, to write a poem is barbaric." Adorno collaborated closely with Walter Benjamin and Herbert Marcuse, the other aphorists of the Frankfurt School. During the time he lived in Vienna, Adorno enthusiastically attended the lectures of Viennese aphorist Karl Kraus, also a virulent critic of consumer culture.

*Essential Aphorisms*

The whole is the false.

The almost insoluble task is to let neither the power of others, nor our own powerlessness, stupefy us.

He who offers for sale something unique that no one wants to buy, represents, even against his will, freedom from exchange.

People know what they want because they know what other people want.

Every work of art is an uncommitted crime.

Love is the power to see similarity in the dissimilar.

True thoughts are those alone which do not understand themselves.

Love you will find only where you may show yourself weak without provoking strength.

Artistic productivity is the capacity for being voluntarily involuntary.

Art is magic delivered from the lie of being truth.

The comfort that flows from great works of art lies less in what they express than in the fact that they have managed to struggle out of existence. Hope is soonest found among the comfortless.

The splinter in your eye is the best magnifying glass.

**AMIEL, HENRI FRÉDÉRIC** (Switzerland, 1821–1881) Despite holding a series of prominent academic posts in Geneva, Amiel was largely unknown as an author during his lifetime. His writing gained widespread recognition only with the posthumous publication of the *Journal Intime*, a record of his life and thoughts that he kept from 1847 until his death.

*Essential Aphorisms*

Spite is anger which is afraid to show itself, it is an impotent fury conscious of its impotence.

To shun one's cross is to make it heavier.

Great men are true men, the men in whom nature has succeeded. They are not extraordinary—they are in the true order. It is the other species of men who are not what they ought to be.

An error is the more dangerous in proportion to the degree of truth which it contains.

A man must be able to cut a knot, for everything cannot be untied; he must know how to disengage what is essential from the detail in which it is enwrapped, for not everything can be equally considered; in a word, he must be able to simplify his duties, his business, and his life.

It is by teaching that we teach ourselves, by relating that we observe, by affirming that we examine, by showing that we look, by writing that we think, by pumping that we draw water into the well.

The fire which enlightens is the same fire which consumes.

The man who insists upon seeing with perfect clearness before he decides, never decides. Accept life, and you must accept regret.

We are never more discontented with others than when we are discontented with ourselves.

We only understand that which is already within us.

Let mystery have its place in you; do not be always turning up your whole soil with the plowshare of self-examination, but leave a little fallow corner in your heart ready for any seed the winds may bring.

Destiny has two ways of crushing us—by refusing our wishes and by fulfilling them.

Work while you have the light. You are responsible for the talent that has been entrusted to you.

In the conduct of life, habits count for more than maxims, because habit is a living maxim, become flesh and instinct. To reform one's maxims is nothing: it is but to change the title of the book. To learn new habits is everything, for it is to reach the substance of life. Life is but a tissue of habits.

## Parallel Lines: Charm

Charm is the quality in others that makes us more satisfied with ourselves.

—AMIEL

You know what charm is: a way of getting the answer yes without having asked any clear question.                                                                    —ALBERT CAMUS

**ARENDT, HANNAH** (Germany, 1906–1975) Arendt, the daughter of secular German Jews, fled Germany in the 1930s as the Nazis came to power. She eventually immigrated to the United States, becoming an American citizen in 1950. In the early 1960s, she covered the trial of Nazi war criminal Adolf Eichmann for the *New Yorker*, and she later published *Eichmann in Jerusalem: A Report on the Banality of Evil*, an exploration of the nature of evil.

*Essential Aphorisms*

There are no dangerous thoughts; thinking itself is dangerous.

Man cannot be free if he does not know that he is subject to necessity, because his freedom is always won in his never wholly successful attempts to liberate himself from necessity.

Forgiveness is the key to action and freedom.

Storytelling reveals meaning without committing the error of defining it.

The most radical revolutionary will become a conservative the day after the revolution.

This is the precept by which I have lived: Prepare for the worst; expect the best; and take what comes.

**ARISTOTLE** (Greece, 384–322 BCE) When teaching at the Lyceum, the school he founded in Athens, Aristotle was in the habit of pacing up and down as he talked, a practice that led to his followers being dubbed *peripatetics*, or "those who walk about." After Aristotle's death, his writings went on something of a walkabout themselves. The collected works were entrusted to the care of Theophrastus, a former student, who in turn passed them on to Neleus, one of his own pupils. When Neleus died, one of his heirs stashed the manuscripts in a vault, apparently to keep them safe from theft. He chose a very effective hiding place, because there the books lay for several generations, completely forgotten until about 100 BCE, when a wealthy book collector happened to discover them and took them back to Athens.

*Essential Aphorisms*

He who has overcome his fears will truly be free.

A likely impossibility is always preferable to an unconvincing possibility.

Inferiors revolt in order that they may be equal; equals revolt that they may be superior.

He who is unable to live in society, or who has no need because he is sufficient for himself, must be either a beast or a god.

We are what we repeatedly do. Excellence, then, is not an act, but a habit.

Humor is the only test of gravity, and gravity of humor; for a subject which will not bear raillery is suspicious, and a jest which will not bear serious examination is false wit.

It is the mark of an educated mind to be able to entertain a thought without accepting it.

The worst form of inequality is to try to make unequal things equal.

To perceive is to suffer.

What it lies in our power to do, it lies in our power not to do.

We live in deeds, not years; in thoughts, not breaths; in feelings, not in figures on a dial. We should count time by heartthrobs. He most lives who thinks most, feels the noblest, acts the best.

It is best to rise from life as from a banquet, neither thirsty nor drunken.

*Parallel Lines: Friends I*

A friend is a second self.                                    —ARISTOTLE

A faithful friend is the medicine of life.              —ECCLESIASTICUS

He who wants more than one friend deserves none.

—CHRISTIAN FRIEDRICH HEBBEL

I destroy my enemies when I make them my friends.

—ABRAHAM LINCOLN

The only reward of virtue is virtue; the only way to have a friend is to
be one.                                    —RALPH WALDO EMERSON

He will never have true friends who is afraid of making enemies.

—WILLIAM HAZLITT

A true friend contributes more to our happiness than a thousand enemies
to our unhappiness.            —MARIE VON EBNER-ESCHENBACH

Your friend is your needs answered.            —KAHLIL GIBRAN

**BENJAMIN, WALTER** (Germany, 1892–1940) Benjamin, whose writing covers
everything from the theory of language to Jewish mysticism, was part of the
Frankfurt School, along with Theodor Adorno and Hannah Arendt. He was close
to playwright Bertolt Brecht and was an acquaintance of both Karl Kraus and
Hugo von Hofmannsthal. Benjamin's father even claimed to be distantly related
to the poet-aphorist Heinrich Heine. Benjamin apparently committed suicide in
the town of Portbou on the Spanish-French border while trying to escape the
Nazis. The group Benjamin was traveling with was denied passage into Spain,
and he may have killed himself to avoid being sent to a concentration camp. The
next day, however, the party was allowed to proceed. Hannah Arendt escaped the
Nazis through Portbou just a few months later.

*Essential Aphorisms*

Opinions are to the vast apparatus of social existence what oil is to
machines: one does not go up to a turbine and pour machine oil all over it;
one applies a little to hidden spindles and joints that one has to know.

To convince is to conquer without conception.

These are the days when no one should rely unduly on his
"competence." Strength lies in improvisation. All the decisive
blows are struck left-handed.

Work on good prose has three steps: a musical stage when it is composed, an architectonic one when it is built, and a textile one when it is woven.

Speech conquers thought but writing commands it.

The work is the death mask of its conception.

To be happy is to be able to become aware of oneself without fright.

Counsel woven into the fabric of real life is wisdom.

## Parallel Lines: Writing Books

Of all the ways of acquiring books, writing them oneself is regarded as the most praiseworthy method . . . Writers are really people who write books not because they are poor, but because they are dissatisfied with the books which they could buy but do not like.    —BENJAMIN

When I want to read a book, I write one.    —BENJAMIN DISRAELI

**BRADLEY, FRANCIS HERBERT** (United Kingdom, 1846–1924) In 1870, Bradley secured for himself what has to be one of the best jobs in the world: fellow at Merton College Oxford, with tenure for life and no requirement to teach. Bradley, a reclusive, mysterious figure, remained a bachelor all of his life. One neighbor, who lived near Bradley for sixteen years, claimed never to have laid eyes on him. Born in Clapham, which was then in the countryside and is now part of south London, Bradley was part of a group known as the British Idealists, philosophers who argued that reality consists of a single, all-encompassing absolute and that there is ultimately no distinction between a thought and its object. Bradley's father, an Evangelical preacher, apparently passed on an interest in mysticism to his son. Bradley's own work is striking for its relentless use of reason to prove what is essentially a mystical feature of many religions: that what we call reality is an ineffable, inexpressible unity that transcends our everyday notions of the world.

## Essential Aphorisms

Unhappy those who seek to revive the intoxication and who cannot renew the mystery.

We begin by trying to alter the faults of those about us, we go on to make the best of them, and perhaps end by loving them.

One said of suicide, "As long as one has brains one should not blow them out." And another answered, "But when one has ceased to have them, too often one cannot."

"Experience," said one, "is the worst of illusions. It has taught me to know, but has not taught me how to avoid."

The force of the blow depends on the resistance. It is sometimes better not to struggle against temptation. Either fly or yield at once.

One was asked, "What is Hell?" And he answered, "It is Heaven—that has come too late."

### Parallel Lines: New Love

One cannot remain in love unless perpetually one falls in love anew.

—BRADLEY

He who is in love is wise and is becoming wiser, sees newly every time he looks at the object beloved, drawing from it with his eyes and his mind those virtues which it possesses.        —RALPH WALDO EMERSON

**CAMUS, ALBERT** (France, 1913–1960) On December 15, 1941, Camus witnessed the execution by the Nazis of Gabriel Péri, a communist member of the French National Assembly and an outspoken opponent of fascism. The killing spurred Camus, who until that time had been a pacifist, to join the French resistance as editor of the underground newspaper *Combat*. Camus's first books, *The Stranger* and *The Myth of Sisyphus*, written that same year, explored the idea of the absurd. He died—along with his friend and publisher, Michel Gallimard—in a car accident.

### Essential Aphorisms

The only real progress lies in learning to be wrong all alone.

A man's work is nothing but this slow trek to rediscover, through the detours of art, those two or three great and simple images in whose presence his heart first opened.

No man is a hypocrite in his pleasures.

After a certain age every man is responsible for his face.

Every revolutionary ends up by becoming either an oppressor or a heretic.

All great deeds and all great thoughts have a ridiculous beginning.

An intellectual is someone whose mind watches itself.

We are all special cases.

What we call basic truths are simply the ones we discover after all the others.

Don't wait for the Last Judgment. It takes place every day.

## Parallel Lines: Friends II

Don't believe your friends when they ask you to be honest with them. All they really want is to be maintained in the good opinion they have of themselves.
—CAMUS

Reprove your friend in secret and praise him openly.
—LEONARDO DA VINCI

A good friend is my nearest relation.
—THOMAS FULLER

We learn our virtues from our friends who love us; our faults from the enemy who hates us. We cannot easily discover our real character from a friend. He is a mirror, on which the warmth of our breath impedes the clearness of the reflection.
—JEAN PAUL RICHTER

Friendship is a sheltering tree.
—SAMUEL TAYLOR COLERIDGE

For when two beings who are not friends are near each other there is no meeting, and when friends are far apart there is no separation.
—SIMONE WEIL

To find a friend one must close one eye—to keep him, two.
—NORMAN DOUGLAS

Life without a friend is like death without a witness.
—ZBIGNIEW HERBERT

**CANETTI, ELIAS** (Bulgaria, 1905–1994) In 1927, Canetti happened to be on the street outside Vienna's Palace of Justice when an angry mob burned the building down. He was swept along with the melee, and the experience formed the basis of what became his best-known work, *Crowds and Power*, a study of mob mentality. Canetti himself, however, was mostly a loner. Born in Bulgaria, in a small town on the Danube, he lived most of his adult life quietly in Hampstead, north London.

*Essential Aphorisms*

We forget nothing, and we forget it less and less.

No massacre protects against the next one.

Seeing something again involves the happy excitement at finding that something *is still there*.

It all depends on this: *with whom we confuse ourselves.*

If prayers were to be answered, they could not be retracted: a highly alarming state of affairs.

Explain nothing. Put it there. Say it. Leave.

**CARLYLE, THOMAS** (Scotland, 1795–1881) Carlyle's belief in the "great men" theory of history—that historical events are driven by exceptional individuals who somehow embody an epoch's social and spiritual aspirations—appealed to a diverse range of thinkers. Ralph Waldo Emerson found in it an echo of his own idea of Representative Men, those artistic and political revolutionaries responsible for the advance of civilization, while Adolf Hitler found it a useful prop in support of his cult of charismatic leadership. Raised in a strictly Calvinist family in Scotland, Carlyle was simultaneously a reactionary and a liberal. He dismissed democracy as little better than mob rule, but he also criticized ideologies (especially laissez-faire capitalism) that he felt dehumanized society and hindered progress.

*Essential Aphorisms*

A man lives by believing something, not by debating and arguing about many things.

When the oak is felled the whole forest echoes with its fall, but a hundred acorns are sown in silence by an unnoticed breeze.

The actual well seen is ideal.

The block of granite which was an obstacle in the pathway of the weak became a stepping-stone in the pathway of the strong.

Weak eyes are fondest of glittering objects.

War is a quarrel between two thieves too cowardly to fight their own battle.

There are good and bad times, but our mood changes more often than our fortune.

Science must have originated in the feeling that something was wrong.

Our main business is not to see what lies dimly at a distance, but to do what lies clearly at hand.

The greatest of all faults is to be conscious of none.

No pressure, no diamonds.

The history of the world is but the biography of great men.

Men do less than they ought, unless they do all that they can.

I do not believe in the collective wisdom of individual ignorance.

He who could foresee affairs three days in advance would be rich for thousands of years.

Be not a slave of words.

Blessed is he who has found his work; let him ask no other blessedness.

What you see but can't see over is as good as infinite.

**DIDEROT, DENIS** (France, 1713–1784) Diderot is responsible for coining that marvelous French phrase *l'esprit de l'escalier* ("the spirit of the staircase"), that moment of belated inspiration when you think of the perfect comeback for a difficult encounter only when you're walking down the stairs after the altercation is over. Diderot himself, though, didn't suffer much from the condition. He was famed as a brilliant conversationalist and, during the twenty years or so he spent editing the twenty-eight volumes of his *Encyclopédie*, wrote hundreds of entries on a bewildering array of topics in agriculture, industry, and science. The *Encyclopédie* became one of the founding documents of the Enlightenment because of its promotion of freedom of thought, religious tolerance, and the importance of scientific inquiry.

## Essential Aphorisms

From fanaticism to barbarism is only one step.

We swallow greedily any lie that flatters us, but we sip only little by little at a truth we find bitter.

It is very important not to mistake hemlock for parsley, but to believe or not believe in God is not important at all.

A thing is not proved just because no one has ever questioned it. What has never been gone into impartially has never been properly gone into. Hence skepticism is the first step toward truth. It must be applied generally, because it is the touchstone.

Distance is a great promoter of admiration!

Evil always turns up in this world through some genius or other.

Happiest are the people who give most happiness to others.

Pithy sentences are like sharp nails which force truth upon our memory.

One may demand of me that I should seek truth, but not that I should find it.

In order to shake a hypothesis, it is sometimes not necessary to do anything more than push it as far as it will go.

**EPICTETUS** (Greece, c. 55–c. 135) Epictetus, a slave who eventually won his freedom, set up his own philosophical school in Nicopolis, where Arrian, one of his most devoted students, recorded his aphorisms in *The Discourses*. The only personal details known about him are that he married late in life, apparently to help raise an orphaned child, and was disabled. Some sources say his disability was the result of rheumatism; others say it was caused by torture. The story goes that

Epictetus's owner was punishing him by twisting his leg. Enduring the pain with typical Stoic composure, he warned that his leg was about to break. When it finally did snap, Epictetus quipped, "I told you so."

*Essential Aphorisms*

Some things are up to us and some are not up to us.

The things that are up to us are by nature free, unhindered, and unimpeded; the things that are not up to us are weak, enslaved, hindered, not our own. So remember, if you think that things that are naturally enslaved are free or that things not your own are your own, you will be thwarted, miserable, and upset, and will blame both gods and men.

What is yours is to play the assigned part well. But to choose it belongs to someone else.

A person's master is someone who has power over what he wants or does not want, either to obtain it or take it away. Whoever wants to be free, therefore, let him not want or avoid anything that is up to others. Otherwise he will necessarily be a slave.

A ship ought not to be fixed to one small anchor, nor life to a single hope.

For both our legs and our hopes, possibility must govern our stride.

The pleasures that come most rarely give the most delight.

An uneducated person accuses others when he is doing badly; a partly educated person accuses himself, an educated person accuses neither someone else nor himself.

Do not seek to have events happen as you want them to, but instead want them to happen as they do happen, and your life will go well.

No man is free who is not master of himself.

*Parallel Lines: Make It So*

Nothing can be otherwise than it already is. What upsets people is not things themselves but their judgments about things.   —EPICTETUS

A road is made by people walking on it; things are so because they are called so. What makes them so? Making them so makes them so. What makes them not so? Making them not so makes them not so.

—CHUANG TZU

Get rid of the judgment, you are rid of the "I am hurt"; get rid of the "I am hurt," you are rid of the hurt itself.                —MARCUS AURELIUS

There is nothing either good or bad, but thinking makes it so.

—WILLIAM SHAKESPEARE

The virtues of a thing do not come from it: they go to it.

—ANTONIO PORCHIA

**EPICURUS** (Greece, c. 341–270 BCE) Epicurus was a practical thinker; he wanted his ideas to work in the real world. So he bought a big house with a large garden and set up a school to put his philosophy into practice. Students lived together in a kind of commune; money from the wealthiest members was redistributed among the poorest so that everybody's basic needs were taken care of. Epicurus himself was said to have had very simple tastes, living mostly on a diet of bread and cheese. But he was also careful not to let his students drift too far from reality, encouraging them to work and manage their affairs outside the commune's walls. Epicurus's diagnosis of the cause of suffering is remarkably similar to that of the Buddha: clinging to desires. Let go of those desires, and you eliminate the suffering.

*Essential Aphorisms*

Pleasure is the beginning and end of the blessed life.

Vain is the word of a philosopher, by which no mortal suffering is healed. Just as medicine confers no benefit if it does not drive away bodily disease, so is philosophy useless if it does not drive away the suffering of the mind.

Self-sufficiency is the greatest of all wealth.

Thanks be to blessed nature for making the necessary easy to secure and the unnecessary difficult to supply.

We must free ourselves from the prison of everyday affairs and politics.

Reduce desires to minimum.

There is nothing dreadful in life for the man who has truly comprehended that there is nothing terrible in not living.

Foolish is the man who says that he fears death, not because it will cause pain when it arrives but because anticipation of it is painful. What is no trouble when it arrives is an idle worry in anticipation.

You ought to do nothing in your life that will make you afraid if it becomes known to your neighbor.

The one who is beaten in a philosophical discussion gains more the more he learns.

Necessity is an evil thing, but there is no necessity to live beneath the yoke of necessity.

We do not need the help of our friends so much as the confidence that our friends will help us.

### Parallel Lines: Enough Is Enough

Nothing is sufficient for the man to whom the sufficient is too little.

—EPICURUS

You never know what is enough unless you know what is more than enough.
—WILLIAM BLAKE

**ERASMUS** (The Netherlands, 1466–1536) Erasmus was an avid collector of aphorisms and proverbs. He compiled all the sayings he could find in the works of the classical Greek and Latin authors he loved, and provided a brief history and explication for each one. The result was *Collectanea, A Collection of Paroemiae or Adages, Old and Most Celebrated, Made by Desyderius Herasmus Roterdamus, a Work Both New and Wonderfully Useful for Conferring Beauty and Distinction on All Kinds of Speech and Writing*. The popularity of what came to be known simply as the *Adages* led to numerous reprintings, and in the 1508 edition Erasmus added an introduction in which he praised aphorisms and proverbs as the ideal vehicle for philosophical thought: "An idea launched like a javelin in proverbial form strikes with sharper point on the hearer's mind and leaves implanted barbs for meditation."

*Essential Aphorisms*

In the land of the blind, the one-eyed man is king.

Heaven grant that the burden you carry may have as easy an exit as it had an entrance.

Don't give your advice before you are called upon.

Give light, and the darkness will disappear of itself.

He who allows oppression shares the crime.

Time takes away the grief of men.

War is delightful to those who have had no experience of it.

A nail is driven out by another nail. Habit is overcome by habit.

The desire to write grows with writing.

Your library is your paradise.

**FONTENELLE, BERNARD LE BOVIER DE** (France, 1657–1757) Fontenelle's uncles were the great French dramatists Pierre and Thomas Corneille, but the talent for writing for the stage apparently did not run in the family. His own dramatic works were abysmal failures. Instead, Fontenelle made his name as an essayist and as a popularizer of the ideas of French philosopher René Descartes. His most enduring work is *Conversations on the Plurality of Worlds*, published in 1686, in which he lucidly explained the latest astronomical discoveries and became one of the first writers to postulate that there could be life on other planets.

*Essential Aphorisms*

Whoever sees Nature as it truly is, simply sees the backstage area of a theater.

An educated mind is, as it were, composed of all the minds of preceding ages.

Truth enters the mind so naturally that learning it for the first time seems merely like remembering it.

If I carried all the thoughts of the world in my hand, I would take care not to open it.

It's no farther from the Earth to the Moon than from the Moon to the Earth.

All philosophy is based on two things only: curiosity and poor eyesight.

**FRANKL, VIKTOR E.** (Austria, 1905–1997) Frankl invented the term *existentialism*, devised his own school of psychoanalysis (called *logotherapy*), once suggested that a Statue of Responsibility be built on the West Coast of the United States to complement the Statue of Liberty on the East Coast, and survived four different Nazi concentration camps. When Frankl, a Viennese psychologist and physician, was arrested in 1942, he hid the manuscript of a book in progress inside the lining of his coat. But the papers were discovered and destroyed by the Nazis. Frankl spent the next three years of his captivity reconstructing the book in his mind and on scraps of paper. His experiences in the Nazi death camps formed the heart of logotherapy: the belief that, even in the midst of the most extreme suffering, life can still have meaning—if the sufferer is determined to find it.

*Essential Aphorisms*

What is to give light must endure burning.

Between stimulus and response there is a space. In that space is our power to choose our response. In our response lies our growth and our freedom.

Ever more people today have the means to live, but no meaning to live for.

Life can be pulled by goals just as surely as it can be pushed by drives.

Live as if you were living a second time, and as though you had acted wrongly the first time.

Ultimately, man should not ask what the meaning of his life is, but rather he must recognize that it is he who is asked.

**GÓMEZ DÁVILA, NICOLÁS** (Colombia, 1913–1994) Gómez Dávila called his aphorisms *escolios*, or "glosses." He is among Colombia's most controversial scholars, despite the fact that he never held a university post or made the slightest effort to publicize his work. He spent most of his time reading, in a private library that reportedly contained more than 30,000 volumes. Gómez Dávila described himself as a "reactionary"; he criticized both democracy and socialism, attacked liberalism in all its forms, and deplored the reform of the Catholic Church instituted by the Second Vatican Council.

## Essential Aphorisms

The one who renounces seems weak to the one incapable of renunciation.

To think like our contemporaries is a recipe for prosperity and stupidity.

In an age in which the media broadcast countless pieces of foolishness, the educated man is defined not by what he knows, but by what he doesn't know.

The punishment of the idealist consists in the triumph of his cause.

Confused ideas and muddy ponds appear deep.

Nowadays public opinion is not the sum of private opinions. On the contrary, private opinions are an echo of public opinion.

## Parallel Lines: Growing Old

The stupidity of an old man imagines itself to be wisdom; that of an adult, experience; that of a youth, genius. —GÓMEZ DÁVILA

Old people are fond of giving good advice; it consoles them for no longer being capable of setting a bad example. —LA ROCHEFOUCAULD

The counsels of the old, like the winter sun, shine, but give no heat.
—LUC DE CLAPIERS, MARQUIS DE VAUVENARGUES

Life: the first half of it consists of the capacity to enjoy without the chance; the last half consists of the chance without the capacity. —MARK TWAIN

Old age is like everything else. To make a success of it, you've got to start young. —THEODORE ROOSEVELT

Growing old is not a problem if you begin on time. —TOON VERHOEVEN

**GUICCIARDINI, FRANCESCO** (Italy, 1483–1540) Guicciardini was a friend of Niccolò Machiavelli, though he surpassed his famous fellow political theorist in the sheer villainy of his views. Guicciardini trained as a lawyer and served in a variety of influential diplomatic posts for the Medicis, during the time when that clan was at the height of its insidious power. His contemporaries all describe him as ambitious, avaricious, wily, and wicked. Guicciardini's thoughts and reflections on politics amount to a do-it-yourself guide for aspiring despots.

*Essential Aphorisms*

Nothing is more fleeting than the memory of benefits received. Therefore, rely more on those whose circumstances do not permit them to fail you than on those whom you have favored. For often they will not remember the favors, or they will suppose them to have been smaller than they were, or they will even claim that you did them almost because you were obliged.

Always deny what you don't want to be known, and always affirm what you want to be believed. For, though there be much—even conclusive— evidence to the contrary, a fervent affirmation or denial will often create at least some doubt in the mind of your listener.

It is a great thing to have authority: if you use it well, men will fear you even more than your powers warrant. Not knowing exactly the extent of your authority, they will quickly decide to yield rather than contest whether you can do what you threaten.

Waste no time with revolutions that do not remove the causes of your complaints but that simply change the faces of those in charge.

Anyone charged with defending a land must make it his principal object to hold out as long as possible. For, as the proverb says, he who has time has life. Delay brings infinite opportunities that at first could not be known or hoped for.

There is no rule or prescription for saving yourself from a bestial and cruel tyrant, except the one that applies for the plague. Run as far and as fast as you can.

Pray to God that you are always on the winning side, for you will get credit for things in which you had no part. If, on the contrary, you are a loser, you will be blamed for an infinite number of things of which you are entirely innocent.

Industries and trades are at their best before many people recognize how profitable they are. As soon as that happens, they decline, for strong competition makes them less profitable. Thus, in all matters, it is wise to get up very early.

It is very easy to ruin a good position, but very hard to acquire it. Therefore, if you are enjoying a good livelihood, make every effort not to let it slip through your fingers.

Although leisure does not give birth to whims, it is indeed true that there can be no whims without leisure.

### Parallel Lines: Good Fortune and Adversity

A man's good fortune is often his worst enemy, for it can make him wicked, lighthearted, insolent. A man's ability to bear good fortune, therefore, is a far better test of him than his ability to bear adversity.

—GUICCIARDINI

Prosperity procures friends, but adversity proves them.

—PUBLILIUS SYRUS

Certainly virtue is like precious odors, most fragrant when they are incensed or crushed; for prosperity doth best discover vice, but adversity doth best discover virtue.

—FRANCIS BACON

**HERACLITUS** (Greece, c. 540–c. 480 BCE) Nothing at all is known about the life of Heraclitus, except what can be deduced from his aphorisms. Like the other ancient Greek philosophers, he strove to identify the one immutable stuff from which the amazing variety of human experience emerged. Heraclitus decided that substance was fire, because only a flame remained constant even while it was continually in flux. And that was the essence of Heraclitean philosophy: everything is caught up in an endless process of change—an insight that also forms the philosophical basis for the aphorisms of the *I Ching*.

### Essential Aphorisms

Change alone is unchanging.

Through contention all things come to be.

One ought not to talk or act as if he were asleep.

The most beautiful order of the world is still a random gathering of things insignificant in themselves.

Character is fate.

Opposites cooperate. The most beautiful harmonies come from opposition. All things repel each other.

Nature is wont to hide herself.

One cannot step twice into the same river, for the water in which you first stepped has flowed on.

The same road goes both up and down.

Even sleeping men are doing the world's business and helping it along.

**HUXLEY, THOMAS HENRY** (United Kingdom, 1825–1895) Huxley was known as "Darwin's bulldog" because of the tenacity with which he defended the theory of evolution against its many critics in the late nineteenth century. Huxley was also a formidable scientist in his own right. He carried out important studies of marine invertebrates and, in his book *Evidence as to Man's Place in Nature*, published in 1863, was the first person to explicitly write that human beings evolved through natural selection. In one famous debate, Huxley faced Bishop Wilberforce, who tried to ridicule evolution by asking Huxley if he was descended from apes on his grandmother's or grandfather's side. "I would rather be the offspring of two apes than be a man and afraid to face the truth," Huxley replied.

*Essential Aphorisms*

Misery is a match that never goes out.

History warns us that it is the customary fate of new truths to begin as heresies and to end as superstitions.

The scientific spirit is of more value than its products, and irrationally held truths may be more harmful than reasoned errors.

Science commits suicide when it adopts a creed.

A man's worst difficulties begin when he is able to do as he likes.

The only people, scientific or other, who never make mistakes are those who do nothing.

The greatest tragedy of science—the slaying of a beautiful hypothesis by an ugly fact.

Do what you can to do what you ought, and leave hoping and fearing alone.

**JAMES, WILLIAM** (United States, 1842–1910) James came from a wealthy and intellectually accomplished family. His father was a distinguished theologian who was devoted to the mystical beliefs of Emanuel Swedenborg; his younger brother, Henry, was a prominent novelist. William James wrote pioneering books on the philosophy of pragmatism and the psychology of religious experience. He even sought out his own mystical experiences through the use of psychoactive drugs like chloral hydrate, nitrous oxide, and peyote. He coined the phrase "stream of thought" as a description of the flexible, flowing nature of consciousness. He also anticipated advances in neurobiology by theorizing that physical states create emotions rather than the other way around. He had personal connections with a variety of fellow aphorists: Ralph Waldo Emerson was his godfather; G. K. Chesterton and Mark Twain were his friends; George Santayana and Gertrude Stein were his students; and Bertrand Russell and Ludwig Wittgenstein were deeply influenced by his ideas.

*Essential Aphorisms*

No matter how full a reservoir of maxims one may possess, and no matter how good one's sentiments may be, if one has not taken advantage of every concrete opportunity to act, one's character may remain entirely unaffected for the better.

Be not afraid of life. Believe that life is worth living, and your belief will help create the fact.

Common sense and a sense of humor are the same thing, moving at different speeds. A sense of humor is just common sense, dancing.

Act as if what you do makes a difference. It does.

Be willing to have it so. Acceptance of what has happened is the first step to overcoming the consequences of any misfortune.

Do every day or two something for no other reason than you would rather not do it, so that when the hour of dire need draws nigh, it may find you not unnerved and untrained to stand the test.

Begin to be now what you will be hereafter.

Man can alter his life by altering his thinking.

When you have to make a choice and don't make it, that is in itself a choice.

Most people never run far enough on their first wind to find out if they've got a second.

The great use of life is to spend it for something that will outlast it.

Wisdom is learning what to overlook.

**JOUBERT, JOSEPH** (France, 1754–1824) Joubert was the least worldly of all the great French aphorists. He abhorred the military, shunned politics, and was more comfortable in his own study than in the Parisian salons. He lived through the Revolution but played no part in it. He devoted himself almost exclusively to literature. His beguiling *pensées*, as recorded in his notebooks between 1774 and 1824, contain Joubert's luminous insights into the art and craft of the aphorism. Joubert was fascinated by the maxim, and his notebooks reveal him to be an accomplished theorist as well as practitioner of the form. Joubert's main influence and model was Michel de Montaigne. But while Montaigne was gregarious and outgoing, Joubert was a prim, fastidious bookworm. Their subject matters were entirely different as well: Montaigne wrote about his life, in all its glorious and grimy detail; Joubert wrote only about his delicate, elegant thoughts.

*Essential Aphorisms*

Genuine good sayings surprise the author as much as the listeners.

A work of genius, whether poetic or didactic, is too long if it cannot be read in one day.

Wisdom is repose in light.

We can sprain our minds as well as our bodies.

In things that are visible and palpable, never prove what is believed already; in things that are certain and mysterious—mysterious by their greatness and by their nature—make people believe them, and do not prove them.

To seek that style which makes one perceive or discover more meanings than it explains.

It is better to stir up a question without deciding it than to decide it without stirring it up.

Everything that is exact is short.

Maxims, because what is isolated can be seen better.

In a moment of insight you can *perceive* everything; but it takes years for exactitude to give it expression.

Writing is closer to thinking than to speaking.

One cannot write simply or naturally except when one has thoughts that are beautiful. Wait for them.

Some men find their sole activity in repose; and others their sole repose in movement.

What is true by lamplight is not always true in the sunshine.

The evening of life brings with it its lamp.

When one has knocked in vain at the door of certain truths, one must try to get in through the window.

To teach is to learn twice.

Poetry has no utility save for the soul's delight.

Maxims are to the intelligence what laws are to action: they do not illuminate, but they guide, they control, they rescue blindly. They are the clue in the labyrinth, the ship's compass in the night.

The poet must not cross an interval with a step when he can cross it with a leap.

To penetrate a thought and to produce a thought are almost the same action.

A thought is a thing as real as a cannon ball.

**KIERKEGAARD, SØREN** (Denmark, 1813–1855) Kierkegaard's father, a profoundly spiritual man, wanted his son to become a pastor. But Kierkegaard, an intensely religious person himself, was unable to conform to the institutional requirements of the priesthood. He was a fierce critic of the Christian church in general, and the Danish State Church in particular, for the way he believed those institutions stifled individual belief and expression. He refused to take communion or have a priest by his bedside as he lay dying. Kierkegaard developed a much more fragmented philosophy than that embraced by the Church, one in which the lone individual constantly hovered between faith and despair.

*Essential Aphorisms*

The tyrant dies and his rule is over, the martyr dies and his rule begins.

The truth is a trap: you cannot get it without its getting you; you cannot get the truth by capturing it, only by its capturing you.

The most painful state of being is remembering the future, particularly one you can never have.

The supreme paradox of all thought is its attempt to discover something that thought cannot think.

What is a poet? An unhappy man who hides deep anguish in his heart, but whose lips are so formed that when the sigh and cry pass through them, it sounds like lovely music.

Aren't people absurd! They never use the freedoms they do have but demand those they don't have; they have freedom of thought, they demand freedom of speech.

Most people are in such a rush to enjoy themselves that they hurry right past it.

A fire broke out backstage in a theater. The clown came out to warn the public; they thought it was a joke and applauded. He repeated it; the acclaim was even greater. I think that's just how the world will come to an end: to general applause from wits who believe it's a joke.

What the philosophers say about reality is often as deceptive as when you see a sign in a second-hand store that reads: Pressing Done Here. If you went in with your clothes to have them pressed you would be fooled; the sign is for sale.

Life must be lived forward, however, it can only be understood backward.

### Parallel Lines: Doors

Alas, the door of fortune does not open inward so that one can force it by charging at it; it opens outward and so there is nothing one can do.

—KIERKEGAARD

Step back: the door opens inward.          —JAMES RICHARDSON

**LICHTENBERG, GEORG CHRISTOPH** (Germany, 1742–1799) Lichtenberg was an accomplished physicist, mathematician, and astronomer and one of the first people in history to conduct actual experiments. He was also something of an amateur psychologist. More than a century before Freud, he scrupulously recorded his dreams and speculated about how dream analysis could reveal our inner lives. He authored numerous scientific papers, edited the *Göttingen Pocket Almanac* for more than twenty years, and produced an early map of the moon. Born in Oberramstadt, near Darmstadt, Germany, Lichtenberg became a lecturer at the University of Göttingen and quickly established a reputation as a scientist and philosopher, known as an eager and entertaining popularizer of the young science of electricity. He erected Göttingen's first lightning rod and gave crowd-pleasing talks at his home that featured spectacular displays of electrical special effects.

### Essential Aphorisms

The great rule: If the little bit you have is nothing special in itself, at least find a way of saying it that is a little bit special.

Imagine the world so greatly magnified that particles of light look like twenty-four-pound cannon balls.

Why does a suppurating lung give so little warning and a sore on the finger so much?

To the wise man nothing is great and nothing small. As the few adepts in such things well know, universal morality is to be found in little everyday penny-events just as much as in great ones.

The most entertaining surface on earth is the human face.

The greatest things in the world are brought about by other things that we count as nothing: little causes we overlook but which at length accumulate.

Prejudices are so to speak the mechanical instincts of men: through their prejudices they do without any effort many things they would find too difficult to think through to the point of resolving to do them.

Be attentive, feel nothing in vain, measure and compare: this is the whole law of philosophy.

What we have to discover for ourselves leaves behind in our mind a pathway that can also be used on another occasion.

We say that someone occupies an official position, whereas it is the official position that occupies him.

The world offers us correction more often than consolation.

The most dangerous untruths are truths slightly distorted.

The sure conviction that we could if we wanted to is the reason so many good minds are idle.

Those who never have time do least.

Do not judge God's world from your own. Trim your hedge as you wish and plant your flowers in the patterns you can understand, but do not judge the garden of nature from your little window box.

Nothing can contribute more to peace of soul than the lack of any opinion whatever.

Truth has a thousand obstacles to overcome before it can get safely down on to paper and from paper back into a head. The liar is the least of its foes.

There exists no bridge that leads beyond our thoughts to the objects of them.

It is impossible to carry the torch of truth through a crowd without singeing someone's beard.

There would be far less soothsaying if there were far more truth-saying.

## Parallel Lines: $2 \times 2 = ?$

Doubt everything at least once, even the proposition that twice two is four.
—LICHTENBERG

One can prove or refute anything at all with words. Soon people will perfect language technology to such an extent that they'll be proving with mathematical precision that twice two is seven.    —ANTON CHEKHOV

Those who have never realized with head and heart that two times two is five have never known passion.    —HANS KUDSZUS

**MACHIAVELLI, NICCOLÒ** (Italy, 1469–1527) Machiavelli was not solely a Dear Abby for despots. The cruel pragmatist who wrote *The Prince*, a manual for winning and retaining power at any cost, also wrote *The Discorsi*, a collection of essays examining the work of the Roman historian Titus Livy that also explores the proper workings of a republic, his preferred form of government. Still, it is in *The Prince* that he composed some of his most stinging aphorisms.

## Essential Aphorisms

A wise prince must devise ways by which his citizens are always and in all circumstances dependent on him and on his authority; and then they will always be faithful to him.

Princes should delegate to others the enactment of unpopular measures and keep in their own hands the means of winning favors.

Violence must be inflicted once for all; people will then forget what it tastes like and so be less resentful. Benefits must be conferred gradually; and in that way they will taste better.

Men worry less about doing an injury to one who makes himself loved than to one who makes himself feared. For love is secured by a bond of gratitude that men, wretched creatures that they are, break when it is to their advantage to do so; but fear is strengthened by a dread of punishment that is always effective.

**MAY, SIMON** (United Kingdom, 1956–  ) May, a fellow in philosophy at Birkbeck College, University of London, was first drawn to aphorisms by a love of riddles. "They offered freedoms that systematic works of science, philosophy, and literature often didn't," he says. "Their style—brief, suggestive, fragmentary—mocked the conceit that one can grasp the world as a totality, or possess the final truth valid for all people at all times. Aphorisms are the enemy of ideologies."

*Essential Aphorisms*

Failure is life's magnifying glass.

One must know what to look for if one is to know what to overlook.

To live in perpetual hope can be a form of resignation.

The ability to forget and the inability to recall are altogether different skills.

To succeed, one must question the value of one's works, but never the value of one's work.

It is tempting to consider what is beyond our power to be beneath our dignity.

**ORTEGA Y GASSET, JOSÉ** (Spain, 1883–1955) Inspired by Friedrich Nietzsche, Ortega y Gasset made iconoclasm the focal point of his philosophy. Born in Madrid and educated as a boy by Jesuits, he was a professor all his life. But he didn't write in academic jargon. His spare, lucid style makes his ideas immediately accessible. Ortega y Gasset rejected Descartes' famous dictum, "I think, therefore I am." Instead, he insisted that a person was more than just his or her thoughts; reality must also include the world and each individual's actions and decisions in it.

*Essential Aphorisms*

Effort is only effort when it begins to hurt.

Excellence means when a man or woman asks of himself more than others do.

Law is born from despair of human nature.

Living is a constant process of deciding what we are going to do.

Our firmest convictions are apt to be the most suspect, they mark our limitations and our bounds. Life is a petty thing unless it is moved by the indomitable urge to extend its boundaries.

Being an artist means ceasing to take seriously that very serious person we are when we are not an artist.

An "unemployed" existence is a worse negation of life than death itself.

To live is to feel oneself lost.

*Parallel Lines: Tell Me Who You Are*

Tell me to what you pay attention and I will tell you who you are.

—ORTEGA Y GASSET

What do you despise? By this you are truly known.    —MICHELANGELO

Show me who thou art with, and I will tell thee what thou art.

—CERVANTES

Tell me what you eat: I will tell you who you are.

—ANTHELME BRILLAT-SAVARIN

Tell me with whom you consort and I will tell you who you are; if I know how you spend your time, then I know what might become of you.

—JOHANN WOLFGANG VON GOETHE

Tell me what you think you are and I will tell you what you are not.

—HENRI FRÉDÉRIC AMIEL

**PLATO** (Greece, c. 428–c. 348 BCE) Plato is said to have started out as a playwright, but after hearing Socrates speak one day he dropped that career and took
up philosophy instead. He retained his playwright's eye for characterization and
ear for dialogue, though, and his writing remains the most reliable and engrossing
source of information about Socrates's life, thoughts, and sayings. Like that of so
many other ancient Greek philosophers, Plato's biography is still very much a
mystery. He was Socrates's most brilliant pupil and Aristotle's teacher. His actual
name may have been Aristocles; the name Plato, which means "broad," was possibly given to him by a wrestling coach as a nickname referring to his physique.
When Socrates died, Plato left Athens, traveling in Europe and perhaps even to
the Middle East. He eventually returned to Athens and founded his school, the
Academy, which took its name from its location amid a grove of trees sacred to
the hero Academus. As a young man, Plato had an interest in the philosophy of
Heraclitus. He is also said to have visited several of Pythagoras's followers in
southern Italy when he traveled there after Socrates died. The influence of these
two thinkers can be seen in Plato's ideas as well as in the terse style in which
he expresses them. But the greatest influence on Plato was, of course, Socrates,
whom Plato described as "the most just man alive."

## Essential Aphorisms

Everything that deceives may be said to enchant.

Wealth is the parent of luxury and indolence, and poverty of meanness and
viciousness, and both of discontent.

No human thing is of serious importance.

No one is more hated than he who speaks the truth.

One of the penalties for refusing to participate in politics is that you end
up being governed by your inferiors.

When the tyrant has disposed of foreign enemies by conquest or treaty, and
there is nothing to fear from them, then he is always stirring up some war
or other, in order that the people may require a leader.

## Parallel Lines: Justice

Mankind censure injustice fearing that they may be the victims of it, and
not because they shrink from committing it.                    —PLATO

Justice is no more than lively fear that our belongings will be taken away from us. This is at the root of men's consideration and respect for all the interests of others, and their scrupulous care never to do them wrong.

—LA ROCHEFOUCAULD

**RUSSELL, BERTRAND** (United Kingdom, 1872–1970) "It is impossible to describe Bertrand Russell except by saying that he looks like the Mad Hatter." That was the way Norbert Wiener, an American mathematician and founder of the field of cybernetics, described the British philosopher and social critic who, along with Albert Einstein, was the most famous intellectual of his day. Russell is remembered as much for his social activism as for his pioneering work in mathematical logic and analytic philosophy. He was an early supporter of women's suffrage, opposed British entry into World War I (for which he was dismissed from Trinity College, Cambridge), and throughout the 1950s and '60s was a passionate campaigner against nuclear weapons and the Vietnam War.

*Essential Aphorisms*

War does not determine who is right—only who is left.

What is wanted is not the will to believe, but the will to find out, which is the exact opposite.

The time you enjoy wasting is not wasted time.

Science is what you know, philosophy is what you don't know.

In all affairs it's a healthy thing now and then to hang a question mark on the things you have long taken for granted.

Democracy is the process by which people choose the man who'll get the blame.

Do not fear to be eccentric in opinion, for every opinion now accepted was once eccentric.

All movements go too far.

**SANTAYANA, GEORGE** (Spain, 1863–1952) Santayana was a quintessential man of letters. An inheritance from his mother allowed him to lead a life of leisure and literature. He taught for a while at Harvard—studying with William James and then teaching T. S. Eliot and Wallace Stevens—then retired to Europe, where he settled in Rome and wrote works of philosophy, an autobiography, and a novel. An atheist, he spent the last ten years of his life in a convent in Rome, cared for by the nuns.

## Essential Aphorisms

Progress, far from consisting in change, depends on retentiveness. Those who cannot remember the past are condemned to repeat it.

The God to whom depth in philosophy brings back men's minds is far from being the same from whom a little philosophy estranges them.

All living souls welcome whatever they are ready to cope with; all else they ignore, or pronounce to be monstrous and wrong, or deny to be possible.

Only the dead have seen an end to war.

The young man who has not wept is a savage, and the older man who will not laugh is a fool.

The Difficult is that which can be done immediately; the Impossible that which takes a little longer.

Sanity is madness put to good uses.

There is no cure for birth and death save to enjoy the interval.

## Parallel Lines: Fanaticism

Fanaticism consists of redoubling your effort when you have forgotten your aim.                                                                —SANTAYANA

A fanatic is one who can't change his mind and won't change the subject.
                                                              —WINSTON CHURCHILL

**SATO, ISSAI** (Japan, 1772–1859) One of Japan's most important nineteenth-century Confucian scholars, Issai was born in Tokyo and held a series of distinguished academic posts until his death.

*Essential Aphorisms*

> There are always people who make big declarations. These are always people of little consequence.

> Historical works all may communicate traces, but they do not communicate truth. One who reads history ought to take these traces, and nudge out the truths concealed within.

> How long is the winter day spent in idleness, but how short the summer day devoted to study. Long and short is in me, and not in the day.

> Treat others like the spring breeze; guard yourself like the autumn frost.

**SCHLEGEL, FRIEDRICH VON** (Germany, 1772–1829) Schlegel practiced the spontaneous combustion method of philosophical composition. In contrast to earlier thinkers like Descartes and Spinoza, who devised elaborate and meticulously argued systems, Schlegel liked to publish his thoughts raw, in the form in which they first occurred to him: as aphorisms. Schlegel jotted down his musings in a notebook and printed them in *Athenaeum*, the literary journal he founded in 1798 with his brother, August Wilhelm. Born in Hanover in 1772, Friedrich von Schlegel was apprenticed to a banker in Leipzig but couldn't confine his mind to the rigid credit and debit columns of finance. So he took up the study of literature, comparative philology, and Greek antiquity, and instead became an early prophet of the Romantic Movement in literature.

*Essential Aphorisms*

> One can only become a philosopher, not be one. As soon as one thinks one is a philosopher, one stops becoming one.

> A fragment, like a miniature work of art, has to be entirely isolated from the surrounding world and be complete in itself like a porcupine.

> In poetry too every whole can be a part and every part really a whole.

> Nothing is more rarely the subject of philosophy than philosophy itself.

> Many witty ideas are like the sudden meeting of two friendly thoughts after a long separation.

> Whatever one cannot say, one does not really know.

**SPINOZA, BARUCH DE** (The Netherlands, 1632–1677) On July 27, 1656, Spinoza, the twenty-three-year-old son of a prominent Amsterdam merchant, was excommunicated from the city's Portuguese-Jewish community. He was thenceforth to be regarded as a permanent outcast. Though the order doesn't list Spinoza's offenses by name, and at the time of his excommunication he hadn't yet published anything, he was already well known as one of the freest thinkers in a famously free-thinking city. Spinoza denied that the human soul was immortal; dismissed heaven and hell as silly superstitions; argued that sacred scripture was not divinely revealed but compiled, edited, and manipulated by human beings; decried organized religions as purveyors of fear, ignorance, and prejudice; and rejected the idea of a personalized, loving God in favor of one that was identical with nature and indifferent to human fate. Spinoza didn't seem to take much notice of his excommunication, though. He took up lens grinding to earn a living, was careful about what he published and with whom he shared his thoughts, and dedicated himself to building on Descartes' ideas about the supremacy of human reason.

*Essential Aphorisms*

Love is nothing else but pleasure accompanied by the idea of an external cause: Hate is nothing else but pain accompanied by the idea of an external cause.

Happiness or unhappiness is made wholly to depend on the quality of the object which we love.

Men believe themselves to be free, simply because they are conscious of their actions, and unconscious of the causes whereby those actions are determined.

Nature abhors a vacuum.

Whatsoever is, is in God, and without God nothing can be, or be conceived.

God is a thinking thing.

Surely human affairs would be far happier if the power in men to be silent were the same as that to speak. But experience more than sufficiently teaches that men govern nothing with more difficulty than their tongues.

So long as a man imagines that he cannot do this or that, so long is he determined not to do it: and consequently, so long is it impossible to him that he should do it.

## Parallel Lines: Hope and Fear

Hope is nothing else but an inconstant pleasure, arising from the image of something future or past, whereof we do not yet know the issue. Fear, on the other hand, is an inconstant pain also arising from the image of something concerning which we are in doubt. If the element of doubt be removed from these emotions, hope becomes confidence and fear becomes despair.

—SPINOZA

Fear is pain arising from the anticipation of evil.     —ARISTOTLE

Hope is the confusion of the desire for a thing with its probability.

—ARTHUR SCHOPENHAUER

**STEIN, GERTRUDE** (United States, 1874–1946) Stein was famous, notorious in some circles, for her playful, impenetrable style. She maintained that style until the very end. According to her lifelong partner, Alice B. Toklas, Stein's last words as she lay in the hospital dying of stomach cancer were, "What is the answer?" When Toklas did not respond, she said, "In that case, what is the question?" There can be no question that Stein was one of the most influential artists of the early twentieth century. Not only was her own work a catalyst in the development of modern art and literature, she was also an early friend and supporter to some of the twentieth century's greatest artists, including the painters Braque, Matisse, and Picasso and the writers Sherwood Anderson, Ernest Hemingway, and Thornton Wilder. Born in Pittsburgh, Stein lived most of her life in France. During World War I, she and Toklas drove supplies to French hospitals; during World War II, Stein, who came from Jewish-German ancestry, initially supported the Vichy government before turning against it later in the conflict. In the 1920s, Stein's apartment in Paris was the center of the avant-garde movement, a gathering place for the "lost generation" of American expatriate artists—a group that Stein herself had named.

## Essential Aphorisms

Everybody gets so much information all day long that they lose their common sense.

Rose is a rose is a rose is a rose.

There is no there there.

The creator of the new composition in the arts is an outlaw until he is a classic.

A real failure does not need an excuse. It is an end in itself.

You are you because your little dog knows you.

It takes a lot of time to be a genius, you have to sit around so much doing nothing, really doing nothing.

Generally speaking anybody is more interesting doing nothing than doing something.

A creator is not in advance of his generation but he is the first of his contemporaries to be conscious of what is happening to his generation.

We are always the same age inside.

**SZASZ, THOMAS** (United States, 1920–    ) Szasz is best known for his book *The Myth of Mental Illness*, in which he argues that psychological disorders such as schizophrenia are not really illnesses at all but labels through which governments and the medical profession try to exercise social control.

*Essential Aphorisms*

Boredom is the feeling that everything is a waste of time; serenity, that nothing is.

If someone does something we disapprove of, we regard him as bad if we believe we can deter him from persisting in his conduct, and as mad if we believe we cannot.

When a person can no longer laugh at himself, it is time for others to laugh at him.

Two wrongs don't make a right, but they make a good excuse.

**TACITUS** (Italy, c. 56–c. 117) It is thanks to the histories of Tacitus that we know so much about the Roman Empire from the years 14 to 96. But he was far less scrupulous in recording the details of his own life. Hardly anything is known about Tacitus's personal history, not even his first name. The few details known for sure are that he studied rhetoric in Rome, was married (bravely, he wrote a biography of his father-in-law), held a seat in the Senate, and was an avid hunter.

*Essential Aphorisms*

A bad peace is even worse than war.

Be assured those will be thy worst enemies, not to whom thou hast done evil, but who have done evil to thee. And those will be thy best friends, not to whom thou hast done good, but who have done good to thee.

Greater things are believed of those who are absent.

He that fights and runs away, may turn and fight another day; but he that is in battle slain, will never rise to fight again.

It belongs to human nature to hate those you have injured.

It is less difficult to bear misfortunes than to remain uncorrupted by pleasure.

The desire for safety stands against every great and noble enterprise.

Things forbidden have a secret charm.

Those in supreme power always suspect and hate their next heir.

To show resentment at a reproach is to acknowledge that one may have deserved it.

**UNAMUNO, MIGUEL DE** (Spain, 1864–1936) Fray Luis Ponce de León, who died in 1591, is one of Spain's greatest lyric poets. He was also an Augustinian monk and professor at the University of Salamanca who was locked up for four years during the Inquisition for translating the *Song of Solomon*. On first returning to the classroom after his release from prison, he began his lecture with the words, "As we were saying yesterday . . ." Some three and a half centuries later, in 1924, Unamuno—a philosopher, playwright, and poet as well as a lecturer at the University of Salamanca—fled the dictatorship of General Miguel Primo de Rivera and didn't return to Spain until 1930. On taking up his teaching post again, he opened his first class with the words, "As we were saying yesterday . . ."

*Essential Aphorisms*

It is sad not to be loved, but it is much sadder not to be able to love.

The devil is an angel too.

The supreme triumph of reason is to cast doubt upon its own validity.

Isolation is the worst possible counselor.

Faith which does not doubt is dead faith.

Consciousness is a disease.

To fall into a habit is to begin to cease to be.

We should try to be the parents of our future rather than the offspring of our past.

**WEIL, SIMONE** (France, 1909–1943) From her earliest youth, Weil believed in the power of suffering with others. At the age of six, she stopped eating sugar to show her solidarity with the French troops fighting in World War I. While working for the French resistance in England in 1943, she refused to eat anything but the most meager rations, arguing that this was all her countrymen in occupied France had to eat. The lack of food, combined with recurrent tuberculosis, resulted in her death at the age of thirty-four. Most of her political and mystical writings were published posthumously.

*Essential Aphorisms*

We must prefer real hell to an imaginary paradise.

A mind enclosed in language is in prison.

Imagination and fiction make up more than three quarters of our real life.

All sins are attempts to fill voids.

Difficult as it is really to listen to someone in affliction, it is just as difficult for him to know that compassion is listening to him.

Force is as pitiless to the man who possesses it, or thinks he does, as it is to its victims; the second it crushes, the first it intoxicates. The truth is, nobody really possesses it.

The highest ecstasy is the attention at its fullest.

Two prisoners whose cells adjoin communicate with each other by knocking on the wall. The wall is the thing which separates them but is also their means of communication. It is the same with us and God. Every separation is a link.

**WHITEHEAD, ALFRED NORTH** (United Kingdom, 1861–1947) Whitehead is remembered today mostly for his work in mathematical logic and the philosophy of science, and for his coauthorship with Bertrand Russell of the massive *Principia Mathematica* in 1910. As a professor at Harvard, Whitehead regularly held open house on Sunday afternoons to which students were invited. Many of Whitehead's aphorisms were uttered during these rambling Sunday-afternoon discussions.

*Essential Aphorisms*

The deepest definition of youth is life as yet untouched by tragedy.

Civilization advances by extending the number of important operations which we can perform without thinking of them.

It is the business of the future to be dangerous; and it is among the merits of science that it equips the future for its duties.

Everything of importance has been said before by somebody who did not discover it.

Not ignorance, but ignorance of ignorance, is the death of knowledge.

Familiar things happen, and mankind does not bother about them. It requires a very unusual mind to undertake the analysis of the obvious.

The art of progress is to preserve order amid change and to preserve change amid order.

There are no whole truths; all truths are half-truths. It is trying to treat them as whole truths that plays the devil.

# STRANGE BEASTS

$S$OME aphorists resist easy categorization. Their personal peculiarities and aphoristic innovations place them in a class by themselves. These writers stand out as unique even among their fellow aphorists, already a pretty eccentric group. And, like Friedrich Nietzsche, they take the aphorism very seriously: "Whoever writes in blood and aphorisms does not want to be read but to be learned by heart. In the mountains the shortest way is from peak to peak: but for that one must have long legs. Aphorisms should be peaks—and those who are addressed tall and lofty." The view from these mountaintops is always exhilarating and often wonderfully askew. When you meet one of these strange beasts in the forest, prepare to be scared, provoked—and amused.

**BIERCE, AMBROSE** (United States, 1842–1914?) The American Civil War shaped both Bierce's literary career and, ultimately, his fate. He fought in some of that conflict's bloodiest battles and was wounded several times, once taking a bullet in the head. The carnage only confirmed his already saturnine view of human nature. After the war, Bierce washed up in San Francisco, penniless and without any prospects. He fell into a job on a local newspaper and rapidly made his name as one of California's fiercest crusading journalists, attacking craven politicians and robber barons. In 1880, Bierce began writing a column for the *Wasp* newspaper called "The Devil's Dictionary." Over the next thirty years, he delighted readers with his diabolical definitions of everything from "abasement" to "zoology." He also started writing short stories, many of which were based on his Civil War experiences and featured occult or supernatural occurrences. Bierce adopted an appropriately dark persona, too. He dressed in black, carried a revolver (for self-defense, he claimed), and displayed a human skull and a box containing the ashes of his deceased son on his desk. In 1913, at the age of seventy-one, Bierce disappeared. Rumors circulated that he was a secret government agent, that he had been killed while fighting alongside Mexican revolutionary Pancho Villa, that he faked his own death and fled to South America. As late as the 1930s, an explorer was said to have encountered a strange white man clad in jaguar skins (presumably Bierce) in the Brazilian jungle, where the local tribe worshiped him as a god. The more likely explanation is that Bierce, after revisiting his old Civil War battle sites, traveled to the Grand Canyon to kill himself, a plan he had mentioned to friends on several occasions. His body has never been found. As a lexicographer, Bierce saw himself as continuing the great tradition of satirical dictionaries pioneered by the likes of Samuel Johnson and Voltaire. He shared Mark Twain's dark humor and dyspeptic view of the human condition. The two men followed similar career paths as well: both Bierce and Twain were printer's assistants and journalists before they became famous for their literary works. And like La Rochefoucauld, Bierce believed all human actions were instinctively selfish, disingenuous, and untrustworthy.

*Essential Aphorisms*

Admiration, n. Our polite recognition of another's resemblance to ourselves.

Aphorism, n. Predigested wisdom.

Back, n. That part of your friend which it is your privilege to contemplate in your adversity.

Consult, v.t. To seek another's approval of a course already decided on.

Corporation, n. An ingenious device for obtaining individual profit without individual responsibility.

Cynic, n. A blackguard whose faulty vision sees things as they are, not as they ought to be.

Day, n. A period of twenty-four hours, mostly misspent.

Destiny, n. A tyrant's authority for crime and a fool's excuse for failure.

Friendship, n. A ship big enough to carry two in fair weather, but only one in foul.

Future, n. That period of time in which our affairs prosper, our friends are true and our happiness is assured.

Hearse, n. Death's baby-carriage.

Misfortune, n. The kind of fortune that never misses.

Oblivion, n. The state or condition in which the wicked cease from struggling and the dreary are at rest. Fame's eternal dumping ground. Cold storage for high hopes. A place where ambitious authors meet their works without pride and their betters without envy. A dormitory without an alarm clock.

Once, adv. Enough.

Opportunity, n. A favorable occasion for grasping a disappointment.

Otherwise, adv. No better.

Pleasure, n. The least hateful form of dejection.

Positive, adj. Mistaken at the top of one's voice.

Really, adv. Apparently.

Self-esteem, n. An erroneous appraisement.

Self-evident, adj. Evident to one's self and to nobody else.

Twice, adv. Once too often.

### Parallel Lines: All Alone

Alone, adj. In bad company.                                    —BIERCE

Alone: not hindered by anyone else's help.    —JULIEN DE VALCKENAERE

**BRILLAT-SAVARIN, ANTHELME** (France, 1755–1826) Brillat-Savarin was a man of many talents: author, lawyer, linguist (he spoke about half a dozen languages), politician, and violinist. But his fame rests on his qualities as a gourmand and on his ability to convey his love for the table in brief, aphoristic meditations à la Michel de Montaigne. Brillat-Savarin was not a chef, but he was far more than a food critic. He regarded the preparation and consumption of meals as both an art and a science. He composed a collection of aphorisms that he intended to serve as the foundation of his philosophy of food.

*Essential Aphorisms*

The fate of nations depends on the way they eat.

The table is the only place where the first hour is never dull.

The pleasures of the table belong to all times and all ages, to every country and every day; they go hand in hand with all our other pleasures, outlast them, and remain to console us for their loss.

The discovery of a new dish does more for the happiness of mankind than the discovery of a star.

The most indispensable quality of a cook is punctuality; it is also that of a guest.

To entertain a guest is to make yourself responsible for his happiness so long as he is beneath your roof.

**CHAZAL, MALCOLM DE** (Mauritius, 1902–1981) De Chazal was a painter as well as an aphorist, and his canvases—mostly seascapes, landscapes, and depictions of the flora and fauna of his native Mauritius—are as vibrant and idiosyncratic as his sayings. Brilliantly colored and executed in quick, strong strokes, his paintings pulse with vitality and life. He developed a philosophical system, Unism, that he believed encompassed both his verbal and his visual art. The basic principle was that "man and nature are entirely continuous and that all parts of the human body and all expressions of the human face, including their feelings, can actually be discerned in plants, flowers, and fruits, and to an even greater extent in our other selves, animals." True to the principles of Unism, De Chazal's aphorisms are almost animistic in the way they impute human traits and characteristics to animals and inanimate objects. De Chazal shunned his family's business interests in the Mauritian sugar industry, concentrating instead solely on his writing, painting, and increasingly esoteric philosophical speculations. He was an irascible character—reclusive, surly, and dictatorial. He hated mirrors, so his hosts had to veil them in his presence. But he was hypersensitive to the sensual world, to the realm of colors, odors, shapes, and textures.

*Essential Aphorisms*

Flowers of various colors set waving by the wind: color shaking a tambourine while it dances on a leafy floor.

A flick of the fingernail tells whether the closed jar is empty or not. One word out of a fool's mouth is enough to convict him.

A flowing river is an infinity of superimposed production belts.

The eyes of the overly fearful stammer.

A moody silence between lovers is a shared widowhood.

A fountain of water is all ball bearings, so perfect in function that it requires no lubrication. Water is the only substance friction will not wear out.

Breasts restrained by a brassiere are like two tennis balls expelled by the rib cage that fall back into the net at each stroke.

Death is the bowel movement of the soul evacuating the body by intense pressure on the spiritual anus.

Light shining on water droplets spaced out along a bamboo stalk turns the whole structure into a flute.

White has the longest arms and the shortest legs: it makes the best semaphore system. Red has the shortest arms and the longest legs: it makes the fleetest messenger.

The act of love turns the spinal column into a finger as if to feel and caress the brain from within.

Age adds a pane of glass each year to the lantern of the eye.

The sun is pure communism everywhere except in cities, where it's private property.

Space is the widest open of all mouths.

Objects and things are needles to the wind's phonograph record, the human ear being the rest of the apparatus.

Beige is orange beaten stiff. Dredge in blue, knead the paste, and you have gray.

Man wants his religion to be above all *comfortable*. Religious intolerance is the sign of religious decline. To fill all the pews, churches have to be easy chairs for the heart and not torture racks for the spirit.

The act of love is a toboggan in which those who are joined become each other's vehicle.

Objects are the clasps on the pockets of space.

Indifference turns the pupil's brilliant glow into a night-light of a look.

At the height of its trajectory a water jet puts hair rollers into the light's tresses; as the water falls back it undoes them, letting the curls tumble down.

The plant uses the seed as a handbag.

**CIORAN, E. M.** (Romania, 1911–1995) Born in Rasinari, a tiny hamlet in the Carpathian Mountains of Romania, Cioran flirted with the far right during the 1930s, for a time even writing articles in praise of the Nazis. During the early years of World War II, he penned fascist political tracts and propaganda for the pro-Hitler Romanian government. But in his late twenties, Cioran abandoned both Romania and his extremist political views and moved to Paris. There he lived for the rest of his life, earning a modest living as a translator and manuscript reader for publishing houses. His favorite pastimes were smoking and hanging out in cemeteries. Cioran, like Arthur Schopenhauer, was a devoted student of Buddhism. Both men endorsed the Buddha's diagnosis that life consisted of suffering, but Cioran drew far gloomier conclusions from that fact than did either Schopenhauer or the Buddha. Cioran was also a big fan of Friedrich Nietzsche, though he did not share the German philosopher's exuberance in the irrational or his belief in the redeeming power of art.

*Essential Aphorisms*

The fact that life has no meaning is a reason to live—moreover, the only one.

A book is a postponed suicide.

We have lost, being born, as much as we shall lose, dying. Everything.

A free man is one who has discerned the inanity of all points of view; a liberated man is one who has drawn the consequences of such discernment.

Only one thing matters: learning to be the loser.

To live is to lose ground.

**COLTON, CHARLES CALEB** (United Kingdom, 1780–1832) In the preface to his *Lacon: or Many Things in Few Words, Addressed to Those Who Think*, Colton wrote, "That writer does the most, who gives his reader the *most* knowledge, and takes from him the *least* time." The book, published in 1820, is a generous sampling of Colton's wit and wisdom; it is several hundred pages in length, but reading it makes you completely forget the clock. Colton described his age as one in which "free thinking [consists] not in thinking freely, but in being *free from thinking*." He was a famously free thinker himself. Educated at Eton and at King's College, Cambridge, he was appointed vicar of Kew, just outside London, in 1812. He was known as an eloquent preacher; that is, when he cared to apply himself to his sermons. At times, he was brilliant and moving. At other times—such as the occasion when he rushed through his talk and leapt from the pulpit with a rifle in each hand because he was late for a hunting expedition—he just went through the motions. He was notorious for his eccentricities, a vicar who loved to hunt, to gamble, and to drink. He was among the earliest cigar smokers and is reported to have stashed a supply of stogies under the pulpit, where he believed the temperature kept them fresh. In 1828, Colton lost his appointment as vicar of Kew, no doubt for the clerical equivalent of dereliction of duty. At various times, his gambling losses reduced him to squalor. But he somehow always managed to maintain a stock of fine wines. One visitor to his rooms wrote, "The appearance of Mr. C. was at once striking and peculiar. There was an indefinable something in the general character of his features, which, without being prepossessing, fixed the attention of a stranger in no ordinary degree . . . The most exaggerated description of the garrets of the poets of fifty years ago would not libel Mr. Colton's apartment." In a drawer underneath his bed, though, Colton kept a cache of outstanding wines, carefully arranged in rows and cushioned in sawdust. At one point, Colton disappeared, believed murdered by one of his less savory gambling associates. In fact, the reverend had merely gone into hiding to avoid his creditors, first to America—where he traveled under an assumed name and little is known of his exploits—and finally to Paris. In France, Colton was a regular at the Palais Royal, where he started winning big at the gaming tables. He upgraded his accommodation accordingly, amassed a collection of valuable paintings, and indulged his passion for fine wines to the full. *Lacon* was a publishing phenomenon when it came out in 1820. Demand for the book was so high that Colton produced a second volume in 1822. But Colton's lifestyle is said to have brought on an illness that required surgery.

Colton, terrified by the prospect of the procedure, blew out his brains instead. One commentator described Colton's suicide as forcing the former vicar to enter "unbidden the presence of Him of whose laws he was so conspicuous a teacher and violator." In his life and his books, however, Colton was true to his own words: "It is much safer to think what we say, than to say what we think; I have attempted both."

## Essential Aphorisms

He that has never suffered adversity is but half acquainted with others, or with himself.

Constant success shows us but one side of the world. For, as it surrounds us with friends, who will tell us only our merits, so it silences those enemies from whom alone we can learn our defects.

The sun should not set upon our anger; neither should he rise upon our confidence. We should forgive freely, but forget rarely. I will not be revenged, and this I owe to my enemy; but I will remember, and this I owe to myself.

He that likes a hot dinner, a warm welcome, new ideas and old wine will not often dine with the great.

There are some men whose enemies are to be pitied much and their friends more.

An act, by which we make one friend and one enemy, is a losing game, because revenge is a much stronger principle than gratitude.

Men spend their lives in anticipations, in determining to be vastly happy at some period or other when they have time. But the present time has one advantage over every other: it is our own. Past opportunities are gone, future have not come. We may lay in a stock of pleasures, as we would lay in a stock of wine; but if we defer the tasting of them too long, we shall find that both are soured by age!

It is only when the rich are sick that they fully feel the impotence of wealth.

Those who have resources within themselves, who can dare to live alone, want friends the least, but, at the same time, best know how to prize them the most. But no company is far preferable to bad, because we are more apt to catch the vices of others rather than their virtues, as disease is far more contagious than health.

An upright minister asks, what recommends a man; a corrupt minister asks, who.

For one man who sincerely pities our misfortunes, there are a thousand who sincerely hate our successes.

If you are under obligations to many, it is prudent to postpone the recompensing of one until it be in your power to remunerate all; otherwise you will make more enemies by what you give than by what you withhold.

The two most precious things on this side of the grave are our reputation and our life. But it is to be lamented that the most contemptible whisper may deprive us of the one and the weakest weapon of the other. A wise man, therefore, will be the more anxious to deserve a fair name than to possess it, and this will teach so to live as not to be afraid to die.

Pedantry crams our heads with learned lumber and takes out our brains to make room for it.

Men will wrangle for religion, write for it, fight for it, die for it; anything but live for it.

No roads are so rough as those that have just been mended, so no sinners are so intolerant as those that have just turned saints.

**DICKINSON, EMILY** (United States, 1830–1886) "Enter a spirit clad in white, figure so draped as to be misty, face moist, translucent alabaster, forehead firmer as of statuary marble. Eyes once bright hazel now melted and fused so as to be two dreamy, wondering wells of expression . . . mouth made for nothing and used for nothing but uttering choice speech, rare thoughts, glittering, starry misty figures, winged words." That's how Joseph Lyman, a journalist from the *New York Times* who visited the Dickinson household frequently during the 1860s, described Emily. Because her closest confidantes were her poetry and her piano, very little is known for certain about Dickinson's life. Apart from one or two apparently unrequited love affairs, her biography is devoid of any momentous events. Born into a prominent family in Amherst, Massachusetts, she rarely ventured beyond her home and garden on North Pleasant Street. She was a vivacious and intelligent teenager who gradually grew estranged from her friends. As they grew up to marry businessmen or missionaries, she withdrew into a private world of books and botany.

*Essential Aphorisms*

Tell all the Truth but tell it slant—
Success in Circuit lies
Too bright for our infirm Delight
The Truth's superb surprise.

As Lightning to the Children eased
With explanation kind
The Truth must dazzle gradually
Or every man be blind.

Count not that far that can be had,
Though sunset lie between—
Nor that adjacent, that beside,
Is further than the sun.

Who goes to dine must take his Feast
Or find the Banquet mean—
The Table is not laid without
Till it is laid within.

To make a prairie it takes a clover and one bee,
One clover, and a bee,
And revery.
The revery alone will do,
If bees are few.

The supper of the heart is when the guest has gone.

**DIOGENES** (Greece, 404–c. 323 BCE) Before arriving in Athens, where he eventually took up residence in a tub and lived with a pack of stray dogs, Diogenes was captured at sea and sold into slavery. During the auction at which he was up for sale, he is said to have pointed his future owner out in the crowd and instructed his captors, "Sell me to that man. He needs a master." Diogenes got the buyer he wanted, and he went on to become the bad boy of ancient Greek philosophy. He famously disdained conventional manners, morality, and metaphysics. The only worthwhile philosophy, he believed, was one that helped people live a good life in the here and now. He went looking for an honest man in Athens and couldn't find one, not even with a lamp in broad daylight. Diogenes was in many ways a wild, ill-mannered, and insolent disciple of Socrates. Both men were subversives who thought the status quo not worth preserving. The difference is that Diogenes was a shock jock, while Socrates was more of a gentle but relentless persuader.

## Essential Aphorisms

The art of being a slave is to rule one's master.

There is no stick hard enough to drive me away from a man from whom I can learn something.

Of what use is a philosopher who doesn't hurt anybody's feelings?

Go about with your middle finger up and people will say you're daft; go about with your little finger out, and they will cultivate your acquaintance.

In the rich man's house there is no place to spit but in his face.

The only real commonwealth is the whole world.

Practice makes perfect.

I was once as young and silly as you are now, but I doubt if you will become as old and wise as I am.

If, as they say, I am only an ignorant man trying to be a philosopher, then that may be what a philosopher is.

Give up philosophy because I'm an old man? It's at the end of a race that you break into a burst of speed.

## Parallel Lines: To Have and To Have Not

To own nothing is the beginning of happiness.                —DIOGENES

A man is wealthy in proportion to the things he can do without.

                                                              —EPICURUS

Who seeks more than he needs hinders himself from enjoying what he has.
— SOLOMON BEN JUDAH IBN GABIROL

The more we increase our needs and possessions the more we expose
ourselves to adversities and to the blows of Fortune.
— MICHEL DE MONTAIGNE

He whom no losses impoverish is truly rich. — JOHANN KASPAR LAVATER

A man is rich in proportion to the number of things which he can afford to
let alone. — HENRY DAVID THOREAU

Whoever possesses little is possessed by that much less.
— FRIEDRICH NIETZSCHE

Complete possession is proved only by giving. All you are unable to give
possesses you. — ANDRÉ GIDE

**EKELUND, VILHELM** (Sweden, 1880–1949) After a few drinks in a Gothenburg
restaurant one night in 1908, Ekelund was feeling pleasantly tipsy. Stepping outside, he found a stray dog and started playing a game of fetch with it. He threw a
stick into a fountain and the dog dutifully jumped in after it. Ekelund trod on
some plants in the process and a stranger upbraided him, whereupon Ekelund pro-
ceeded to beat the man up. It was not until the next day that the young Swedish
poet learned that the man he had assaulted was actually the Gothenburg district
police superintendent. He was sentenced to a month in prison, but he fled to Berlin
and stayed away from Sweden for the next twelve years, until the statute of limitations expired. For Ekelund, who at the time was one of Sweden's best-known poets, the episode was symptomatic of his relationship with his native country. When
Ekelund switched from poetry to aphoristic prose in his late twenties, his Swedish
contemporaries shunned him. His self-imposed exile proved harsh, too. In Germany, he tried to earn a living from freelance writing but without much success.
He quickly descended into poverty and moved to Hamburg in a bid to reverse his
fortunes. Instead, he was briefly detained on suspicion of murder. Ekelund was
promptly cleared of the charges, but, now living in fear of both the German and
the Swedish police, he became a vagrant, moving constantly from place to place
under a variety of pseudonyms. He returned to Sweden in 1921 but failed to endear
himself to his countrymen. Always prone to fits of temper, he once threw an ash-
tray at a couple whose dancing style displeased him. Invited to a dinner party in his
honor by a member of the Swedish Academy of Letters, Ekelund is said to have
spent the entire evening with his nose in a book. He even continued reading while

eating. When he was finished, Ekelund snapped the book shut, looked up, and said, "One shouldn't socialize." Then he left. Ekelund regarded Friedrich Nietzsche as a role model and kindred spirit. Like Nietzsche, Ekelund rejected convention, whether in literature or morality. Yet his aphorisms are far more sedate than Nietzsche's, perhaps because Ekelund was at heart a contemplative while his German counterpart was much more of a revolutionary. Both men were also among the best writers of aphorisms about aphorisms.

*Essential Aphorisms*

To live poetically is to densify life.

To read fast is as bad as to eat in a hurry.

Solid unpopularity is the only road to great influence.

To find is to grow morally: one never finds anything except what one is worthy of finding. Walls are covered with books; but all they secretly whisper is only this: grow!

There is no deeper defiance than the ability to grant that you were wrong. Guilt—if you put it on yourself—can give you strength and foothold. If you put the blame on somebody else, it becomes not only wasted capital—it becomes the thicket and you get stuck in its thorns.

One has never really triumphed over one's enemies except in one way: by having no time for them!

He who cherishes the beginning—*awaiting himself*; is on the track of the art of living.

You are never any higher—than at a beginning. Better to crawl—than to swell!

In order to understand, one has to get completely lost in the thicket . . . Bad examples are of no use; you have to be on the brink of becoming one yourself before you will see clearly.

To act presumptuous won't do—but it may well pay to stretch your thoughts beyond the toes you are going to turn up one day in the four planks of a wooden box.

There is a muscle in your soul which will forever languish, unless you understand to keep up your *hunger*—hunger in every sense of the word. And life depends on this muscle.

Everything beautiful wants to tell you something. Everything beautiful wants to become thought.

### Parallel Lines: Vilhelm Ekelund and Friedrich Nietzsche

People of solitude always love the aphorism. It gives distraction to the hypochondriac, it gives an air of composure and calm to the nervous, it gives the illusion of productivity to the thinker and the poet in times of barrenness and nonproductivity. —EKELUND

In praise of the max.—A good maxim is too hard for the teeth of time and whole millennia cannot consume it, even though it serves to nourish every age: it is thus the great paradox of literature, the imperishable in the midst of change, the food that is always in season, like salt—though, unlike salt, it never loses its savor. —NIETZSCHE

**ELUARD, PAUL** (France, 1895–1952) and **Benjamin Péret** (France, 1899–1959) Eluard, whose real name was Eugène Grindel, and Péret were prominent poets of the Parisian Surrealist movement. Eluard was a member of the Communist Party, wrote political tracts praising Stalin, and was involved in the French resistance during World War II. Péret left the Dada movement to join the Surrealists, became editor of the influential journal *La Révolution surréaliste*, and fought in the Spanish Civil War. Their *152 Proverbs Adapted to the Taste of the Day* is a surrealistic parody of popular nostrums.

### Essential Aphorisms

No one goes swimming in a deep forest.

The sun shines for no one.

Who stirs in it gets lost in it.

When reason's away, the mice will play.

There's always a pearl in your mouth.

When the road has been traveled, it must be traveled again.

**GÓMEZ DE LA SERNA, RAMÓN** (Spain, 1888–1963) Gómez de la Serna claimed he invented a new form of literature. Born in the Rastro district of Madrid, Ramón (as he was invariably known) devised *greguerías*—acute observations of everyday life tinged by his surrealistic wit and then distilled into brief, aphoristic insights. In one of his several autobiographies, he says he coined the term *greguerías* (which means an irritating noise, gibberish, or hubbub) around 1910. He was visiting Florence in that year, gazing at the river Arno from his hotel window, when he suddenly imagined that the banks of the river wanted to swap sides. This kind of whimsical perception became characteristic of Ramón's aphorisms. He even devised a formula for their creation: "metaphor + humor = *greguerías*." He dubbed his peculiar writing style *ramonismo*. Gómez de la Serna wrote dozens of books, including novels, biographies of El Greco and Goya, poems, criticism, and a taxonomy of all possible types of human breast. Plus, he managed to pen thousands and thousands of *greguerías*. He was something of an eccentric, too; at one point, he had business cards printed up identifying himself as a "circus critic." And he was precocious as well as prolific. His first book was published when he was only sixteen; in his early twenties he was editing his own literary magazine, *Prometeo*, in which he published authors like Anatole France and Oscar Wilde. He enjoyed modest fame for a few years in the late 1920s, after the French Surrealists discovered and championed his writing. But in 1936, in the midst of the Spanish Civil War, he fled to Argentina, where he remained for most of the rest of his life, except for an ill-advised return to his homeland in 1949, when he was seen to be lending credibility and support to the regime of dictator Francisco Franco. He died in Buenos Aires, largely forgotten. The French surrealists feted both Gómez de la Serna and Malcolm de Chazal as honorary members of their movement. But there is nothing even remotely surreal about either man's aphorisms. If anything, their sayings are hyper-realistic: intense depictions of actual physical sensations and objects. Both men anthropomorphize nature and find all too human analogies for what goes on in the natural world. Their taut descriptions are so precise, and their imagery so striking, that commonplaces suddenly take a new, entirely numinous existence.

*Essential Aphorisms*

A carbon copy is taken of everything said in the dark.

After helping a blind man across the road, we remain slightly undecided.

It is haste that carries us so precipitately toward death.

In the interval of the play, we have to administer the kiss of life to our own existence.

The painter should not sign his landscapes, seeing that God didn't.

Ants rush about as though the shops were just closing.

The giraffe is a horse elongated by curiosity.

How quickly they pack suitcases in films!

Life is saying good-bye into a mirror.

Fleas make a dog into a guitarist.

When we stoop for a fallen glove, we help death up.

When the restaurant service is especially slow we become xylophonists of impatience.

It is easier to shear a sheep than undress a sleeping child.

Fish are always in profile.

Some husbands take their wife by the arm as if accompanying them to the police station.

Tombs should be made with periscopes.

Trees only realize that they exist thanks to their shade.

A diamond is a piece of coal that realized its ambitions.

The owl is the table-lamp of the wood at night.

When you open a nutshell, there is an ear inside.

Sunflowers: pocket-mirrors of the sun.

Love is believing you have managed to persuade time not to pass.

**KAFKA, FRANZ** (Czech Republic, 1883–1924) Before his death, Kafka left strict instructions for his friend Max Brod to burn all of his diaries, letters, and manuscripts. Kafka was virtually unknown at the time, and the only works he wished to preserve were a few of his shorter pieces, including *The Metamorphosis*, the tragic tale of Gregor Samsa's life as an insect. But Brod did nothing of the kind. Instead, he systematically published everything of Kafka's he could find, including the brief collection of aphorisms Kafka entered in his diary between January 6 and February 29, 1920. For most of his adult life, Kafka was an employee of the Worker's Accident Insurance Institute for the Kingdom of Bohemia. Like the huge, faceless organizations he parodied in his writings, the Worker's Accident Insurance Institute was an enormous bureaucracy. But Kafka got on well there; he was well liked and good at his job, earning several promotions before he was forced to retire due to ill health. Many of Kafka's afflictions—migraines, insomnia, boils—seem to have been brought on by anxiety. He tried to make lifestyle changes, such as becoming a vegetarian, to combat these regular bouts of illness, but merely altering his diet was futile against the tuberculosis he contracted in 1917. Kafka's short, troubled life consisted of a series of interruptions: periods of intense creativity were punctuated by spells of sickness and listlessness; attempts to reconcile with his overbearing father were negated by fresh rebuffs; a series of romantic relationships was broken off by Kafka's own uncertainty and indecisiveness. None of his novels was ever finished. As his tuberculosis worsened, Kafka developed lesions inside his throat that made it too painful for him to eat or drink. He died of starvation in a sanatorium near Vienna.

*Essential Aphorisms*

The true way leads along a tightrope, which is not stretched aloft but just above the ground. It seems designed more to trip one than to be walked along.

Beyond a certain point there is no return. This point has to be reached.

A first sign of the beginning of understanding is the wish to die. This life seems unbearable, another unattainable. One is no longer ashamed of wanting to die; one begs to be moved out of the old cell, which one hates, into a new one which one must first learn to hate. One is also moved by a certain residual faith that, during transport, the master will happen to come along the corridor, look at the prisoner and say: "This man is not to be locked up again. He comes to me."

Like a path in autumn: scarcely has it been swept clear when it is once more covered with dry leaves.

You are the task. No pupil far and wide.

It is only our conception of time that makes us call the Last Judgment by that name; in fact it is a permanent court-martial.

He runs after facts like a beginner learning to skate, who is furthermore practicing somewhere where it is forbidden.

Human intercourse tempts one to introspection.

### Parallel Lines: Books

We need the books that affect us like a disaster, that grieve us deeply, like the death of someone we loved more than ourselves, like being banished into forests far from everyone, like a suicide. A book must be an axe for the frozen sea inside us.                                          —KAFKA

What we find in books is like the fire in our hearths. We fetch it from our neighbor's, we kindle it at home, we communicate it to others, and it becomes the property of all.                                          —VOLTAIRE

A book is a mirror: if an ape looks into it an apostle is unlikely to look out.
                                          —GEORG CHRISTOPH LICHTENBERG

'Tis the good reader that makes the good book; in every book he finds passages which seem confidences or asides hidden from all else and unmistakenly meant for his ear; the profit of books is according to the sensibility of the reader; the profoundest thought or passion sleeps as in a mine, until it is discovered by an equal mind and heart.
                                          —RALPH WALDO EMERSON

Buying books would be a good thing if one could also buy the time to read them in: but as a rule the purchase of books is mistaken for the appropriation of their contents.                      —ARTHUR SCHOPENHAUER

A great book contains a whole life.      —MARIE VON EBNER-ESCHENBACH

Certain books form a treasure, a basis, once read they will serve you for the rest of your lives.
—EZRA POUND

A book should open old wounds, even inflict new ones. A book should be a *danger*.
—E. M. CIORAN

**NIETZSCHE, FRIEDRICH** (Germany, 1844–1900) The son of a pious Lutheran minister, Nietzsche was a devout and obedient child who could recite biblical verses from memory and often sang church hymns to himself. Fellow students called him the "little pastor." Nietzsche was plagued by ill health—migraines, dysentery, diphtheria, and syphilis—throughout his life. Illness began to get the better of him in the late 1870s, when he resigned his teaching post and roamed around northern Italy and the Swiss Alps in search of a place that would restore his health and allow him the time and solitude in which to write. He had a nervous breakdown in Turin in January 1889 and was taken back to Germany to live with his family. There his madness finally won him fame. Nietzsche's sister Elisabeth took control of his literary affairs and dressed him up in a white robe to exhibit him to tourists as the mad prophet. His books, which had never sold well, now flew off the shelves. In 1865, at the age of twenty-one, Nietzsche came across a copy of Arthur Schopenhauer's *The World as Will and Representation*. It immediately changed his life. Nietzsche embraced Schopenhauer's assertion that there is no god and no meaning inherent in the universe except what we give to it. He also adapted and incorporated Schopenhauer's ideas about the will and redemption through art into his own philosophy. Nietzsche was also enormously influenced by the seventeenth-century French moralists, particularly Sébastien-Roch-Nicolas Chamfort, Michel de Montaigne, and François de la Rochefoucauld, and shared their contempt for social convention, moral hypocrisy, and received wisdom.

*Essential Aphorisms*

Truths are illusions of which one has forgotten that they *are* illusions.

He whom you cannot teach to fly, teach to fall faster!

Good and evil are the prejudices of God.

Whoever must be a creator always annihilates.

Morality is herd-instinct in the individual.

Blessed are the sleepy ones: for they shall soon drop off.

Before the effect one believes in causes different from those one believes in after the effect.

Every habit makes our hand more witty and our wit less handy.

Better to remain in debt than to pay with a coin that does not bear our image!

All one needs in order to be a poet is the ability to have a lively action going on before one continually, to live surrounded by hosts of spirits.

We possess *art* lest we *perish of the truth*.

One must learn to be a sponge if one wants to be loved by hearts that overflow.

Once you know that there are no purposes, you also know that there is no accident.

One repays a teacher badly if one always remains nothing but a pupil.

We are all growing volcanoes approaching their hour of eruption.

When you look long into an abyss, the abyss looks into you.

*Parallel Lines: Laughter*

We should consider every day lost on which we have not danced at least once. And we should call every truth false which was not accompanied by at least one laugh.                                    —NIETZSCHE

We must laugh before we are happy, for fear of dying before we have laughed.                                    —JEAN DE LA BRUYÈRE

That of all days is most completely wasted in which one did not once laugh.                          —SÉBASTIEN-ROCH-NICOLAS CHAMFORT

The man who understands finds almost everything laughable, the man of reason practically nothing.          —JOHANN WOLFGANG VON GOETHE

Laughter is the sensation of feeling good all over and showing it principally in one place.
—JOSH BILLINGS

**PASCAL, BLAISE** (France, 1623–1662) Pascal was a peculiar prodigy. As a young boy, he became extremely agitated every time he saw his parents together, although seeing each of them separately didn't upset him. He also couldn't stand the sight of water. Though Pascal demonstrated an early brilliance in mathematics, his father worried that advanced studies might overwhelm his son's sensitive nature— until he strolled into the boy's room one day to discover that Pascal had independently proved Euclid's geometric theorems by drawing figures on the wall. The elder Pascal promptly gave his son a copy of Euclid's *Elements*. Pascal was a scientist and inventor as well as a mathematician: he developed the first calculator, came up with the idea for the wristwatch, and devised Paris's first public transport system, a network of horse-drawn carriages that traveled along specific routes during specific times. Pascal's aphorisms are contained in the *Pensées*, a collection of fragmentary thoughts and musings he hoped to use as the basis for a grand defense of Christianity. Though Pascal was a scientist, he believed that human reason could not prove the existence of God—or the worthiness of human life. For that, only faith was sufficient. As a young man, Pascal became a follower of Jansenism, a Christian sect that stressed prayer and introspection and regarded human nature as thoroughly corrupt. He gradually became more and more austere in his spiritual views, giving away all his money and possessions to the poor and renouncing even the simplest sensual pleasures, such as fruit or sauces on his food. He even urged his sister not to hug her children. Toward the end of his life, Pascal wore a belt studded with steel spikes under his shirt, which he would press into his flesh whenever he was enjoying himself. Pascal's biggest influences were Epictetus and Michel de Montaigne, though his beliefs were diametrically opposed to theirs. Epictetus praised the acceptance of fate as the key Stoic virtue; Pascal interpreted this as submission to God's will. Pascal shared Montaigne's essential skepticism—How do I know what I know?—but unlike his fellow Frenchman decided that God and not man was the measure of all things. Like his contemporary La Rochefoucauld, Pascal thought *amour-propre* (self-love) was the driving force behind all our actions. La Rochefoucauld analyzed the effects of *amour-propre* on ordinary lives; Pascal more or less equated it with original sin.

*Essential Aphorisms*

The heart has its reasons which reason itself does not know.

Concupiscence and force are the basis of all our actions. Concupiscence causes voluntary actions, force involuntary ones.

What a figment of the imagination human beings are! What a novelty, what monsters! Chaotic, contradictory, prodigious, judging everything, mindless worm of the earth, storehouse of truth, cesspool of uncertainty and error, glory and reject of the universe.

There is enough light for those whose only desire is to see, and enough darkness for those of the opposite disposition.

The most important thing in our life is the choice of a career: chance decides it.

Everything that cannot be understood does nevertheless not cease to exist.

We run carelessly over the precipice after having put something in front of us to prevent us seeing it.

To have no time for philosophy is truly to philosophize.

We do not show greatness by being at one extreme, but rather by touching both at once and filling all the space in between.

It is much better to know something about everything, than everything about something.

It is easier to put up with death without thinking about it, than with the idea of death when there is no danger of it.

Having been unable to strengthen justice, we have justified strength.

Little things comfort us because little things distress us.

Anyone who does not see the vanity of the world is very vain himself.

Man's greatness lies in his capacity to recognize his wretchedness.

The last thing one discovers in composing a work is what has to be put first.

A human being is only a reed, the weakest in nature, but he is a thinking reed.

Take comfort; it is not from yourself that you must expect it, but on the contrary by expecting nothing from yourself that you should expect it.

## Parallel Lines: A Room of One's Own

On the occasions when I have pondered over men's various activities, the dangers and worries they are exposed to at court or at war, from which so many quarrels, passions, risky, often ill-conceived actions and so on are born, I have often said that man's unhappiness springs from one thing alone, his incapacity to stay quietly in one room.          —PASCAL

Nothing, to my way of thinking, is a better proof of a well-ordered mind than a man's ability to stop just where he is and pass some time in his own company.                                        —SENECA

Abba Anthony said also, "Just as fish die if they stay too long out of water, so the monks who loiter outside their cells or pass their time with men of the world lose the intensity of inner peace. So like a fish going towards the sea, we must hurry to reach our cell, for fear that if we delay outside we will lose our interior watchfulness."       —APOPHTHEGMATA PATRUM

Do not go far away: you have plenty to do at home! The only reason why they seek occupation is to be occupied.       —MICHEL DE MONTAIGNE

All mischief comes from our not being able to be alone; hence play, luxury, dissipation, wine, ignorance, calumny, envy, forgetfulness of one's self and of God.                                  —JEAN DE LA BRUYÈRE

All the inducements of early society tend to foster immediate action; all its penalties fall on the man who pauses; the traditional wisdom of those times was never weary of inculcating that "delays are dangerous," and that the sluggish man—the man "who roasteth not that which he took in hunting"—will not prosper on the earth, and indeed will very soon perish out of it. And in consequence an inability to stay quiet, an irritable desire to act directly, is one of the most conspicuous failings of mankind.
                                        —WALTER BAGEHOT

It is not necessary that you leave the house. Remain at your table and listen. Do not even listen, only wait. Do not even wait, be wholly still and alone. The world will present itself to you for its unmasking, it can do no other, in ecstasy it will writhe at your feet.       —FRANZ KAFKA

**PORCHIA, ANTONIO** (Argentina, 1886–1968) Porchia was born in or around the village of Conflenti in southern Italy. His father died when he was twelve and his mother decided to move the family—Antonio and six siblings—to Argentina. The Porchias settled in one of the many Buenos Aires barrios that were filling up with Italian immigrants looking to escape the poverty of their homeland. Porchia took a variety of odd jobs after his arrival, including as a dockworker, carpenter, and basket weaver. He eventually bought a printing press and until 1936, when he retired to his garden and to his writing, ran a small printing business with his brothers. Porchia was well into his sixties before anyone outside his immediate circle of friends knew anything about his aphorisms. Porchia seems to have not been particularly well read. But his aphorisms are imbued with a Taoist approach to life reminiscent of Lao Tzu, and many of his sayings bear a striking resemblance to those of the Buddha.

*Essential Aphorisms*

He who has seen everything empty itself is close to knowing what everything is filled with.

The little things are what is eternal, and the rest, all the rest, is brevity, extreme brevity.

The loss of a thing affects us until we have lost it altogether.

The fear of separation is all that unites.

My poverty is not complete: it lacks me.

If you do not raise your eyes you will think that you are the highest point.

A large heart can be filled with very little.

One learns not to need by needing.

In no one did I find who I should be like. And I stayed like that: like no one.

You will find the distance that separates you from them by joining them.

You think you are killing me. I think you are committing suicide.

Would there be this eternal seeking if the found existed?

We tear life out of life to use it for looking at itself.

We become aware of the void as we fill it.

I know what I have given you. I do not know what you have received.

All that I have lost I find at every step and remember that I have lost it.

When I have nothing left, I will ask for no more.

When I throw away what I don't want, it will fall within reach.

I stop wanting what I am looking for, looking for it.

A full heart has room for everything and an empty heart has room for nothing. Who understands?

I keep my hands empty for the sake of what I have had in them.

He who makes a paradise of his bread makes a hell of his hunger.

When I die, I will not see myself die, for the first time.

I began my comedy as its only actor, and I come to the end of it as its only spectator.

## Parallel Lines: The Cost of Living

What we pay for with our lives never costs too much.          —PORCHIA

No mortal thing can bear so high a price,
But that with mortal thing it may be bought.          —WALTER RALEIGH

We are apt to value many things for what they have cost us, before we take the trouble of calculating their intrinsic worth.
          —WALTER SAVAGE LANDOR

However much you paid for a beautiful illusion, you got a bargain.
          —MARIE VON EBNER-ESCHENBACH

We often make people pay dearly for what we think we give them.

—MARIE-JOSEPHINE DE SUIN DE BEAUSACQ

Where quality is the thing sought after, the thing of supreme quality is cheap, whatever the price one has to pay for it.   —WILLIAM JAMES

Every profound experience has to be paid for with one's own life—and with that of others.   —CHRISTIAN MORGENSTERN

What we buy belongs to us only when the price is forgotten.

—ELIZABETH BIBESCO

Sometimes one pays most for the things one gets for nothing.

ALBERT EINSTEIN

Love's worth is love's cost.   —KAROL BUNSCH

**POUND, EZRA** (United States, 1885–1972) Pound was in classic form at the premiere of *Ballet Mécanique*, George Antheil's experimental music composition. When the piece was first performed in Paris in 1925, the audience was studded with the stars of Modernism, including Pound, James Joyce, T. S. Eliot, and Sylvia Beach, the publisher of *Ulysses*. As soon as the first notes were struck, though, there was a riot. Antheil's composition involved industrial noises (like the sound of actual airplane propellers) as well as more conventional instrumentation, and some in the crowd didn't like it. There was shouting and yelling from all over the theater, fistfights broke out, and, according to Beach, the gusts from the propellers blew a man's toupee all the way to the back of the house. Through all the chaos, Pound was observed hanging upside down from the gallery, denouncing the philistines who were drowning out Antheil's music. Pound was a great propagandist and *provocateur*. He was a leading proponent and practitioner of some of the most important artistic movements of the early twentieth century, including Imagism, Vorticism, and Modernism. He was also responsible for helping to bring to public attention such major figures as Robert Frost, Ernest Hemingway, Joyce, D. H. Lawrence, Wyndham Lewis, Marianne Moore, William Carlos Williams, and sculptor Henri Gaudier-Brzeska. As both an author and critic, he was a defining influence on literature in English. Born in Hailey, Idaho, Pound moved to Europe in 1908 and, except for twelve years spent in an insane asylum in the United States, made the Continent his home for the rest of his life. In the 1920s, Pound lived in Paris and hung out with Dadaist and Surrealist artists like Tristan Tzara and Marcel Duchamp. He then moved to Rapallo, Italy, where he became a supporter of and apologist for fascist dictator Benito Mussolini. During

World War II, he appeared on Italian radio, criticizing American involvement in the conflict and making anti-Semitic remarks. After Mussolini's defeat, Pound was arrested by the U.S. Army and interred in a detention camp near Pisa. For the first twenty-five days of his confinement, he was held outdoors in a cage that was exposed to the elements. Pound was brought back to the United States to face charges of treason, but he was found unfit to stand trial due to insanity. He spent the next twelve years at St. Elizabeth's Hospital in Washington, D.C., where he continued to write books and received a steady stream of literary pilgrims. On his release in 1958, he returned to Italy. Like Mark Twain, Pound was a shrewd and well-traveled expatriate who enjoyed playing off his persona as an innocent abroad. Both men spent large stretches of their writing lives in Europe, and both reveled in their brash, pugnacious, and antiestablishment styles. And both men spent a lot of time thinking—and aphorizing—about what makes great writing.

## Essential Aphorisms

Religion is the root of all evil, or damn near all.

It is better to present one image in a lifetime than to produce voluminous works.

The life of the race is concentrated in a few individuals.

The only thing one can give an artist is leisure in which to work. To give an artist leisure is actually to take part in his creation.

The arts are, when they are healthy, succinct.

All good art is realism of one sort or another.

Artists are the antennae of the race.

Critics should know more and write less.

A writer dies when he ceases to have, and exercise, omnivorous curiosity.

Man reading should be man intensely alive. The book should be a ball of light in one's hand.

The function of poetry is to debunk by lucidity.

Without constant experiment literature dies.

Be influenced by as many great artists as you can, but have the decency to either acknowledge the debt outright, or to try to conceal it.

Poetry is a sort of inspired mathematics, which gives us equations, not for abstract figures, triangles, spheres, and the like, but equations for the human emotions.

A sound poetic training is nothing more than the science of being discontented.

If a man isn't willing to take some risks for his opinions, either his opinions are no good or he's no good.

## Parallel Lines: Ezra Pound and Mark Twain

Great literature is simply language charged with meaning to the utmost possible degree.                                                    —POUND

The difference between the almost-right word and the right word is really a large matter—it's the difference between the lightning bug and the lightning.                                                                        —TWAIN

Good writers are those who keep the language efficient.            —POUND

As to the Adjective: when in doubt, strike it out.                   —TWAIN

**PRUTKOV, KOZMA** (Russia, c. 1852–1863) He is one of Russia's greatest dramatists, poets, and thinkers, a writer whose wise and witty sayings are still quoted daily by Russians from all walks of life. Not bad for an author who never actually existed. Kozma Prutkov is Russia's most elaborate literary practical joke, the creation of the civil servant and minor aristocrat Aleksei Tolstoy and his two cousins, Aleksei and Vladimir Zhemchuzhnikov. Tolstoy and the Zhemchuzhnikov brothers invented Prutkov as a satire on the rigidity and bureaucracy of Tsar Nicholas I's reign. Prutkov was the archetypal bureaucrat, head of the fictional Bureau of Assay, a caricature of the dedicated apparatchik who has so completely internalized the party line that he is unable to think in anything but the most hackneyed clichés. As a result, Prutkov's pronouncements are really parodies of aphorisms, burlesques of what passed for wisdom under Nicholas I. With quintessentially bitter Russian wit, Tolstoy and co. punctured the venality and pomposity of their times.

*Essential Aphorisms*

Zeal conquers all.

No one can embrace the unembraceable.

Death is placed at the end of life so that it can be prepared for most conveniently.

Nails and hair are given to man in order to provide him with a continual but light occupation.

The man wishing to dine too late risks dining the next morning.

Where is the beginning of that end with which the beginning is ended?

The official dies, and his decorations remain on the face of the earth.

Even oysters have enemies.

Only in government service do you learn to know the truth.

A specialist is like a swollen cheek: his fullness is one-sided.

I do not fully understand why many people call fate a turkey, and not some other bird more similar to fate.

A good cigar is like the globe: it turns for the contentment of man.

**SCHOPENHAUER, ARTHUR** (Germany, 1788–1860) It was Schopenhauer's aphorisms—published in 1851 as part of the essays and reflections contained in his second and last book, *Parerga and Paralipomena*—that first won him popular acclaim. During the previous thirty-two years, he and his philosophy had been thoroughly ignored. His fellow thinkers dismissed him as a crank and curmudgeon, while what he considered his masterpiece—*The World as Will and Representation*—went almost completely unread. In the 1820s, during an ill-fated career as a university lecturer, he couldn't attract a single student to his classes; by the 1850s, people would crowd into the Englischer Hof, Schopenhauer's favorite Frankfurt restaurant, just to watch the eccentric thinker eat lunch. As part of a daily routine that rarely varied during the twenty-seven years he lived in Frankfurt, Schopenhauer rose every day at seven a.m., took a bath, drank a cup of coffee, and wrote until noon. Then he played the flute for an hour and headed to the Englischer Hof for lunch. After his meal, he read until four and then went for a brisk two-hour constitutional, accompanied by his poodle. At six p.m. he stopped by the library to read the London *Times* and in the evening had dinner at a restaurant, attended the theater or a concert, and was in bed by ten p.m. This life of literature and leisure was made possible by Schopenhauer's father, a wealthy merchant who committed suicide by throwing himself out of the window of one of his Hamburg warehouses. As a result, when Schopenhauer turned twenty-one, he inherited a small fortune that allowed him to focus on philosophy without having to worry about earning a living. He could now afford to declare, "Life is an unpleasant business; I have resolved to spend it reflecting upon it." Like Baltasar Gracián—whose work he loved, translating it into German in the 1820s—Schopenhauer was a practitioner of the long-form aphorism. Schopenhauer was also deeply influenced by Buddhist philosophy, writing in 1832, "In my seventeenth year, without any learned school education, I was gripped by the misery of life as Buddha was in his youth when he saw sickness, old age, pain and death." In *The World as Will and Representation*, he even recommends a practice of focused attention that is very similar to Buddhist meditation.

*Essential Aphorisms*

The good things we possess, or are certain of getting, are not felt to be such; because all pleasure is in fact of a negative nature and effects the relief of pain, while pain or evil is what is really positive; it is the object of immediate sensation.

A good supply of resignation is of the first importance in providing for the journey of life. It is a supply which we shall have to extract from disappointed hopes; and the sooner we do it, the better for the rest of the journey.

A man is wise only on condition of living in a world full of fools.

The reason the impressions we receive in youth are so significant, the reason why in the dawn of life everything appears to us in so ideal and transfigured a light, is that we then first become acquainted with the genus, which is still new to us, through the individual, so that every individual thing stands as a representative of its genus: we grasp therein the (Platonic) *Idea* of this genus, which is essentially what constitutes beauty.

The task of the novelist is not to narrate great events but to make small ones interesting.

Every parting is a foretaste of death, and every reunion a foretaste of resurrection. That is why even people who were indifferent to one another rejoice so much when they meet again after twenty or thirty years.

If you want to know how you really feel about someone take note of the impression an unexpected letter from him makes on you when you first see it on the doormat.

A precondition for reading good books is not reading bad ones: for life is short.

If [a man] wants to think only, and not act and do business, the disposition to the latter is not thereby destroyed all at once; but as long as the thinker lives, he has every hour to keep on killing the acting and pushing man that is within him; always battling with himself, as though he were a monster whose head is no sooner struck off than it grows again. In the same way, if he is resolved to be a saint, he must kill himself so far as he is a being that enjoys and is given over to pleasure; for such he remains as long as he lives. It is not once for all that he must kill himself: he must keep on doing it all his life.

A man's nature is in harmony with itself when he desires to be nothing but what he is; that is to say, when he has attained by experience a knowledge of his strength and of his weakness, and makes use of the one and conceals the other, instead of playing with false coin, and trying to show a strength which he does not possess. It is a harmony which produces an agreeable and rational character; and for the simple reason that everything which makes the man and gives him his mental and physical qualities is nothing but the manifestation of his will; is, in fact, what he wills. Therefore it is the greatest of all inconsistencies to wish to be other than we are.

Obstinacy is the result of the will forcing itself into the place of the intellect.

A true philosophy cannot be spun out of mere abstract concepts, but has to be founded on observation and experience, inner and out.

The sublime melancholy which leads us to cherish a lively conviction of the worthlessness of everything, of all pleasures and of all mankind, and therefore to long for nothing, but to feel that life is merely a burden which must be borne to an end that cannot be very distant, is a much happier state of mind than any condition of desire, which, be it never so cheerful, would have us place a value on the illusions of the world, and strive to attain them.

Life is known to be a process of combustion; intellect is the light produced by this process.

**WITTGENSTEIN, LUDWIG** (Austria, 1889–1951) Wittgenstein was a profoundly spiritual man, an odd combination of mendicant and mathematician. Born into one of the wealthiest and most highly cultured families in Hapsburg Vienna, Wittgenstein renounced his family's money and led a frugal, ascetic existence, living off the stipend he received from Cambridge University and whatever he earned from his periodic employment outside academia. After the publication of *Tractatus Logico-Philosophicus* in 1922, the only one of his books to appear in his lifetime, he renounced his work on logic and mathematics, too, and left Cambridge to teach in elementary schools in rural Austria. He loved crime fiction and Hollywood B-movies, particularly westerns and musicals. He was a virtuoso whistler. After his return to academic life in 1929, Wittgenstein focused on metaphysics, ethics, aesthetics, and especially the philosophy of language. Wittgenstein adopted the terse, declarative style of Benedict Spinoza. Like Spinoza's axioms, Wittgenstein's aphorisms are stripped down to the essentials; all excess description has been pared away. Each one is its own proof.

*Essential Aphorisms*

Philosophical problems arise when language goes on holiday.

When the answer cannot be put into words, neither can the question be put into words. The riddle does not exist. If a question can be framed at all, it is also possible to answer it.

The solution of the problem of life is seen in the vanishing of the problem.

Philosophy is a battle against the bewitchment of our intelligence by means of our language.

Philosophy is not a body of doctrine but an activity.

Resting on your laurels is as dangerous as resting when hiking through snow. You doze off and die in your sleep.

The world of the happy man is a different one from that of the unhappy man.

A good simile refreshes the intellect.

Strike a coin from every mistake.

Genius is courage in one's talent.

Words are deeds.

Uttering a word is like striking a note on the keyboard of the imagination.

The world is all that is the case.

The limits of my language mean the limits of my world.

**WORTH, PATIENCE** (United Kingdom, 1649–c. 1680s) Born in England, Worth traveled to America with some of the early English settlers when she was in her thirties. By her own account, she had a feisty, witty personality and held some unconventional views for her time, especially about religion. She was apparently killed in a skirmish with Native Americans. At least, that's what Pearl Lenore Curran says Patience Worth told her over a period of about twenty-five years, beginning in 1912. Curran, a St. Louis, Missouri, housewife who died in 1937, claimed to have been in telepathic contact with Patience Worth some 260 years after the latter's death—and to have taken posthumous dictation, with the help of a Ouija board, of Worth's poems, novels, and "proverbs." Proverbs is the right word to describe these sayings; the language is archaic and the themes very Old Testament. In the book *The Case of Patience Worth*, Walter Franklin Prince writes, "almost immediately after Patience Worth announced herself . . . she began to make replies, which in pith, wit, wisdom and generally in terseness, resemble the proverbs of old time."

*Essential Aphorisms*

A fiery tongue belongs to one worth burning.

A basting but toughens an old goose.

A lollipop is but a breeder of pain.

A pot of wisdom would boil to nothing ere a doubter deemeth it worth tasting.

Prod ye the donkey's rump ye are sure of a kick.

It taketh a wise man to be a good fool.

# AFTERISMS

It is no exaggeration to say that I have been working on this book since 1970 when, at the age of eight, I first became obsessed with aphorisms. The actual composition, however, took place during 2006. I spent a lot of that year at the British Library in London, where I went through the entire catalog of more than 1,400 volumes that came up under the search term "aphorism." I personally looked at every book that was in a language I could read (basically, English, Dutch, and German). For the rest, I compiled a list of authors and titles and sought out translators proficient in those languages to help me. I am very grateful to the following for their resourceful research and deft translations: Emily Anderson (Japanese), Alex Brenner (Chinese), Mohamed Elsamahi (Arabic), Michael Gilleland (from the Spanish of Nicolás Gómez Dávila), Isolde Grabenmeier (Polish), Linda Hoetink (French, German, and some help with Dutch), Boris Mitic (Serbian), Peter Robinson (Italian), Ursula Sautter (German, Italian, and Spanish), Maria Shpikalova (Russian), Mirja Siltala (Finnish), Jan Stojaspal (Czech), and Lothaire de Vargas (French). Except for some of Multatuli's aphorisms, all translations from the Dutch are my own.

Each of these translators made a vital contribution to the book. All mistakes—whether of omission, commission, translation, interpretation, or attribution—are my own. I welcome comments and corrections through my Web site, www.jamesgeary.com.

I am aware that my limited knowledge of many of the world's languages and cultures means that I have not given an adequate representation of their aphorisms. Perhaps I can rectify that in future editions of this book. In the meantime, I welcome information about any and all aphorists through the Aphorism Alert section on my Web site.

Two previous anthologies were important research and reference sources: *The Faber Book of Aphorisms*, edited by W. H. Auden and Louis Kronenberger, and *The Oxford Book of Aphorisms*, edited by John Gross. Both books saved me from a number of glaring omissions.

Many people were extremely generous in providing tips about new aphorists and assistance in tracking down obscure authors. For this, I thank: Viveca Bachrach, Michael Bourdaghs, Stephen Clucas, Les Coleman, Markku Envall, Ferial Ghazoul, Bobby Ghosh, Patrick Hughes, Jeff Israely, Susie Jakes, Yahia Labibidi, Sara Levine, Daniel Liebert, Paul Quinn-Judge, James Richardson, Ian Sansom, Sarah Teslik, Sarah Whitfield, Hannah Whitley, and Yuri Zarakhovich.

I am indebted to Michael Brunton for his amazing literary sleuthing and to Max Brockbank, proprietor and presiding genius of www.sceneonthenet.com, who designed and maintains my Web site.

I thank Gillian Blake of Bloomsbury USA and Katinka Matson of Brockman Inc. for making this book possible and, in turn, for making it possible for me to spend an entire year of my life doing what I love best: reading and writing about aphorisms.

And Linda, Gilles, Tristan, and Hendrikje—because words fail me.

# BIBLIOGRAPHY

Wherever possible and practical, I relied on published works in the preparation of this book. I consulted a range of print and online sources in the composition of the biographies. In some cases, my only source for aphorisms was online; this is indicated below. In addition, I often include an online reference for readers who might like to see more from a particular author.

## COMICS, CRITICS, AND SATIRISTS

**Allen, Woody.** Woody Allen's aphorisms can be found at en.wikiquote.org/wiki/Woody_Allen.

**Baljak, Aleksandar.** *Ubedili ste boga u meni.* Belgrade: Sic, 1982.

―――. *U granicama demokratije.* Belgrade: Filip Visnjic, 1988.

―――. *Krvavi provod.* Belgrade: Srpska Rec, 1995.

―――. *Sumnjivo okupljanje reci.* Belgrade: Gutembergova Galaksija, 2000.

―――. *Rat je prvi poceo.* Belgrade: Agora, 2007.

**Balzac, Honoré de.** *Epigrams on Men, Women, and Love.* Selected and translated by Jacques Le Clercq, with wood engravings by Derrick Harris. Mount Vernon, NY: Peter Pauper Press, 1959.

**Banksy.** Banksy's aphorisms can be found at www.banksy.co.uk.

**Beerbohm, Max.** *The Incomparable Max.* A selection introduced by S. C. Roberts. London: Heinemann, 1962. Additional aphorisms can be found at www.brainyquote.com/quotes/authors/m/max_beerbohm.html.

**Billings, Josh.** *The Complete Works of Josh Billings, with One Hundred Illustrations by Thomas Nast and Others, and a Biographical Introduction.* New York: G. W. Dillingham Co., 1876.

―――. *Life and Adventures of Josh Billings with A Sketch of the Humorist, by Francis S. Smith, Also One Hundred Illustrated Aphorisms.* New York: G. W. Carleton & Co., Publishers, 1883.

―――. *Josh Billings' Old Farmer's Allminax: Perhaps Rain, Perhaps Not.* New York: G. W. Dillingham Co., 1902.

————. Cited in Kesterson, David B. *Josh Billings*. New York: Twayne Publishers, 1973. Additional aphorisms can be found at www.brainyquote.com/quotes/authors/j/ josh_billings.html.

**Börne, Ludwig.** *The State Paper of the Heart: Fragmente und Aphorismen.* Werner Ehrenforth, ed. Berlin: Eulenspiegel Verlag, 1986.

**Boyd, Andrew.** *Life's Little Deconstruction Book: Self-Help for the Post-Hip.* New York: W. W. Norton & Company, 1998.

————. *Daily Afflictions: The Agony of Being Connected to Everything in the Universe.* New York: W. W. Norton & Company, 2002.

**Brie, André.** *Nur die nackte Wahrheit geht mit keiner Mode.* Berlin: Eulenspiegel Verlag, 2000.

**Brilliant, Ashleigh.** Ashleigh Brilliant's aphorisms can be found at www.ashleighbril liant.com/index.html.

**Brudzinski, Wieslaw.** Cited in *Wspólczesna aforystyka polska.* Zebral, opracowal i wstepem opatrzyl Joachim Glensk. Antologia 1945–1984. Lódz: Wydanictwo Lódzkie, 1986.

————. Cited in *Katzenjammer: Aphorismen.* Herausgegeben und aus dem Polnischen übersetzt von Karl Dedecius. Frankfurt/Main: Edition Suhrkamp, 1966.

————. Cited in *A Treasury of Polish Aphorisms.* A bilingual edition compiled and translated by Jacek Galazka. Cornwall Bridge, CT: Polish Heritage Publications, 1997.

**Butler, Samuel.** *Hudibras Parts I and II and Selected Other Writings.* John Wilders and Hugh de Quehen, eds. Oxford: Clarendon Press, 1973.

————. Cited in *The Oxford Book of Aphorisms.* John Gross, ed. Oxford: Oxford University Press, 2003. Additional aphorisms can be found at en.wikiquote.org/wiki/Samuel_Butler_%281612-1680%29.

**Butler, Samuel.** *The Note-Books of Samuel Butler.* London: Jonathan Cape, 1921.

**Byrne, David.** *Your Action World.* San Francisco: Chronicle Books, 1991.

————. *The New Sins.* Brooklyn, NY: McSweeney's, 2001.

**Chamfort, Sébastien-Roch-Nicolas.** *Products of the Perfected Civilization.* Selected Writings of Chamfort. Translated and with an Introduction by W. S. Merwin. Foreword by Louis Kronenberger. San Francisco: North Point Press, 1984. © 1984 by W. S. Merwin. By permission of The Wylie Agency.

————. *Maxims and Considerations of Chamfort.* Translated and with an Introduction by E. Powys Mathers. London: Golden Cockerel Press, 1926.

**Coleman, Les.** *Unthoughts.* London: Ink Sculptors, 1992.

————. *Unthinking.* Todmorden, England: Littlewood Arc, 1993.

**Connolly, Cyril.** *Enemies of Promise.* London: Andre Deutsch, 1996.

————. (Palinurus) *The Unquiet Grave.* London: Hamish Hamilton, 1945.

**Čotrić, Aleksandar.** *Dacemo mi vama demokratiju.* Belgrade: Knjizevna Omladina Srbije, 1993.

————. *Peta kolona.* Belgrade: Srpska Rec, 1997.

————. *Nedozvoljene misli.* Belgrade: Srpska Rec, 2000.

————. *Kratki rezovi.* Belgrade: Srpska Rec, 2004.

**Dard, Frédéric.** *Les Pensées de San Antonio.* Paris: Le Cherche Midi Éditeur, 1996.

**Dovlatov, Sergei.** Sergei Dovlatov's aphorisms are from *Solo na Underwude* (1980) and can be found, in Russian, at www.lib.ru/DOWLATOW/dowlatow.txt.

**Fiori, Fulvio.** Fulvio Fiori's aphorisms are from *Vivere Mi Piace da Morire* (1993) and *Riflessioni Trasparenti* (1994).

**Fredro, Aleksander.** Cited in *A Treasury of Polish Aphorisms*. A bilingual edition compiled and translated by Jacek Galazka. Cornwall Bridge, CT: Polish Heritage Publications, 1997.

―――. Cited in *Aforyzmy Polskie. Antologia*. Danuta i Wlodzimierz Maslowscy, eds. Introduction by Jan Miodek. Kety: Wydawnictwo Antyk, 2001. Additional aphorisms can be found, in Polish, at www.mysli.com.pl/ludzie.php?autor=2289&l=N.

**Gervaso, Roberto.** Roberto Gervaso's aphorisms can be found, in Italian, at www.drzap .it/O_Gervaso.htm.

**Griboyedov, Alexander Sergeevich.** *Woe from Wit*. Edited with introduction, bibliography, and vocabulary by Richard Peace. Notes by D. P. Costello. London: Bristol Classics Press, 2003. *Woe from Wit* can also be found, in English, at spintongues .msk.ru/griboyedov.htm.

**Guberman, Igor.** The *gariki* of Igor Guberman can be found, in Russian, at www.guber man.bibliadore.com/stihi.htm.

**Holzer, Jenny.** *Jenny Holzer*. Text by David Joselit, Joan Simon, and Renata Salecl. London: Phaidon Press, 2001. © 2007 Jenny Holzer, member Artists Rights Society, NY.

**Hubbard, Elbert.** *The Notebook of Elbert Hubbard: Mottoes, Epigrams, Short Essays, Passages, Orphic Sayings and Preachments*. Gathered together by Elbert Hubbard II. New York: Wm. H. Wise & Co., 1927. Additional aphorisms can be found at www.brainyquote.com/quotes/authors/e/elbert_hubbard.html.

**Hubbard, Frank McKinney.** *Abe Martin's Wisecracks*. Selected by E. V. Lucas. London: Methuen & Co., 1930. Additional aphorisms can be found at en.wikiquote.org/ wiki/Kin_Hubbard.

**Jackson, Holbrook.** *Platitudes Undone, A Facsimile Edition of Platitudes in the Making: Precepts and Advices for Gentlefolk*. With the original handwritten responses of G. K. Chesterton. San Francisco: Ignatius Press, 1997.

**Kraus, Karl.** *Dicta and Contradicta*. Jonathan McVity, trans. Urbana and Chicago: University of Illinois Press, 2001.

**Kruger, Barbara.** *Love for Sale: The Words and Pictures of Barbara Kruger*. Text by Kate Linker. New York: Harry N. Abrams, 1996. By permission of the Mary Boone Gallery, New York.

**Kuppner, Frank.** *A God's Breakfast*. London: Carcanet, 2004.

**Laub, Gabriel.** *Denken verdirbt den Charakter: Alle Aphorismen*. Munich and Vienna: Carl Hanser, 1984.

**Lec, Stanislaw J.** *Unkempt Thoughts*. Jacek Galazka, trans.; introduction by Clifton Fadiman; illustrated by Barbara Carr. New York: St. Martin's Press, 1962.

―――. *More Unkempt Thoughts*. Jacek Galazka, trans.; illustrated by David Pascal. New York: Funk & Wagnalls, 1968.

**Mencken, H. L.** *The Gist of Mencken: Quotations from America's Critic Gleaned from Newspapers, Magazine, Books, Letters and Manuscripts by Mayo DuBasky*. Metuchen, N.J.: Scarecrow, 1990. Additional aphorisms can be found at www.brainyquote .com/quotes/authors/h/h_l_mencken.html.

**Mestrum, Theo.** *Kleren voor de Keizer: Aforismen*. Amsterdam: De Beuk, 1997.

Morgenstern, Christian. *Epigramme und Sprüche. Collected Works: Volume 14.* Basel: Zbinden, 1977.

Paronen, Samuli. Cited in *Aforismin Vuosisata.* Markku Envall, ed. Juva, Finland: WSOY, 1997.

Pope, Alexander. *Complete Poetical Works.* Oxford: Oxford University Press, 1983. By permission of Oxford University Press.

Ranevskaya, Faina. *Sluchai, Shutki, Aphorizmy.* Collected by Igor Zakharov. Moscow: Zakharov Publishers, 2002. Ranevskaya's aphorisms can also be found, in Russian, at www.lib.ru/MEMUARY/RANEWSKAQ/shutki.txt.

Rogers, Will. *The Wit and Wisdom of Will Rogers.* Alex Ayres, ed. New York: Meridian, 1993. Additional aphorisms can be found at www.willrogers.org/.

Scutenaire, Louis. Cited in *Surrealist Painters and Poets: An Anthology.* Mary Ann Caws, ed. Boston: MIT Press, 2002. Also cited in *Les Levres Nues,* No. 2, August 1954, pp. 15–19 and No. 5, June 1955, pp. 29–31.

Shenderovich, Victor. Shenderovich's aphorisms can be found, in Russian, at www.shender.ru/shendevr/.

Swift, Jonathan. *Thoughts on Various Subjects* is available at etext.library.adelaide.edu.au/s/swift/jonathan/s97th/.

Tucholsky, Kurt. Cited in *Deutsche Aphorismen.* Gerhard Fieguth, ed. Stuttgart: Reclam, 1978.

———. Cited in *Deutsche Aphorismen aus drei Jahrhunderten.* Selected by Federico Hindermann and Bernhard Heinser. Zurich: Manesse, 1987.

Twain, Mark. *Tales, Sketches, Speeches, & Essays 1891–1910.* "More Maxims of Mark." New York: The Library of America, 1976.

———. *The Quotable Mark Twain: His Essential Aphorisms, Witticisms & Concise Opinions.* Edited by R. Kent Rasmussen. Chicago: Contemporary Books, 1998.

Valckenaere, Julien de. *Flitsen in de Duisternis.* Brugge: Uitgeverij Orion, 1974.

Verhoeven, Toon. *Terzijde.* Amsterdam: B.V. Weekbladpers/Vrij Nederland, 1990.

Voltaire. *Selected Works of Voltaire.* Joseph McCabe, trans. London: Watts & Co., 1948.

———. *Philosophical Dictionary.* Theodore Besterman, ed. and trans. London: Penguin Books, 1972.

———. *Candide.* Ware: Wordsworth Classics, 1993.

Additional aphorisms can be found at en.wikiquote.org/wiki/Voltaire.

Weller, Mikhail. Mikhail Weller's aphorisms are from *All About Life* (1998) and can be found, in Russian, at www.lib.ru/WELLER/life.txt.

Werich, Jan. Werich's aphorisms can be found, in Czech, at www.mraveniste.org/ego/jan-werich-citaty.html.

Wright, Steven. Steven Wright's aphorisms can be found at www.weather.net/zarg/ZarPages/stevenWright.html.

Zakić, Rastko. *Kuda nas modni kreatori vode.* Belgrade: Zapis, 1978.

———. *Ukrstene reci.* Belgrade: KRRZ, 1984.

———. *Drzavne brige.* Belgrade: KRRZ, 1986.

———. *Druge dzavne brige.* Belgrade: KRRZ, 1987.

———. *Pristojnost nalaze da se pobunimo.* Belgrade: Srpska Rec, 1998.

## ICONS AND ICONOCLASTS

Ali, Muhammad. Muhammad Ali's aphorisms can be found at en.wikiquote.org/wiki/ Muhammad_Ali.

Bagehot, Walter. *The Best of Bagehot*. Edited with an introduction by Ruth Dudley Edwards. London: Hamish Hamilton, 1993. Additional aphorisms can be found at en.wikiquote.org/wiki/Walter_Bagehot.

Baruch, Bernard. *My Own Story*. London: Odhams Press, 1958. Additional aphorisms can be found at www.brainyquote.com/quotes/authors/b/bernard_baruch.html.

Burke, Edmund. *The Wisdom of Edmund Burke*. Extracts from his speeches and writings, selected and arranged by Edward Alloway Pankhurst. London: John Murray, 1886.

———. *Maxims and Reflections of Burke*. Selected and edited by F. W. Raffety. London: T. S. Clark & Co., 1909. Additional aphorisms can be found at www.brainyquote.com/quotes/authors/e/ed mund_burke.html.

Churchill, Winston. *The Wisdom of Winston Churchill*. F. B. Czarnomski, ed. London: George Allen and Unwin, 1956.

———. *The Irrepressible Churchill*. Compiled by Kay Halle. London: Robson Books, 1987.

Cicero. *On the Good Life*. London: Penguin Books, 2001.

———. *Selected Works*. London: Penguin Books, 1974. Additional aphorisms can be found at en.wikiquote.org/wiki/Cicero and www.brainy quote.com/quotes/authors/m/marcus_tullius_cicero.html.

Clausewitz, Carl von. *The Essential Clausewitz: Selections from On War*. Joseph I. Greene, ed. Mineola, NY: Dover Publications, 2003. Additional aphorisms can be found at www.clausewitz.com/CWZHOME/Quotations .html.

Cruijff, Johan. Johan Cruijff's aphorisms can be found at en.wikiquote.org/wiki/Jo han_Cruyff.

Disraeli, Benjamin. *The Sayings of Disraeli*. Edited by Robert Blake. London: Duckworth, 1992.

———. *Selected Speeches of the Late Right Honourable the Earl of Beaconsfield*. Arranged and edited, with introduction and explanatory notes, by T. E. Kebbel. London: Longmans, Green, & Co., 1882. Additional aphorisms can be found at en.wikiquote.org/wiki/Benjamin_Disraeli% 2C_1st_Earl_of_Beaconsfield.

Dylan, Bob. The aphorisms of Bob Dylan can be found in his song lyrics, available at bobdylan.com/songs/.

Edison, Thomas Alva. *The Diary and Sundry Observations of T. A. Edison*. D. D. Runes, ed. New York: Philosophical Library, 1948. Additional aphorisms can be found at en.wikiquote.org/wiki/Thomas_Edison.

Einstein, Albert. *The Expanded Quotable Einstein*. Collected and edited by Alice Calaprice, with a foreword by Freeman Dyson. Princeton: Princeton University Press, 2000. Additional aphorisms can be found at en.wikiquote.org/wiki/Albert_Einstein.

Emerson, Ralph Waldo. *Selected Prose and Poetry*. New York: Holt, Rinehart and Winston, 1969.

————. *The Heart of Emerson's Journals.* Bliss Perry, ed. New York: Dover Publications, 1995.

Ford, Henry. The aphorisms of Henry Ford can be found at en.wikiquote.org/wiki/Henry_Ford.

Gandhi, Mohandas K. *The Wit and Wisdom of Gandhi.* Edited, with an introduction, by Homer A. Jack. Preface by John Haynes Holmes. Boston: Beacon Press, 1951.

————. *The Sayings of Mahatma Gandhi.* Singapore: Graham Brash, 2000.

Hippocrates. Hippocrates' aphorisms can be found at http://classics.mit.edu/Hippocrates/aphorisms.html.

Holmes, Oliver Wendell, Jr. *The Essential Holmes: Selections from the Letters, Speeches, Judicial Opinions, and Other Writings of Oliver Wendell Holmes, Jr.* Edited and with an introduction by Richard A. Posner. Chicago: University of Chicago Press, 1992.

Additional aphorisms can be found at www.brainyquote.com/quotes/authors/o/oliver_wendell_holmes_jr.html and en.wikiquote.org/wiki/Oliver_Wendell_Holmes%2C_Jr.

Kennedy, John Fitzgerald. John F. Kennedy's aphorisms can be found at en.wikiquote.org/wiki/John_F_Kennedy.

King, Martin Luther, Jr. *In My Own Words.* Selected and introduced by Coretta Scott King. London: Hodder & Stoughton, 2002.

Additional aphorisms can be found at en.wikiquote.org/wiki/Martin_Luther_King_Jr.

Lincoln, Abraham. *Of the People, By the People, For the People and Other Quotations by Abraham Lincoln.* New York: Columbia University Press, 1996.

Additional aphorisms can be found at en.wikiquote.org/wiki/Abraham_Lincoln.

Montesquieu, Charles de Secondat, Baron de. *Selected Political Writings.* Melvin Richter ed. and trans. Indianapolis: Hackett, 1990.

Additional aphorisms can be found at en.wikiquote.org/wiki/Charles_de_Secondat%2C_Baron_de_Montesquieu and en.thinkexist.com/quotes/charles_de_montesquieu/4.html.

Napoleon. *Aphorisms of Napoleon in French and English.* James Alexander Manning, trans. London: Ackermann and Co., 1852.

Paine, Thomas. *Aphorisms, Opinions and Reflections of T. Paine, to which is prefixed an Essay on his Life.* London, 1826.

Raleigh, Walter. *Selected Prose and Poetry.* Agnes M. C. Latham, ed. London: Athlone Press, 1965.

Additional aphorisms can be found at www.giga-usa.com/gigaweb1/quotes2/quautraleigh1walterx001.htm and www.bartleby.com/100/124.html.

Roosevelt, Eleanor. Eleanor Roosevelt's aphorisms can be found at en.wikiquote.org/wiki/Eleanor_Roosevelt.

Roosevelt, Franklin Delano. *Nothing to Fear: The Selected Addresses of Franklin Delano Roosevelt, 1932–1945.* Edited, with an introduction and historical notes, by B. D. Zevin. London: Hodder & Stoughton, 1947.

Additional aphorisms can be found at en.wikiquote.org/wiki/Franklin_Delano_Roosevelt.

Roosevelt, Theodore. *The Real Roosevelt: His Forceful and Fearless Utterances on Various Subjects.* Selected and arranged by Alan Warner. With a foreword by Lyman Abbott. New York: G. P. Putnam's & Sons, 1910.

Additional aphorisms can be found at en.wikiquote.org/wiki/Theodore_Roosevelt.

**Schreiner, Olive.** Cited in Stewart, Julia. *Stewart's Quotable Africa.* London: Penguin Books, 2004.
Additional aphorisms can be found at en.thinkexist.com/quotes/olive_schreiner/.
**Sun Tzu.** *The Art of War.* Thomas Cleary, trans. Boston and London: Shambhala, 1988.
**Thoreau, Henry David.** *Walden and "Civil Disobedience."* New York: New American Library, 1960.
————. *The Heart of Thoreau's Journals.* Odell Shepard, ed. New York: Dover Publications, 1961.
**Tocqueville, Alexis de.** *Democracy in America.* New York: Mentor Books, 1984.
Additional aphorisms can be found at en.wikiquote.org/wiki/Alexis_de_Tocqueville and www.brainyquote.com/quotes/authors/a/alexis_de_tocqueville.html.
**Truman, Harry S.** Harry S. Truman's aphorisms can be found at en.wikiquote.org/wiki/Harry_Truman.
**Tutu, Desmond.** Cited in Stewart, Julia. *Stewart's Quotable Africa.* London: Penguin Books, 2004.
Additional aphorisms can be found at en.wikiquote.org/wiki/Desmond_Tutu.
**Warhol, Andy.** *The Philosophy of Andy Warhol (From A to B and Back Again).* New York: Harcourt Brace Jovanovich, 1975.
Additional aphorisms can be found at en.wikiquote.org/wiki/Andy_Warhol.
**Washington, George.** *Rules of Civility: The 110 Precepts That Guided Our First President in War and Peace.* Edited and with a new preface by Richard Brookhiser. Charlottesville: University of Virginia Press, 2003.
**West, Mae.** Mae West's aphorisms can be found at en.wikiquote.org/wiki/Mae_West.

## MORALISTS, MAJOR AND MINOR

### THE MAJOR MORALISTS

**Amenemope.** *Ancient Egyptian Literature, A Book of Readings. Volume II: The Old and Middle Kingdoms.* Miriam Lichtheim, trans. Berkeley: University of California Press, 1976. By permission of the University of California Press.
**Bacon, Francis.** *The Major Works.* Edited with an introduction and notes by Brian Vickers. Oxford: Oxford University Press, 2000.
————. *The Essays or Counsels Civil and Moral, including also his Apophthegms, Elegant Sentences and Wisdom of the Ancients.* New York: William L. Allison Company, 1897.
**Bruyère, Jean de la.** *La Bruyère and Vauvenargues: Selections from the Characters, Reflexions and Maxims.* Translated with introductory notes and memoirs by Elizabeth Lee. London: Archibald Constable & Co., 1903.
Additional aphorisms can be found at en.wikiquote.org/wiki/Jean_de_La_Bruyere.
**Bunsch, Karol.** Cited in *Wspólczesna aforystyka polska.* Zebral, opracowal i wstepem opatrzyl Joachim Glensk. Antologia 1945–1984. Lódz: Wydanictwo Lódzkie, 1986.
————. Cited in *A Treasury of Polish Aphorisms.* A bilingual edition compiled and translated by Jacek Galazka. Cornwall Bridge, CT: Polish Heritage Publications, 1997.
Additional aphorisms can be found, in Polish, at www.mysli.com.pl/ludzie.php?autor=2289&l=N.

Chesterton, G. K. *More Quotable Chesterton: A Topical Compilation of the Wit, Wisdom and Satire of G. K. Chesterton.* George J. Marlin, et al., eds. San Francisco: Ignatius Press, 1988. By permission of A. P. Watt on behalf of the Royal Literary Fund. Additional aphorisms can be found at www.chesterton.org/discover/quotations.html.

Ebner-Eschenbach, Marie von. *Aphorisms.* Mrs. A. L. Wister, trans. Philadelphia: J. P. Lippincott and Co., 1883.

————. *Aphorisms.* Translated and introduced by David Scrase and Wolfgang Meider. Riverside, CA: Ariadne Press, 1994.

Franklin, Benjamin. *Wit and Wisdom from Poor Richard's Almanack.* Steve Martin, series editor; introduction by Dave Barry. New York: Modern Library, 2000. Additional aphorisms can be found at en.wikiquote.org/wiki/Benjamin_Franklin.

Gracián, Baltasar. *The Art of Worldly Wisdom.* Joseph Jacobs, trans. Boston: Shambhala, 1993. Reprinted by arrangement with Shambhala Publications, Inc.

Johnson, Samuel. *The Sayings of Dr. Johnson.* Compiled by James Reeves. London: John Baker, 1968.

Additional aphorisms can be found at en.wikiquote.org/wiki/Samuel_Johnson.

Lavater, Johann Kaspar. *Aphorisms on Man.* Dublin: Chamberlaine and Rice, 1790.

Montaigne, Michel de. *The Complete Essays.* Translated and edited with an introduction and notes by M. A. Screech. London: Penguin Books, 1991. By permission of Penguin Books, Ltd.

Ptah-Hotep. *The Instructions of Ptah-Hotep* can be found at www.kenseamedia.com/ency clopedia/ppp/instructions_ptah_hotep.htm.

Rochefoucauld, François, Duc de la. *Maxims.* Translated with an introduction by Leonard Tancock. London: Penguin Books, 1959. By permission of Penguin Books, Ltd.

Sablé, Madeleine de Souvré, Marquise de. The aphorisms of Madame de Sablé can be found at charon.sfsu.edu/sablefolder/newsable.php.

Seneca. *Letters from a Stoic.* Selected and translated with an introduction by Robin Campbell. London: Penguin Books, 1969. By permission of Penguin Books, Ltd.

Staël-Holstein, Anne-Louise-Germaine Necker de. *An Extraordinary Woman: Selected Writings of Germaine de Staël.* Translated and with an introduction by Vivian Folkenflik. New York: Columbia University Press, 1987.

Additional aphorisms can be found at www.brainyquote.com/quotes/authors/m/ madame_de_stael.html and en.thinkexist.com/quotes/madame_de_stael.

Tolstoy, Leo. *Walk in the Light While Ye Have Light, Thoughts and Aphorisms, Letters, Miscellanies. Volume XIX of the Complete Works of Count Tolstoy.* Leo Wiener, ed. and trans. London: J. M. Dent & Co., 1905.

Vauvenargues, Luc de Clapiers, Marquis de. *Maximes.* London: Arthur L. Humphreys, 1903.

## THE MINOR MORALISTS

Al-Siqilli, Muhammad ibn Zafar. *The Just Prince: A Manual of Leadership.* Joseph A. Kechichian and R. Hrair Dekmejian, trans. London: Saqi, 2003.

Beausacq, Marie-Josephine de Suin de. *Maximes de la Vie.* Paris: Paul Ollendorff Éditeur, 1987.

————. Cited in Grierson, Francis. *Parisian Portraits.* London: Stephen Swift, 1911.

————. Cited in *The Oxford Book of Aphorisms.* John Gross, ed. Oxford: Oxford University Press, 2003.

Burdin, Francesco. *Un Milione di Giorni: Aforismi.* Gino Ruozzi, ed. Venice: Marsilio, 2001.

Collins, John Churton. Cited in *A Treasury of English Aphorisms.* Logan Pearsall Smith, ed. London: Constable and Company, 1947.
Additional aphorisms can be found at www.quotationspage.com/quotes/John_Chur ton_Collins, www.jimpoz.com/quotes/speaker.php?speakerid=846 and www.quota tionsbook.com/authors/1624/John_Churton_Collins.

Ecclesiasticus. Aphorisms from Ecclesiasticus are taken from the King James Bible.

Eckermann, Johann Peter. *Aphorismen.* Sander L. Gilman, ed. Berlin: Erich Schmidt, 1984.

Fort, Gertrud von le. *Aphorismen.* Munich: Franz Ehrenwirth Verlag, 1962.

Fuller, Thomas. *Wise Words and Quaint Counsels of Thomas Fuller.* Selected and Arranged with a Short Sketch of the Author's Life by Augustus Jessop. Oxford: Clarendon Press, 1892.
Additional aphorisms can be found at en.wikiquote.org/wiki/Thomas_Fuller.

Fuller, Thomas. *Gnomologia: Adagies and Proverbs; Wise Sentences and Witty Sayings, Ancient and Modern, Foreign and British.* London: B. Barker and A. Bettesworth and C. Hitch, 1732.

———. *Introductio ad Sapientiam: or, The Art of Right Thinking, Assisted and Improved by such Notions as Men of Sense and Experience Have Left Us in Their Writings in order to Eradicate Error, and Plant Knowledge.* London: W. Innys, 1731.
Additional aphorisms can be found at www.quotationspage.com/quotes/Dr._Thomas _Fuller/ and www.brainyquote.com/quotes/authors/t/thomas_fuller.html.

Hammarskjöld, Dag. *Markings.* Leif Sjoberg and W. H. Auden, trans. With a Foreword by W. H. Auden. New York: Alfred A. Knopf, 1966.

Hazlitt, William. *Characteristics in the Manner of Rochefoucault's Maxims.* With introductory remarks by R. H. Horne. London: Bodoni Series, Elkin Mathews & Marrot, 1927.

Herbert, George. *Jacula Prudentum, or Outlandish Proverbs, Sentences, etc, Selected by Mr. George Herbert.* London: T. Garthwait, 1651.

———. *Poems and Proverbs of George Herbert.* London: Rivingtons, 1871.

———. *The Complete English Poems.* London: Penguin, 1991.

Hiddema, Frans. *Associatief: Aforismen.* Amsterdam: De Beuk, 1991.

———. *Niets Spreekt Vanzelf: Aforismen.* Amsterdam: Ad Donker, 1995.

Hoffer, Eric. *Reflections on the Human Condition.* London: Millington, 1973.

———. *Between the Devil and the Dragon.* New York: Harper & Row, 1982.

Inge, William Ralph. *Assessments and Anticipations.* London: Cassell & Co., 1929. Additional aphorisms can be found at www.brainyquote.com/quotes/authors/w/ william_ralph_inge.html.

Jünger, Ernst. *Tagebücher.* In: *Werke, Vol. 2/3.* Stuttgart: Klett, 1962.

Jünger, Friedrich Georg. *Gedanken und Merkzeichen.* Frankfurt/Main: Vittorio Klostermann, 1949.

Kudszus, Hans. *Jaworte, Neinworte: Aphorismen.* Frankfurt/Main: Suhrkamp, 1970.

Kurz, Isolde. *Im Zeichen des Steinbocks.* Munich and Leipzig: Georg Müller, 1909.

Marcuse, Ludwig. *Argumente und Rezepte: Ein Wörterbuch für Zeitgenossen.* Zurich: Diogenes, 1973.

**Morandotti, Alessandro.** Alessandro Morandotti's aphorisms can be found, in Italian, at www.aforismieaforismi.it.

**Multatuli.** *Barbertje Moet Hangen: Verhalen, Parabelen, Aforismen.* Verzameld en ingeleid door Garmt Stuiveling. Den Haag/Antwerpen: Daamen N.V./De Sikkel, 1955.

———. *The Oyster and the Eagle: Selected Aphorisms and Parables.* Translated, edited and annotated with an introductory essay by E. M. Beekman. Amherst: University of Massachusetts Press, 1974.

**Musil, Robert.** *Tagebücher, Aphorismen, Essays und Reden.* Adolf Frisé, ed. Hamburg: Rowohlt, 1955.

**Paasilinna, Erno.** Cited in *Aforismin Vuosisata.* Markku Envall, ed. Juva, Finland: WSOY, 1997.

**Penn, William.** *The Fruits of Solitude and Other Writings.* London: J. M. Dent & Sons, 1942.

**Prescott, Joseph.** *Aphorisms and Other Observations, Second Series.* New York: privately printed, 1995.

**Rivarol, Antoine de.** *Pensées diverses.* Paris: Les Editions Desjonquières, 1998.

**Saint-Beuve, Charles-Augustin.** Cited in *1000 Flashes of French Wit, Wisdom and Wickedness.* Edited by J. De Finod. New York: D. Appleton and Company, 1897.

**Samozwaniec, Magdalena.** Cited in *Panorama der polnischen Literatur des 20. Jahrhunderts. Bd. III: Pointen. 1,000 Aphorismen, Epigramme, Feuilletons, Grotesken, Glossen von 100 Autoren.* Hg. u. übertragen von Karl Dedecius. Zürich: Ammann Verlag, 1997.

———. Cited in *Aforyzmy Polskie. Antologia.* Danuta i Wlodzimierz Maslowscy, eds. Introduction by Jan Miodek. Kety: Wydawnictwo Antyk, 2001.

———. Cited in *A Treasury of Polish Aphorisms.* A bilingual edition compiled and translated by Jacek Galazka. Cornwall Bridge, CT: Polish Heritage Publications, 1997.

Additional aphorisms can be found, in Polish, at www.mysli.com.pl/ludzie.php?au tor=2289&l=N.

**Savile, George, Marquis of Halifax.** Cited in Smith, Logan Pearsall. *Reperusals and Re-Collections.* London: Constable and Company, 1936.

**Schnitzler, Arthur.** *Aphorismen und Betrachtungen.* Robert O. Weiss, ed. Frankfurt am Main: S. Fischer Verlag, 1976.

**Selden, John.** *Table-Talk: Being the Discourses of John Selden, Esq.; or His Sense of Various Matters of Weight and High Consequence Relating Especially to Religion and State.* Edited by R. Milward. London, 1689.

Additional aphorisms can be found at en.wikiquote.org/wiki/John_Selden.

**Seume, Johann Gottfried.** *Ausgewahlte Werke Seumes.* Wilhelm Hausenstein, ed. Leipzig: Leipziger Buchdruckerei AG, 1912.

**Smith, Logan Pearsall.** *All Trivia.* London: Penguin Press, 1986.

**Smith, Sydney.** *Selected Writings of Sydney Smith.* Edited and with an introduction by W. H. Auden. London: Faber & Faber, 1957.

Additional aphorisms can be found at en.wikiquote.org/wiki/Sydney_Smith.

**Stanhope, Philip, Fourth Earl of Chesterfield.** *The Principles of Politeness and of Knowing the World.* London: J. Bell, 1775.

———. Cited in Smith, Logan Pearsall. *Reperusals and Re-Collections.* London: Constable and Company, 1936.

Additional aphorisms can be found at en.wikiquote.org/wiki/Philip_Stanhope.

**Wagensberg, Jorge.** *Si la naturaleza es la respuesta, ¿cuál era la pregunta?* Barcelona: Tusquets, 2002.

———. *A más cómo, menos por qué.* Barcelona: Tusquets, 2006.

**Whichcote, Benjamin.** *Moral and Religious Aphorisms.* London: Elkin Mathews & Marrot, 1930.

**Wotton, Sir Henry.** *A Philosophical Survey of Education or Moral Architecture and The Aphorisms of Education.* London: Hodder & Stoughton, 1938.

**Zimmerman, Johann Georg Ritter von.** *Aphorisms and Reflections on Men, Morals and Things.* London: Associated, 1800.


## NOVELISTS AND PLAYWRIGHTS

NOVELISTS

**Bach, Richard.** *Illusions: The Adventures of a Reluctant Messiah.* New York: Dell Publishing Co., 1977.

———. *Messiah's Handbook: Reminders for the Advanced Soul.* Charlottesville, VA: Hampton Roads Publishing Company, 2004.

**Béalu, Marcel.** *Le Vif.* Quimper: Les Éditions Calligrammes, 1987.

**Bibesco, Elizabeth.** *Haven: Short Stories, Poems and Aphorisms.* London: James Barrie, 1951.

**Bowen, Elizabeth.** *The Mulberry Tree: Writings of Elizabeth Bowen.* Selected and introduced by Hermione Lee. London: Vintage, 1999.

Additional aphorisms can be found at www.brainyquote.com/quotes/authors/e/elizabeth_bowen.html.

**Bulgakov, Mikhail.** *The Master and Margarita.* Mirra Ginsburg, trans. New York: Grove Press, 1967.

Additional aphorisms, in Russian, can be found at www.lib.ru/BULGAKOW/dogheart .txt, www.kulichki.com/inkwell/text/hudlit/ruslit/bulg/bulgakov.htm, and www .aphorism.ru/author/a494.shtml.

**Bulwer-Lytton, Edward.** *The Bulwer Lytton Birthday Book: Quotations, in Prose and Verse, from the Works of Lord Lytton for Every Day in the Year.* London: G. Routledge & Sons, 1879.

Additional aphorisms can be found at http://en.wikiquote.org/wiki/Edward_Bulwer-Lytton and www.brainyquote.com/quotes/authors/e/edward_bulwerlytton.html.

**Cervantes, Miguel de.** *Wit and Wisdom of Don Quixote.* Boston: Roberts Brothers, 1882.

**Chateaubriand, François-René de.** Cited in *1000 Flashes of French Wit, Wisdom and Wickedness.* J. De Finod, ed. New York: D. Appleton and Company, 1897.

**Douglas, Norman.** *An Almanac.* London: Chatto & Windus, 1945.

Additional aphorisms can be found at www.brainyquote.com/quotes/authors/n/norman_douglas.html.

**Eliot, George.** *Adam Bede.* Edinburgh and London: William Blackwood and Sons, 1859.

Additional aphorisms can be found at en.wikiquote.org/wiki/George_Eliot.

**France, Anatole.** *The Wisdom of Anatole France.* Being Selected Passages from His Works, Chosen with An Introduction by J. Lewis May. London: John Lane, 1932.

Additional aphorisms can be found at en.wikiquote.org/wiki/Anatole_France.

**Gicgier, Tadeusz.** Cited in *Współczesna aforystyka polska*. Zebral, opracowal i wstepem opatrzyl Joachim Glensk. Antologia 1945–1984. Lódz: Wydanictwo Lódzkie, 1986. Additional aphorisms can be found, in Polish, at http://www.mysli.com.pl/ludzie.php?au tor=2289&l=N.

**Gide, André.** *Journals 1889–1949.* Translated, selected, and edited by Justin O'Brien. London: Penguin, 1967. Additional aphorisms can be found at en.wikiquote.org/wiki/Andr%C3%A9_Gide.

**Gombrowicz, Witold.** *Possessed.* English version by J. A. Underwood. London and New York: Marion Boyars Publishers, 1988.

————. *Cosmos and Pornografia.* Eric Mosbacher and Alastair Hamilton, trans. New York: Grove Press, 1985.

————. Cited in *A Treasury of Polish Aphorisms.* A bilingual edition compiled and translated by Jacek Galazka. Cornwall Bridge, CT: Polish Heritage Publications, 1997.

————. Cited in *Współczesna aforystyka polska.* Zebral, opracowal i wstepem opatrzyl Joachim Glensk. Antologia 1945–1984. Lódz: Wydanictwo Lódzkie, 1986.

————. Cited in *Aforyzmy Polskie. Antologia.* Danuta i Wlodzimierz Maslowscy, eds. Introduction by Jan Miodek. Kety: Wydawnictwo Antyk, 2001.

————. Cited in *Panorama der polnischen Literatur des 20. Jahrhunderts. Bd. III: Pointen. 1,000 Aphorismen, Epigramme, Feuilletons, Grotesken, Glossen von 100 Autoren.* Hg. u. übertragen von Karl Dedecius. Zürich: Ammann Verlag, 1997.

**Huxley, Aldous.** *Crome Yellow.* New York: Harper & Row, Publishers, 1974.

————. *The Doors of Perception and Heaven and Hell.* London: Penguin Books, 1972.

Additional aphorisms can be found at en.wikiquote.org/wiki/Aldous_Huxley and www.brainyquote.com/quotes/authors/a/aldous_huxley.html.

**Irzykowski, Karol.** Cited in *Aforyzmy Polskie. Antologia.* Danuta i Wlodzimierz Maslowscy, eds. Introduction by Jan Miodek. Kety: Wydawnictwo Antyk, 2001.

————. Cited in *Panorama der polnischen Literatur des 20. Jahrhunderts. Bd. III: Pointen. 1,000 Aphorismen, Epigramme, Feuilletons, Grotesken, Glossen von 100 Autoren.* Hg. u. übertragen von Karl Dedecius. Zürich: Ammann Verlag, 1997.

**Kourouma, Ahmadou.** Cited in Stewart, Julia. *Stewart's Quotable Africa.* London: Penguin Books, 2004.

**Lermontov, Mikhail.** *Complete Works.* Moscow: State Publishing House of Fiction, 1956. Additional aphorisms can be found in the novel *A Hero of Our Time*, in Russian, at www.lib.ru/LITRA/LERMONTOW/geroi.txt.

**Li Ao.** *The Mottos of Li Ao.* Shanghai: Shanghai Guji Press, 2000.

**Lu Xun.** *Panghuang.* Beijing: Renmin Wenxue Chubanshe, 1979.

————. *Zawen Quanbian.* Xi'an: Shaanxi Shifan Daxue Chubanshe, 2006.

**Meredith, George.** *The Ordeal of Richard Feverel: A History of Father and Son.* Leipzig: Bernard Tauchnitz, 1875. Additional aphorisms can be found at http://en.thinkexist.com/quotes/george_meredith.

**Natsume, Soseki.** *Nihon no shisoka meigen jiten.* Tokyo: Yuzankaku, 1983.

————. *Nihon meigen meiku no jiten.* Tokyo: Shogakukan, 1988.

**Pavese, Cesare.** *This Business of Living: Diaries, 1935–1950.* Translated from the Italian by A. E. Murch, with Jeanne Molli. London: Quartet Books, 1980.

Additional aphorisms can be found at en.thinkexist.com/quotes/cesare_pavese.

**Renard, Jules.** The aphorisms of Jules Renard can be found at www.brainyquote.com/quotes/authors/j/jules_renard.html.

**Richter, Jean Paul.** Jean Paul Richter's aphorisms can be found at www.brainyquote.com/quotes/authors/j/jean_paul_richter.html.

**Roa Bastos, Augusto.** *Metaforismos*. Barcelona: Edhasa, 1996.

**Shimazaki, Toson.** *Nihon no shisoka meigen jiten*. Tokyo: Yuzankaku, 1983.

———. *Nihon meigen meiku no jiten*. Tokyo: Shogakukan, 1988.

**Stevenson, Robert Louis.** *The Stevenson Birthday Book*. London: Marcus Ward and Co., 1897.

———. Cited in Smith, Logan Pearsall. *Reperusals and Re-Collections*. London: Constable and Company, 1936.

Additional aphorisms can be found at en.wikiquote.org/wiki/Robert_Louis_Stevenson.

**Toomer, Jean.** *Essentials*. Rudolph P. Byrd, ed. Athens and London: University of Georgia Press, 1991.

**Zomeren, Koos van.** *De Wereld Vereenvoudigen: Zinnen en Passages 1965–2005*. Amsterdam: Uitgeverij De Arbeiderspers, 2005.

PLAYWRIGHTS

**Bahr, Hermann.** *Mensch, werde wesentlich*. Selected by Anna Bahr-Mildenburg, arranged by Paul Thun-Hohenstein. Graz: Styria, 1934.

**Brecht, Bertolt.** *Selected Poems*. Translation and introduction by H. R. Hays. New York: Grove Press, 1959.

Additional aphorisms can be found at en.wikiquote.org/wiki/Bertolt_Brecht.

**Chekhov, Anton.** The aphorisms of Anton Chekhov can be found at en.wikiquote.org/wiki/Anton_Chekhov and en.thinkexist.com/quotes/anton_chekhov.

**Grillparzer, Franz.** Cited in *Deutsche Aphorismen*. Gerhard Fieguth, ed. Stuttgart: Reclam, 1978.

**Hebbel, Christian Friedrich.** *Läuse der Vernunft*. Jens Sparschuh, ed. Cologne: Bund Verlag, 1989.

**Ibsen, Henrik.** *The Sayings of Henrik Ibsen*. London: Duckworth, 1996.

**Jardiel Poncela, Enrique.** *Máximas mínimas y otros aforismos*. Barcelona: Edhasa, 2002.

**Kaiser, Georg.** *Werke, Vol. 4*. Walther Huder, ed. Frankfurt/Main, Berlin, Vienna: Propyläen, 1971.

**Molina, Tirso de.** *Aforismos*. Xavier A. Fernández, ed., in collaboration with Rosa Ribas. Kassel: Edition Reichenberger, 1995.

**Schiller, Friedrich von.** *Kleines Lexikon der Schiller-Zitate*. München: Deutscher Taschenbuch Verlag, 2004.

Additional aphorisms can be found at www.brainyquote.com/quotes/authors/f/friedrich_schiller.html.

**Shakespeare, William.** *The Wordsworth Dictionary of Shakespeare Quotations*. Compiled by G. F. Lamb. Ware, Hertfordshire: Wordsworth Editions, 1996.

**Shaw, George Bernard.** *Man and Superman*. "Maxims for Revolutionists." London: Penguin Books, 2000.

**Terence.** The aphorisms of Terence can be found at en.wikiquote.org/wiki/Terence.

Wilde, Oscar. *Nothing . . . Except My Genius: A Celebration of His Wit and Wisdom.* Compiled by Alastair Rolfe. With an introductory essay, "Playing Oscar," by Stephen Fry. London: Penguin Books, 1997.


## OLD SOULS AND ORACLES

Al-Deen, Muhammad Shems. *Moral Aphorisms in Arabic and a Persian Commentary in Verse.* Translated from the original with specimens of Persian poetry, likewise additions to the author's conformity of the Arabic and Persian with the English language by Stephen Weston. London: S. Rousseau, 1805.

Al-Iskandari, Abu al-Fadl ibn Ata'Allah. *Sufi Aphorisms (Kitab al-Hikam).* Translated with an introduction and notes by Victor Danner. Leiden: E. J. Brill, 1973.

Anonymous. *The Cloud of Unknowing and Other Works.* Translated into modern English with an introduction by Clifton Wolters. London: Penguin, 1978. By permission of Penguin Books, Ltd.

Augustine. *The Confessions.* Translated by Maria Boulding. London: Hodder & Stoughton, 1997.

Additional aphorisms can be found at en.wikiquote.org/wiki/Saint_Augustine.

Berra, Yogi. *The Yogi Book: I Really Didn't Say Everything I Said.* New York: Workman Publishing, 1998.

Bhagavad Gita. Translated with an introduction and notes by W. J. Johnson. Oxford: Oxford University Press, 1994.

Buddha. *Dhammapadda: The Sayings of the Buddha.* Thomas Byrom, trans. Boston and London: Shambhala, 1993.

Christian Fathers. *The Sayings of the Desert Fathers: The Alphabetical Collection.* Benedicta Ward, trans. Kalamazoo, MI: Cistercian Publications, 1975.

Chuang Tzu. *The Complete Works of Chuang Tzu.* Burton Watson, trans. New York: Columbia University Press, 1968.

Confucius. *Confucian Analects, the Great Learning and the Doctrine of the Mean.* Translated by James Legge. New York: Dover, 1971.

Ecclesiastes. Aphorisms from Ecclesiastes are taken from the King James Bible.

Eckhart, Johannes. *Selected Writings.* London: Penguin, 1994.

Additional aphorisms can be found at en.wikiquote.org/wiki/Meister_Eckhart, en.thinkexist.com/quotes/meister_eckhart, and www.brainyquote.com/quotes/authors/m/meister_eckhart.html.

Eno, Brian, and Peter Schmidt. *Oblique Strategies: Over One Hundred Worthwhile Dilemmas.* Fifth edition, 2001. Copyright Opal Ltd. www.enoshop.co.uk.

Gabirol, Solomon ben Judah ibn. *Choice of Pearls.* Translated from the Hebrew with Introduction and Annotations by the Rev. A. Cohen. New York: The Bloch Publishing Company, 1925.

Gardner, Jack. *Words Are Not Things.* London: Foulsham, 2005.

———. "Wot Iz Lojik?" Forthcoming.

———. "Everything Fades to Blue." Forthcoming.

Gurdjieff, George Ivanovitch. The aphorisms of Gurdjieff can be found at en.wikiquote.org/wiki/G._I._Gurdjieff.

Hávamál. *The Sayings of the Vikings.* Björn Jónasson, trans. Reykjavík: Gudrun, 1992.

Hellinger, Bert. *On Life and Other Paradoxes: Aphorisms and Little Stories.* Phoenix, AZ: Zeig, Tucker & Theisen, 2002.

I Ching. *The I Ching or Book of Changes.* Richard Wilhelm, trans. Princeton, NJ: Princeton University Press, 1985.

Jesus. The Gospel of Thomas. *The Other Bible.* Edited by Willis Barnstone. San Francisco: Harper & Row, 1984.

———. *The Muslim Jesus: Sayings and Stories in Islamic Literature.* Tarif Khalidi, ed. and trans. Cambridge, MA: Harvard University Press, 2001.

Jewish Fathers. *Sayings of the Jewish Fathers.* Translated, with an introduction and notes by Joseph I. Gorfinkle. Kessinger Publishing. The *Pirqe Aboth* is also available at www.sacred-texts.com/jud/sjf/index.htm.

Kang Hsi. Cited in *The Wisdom of the Chinese: Their Philosophy in Sayings and Proverbs.* New York: Garden City Publishing Co., 1938.

Kempis, Thomas à. *The Imitation of Christ.* Edited with an introduction by Harold C. Gardiner, S.J. Garden City, NY: Image Books, 1955.

Lao Tzu. *The Way and Its Power: A Study of the Tao Te Ching and Its Place in Chinese Thought.* Arthur Waley, trans. New York: Grove Press, 1958.

Marcus Aurelius. *Meditations.* Oxford: Oxford University Press, 1998. By permission of Oxford University Press.

Mencius. *Mencius.* London: Penguin Books, 1970.

Muhammad. *The Sayings of Muhammad.* Abdullah al-Mamun Al-Suhrawardy, trans. London: Constable & Co., 1910.

———. *The Wisdom of the Prophet: Sayings of Muhammad, Selections from the Hadith.* Thomas Cleary, trans. Boston: Shambhala Publications, 2001. Reprinted by arrangement with Shambhala Publications, Inc.

Proverbs. The Proverbs are taken from the King James Bible.

Publilius Syrus. *The Fragments of Publilius Syrus.* London, 1776.

Pythagoras. Cited in Gutas, Dimitri. *Greek Wisdom Literature in Arabic Translation: A Study of the Graeco-Arabic Gnomologia.* New Haven, CT: American Oriental Society, 1975.
Additional aphorisms can be found at en.wikiquote.org/wiki/Pythagoras.

Socrates. *The Collected Dialogues of Plato.* Princeton: Princeton University Press, 1973.
Additional aphorisms can be found at en.wikiquote.org/wiki/Socrates.

Somadeva. Cited in Sternbach, Ludwik. *Aphorisms and Proverbs in the Katha-Sarit-Sagara.* Lucknow: Akhila Bharatiya Sanskrit Parishad, 1980.

Talib, Ali ibn Abi. *Sentences of Ali, Son-in-Law of Mahomet and his Fourth Successor.* Simon Ockley, trans. London: Bernard Lintot, 1717.

Upanishads. *The Spirit of the Upanishads.* Compiled by Yogi Ramacharaka. Chicago: Yogi Publication Society, 1907.

———. *Upanishads.* Swami Prabhavananda and Frederick Manchester, trans. New York: Mentor Books, 1948.

Zen Masters. *Two Zen Classics: Mumonkan and Hekiganroku.* Translated with commentaries by Katsuki Sekida. Edited and introduced by A. V. Grimstone. New York: Weatherhill, 1977. By arrangement with Weatherhill, an imprint of Shambhala Publications, Inc., Boston.

## PAINTERS AND POETS

### PAINTERS

Allston, Washington. *Lectures on Art and Poems*. Richard Henry Dana Jr., ed. New York: Baker and Scribner, 1850.

Delacroix, Eugène. *The Journal of Eugène Delacroix*. Walter Pach, trans. New York: Hacker Art Books, 1937.
Additional aphorisms can be found at en.thinkexist.com/quotes/eugene_delacroix.

Leonardo da Vinci. *The Notebooks of Leonardo da Vinci*. Jean Paul Richter, trans. New York: Dover, 1989.
Additional aphorisms can be found at en.wikiquote.org/wiki/Leonardo_da_Vinci and www.brainyquote.com/quotes/authors/l/leonardo_da_vinci.html.

Mariën, Marcel. *Crystal Blinkers*. John Lyle, trans. Harpford: Transformaction, 1973.

Michelangelo. The aphorisms of Michelangelo can be found at en.wikiquote.org/wiki/Michelangelo and www.brainyquote.com/quotes/authors/m/michelangelo.html.

Picabia, Francis. *Yes No: Poems & Sayings*. Rémy Hall, trans. Madras and New York: Hanuman Books, 1990.

Rosa, Salvator. *Il Teatro della Politica: Sentenziosi aforismi della prudenza*. Giorgio Baroni, ed. Bologna: Commissione per Testi di Lingua, 1991.

### POETS

Al-Ma'ari, Abul Ala. *Studies in Islamic Poetry*. "The Meditations of Ma'ari." R. A. Nicholson, trans. Cambridge: Cambridge University Press, 1921.
———. *Luzum Ma La Yalzam: Luzumiat* ("Unnecessary Necessities"). Beirut: Dar Beirut for Printing and Publishing, 1983.

Auden, W. H. *The Prolific and the Devourer*. Hopewell, NJ: Ecco Press, 1981. © 1981 by W. H. Auden.
Additional aphorisms can be found at www.mrbauld.com/audenwr.html.

Baudelaire, Charles. *Paris Spleen*. Louise Varese, trans. New York: New Directions, 1970.
Additional aphorisms can be found at en.wikiquote.org/wiki/Charles_Baudelaire.

Bergamín, José. *Aforismos de la Cabeza Parlante*. Madrid: Ediciones Turner, 1983.

Blake, William. *The Complete Poems*. London: Penguin Books, 1981.

Char, René. *Hypnos Waking: Poems and Prose by René Char*. Jackson Mathews, trans. New York: Random House, 1956.

Cocteau, Jean. The aphorisms of Jean Cocteau can be found at en.wikiquote.org/wiki/Jean_Cocteau.

Cohen, Leonard. The aphorisms of Leonard Cohen can be found at en.wikiquote.org/wiki/Leonard_Cohen and www.serve.com/cpage/LCohen/lyrics/.

Coleridge, Samuel Taylor. *The Letters, Conversations and recollections of S. T. Coleridge*. With a preface by the editor, Thomas Allsop. London, 1864.
———. *Specimens of the Table Talk of S. T. Coleridge*. London: John Murray, 1836.
Additional aphorisms can be found at en.wikiquote.org/wiki/Samuel_Taylor_Coleridge and www.brainyquote.com/quotes/authors/s/samuel_taylor_coleridge.html.

Corn, Alfred. *The Pith Helmet*. Omaha, NE: The Cummington Press, 1992.

Envall, Markku. Cited in *Aforismin Vuosisata*. Markku Envall, ed. Juva, Finland: WSOY, 1997.

FitzGerald, Edward. *Polonius: A Collection of Wise Saws and Modern Instances*. London: Alexander Moring, De La More Press, 1905.

Frost, Robert. *Selected Poems*. Avenel, NJ: Gramercy Books, 1992.

Additional aphorisms can be found at en.wikiquote.org/wiki/Robert_Frost.

Gibran, Kahlil. *The Prophet*. New York: Alfred A. Knopf, 1980.

Goethe, Johann Wolfgang von. *Maxims and Reflections*. London: Penguin Books, 1998.

Gourmont, Remy de. Remy de Gourmont's aphorisms can be found in *Promenades littéraires (1904–27)* and *Promenades philosophiques (1905–1909)*, and at www.brainyquote.com/quotes/authors/r/remy_de_gourmont.html.

Hein, Piet. *Grooks*. London: Hodder Paperbacks, 1969.

Additional aphorisms can be found at chat.carleton.ca/~tcstewar/grooks/grooks.html.

Heine, Heinrich. *Works of Prose*. Hermann Kesten, ed. E. B. Ashton, trans. London: Secker & Warburg, 1943.

Additional aphorisms can be found at www.brainyquote.com/quotes/authors/h/heinrich_heine.html and en.thinkexist.com/quotes/heinrich_heine/.

Herbert, Zbigniew. Cited in *Aforyzmy Polskie. Antologia*. Danuta i Wlodzimierz Maslowscy, eds. Introduction by Jan Miodek. Kety: Wydawnictwo Antyk, 2001.

———. Cited in *Wspólczesna aforystyka polska*. Zebral, opracowal i wstepem opatrzyl Joachim Glensk. Antologia 1945–1984. Iódz: Wydanictwo Lódzkie, 1986.

Hernández, Miguel. *Prosas líricas y Aforismos*. Madrid: Ediciones de la Torre, 1986.

Hoffenstein, Samuel. *The Complete Poetry of Samuel Hoffenstein*. New York: Modern Library, 1954.

Hofmannsthal, Hugo von. *Buch der Freunde* and *Aus dem Nachlass*. Cited in *Deutsche Aphorismen*. Gerhard Fiegguth, ed. Stuttgart: Reclam, 1978.

Holmes, Oliver Wendell, Sr. *The "Breakfast-Table" Series*. London: George Routledge & Sons, 1886.

Additional aphorisms can be found at en.wikiquote.org/wiki/Oliver_Wendell_Holmes %2C_Sr and www.litquotes.com/quote_author_resp.php?AName=Oliver%20 Wendell%20Holmes,%20Sr.

Horace. *Three Hundred & Sixty-Five Short Quotations from Horace*. With modern titles and varied metrical versions in English by H. Darnley Naylor. Shaftesbury: High House Press, 1935.

Additional aphorisms can be found at www.brainyquote.com/quotes/authors/h/horace .html.

Khayyám, Omar. *Rubaiyat*. Translated into English Quatrains by Edward FitzGerald. Edited with an introduction by Louis Untermeyer. New York: Random House, 1947.

Kipling, Rudyard. *The Sayings of Rudyard Kipling*. London: Duckworth, 1994.

Lababidi, Yahia. *Signposts to Elsewhere*. St. Joseph, MO: Sun Rising Press, 2006.

Landor, Walter Savage. *Aphorisms*. Selected from his works by R. Brimley Johnson. London: George Allen, 1897.

León González, Francisco. *El Gesto de la Agusttia: Aforismos*. Xochimilco, Mexico: Serie Alterna, 1987.

Leopardi, Giacomo. *Pensieri*. W. S. Di Piero, trans. Oxford: Oxford University Press, 1984. Additional aphorisms can be found at en.thinkexist.com/quotes/giacomo_ leopardi/ and www.brainyquote.com/quotes/authors/g/giacomo_leopardi.html.

**Liebert, Daniel.** Daniel Liebert's aphorisms have appeared in *Barrow Street* (Winter 2006) and the *Yale Review* (Spring 2007, Vol. 95, No. 2).

**Machado, Antonio.** *Juan de Mairena: Epigrams, Maxims, Memoranda, and Memoirs of an Apocryphal Professor. With an Appendix of Poems from the Apocryphal Songbooks.* Ben Belitt, ed. and trans. Berkeley: University of California Press, 1963.

**Martial.** *Epigrams.* Selected and translated by James Michie. Introduction by Shadi Bartsch. New York: Modern Library, 2002.

**Narosky, José.** *Brisas: Aforismos.* Buenos Aires: Javier Vergara Editores, 1987.

**Nash, Ogden.** *Collected Verse.* London: J. M. Dent & Sons, 1961. © Reprinted by permission of Curtis Brown.

Additional aphorisms can be found at en.wikiquote.org/wiki/Ogden_Nash and www .brainyquote.com/quotes/authors/o/ogden_nash.html.

**Novalis.** *Aphorismen.* Michael Brucker, ed. Frankfurt/Main and Leipzig: Insel, 1992.

**Parker, Dorothy.** *The Collected Poetry of Dorothy Parker.* New York: Modern Library, 1959.

**Paterson, Don.** *The Book of Shadows.* London: Picador, 2004.

**Péguy, Charles.** *Pensées.* Paris: Gallimard, 1934.

Additional aphorisms can be found at www.brainyquote.com/quotes/authors/c/charles _peguy.html.

**Pessoa, Fernando.** *The Book of Disquietude.* Translated with an introduction by Richard Zenith. Manchester: Carcanet, 1991.

**Pushkin, Alexander.** *Eugene Onegin.* Walter Arndt, trans. New York: E. P. Dutton, 1963.

**Quevedo, Francisco de.** *Sentencias.* Paloma Fanconi, ed. Madrid: Ediciones Temas de Hoy, 1995.

**Richardson, James.** *Vectors: Aphorisms and Ten-Second Essays.* Keene, NY: Ausable Press, 2001.

———. *Interglacial: New and Selected Poems and Aphorisms.* Keene, NY: Ausable Press, 2004.

**Robinson, Peter.** *Untitled Deeds.* Cambridge, U.K.: Salt Publishing, 2004.

Additional aphorisms can be found at jacketmagazine.com/28/robin-aphor.html.

**Roy, Claude.** *Temps variable avec éclaircies.* Paris: Editions Gallimard, 1984.

**Rustavelli, Shota.** *The Knight in the Panther's Skin* can be found at rustaveli .tripod.com/knight/engindex.html.

**Saavedra Weise, Carlos.** *Metaforismos y líneas.* Santa Cruz: Editorial Sirena Color, 1997.

**Saba, Umberto.** *Scorciatoie e raccontini, Tutte le prose.* Arrigo Stara, ed. Milan: Mondadori, 2001.

**Schröder, Rudolf A.** *Aphorismen und Reflexionen.* Richard Exner, ed. Frankfurt am Main: Suhrkamp, 1977.

**Seuss, Dr.** *Did I Ever Tell You How Lucky You Are?* London: HarperCollins, 1990.

———. *Oh, the Places You'll Go!* London: HarperCollins, 1990.

**Sidney, Philip.** *Aphorisms of Sir Philip Sidney.* London: Longman, Hurst, Rees, and Orme, 1807.

**Spaziani, Maria Luisa.** *Aforismi. Scrittori italiani di aforismi, Volume secondo: Il Novecento.* Gino Ruozzi, ed. Milan: Mondadori, 1996.

**Stevens, Wallace.** *Opus Posthumous.* "Adagia." New York: Vintage Books, 1982.

**Tagore, Rabindranath.** *Stray Birds.* London: Macmillan and Co., 1919.

Taylor, Henry. Cited in Smith, Logan Pearsall. *Reperusals and Re-Collections*. London: Constable and Company, 1936.
———. Cited in Gross, John. *The Oxford Book of Aphorisms*. Oxford: Oxford University Press, 2003.
Additional aphorisms can be found at www.brainyquote.com/quotes/authors/h/henry_taylor.html.
Theognis of Megara. *Greek Lyric: An Anthology in Translation*. Andrew M. Miller, trans. Indianpolis: Hackett, 1996. Additional aphorisms can be found at cc.purdue.edu/~corax/theognis.html.
Valéry, Paul. *The Collected Works of Paul Valéry. Volume 1: Poems*. Jackson Mathews, ed. London: Routledge & Kegan Paul, 1970.
———. *The Collected Works of Paul Valéry. Volume 14: Analects*. Jackson Mathews, ed. London: Routledge & Kegan Paul, 1970.

## PHILOSOPHERS AND THEORISTS

Adorno, Theodor. *Minima Moralia: Reflections from a Damaged Life*. E. F. N. Jephcott, trans. London: Verso, 1978.
Amiel, Henri Frédéric. *Journal Intime*. Mary Augusta Ward, trans. London: Macmillan and Co., 1913.
Additional aphorisms can be found at en.wikiquote.org/wiki/Henri-Fr%C3%A9d%C3%A9ric_Amiel. The *Journal Intime* is online at www.gutenberg.org/etext/8545.
Arendt, Hannah. *The Portable Hannah Arendt*. Edited with an introduction by Peter Baehr. London: Penguin, 2000.
Additional aphorisms can be found at www.brainyquote.com/quotes/authors/h/hannah_arendt.html.
Aristotle. Cited in Gutas, Dimitri. *Greek Wisdom Literature in Arabic Translation: A Study of the Graeco-Arabic Gnomologia*. New Haven: American Oriental Society, 1975.
Additional aphorisms can be found at en.wikiquote.org/wiki/Aristotle.
Benjamin, Walter. *Reflections: Essays, Aphorisms, Autobiographical Writings*. Edited and with an introduction by Peter Demetz. New York: Schocken Books, 1986.
Additional aphorisms can be found at en.wikiquote.org/wiki/Walter_Benjamin.
Bradley, F. H. *The Presuppositions of Critical History and Aphorisms*. Bristol, U.K.: Thoemmes Press, 1993.
Camus, Albert. *The Fall*. Justin O'Brien, trans. New York: Alfred A. Knopf, 1956.
Additional aphorisms can be found at www.brainyquote.com/quotes/authors/a/albert_camus.html.
Canetti, Elias. *The Secret Heart of the Clock: Notes, Aphorisms, Fragments 1973–1985*. Joel Agee, trans. London: Andre Deutsch, 1991.
———. *Notes from Hampstead: The Writer's Notes, 1954–1971*. John Hargraves, trans. New York: Farrar, Straus and Giroux, 1998.
Carlyle, Thomas. *The Sayings of Thomas Carlyle*. Selected by Brendan King. London: D.O.R. Books, 1993.

Additional aphorisms can be found at www.brainyquote.com/quotes/authors/t/ thomas_carlyle.html.

Diderot, Denis. *Rameau's Nephew and Other Works*. Jacques Barzun and Ralph H. Bowen, trans., with an introduction by Ralph H. Bowen. Indianapolis: Hackett Publishing Company, 2001.

Additional aphorisms can be found at en.wikiquote.org/wiki/Denis_Diderot.

Epictetus. *The Handbook (The Encheiridion)*. Translated, with an introduction and annotations, by Nicholas P. White. Indianapolis/Cambridge: Hackett Publishing Company, 1983.

————. *The Discourses of Epictetus*. London: J. M. Dent, 1995.

Epicurus. *The Essential Epicurus: Letters, Principal Doctrines, Vatican Sayings, and Fragments*. Translated, with an introduction, by Eugene O'Connor. Amherst, NY: Prometheus Books, 1993.

Erasmus. *The Adages of Erasmus*. Selected by William Barker. Toronto: University of Toronto Press, 2001.

Additional aphorisms can be found at www.brainyquote.com/quotes/authors/d/desiderius_ erasmus.html.

Fontenelle, Bernard le Bovier de. *Conversations on the Plurality of Worlds*. H. A. Hargreaves, trans. Introduction by Nina Rattner Gelbart. Berkeley: University of California Press, 1990.

————. Cited in Auden, W. H., and Louis Kronenberger. *The Viking Book of Aphorisms*. New York: Penguin Books, 1983.

Additional aphorisms can be found at www-history.mcs.st-andrews.ac.uk/Quotations/ Fontenelle.html.

Frankl, Viktor E. *Man's Search for Meaning: An Introduction to Logotherapy*. New York: Pocket Books, 1963.

Additional aphorisms can be found at www.brainyquote.com/quotes/authors/v/viktor_ e_frankl.html.

Gómez Dávila, Nicolás. *Escolios a un texto implícito*. Bogotá: Instituto Colombiano de Cultura, Subdirección de Comunicaciones Culturales, División de Publicaciones, 1977.

Guicciardini, Francesco. *Maxims and Reflections (Ricordi)*. Mario Domandi, trans. Introduction by Nicolai Rubinstein. Philadelphia: University of Pennsylvania Press, 1992.

Heraclitus. *Herakleitos and Diogenes*. Guy Davenport, trans. San Francisco: Grey Fox Press, 1979.

Huxley, Thomas Henry. *Aphorisms and Reflections from the Works of T. H. Huxley*. Selected by Henrietta A. Huxley. London: Macmillan and Co., 1907.

James, William. *The Varieties of Religious Experience*. New York: Macmillan Publishing Company, 1961.

————. *Pragmatism and Other Essays*. New York: Washington Square Press, 1963.

Additional aphorisms can be found at www.brainyquote.com/quotes/authors/w/ william_james.html and en.wikiquote.org/wiki/William_James.

Joubert, Joseph. *Pensées and Letters of Joseph Joubert*. Translated with an introduction by H. P. Collins. London: George Routledge & Sons, 1928.

————. *The Notebooks of Joseph Joubert: A Selection*. Paul Auster, ed. and trans. San Francisco: North Point Press, 1983.

Kierkegaard, Søren. *Either/Or: A Fragment of Life*. London: Penguin Books, 1992. Additional aphorisms can be found at en.wikiquote.org/wiki/Soren_Aabye_Kierkegaard.

Lichtenberg, Georg Christoph. *The Lichtenberg Reader: Selected Writings of Georg Christoph Lichtenberg*. Translated, edited, and introduced by Franz Mautner and Henry Hatfield. Boston: Beacon Press, 1959.

———. Cited in Brinitzer, Carl. *A Reasonable Rebel: Georg Christoph Lichtenberg*. London: George Allen & Unwin, 1960.

———. *The Waste Books*. Translated and with an introduction by R. J. Hollingdale. New York: New York Review Books, 2000.

Machiavelli, Niccolò. *The Prince*. Translated with notes by George Bull. With an introduction by Anthony Grafton. London: Penguin Books, 1999.

May, Simon. *The Little Book of Big Thoughts: A Handbook of Aphorisms*. London: Metro Publishing, 2005.

Ortega y Gasset, José. The aphorisms of José Ortega y Gasset can be found at en.wikipedia.org/wiki/Jos%C3%A9_Ortega_y_Gasset.

Plato. Cited in Gutas, Dimitri. *Greek Wisdom Literature in Arabic Translation: A Study of the Graeco-Arabic Gnomologia*. New Haven: American Oriental Society, 1975. Additional aphorisms can be found at en.wikiquote.org/wiki/Plato.

Russell, Bertrand. The aphorisms of Bertrand Russell can be found at www.brainyquote.com/quotes/authors/b/bertrand_russell.html.

Santayana, George. *Little Essays*. Drawn from the writings of George Santayana by Logan Pearsall Smith. London: Constable, 1924.

———*Obiter Scripta: Lectures, Essays and Reviews*. Justus Buchler and Benjamin Schwartz, eds. New York: C. Scribner's Sons, 1936. Additional aphorisms can be found at en.wikiquote.org/wiki/George_Santayana.

Sato, Issai. *Shinpen kakugen kotowaza jiten*. Osaka: Musashishobo, 1971.

———. *Nihon no shisoka meigen jiten*. Tokyo: Yuzankaku, 1983.

———. *Nihon meigen meiku no jiten*. Tokyo: Shogakukan, 1988

Schlegel, Friedrich von. *Philosophical Fragments*. Peter Firchow, trans. Foreword by Rodolphe Gasché. Minneapolis: University of Minnesota Press, 1991.

Spinoza, Benedict (Baruch) de. *On the Improvement of the Understanding, The Ethics, Correspondence*. Translated from the Latin with an introduction by R. H. M. Elwes. New York: Dover Publications, 1955.

Stein, Gertrude. *How To Write*. New York: Dover Publications, 1975.

———. *Look at Me Now and Here I Am: Writings and Lectures 1911–1945*. London: Penguin Books, 1971. Additional aphorisms can be found at en.wikiquote.org/wiki/Gertrude_Stein.

Szasz, Thomas. *The Untamed Tongue: A Dissenting Dictionary*. La Salle, IL: Open Court, 1991. Reprinted by permission of Open Court Publishing Company. © by Thomas Szasz.

Tacitus. The aphorisms of Tacitus can be found at www.brainyquote.com/quotes/authors/t/tacitus.html.

Unamuno, Miguel de. The aphorisms of Miguel de Unamuno can be found at en.wikiquote.org/wiki/Miguel_de_Unamuno.

Weil, Simone. *Gravity and Grace*. With an Introduction by Gustave Thibon. London: Routledge and Kegan Paul, 1972.

Additional aphorisms can be found at www.brainyquote.com/quotes/authors/s/simone
_weil.html.

**Whitehead, Alfred North.** *Dialogues of Alfred North Whitehead, as recorded by Lucien Price.* London: Max Reinhardt, 1954.

Additional aphorisms can be found at www.brainyquote.com/quotes/authors/a/alfred
_north_whitehead.html and en.wikiquote.org/wiki/Alfred_North_Whitehead.


## STRANGE BEASTS


**Bierce, Ambrose.** *The Devil's Dictionary.* With an introduction by Roy Morris Jr. New York: Oxford University Press, 2002.

**Brillat-Savarin, Anthelme.** *The Philosopher in the Kitchen.* Anne Drayton, trans. London: Penguin Books, 1981.

**Chazal, Malcolm de.** *Sens-Plastique.* Irving Weiss, ed. and trans. New York: Sun, 1979.

———. *Plastic Sense.* Irving Weiss, ed. and trans. Introduction by W. H. Auden. New York: Herder and Herder, 1971.

**Cioran, E. M.** *Anathemas and Admirations.* Richard Howard, trans. New York: Arcade Publishing/Little, Brown and Company, 1991.

———. *The Trouble with Being Born.* Richard Howard, trans. New York: Arcade Publishing, 1998.

**Colton, Charles Caleb.** *Lacon: Or Many Things in Few Words, Addressed to Those Who Think.* London: Longman, Hurst, Rees, Orme, and Brown, 1820.

———. *Lacon.* Edited by George J. Barbour. Cambridgeshire: Melrose Books, 2001.

**Dickinson, Emily.** *The Complete Poems of Emily Dickinson.* Thomas H. Johnson, ed. Boston: Little, Brown and Company, 1960. © 1951, 1955, 1979, 1983 by the President and Fellows of Harvard College.

**Diogenes.** *Herakleitos and Diogenes.* Guy Davenport, trans. San Francisco: Grey Fox Press, 1979.

**Ekelund, Vilhelm.** *Agenda.* Lennart Bruce, trans. Berkeley, CA: Cloud Marauder Press, 1976.

———. *The Second Light.* Translated and with an introduction by Lennart Bruce, with an afterword by Eric O. Johannesson. San Francisco: North Point Press, 1986.

**Eluard, Paul, and Benjamin Péret.** *152 Proverbs Adapted to the Taste of the Day.* English version by John Robert Colombo and Irene Currie. Oakville, Ont.: Oasis Publications, 1977.

**Gómez de la Serna, Ramón.** *Greguerías: The Wit and Wisdom of Ramón Gómez de la Serna.* Selected, introduced and translated by Philip Ward. Cambridge and New York: Oleander Press, 1982.

———. *Aphorisms.* Translated with an introduction by Miguel Gonzalez-Gerth. Pittsburgh: Latin American Literary Review Press, 1989.

**Kafka, Franz.** *The Great Wall of China and Other Short Works.* London: Penguin, 2002.

**Nietzsche, Friedrich.** *The Gay Science.* Bernard Williams, ed.; Josefine Nauckhoff, trans.; poems translated by Adrian Del Caro. Cambridge: Cambridge University Press, 2001. By permission of Cambridge University Press.

———. *Thus Spoke Zarathustra.* Translated and with a preface by Walter Kaufmann. New York: Penguin Books, 1981.

**Pascal, Blaise.** *Pensées and Other Writings.* Translated by Honor Levi, edited with an introduction and notes by Anthony Levi. Oxford: Oxford University Press, 1999.

**Porchia, Antonio.** *Voices.* Aphorisms. Selected and translated by W. S. Merwin. New York: Alfred A. Knopf, 1988. © 1988 by W. S. Merwin. By permission of The Wylie Agency.

**Pound, Ezra.** *ABC of Reading.* New York: New Directions, 1960.

———. *Guide to Kulchur.* New York: New Directions, 1970.

———. *Literary Essays of Ezra Pound.* London: Faber and Faber, 1974.

———. *The Sayings of Ezra Pound.* London: Duckworth, 1994.

**Prutkov, Kozma.** *Thoughts and Aphorisms from the Fruits of Meditation of Kozma Prutkov.* Illustrations by Quentin Blake. London: Royal College of Art, circa 1975.

———. Cited in Heldt Monter, Barbara. *Kozma Prutkov: The Art of Parody.* The Hague and Paris: Mouton, 1972.

**Schopenhauer, Arthur.** *Essays from the Parerga and Paralipomena.* T. Bailey Saunders, trans. London: George Allen and Unwin, 1951.

———. *Essays and Aphorisms.* Selected and translated with an introduction by R. J. Hollingdale. London: Penguin Books, 1970.

**Wittgenstein, Ludwig.** *Tractatus Logico-Philosophicus.* D. F. Pears and B. F. McGuinness, trans., with the introduction by Bertrand Russell. London: Routledge, 1993.

———. *Culture and Value.* G. H. von Wright in collaboration with Heikki Nyman, eds. Revised edition of the text by Alois Pichler. Peter Winch, trans. Oxford: Blackwell Publishing, 2002.

**Worth, Patience.** The proverbs of Patience Worth can be found at www.patienceworth.org.

# INDEX OF APHORISTS

Bold page numbers refer to the main entry for each aphorist.

# INDEX OF THEMES